TELEVISION IN NEW ZEALAND

TELEVISION in New Zealand

PROGRAMMING

THE NATION

EDITED BY

Roger Horrocks & Nick Perry

OXFORD

UNIVERSITY PRESS

OXFORD

UNIVERSITY PRESS

253 Normanby Road, South Melbourne, Victoria 3205, Australia

Oxford University Press is a department of the University of Oxford.
It furthers the University's objective of excellence in research, scholarship,
and education by publishing worldwide in

Oxford New York

Auckland Bangkok Buenos Aires Cape Town Chennai
Dar es Salaam Delhi Hong Kong Istanbul Karachi Kolkata
Kuala Lumpur Madrid Melbourne Mexico City Mumbai Nairobi
São Paulo Shanghai Taipei Tokyo Toronto

OXFORD is a trade mark of Oxford University Press
in the UK and in certain other countries

National Library of New Zealand
Cataloguing-in-Publication data

    Television in New Zealand: programming the nation/
    edited by Roger Horrocks and Nick Perry.
    Includes bibliographical references and index.
    ISBN 0 19 558447 3
    1. Television—New Zealand. I. Horrocks, Roger. II. Perry, Nick, 1942–

    384.550993—dc 21

Typeset by Cannon Typesetting
Printed by Bookpac Production Services, Singapore

Contents

PART 2: Between the Mainstream and the Margins

PART 3: Between International Formats and Local Meanings

Acknowledgments

This book has grown out of a research project on 'New Zealand Television and National Identity', which received a generous grant from the Marsden Fund of the Royal Society of New Zealand (Te Pūtea Rangahau a Marsden). This encouragement was very important, particularly as the Fund is dedicated to 'research that is purely curiosity driven' or 'research for its own sake'.

We also want to thank our referees and others associated with the Marsden grant, such as Greg Bennett and David Scott who provided expert technical assistance; Adam White who helped with organisation; secretarial staff Cathy Cassidy and Suzanne Gomes; graduate students such as Amy West and Susan Pointon; and Gaynor van Beurden and members of the service and administrative staff at the University of Auckland.

Our research was based in the Department of Film, Television and Media Studies at the University of Auckland, and we want to mention the exceptionally collaborative way in which staff worked on the project, including a great deal of informal discussion and a seminar series. This collegial spirit was also shown by other contributors not part of the Marsden project, such as Tainui Stephens, Dr Geoff Lealand of Waikato University, and Dr Trisha Dunleavy of Victoria University. Our thanks to all contributors for their hard work and commitment.

Scott Wilson made a special contribution to the book by helping us prepare the final manuscript. The project benefited greatly from his careful editorial work, computer skills, and calm efficiency.

Our thanks to the many individuals and organisations that have provided photos. We are particularly grateful to Jim Blackman (Triangle), Melanya

Burrows (South Pacific Pictures), Arani Cuthbert (Diva Productions), Kim Peacock (TV3), Zara Potts (TVNZ), and Karin Reinink (*Shortland Street*).

An earlier version of the chapter by Luke Goode and James Littlewood appeared in the *Journal of International Communication* vol. 8(2) pp. 46–63. Our thanks to the editors of that journal for their cooperation. All other chapters were written specifically for the present book.

We are extremely grateful to our publishers, Oxford University Press (Melbourne), for their interest and expertise. Heather Fawcett has been a patient and thoughtful editor, and we would also like to mention Jill Henry and Maggie Way with whom we initially discussed the book. The production owed much to Liz Filleul and Chris Wyness. Our thanks also to the (anonymous) readers of the manuscript who were willing to offer rapid feedback.

Contributors

Annie Goldson, Luke Goode, Margaret Henley, Roger Horrocks, Misha Kavka, Shuchi Kothari, Sarina Pearson, Nick Perry, Laurence Simmons, and **Nabeel Zuberi** are all members of the Department of Film, Television and Media Studies at the University of Auckland. Perry is Head of the Department. Goldson, Henley, Horrocks, Kothari, and Pearson have all been involved in various aspects of the television and film industries.

Sue Abel lectures in the School of Social and Cultural Studies at Massey University, Albany Campus.

Stephen Crofts is a Visiting Fellow at the Centre for Critical and Cultural Studies at the University of Queensland.

Trisha Dunleavy lectures in the School of English Film and Theatre at Victoria University of Wellington.

Geoff Lealand lectures in the Department of Screen and Media Studies at the University of Waikato. He has been a consultant for children's television series.

James Littlewood is a former graduate student of the Department of Film, Television and Media Studies, University of Auckland who now works in market research.

Tanui Stephens, of Te Rarawa, is a producer and director with many film and television credits.

Stephen Turner lectures in the Department of English at the University of Auckland.

Introduction

This book offers a range of chapters by academics and practitioners with thoughtful and passionate perspectives on the medium of television and its relationship with New Zealand. All the chapters (with one exception) are new. We have designed *Television in New Zealand* both as a textbook for the media student and as a general book for any reader with an in-depth interest in New Zealand popular culture, a topic that is still seldom documented and analysed.

Although the focus of the book is television today, and it does offer some detailed discussion of current programs (in such areas as drama, 'reality', and sports), we have tried to avoid writing a book that will go rapidly out of date by concentrating on long-term trends and generic continuities, on the underlying dynamics of New Zealand television. In focusing on the present we have also felt the strong pressure of the future, for television is passing through an exceptional period of change. Many contributors are also concerned to derive lessons from the past, particularly the so-called 'New Zealand experiment', the turbulent years between 1984 and 1999 when successive governments pushed television ever more deeply into commercialism. Tainui Stephens comments in his chapter: 'Māori custom tells us that we in fact walk into the future backwards, our past is always before us, and our future is behind us'. Much of our book proceeds in that spirit.

The academic study of television today offers a variety of possible approaches. We have tried deliberately to cover a wide range, though no book can represent all of them. Included here are examples of 'close reading' or textual analysis (as in chapters by Crofts and Goldson), textual analysis combined with content analysis (Crofts), discourse analysis (Abel and Crofts), studies of a genre (Kavka and Lealand), audience and reception

(Abel), representation (Turner), historical research (Dunleavy and Simmons), political economy and industrial studies (Horrocks and Perry), race and ethnic issues (Abel, Kothari, Pearson, Stephens, and Zuberi), gender issues (Henley), indigenous media (Stephens), cultural studies and cultural theory (Turner), media in everyday life and the domestic environment (Simmons), technological change (Goode and Littlewood), public policy (Horrocks), and so on. Of course, most of our contributors consider it important to employ more than one of these perspectives. Talking about the media inevitably involves technical terms, so we have added a full glossary. Terms are printed in bold on the first occasion they appear.

We would also highlight the variety of today's possible approaches by observing that contributors have gathered their information not only by a great deal of television viewing but also by detailed analysis (including number crunching), interviews (with broadcasters, program makers, and advertisers), ethnographic and focus group study (spending time in a community learning how viewers use and respond to television), international comparisons (gathering information via industry publications, the Internet, and overseas travel), or participant observation (involvement in production, scriptwriting, and funding). These are among the standard methods of media studies today. One way to sum this up in a single sentence would be to say: 'We can study television through the governments that regulate it, the industries that organise it, the programs that embody it, the audiences that recognise it, and the meanings that circulate between all those locations.'

It is important to combine different disciplines and to compare different perspectives, and the chapters of this book should be seen as talking to one another. Their interaction includes some healthy debates and disagreements. Inevitably there is some overlap of information since the same political and organisational changes impinge on every area of television; but with their different contexts, emphases, points of view, and styles, the chapters add up to a many-dimensioned picture of New Zealand television.

PART 1

The New Zealand
Television System

Introduction

The chapters in Part 1 concentrate on the 'big picture', discussing the New Zealand television system as a whole from various angles. We recommend that this Part be read in sequence as the early chapters set up the main ideas and issues. They lay groundwork that will enable the reader to make the most of the later chapters in the section, which are more theoretical and take more knowledge for granted.

The opening chapter by Roger Horrocks provides an overview of the book's 'themes, methods, and perspectives'. His second chapter is a survey (and personal interpretation) of the history of New Zealand television, again stressing key themes. Particular attention is paid to the years since 1984. Though highly critical in some respects, Horrocks seeks to dig deeper than the previous polarised or polemical accounts of the period by identifying positive as well as negative trends.

Laurence Simmons's chapter focuses on one phase of that history. It's a rich description of the hopes and fears associated with the introduction of television. Such debates about morality, politics, and aesthetics still frame the medium today. The chapter demonstrates how an international technology took on its particular local form, and is equally striking in its documentation of how television entered the New Zealand home and domestic space (an aspect of television history that has been relatively neglected until recent years).

Nick Perry's wide-ranging chapter develops the important idea that television has not only adapted to the particular circumstances of local culture but has also been actively involved in shaping New Zealand as we know it, through its specific choices and ways of organising the world. Perry sees New Zealand in its complex particularity as challenging the usual labels. It is 'a third term', not conforming to either side of the binary oppositions between the global and the local, or between commercial and **public service broadcasting**, which have dominated overseas debate.

The final chapter, by Stephen Turner, is the work of one of New Zealand's most original and provocative theorists. It adds further nuances and implications to an idea that has been building up through the section about television's role in shaping our nation, our **'imagined community'**, by offering particular solutions to the kinds of colonial anxiety that have permeated our culture since the days of pioneer settlement. He explores these ideas in relation to New Zealand television advertisements from Toyota's 'Bugger' to Adidas's All Black haka.

1 Studying New Zealand Television:

Themes, Methods, Perspectives

ROGER HORROCKS

Why study or analyse New Zealand television? Analysis may seem an odd process to apply to a medium regarded by many people as a vehicle for relaxation or entertainment, company or sociability, distraction or escape. But to analyse television is not to cease to value such uses—indeed, as even the most hostile critics have come to recognise, it would be a strange study of television that did not acknowledge its pleasures. What analysis offers is another dimension of understanding for those who seek it—such as those who work in the industry (as broadcasters or program-makers), or those who would like to do so; those involved in media public policy; those who see television as having informational or cultural as well as entertainment aspects; or any viewer who is simply curious to understand more about the behind-the-scenes processes of television.

As a medium that is now busily at work twenty-four hours every day of the year, with the average New Zealander watching an average of two hours forty-eight minutes per day (or approximately a sixth of waking life), television is obviously a major force in our culture.[1] For better or worse, its power to promote change and magnify trends has reshaped many areas of New Zealand life, such as politics, sport, marketing, and entertainment. Television contributes constantly to our common culture, our social vocabulary or 'social coin of exchange', such as the thoughts we share with workmates round the water cooler or with family members in the lounge.

More broadly, theorists such as Niklas Luhmann (2000) have argued that mass media such as television provide the frame of reference or cognitive system through which modern society constructs the illusion of its own reality. Television produces a continuous description and ordering of the world in television terms that we absorb all our lives. Other theorists speak similarly of television as helping to shape our '**social imaginary**', our vision of the large social units to which we (mysteriously) belong, such as our nation, our generation, our ethnic group.[2] These are a few of the ideas that will be illustrated and explored in the course of our study of New Zealand television. Of course, this is not to attribute unchallenged power to television, since it is only one force within the complex field of society and must compete for attention or interact with many other media such as radio, print, cinema, and the Internet. There is a lively, ongoing debate about the precise scope of its influence, but no commentator can afford to ignore the prominent part television has played in the daily life of our society over the past forty years.

Another motive for analysing New Zealand television is a desire to change it. This is an attitude many of us share, but since television criticism is so often dominated by moralising and by personal likes and dislikes, we have attempted to delay value judgments until some careful analysis has been done. We see 'analysis first' as an important motto for study of the mass media (while acknowledging that analysis must at the same time keep questioning its own values and assumptions).

Some analysis has always been a natural part of everyday viewing, and anyone who follows the letters column of a magazine like *TV Guide* will be well aware of the thoughtful and passionate relationship many viewers have with television. Fans develop a knowledge of **genres** matched by few academic experts. Fan communities have themselves become a subject of academic research, and the producers of established **series** have picked up new ideas from them. Yet what remains scarce outside of the industry is an awareness of production processes, including technological and economic factors. Because film and television are expensive and technically demanding media, often a practical understanding of how such '**texts**' are made is necessary for a clear and fair judgment. In addition, the academic world has its own forms of analysis providing insights into such matters as style and genre, representation and stereotype, politics and **ideology**. Above all, since television is a complex medium, analysis benefits from the combining of different perspectives—understanding how a program has been made, how it relates to others of its genre, where and why it has been scheduled, and what is interesting about it in social and political as well as creative and technical terms, to mention only a few of the dimensions. This multi-dimensional or 'big picture' approach is the basis of our book.

Why analyse television in national terms?

If we proceed to a study of 'New Zealand television,' the first question is: why think of the medium in national terms? Obviously other contexts are possible. This is a time of increasing **globalisation** and rapid technological change, and it is not uncommon for commentators, particularly in the USA, to assume that national boundaries now have little relevance. In its most extreme form such an attitude is based on a kind of utopian optimism about technology, or a belief that talk of nations is backward-looking and linked inevitably to jingoistic forms of nationalism. It is one of the ironies of globalisation that it has made us more aware of the ways in which universal claims are often merely an expanded version of some local perspective on the world.

While we need always to remember that 'New Zealand television' is a term with complex boundaries, there are dozens of ways in which it is still meaningful in our everyday lives. When viewers turn on television in this country they are presented with a local menu of options. This has to do first with the practical realities of 'reach' or 'coverage', including authorisation by the New Zealand government for television channels to use specific frequencies. Even a satellite has a limited range or '**footprint**', and cable or terrestrial (line-of-sight) transmission has a particular geographic focus. Legally, the screening rights of programs tend to be sold on the basis of national territories. The main networks (TV ONE and TV2, TV3 and TV4, and SKY) still operate primarily on a national basis, each of them transmitting their signal to most parts of the country. It is also important to realise that the small size of New Zealand's population (just under four million) means that our biggest national audiences are equivalent to regional or niche audiences in larger countries. Since television is expensive, and public funding is scarce in New Zealand, most of the industry regards a national audience as the only viable economic unit, though regional 'breakouts' (which allow the insertion of local advertising) offer a partial compromise.

When new television technologies arrive, there are often competing versions so that each country must decide which version to adopt as its 'standard'—such as New Zealand's adoption of the PAL video system (shared by the UK but not by the USA, which opted for the NTSC system). Generally a small country like New Zealand can not afford to risk the chaos that may result from competing systems. The introduction of high-definition, wide-screen forms of television will require similar choices.

Other national regulatory systems come into play, such as television censorship (administered in New Zealand by the **Broadcasting Standards Authority**). Some funding is available to the production industry on a national basis (through New Zealand On Air). And then there are the preferences and loyalties of local audiences, with their particular interest in national news, politics, and sport, and their responsiveness to local symbols and celebrities. Overseas readers may be surprised to learn of the extent to which New Zealand's cultural interests differ even from those of its closest neighbour, Australia—reflected in the fact that its television system is very different. Only a few of New Zealand's prime-time programs (or its favourite films) come from Australia, and even fewer New Zealand programs are purchased by Australian broadcasters.

To what extent television has merely reflected and served national interests, and to what extent it has been the very means by which these interests were created, are matters of vigorous debate, to be addressed by some of the essays in this book. What is clear is that the concept of the nation still matters in the world of television, though it should be emphasised that we see the nation as something fluid—an identity constructed legally, socially, and historically, which is engaged in a continuous process of re-definition (with television playing a significant role in that process). Some of our contributors prefer to speak of '**Aotearoa** New Zealand' as an explicit acknowledgement that this is a bicultural nation, and Tainui Stephens shifts (according to context) between 'New Zealand' and 'Aotearoa **Te Wai Pounamu**' (an acknowledgment of separate islands). In general, our approach is national rather than nationalist, avoiding the kinds of moralising or unhistorical talk associated with extreme (or 'essentialist') forms of nationalism. We should note, also, that while this book focuses on the nation, the global sweep of the media industries makes it necessary to keep relating New Zealand to other territories. It is equally important to acknowledge the diversity within New Zealand, and the achievements of regional and niche television as well as mainstream broadcasters. One reason why the idea of nation has been viewed with suspicion is the way it can be used selectively to suppress disagreement and difference. We are usefully reminded of difference by the many meanings of a term such as 'local'. While '**local content**' is an official term describing all the programs made in New Zealand, South Islanders are more likely to think of 'local' as referring to the South Island (whose media industry sees itself as an underdog in relation to the big companies of the North).

Is this study only of interest to New Zealanders?

New Zealand television provides an interesting case study in international terms for reasons such as these:

1) *The possibility of studying television as a system.* Even taking its regional differences into account, New Zealand is a reasonably self-contained country with a relatively small population, and this has the advantage of

allowing us to see and study television as an overall system. The system is still too complex to hope to grasp it fully, but we can observe its dynamics more clearly than we could in a larger country.

2) *Small country differences.* The systems of large countries have traditionally provided the models for the study of smaller systems. This approach has often been superficial and simplistic as in the case of visiting commentators who assume that New Zealand is merely a condensed or diluted version of British or American television. A closer look at New Zealand reveals the need for different forms of television theory that can adequately describe the distinctive field of forces within a smaller television system.

New Zealand is metaphorically as well as literally a small island nation open to whatever weather sweeps in from the rest of the globe. The political restructuring after 1984 removed so many layers of legal and economic protection that this country is highly exposed to change. Thus, it is a useful test culture for observing the impact of new trends or technologies. The waves produced by 'the storm of progress' (in Walter Benjamin's phrase) may splash against large countries and modify their landscapes but there is no danger of submersion. For New Zealand, change can become a tidal wave. Boundless optimism about new trends and technologies tends to be a large country attitude whereas small countries know the effects are not always positive. A dramatic example was the introduction of sound-on-film at the end of the 1920s which effectively wiped out the existing New Zealand feature film industry by doubling the cost and the equipment required. The industry was too fragile to adapt to the change, which was further complicated by the legal issues around patents, and feature film production did not recover to the same level in New Zealand for nearly fifty years (though a few resourceful technicians managed to develop their own sound cameras). Another example of the cost of change was the arrival of colour television in 1973, which necessitated a temporary cutback in local production. Today digitisation presents the country with a similar mixture of threats and opportunities as local broadcasters re-equip themselves and agonise over the cost of a suitable transmission system.

New Zealand can also be seen as an interesting test case for assessing the benefits and costs of globalisation. For better or worse, the mostly overseas-owned, pay television service SKY has taken control of major local sporting events and is leading the trend to digitisation. A large-scale strategic battle is being fought, with complex, shifting alliances between local and global interests as SKY attempts to position itself for the future as the dominant force in the New Zealand television market.

3) *New Zealand's **postcolonial** history.* Like other former British colonies, New Zealand has struggled to create a culture that is distinctively its own. This has been a difficult task because of the country's small size, economic dependency, and deeply ingrained sense of inferiority or '**cultural cringe**'.

(Ironically, the very term 'cultural cringe'—which refers to the way of think-ing that assumes a local product can never be as good as one from Britain, the USA, or other large countries—is itself borrowed from Australia.) Such problems add drama to the struggle to sustain and grow the local television and film industries. Leading participants have seen local production not merely as a business but as something of a crusade; and the New Zealand industry is noted for the resourcefulness and versatility of its technicians and its ability to make the most of small budgets.

These are important issues as New Zealand has one of the lowest levels of local content in the world. An analysis of its main free-to-air television channels in 2002 showed that New Zealand-made programs occupied 27.4 per cent of airtime (New Zealand On Air 2003) as the overall average, and this was the highest figure for a decade. Most pay television channels have no local content at all. Even for the free-to-air channels, New Zealand material appears to have existed from the beginning at a low level—sometimes as low as 20 per cent, sometimes as high as 30 per cent, but always small in com-parison with the more than 70 per cent figure that is customary for local content in the UK, or more than 90 per cent in the USA (New Zealand On Air 1999; Dunleavy 1999, pp. I 33, I 72, II 215–17, 283). It also falls far short of the more than 55 per cent figure in Australia where quota regulations ensure that local material represents the norm or default setting. In New Zealand it is American **programming** that occupies half the **schedule**, and there is as much British as local material.[3] Though the underlying causes are complex, such facts make New Zealand's television production industry a fascinating example of a postcolonial struggle for survival and independence.

4) *New Zealand's unique cultural mix.* The strength of both British and American influences in New Zealand is unusual. The competition between them shapes every area of the culture, from popular music to literature, and the television system provides a particularly interesting example. In the early days television presenters were required to have **BBC** accents and program-mers made a conscious effort to maintain a balance between British and American material. Today the American influence is stronger but **TVNZ** programs its channels to cater to both tastes. TV ONE's emphasis on British programs makes it the channel of choice for those over 40, while TV2's emphasis on American programs makes it the popular channel for younger viewers. Australian material is screened on both channels but generally fits more comfortably with American programs (reflecting the fact that Australia has gone further than New Zealand in distancing itself from British influence).

New Zealand's indigenous Māori culture has contributed some of the most distinctive aspects of local production, as shown by documentary series such as *Tangata Whenua* and *Waka Huia*, drama series such as *Makutu*, 'one-off' dramas such as *Fish Skin Suit*, animation series such as *Mokotoa*, and music programs such as *Mai Time*. The present government has set aside money for a Māori Television Service, a dedicated channel with strong emphasis on Māori language (**te reo**).

While coming to terms with the responsibilities of biculturalism (an important dimension of New Zealand's postcolonial history), local television is also being called upon to provide better coverage of the country's multi-cultural diversity. It is interesting to follow the evolution of the broadcasting system as it seeks to balance such needs with the traditional Anglo-American tastes of its mainstream audiences.

5) *Local conflicts over public service broadcasting.* Internationally the perennial competition between two organisational models—commercial broadcasting (the typical American approach) and public service broadcasting (the British approach known as the '**Reithian tradition**' after its founding figure Lord Reith)—has become particularly fierce over the past two decades because of the upsurge in **neo-liberal** (or pro-commercial) political thinking. New Zealand provides one of the most dramatic examples of this, since the Labour governments of the 1980s and the National governments of the 1990s both embraced extreme forms of commercialism and deregulation, a phase of our history described by Jane Kelsey (1995) as 'the New Zealand experiment'. What remained of public service broadcasting was re-packaged in an innovative form as New Zealand On Air. These changes and the results they produced make a striking case study. Since the end of the 1990s, a Labour government—concerned that things have gone too far—has attempted to reconstruct some semblance of public service in television, for example by requiring TVNZ to operate in accordance with a Charter. Debate as to whether this attempt to reverse commercial trends can possibly succeed has ensured that 'the New Zealand experiment' continues to be observed with interest.

These are some of the ways in which the New Zealand television case study casts light on current issues in international broadcasting (such as the debates over globalisation and public broadcasting). Some features of the New Zealand system are, however, relevant only to small countries (such as the exaggerated impact of technological change), and some aspects are unique to New Zealand (such as the cultural mix).

Methods of studying New Zealand television

How should we undertake a serious study of New Zealand television? Some academics in other fields find it hard to imagine—is it simply a matter of watching lots of programs? We need to do that, but it is only one dimension of television. The challenge is to do justice to the complexity of the medium. Television programs may present themselves as simple and accessible, but the processes of production and broadcasting tend to be complex, as indicated by the many specialists listed in program credits.

More generally, it is useful to keep in mind the fact that television has many 'stakeholders'—many groups with their own sets of interests, their own kind of intense involvement with the medium. On the industry side there are broadcasting companies and production companies (and in New Zealand it is important to keep those two groups separate because a great deal of production has, over the past fifteen years, been 'outsourced' to independent companies). There are also presenters, guests, and other forms of 'talent'; overseas suppliers of television programs; organisations selling sports rights; and companies that supply **ratings** and other forms of audience research. Other important groups are the technicians and the suppliers of technical services (such as the owners of satellites). Then there are advertisers who represent television's main source of income. And viewers—a hugely varied group since almost every New Zealander does some viewing. The government has its own strong interests in television as it regulates the television environment, owns a network, sells frequencies, and provides funding for certain forms of 'public good'. Many other groups may be added to this analysis of stakeholders, such as the owners of other media and other forms of entertainment, who are linked with television as allies or competitors.

None of these groups is monolithic—there are tensions between large and small production companies and fierce competition between broadcasters, to mention only two of the further divisions, so there are numerous opportunities for coalition or conflict. Furthermore, the categories overlap since an individual or institution can play more than one role. The important thing is to understand how broad the range of perspectives can be and how passionately they can be held. This powerful and expensive medium excites hopes, ambitions, and disappointments—consider the angry letters to newspapers, the complaints to the Broadcasting Standards Authority, the debates in industry magazines such as *Onfilm*, or the battles between commercial organisations (such as TVNZ, TV3, and SKY). Each opinion may appear justified and coherent in terms of where its advocate is standing; but rather than align ourselves with a single interest, it is the aim of our book to assemble and compare perspectives, enabling us to perceive the overall field of forces.

Aspects of the medium

As another way to grasp the complexity, we may turn from the many groups with a stake in television to the medium itself. What are its main aspects and what methods of analysis are associated with each of them?

a) Textual aspects. This term refers to the nature of television programs as communication, as a message shaped creatively and then 'read' or 'decoded'. Textual analysis involves detailed study in a variety of forms—from the kind of close attention a fan devotes to a favourite program, to interpretation by a specialist in **semiotics** or cultural studies. In an academic context, such close **reading** draws upon the skills associated with the study of literature and language but adds an understanding of other elements such as images and soundtracks, together with the kinds of cultural analysis developed by sociology and anthropology. Program-makers also have their own styles of analysis, using technical terms known to production people round the world. The television industry and the academic world tend to be unfamiliar with (and suspicious of) each other's approaches—one group focuses on making programs, the other on reading them—but for the best results, textual study draws on both traditions.

Television raises new questions about the nature of texts because the medium consists not only of individual programs but also, typically, of series, and of the endless **flow** of the schedule, the so-called television 'supertext' (which will be discussed in our chapter on programming). The term '**intertextuality**' draws our attention to the intricate relationships between texts, both inside and outside the television medium. 'Genre' is an important concept for sorting out the similarities and differences between myriad programs. And by emphasising the complex nature of communication, post-structural, psychoanalytical, and **reception** theorists can protect us from becoming so straightforward and literal in our reading that we fail to consider subtle nuances, multiple meanings, and subconscious energies.

Assisted by the video recorder and a recognition that one needs to pay one's dues by watching week after week, this kind of textual and cultural analysis is a crucial dimension of television study. Any understanding of texts should, however, be complemented by an understanding of their *contexts*—social, political, economic, and technological—and the shifting relations between them. The contexts (represented by the next four categories) provide us with other explanations of how and why texts have come to take on their particular shape.

b) Social aspects. Television both mirrors and influences the organisation of social life, in the way it relates its programming to different times of day and different times of year. The term 'social' also draws our attention to the 'uses and gratifications' that television provides for various groups in society. Indeed, the attempt to understand more about the complex nature of audiences has been a central concern of media academics and broadcasters over the past decade. Such research can be either quantitative or qualitative. Broadcasters have focused on market research, particularly the development of quantitative measures such as ratings, whereas recent academic work has tended to focus on ethnographic or qualitative approaches. This is not to suggest that broadcasters do not also use qualitative research (such as focus groups), or that academics do not value quantitative data (which has played an important role in the mass communications tradition).

The study of audiences focuses both on reception (the ways in which people experience, interpret, and respond to television) and on functionality (the ways in which the medium functions in the lives of viewers). Laurence Simmons's chapter in this book illustrates the second of these approaches in its account of how New Zealanders in the 1960s chose to integrate the new medium into their everyday lives and domestic spaces.

c) Political aspects. Because of the power of the mass media, all governments have been concerned to develop some rules to regulate broadcasting standards, unfair trade practices, and access to scarce resources such as broadcasting frequencies. To understand the New Zealand television system it is important to be aware of the relevant government ministers and ministries, and key items of legislation such as the 1989 Broadcasting Act that define the current rules of the broadcasting game.

While the New Zealand government owns a television network (TVNZ), it does not overtly interfere with program context, apart from establishing the general orientation it wants the network to adopt ('more commercial' during the 1980s and 1990s and 'more public service' after 1999). Some overseas governments intervene very directly in television news coverage, and immigrants from those parts of the world may initially be puzzled by the 'arm's length' relationship between television and government in New Zealand. This is not to suggest that our politicians have never tried to influence television—some Prime Ministers have made blatant attempts, and in more subtle terms all the main political parties employ specialists or 'spin doctors' to help them to play the media game as effectively as possible within the rules.

There are many ways that our television system has a rich political dimension, including its role as an arena for national politics. Political studies of television range from detailed scrutiny of news and current affairs programs to analysis of the ideological implications of popular drama series.

d) Economic aspects. Since television is a highly expensive, competitive, and risky medium, economic pressures influence almost every aspect of production and broadcasting. It is a sobering thought that currently all of New Zealand's television networks (including SKY and TV3/TV4) are either losing money or at best making only a modest profit (like TVNZ). Many channels have come and gone (such as the original TV3, surviving only six months in 1989–90 before its dramatic meltdown). There is an obvious need for 'industrial' studies of television, examining commercial, organisational, and strategic aspects. Recent work on 'the creative industries' has attempted to expand economic analysis to take account of less tangible issues such as 'intellectual property' or 'cultural capital'.

Another aspect of economics is advertising, which for many years has been the main source of revenue for free-to-air television in New Zealand, though commercial sponsorship is also important. This situation has far-reaching implications since advertising and sponsorship have influenced the viability of programs, their budgets, the slots in which they are scheduled, the '**target audiences**' sought, their structure (e.g. dramas written and documentaries edited in 'five acts' to allow for the four ad breaks per hour, including 'cliff-hangers' to prevent the viewer from changing channel during the breaks), and so on. The ups and downs of the advertising market also influence the financial health of channels and their ability to undertake new projects. Of course, other sources of income also need to be considered such as overseas sales or co-productions, or public funding through New Zealand On Air.

e) Technological aspects. Television depends upon the appropriate use of sophisticated forms of technology. For example, anyone with a serious interest in television needs to understand the technical and stylistic differences between (a) multi-camera studio production (such as a **soap opera**), (b) single-camera location filming (such as a drama series with 'high **production values**'), and (c) '**OB**' or outside broadcast (such as a football game).

Television has been transformed by such inventions as videotape (replacing film that was still being used by TVNZ for news gathering into the 1980s), satellites (providing a constant 'feed' of news from round the world), and small digital cameras (helping to make possible the current flood of 'reality programs' and 'fly on the wall documentaries'). Today, as the world is living through a period of accelerated technological change, television is struggling to come to terms with the Internet, **interactivity**, high definition images, digital personal video recorders (such as TiVo), and many other developments.

Marshall McLuhan's famous slogan 'The medium is the message' (1967) usefully focused attention on the distinctive aspects of television as a medium; but subsequent work has modified or challenged McLuhan's approach by emphasising the particular ways in which a medium such as television gets shaped and re-shaped by social, economic, and political circumstances (Winston 1986, 1998). Simmons's chapter again provides a good example in its account of the introduction of television into New Zealand. A similar interest in the ways a technology or medium is socially constructed informs other chapters also, such as James Littlewood and Luke Goode's discussion of the digital transformation of New Zealand television.

The five aspects listed above are necessary for any comprehensive understanding of how television in general, or an individual program, comes to take its particular shape:

Figure 1.1

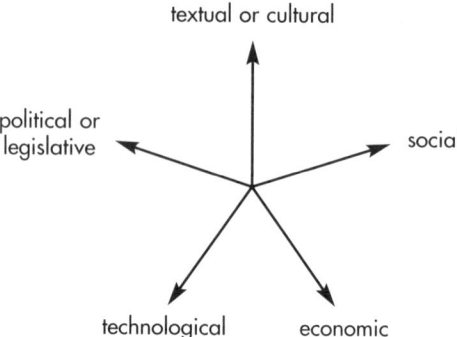

Of course there is some overlap between these factors, and ultimately they represent differences of emphasis rather than discrete categories, but a multi-disciplinary approach of this kind ensures that we look at events from more than one angle. Every major decision by broadcasters or program-makers is likely to have taken into account at least several of these factors. A new series, for example, will have been carefully considered in terms of its budget and potential sales, its technical requirements and problems, and its suitability for a time-slot and target audience on a particular channel, in addition to its creative or cultural aspects. Legislation may also have played a part—such as the need for TVNZ to consider the relevance of a program to the government's Charter requirements or its acceptability in terms of broadcasting standards. In other words, what happens on television is 'over-determined' (that is, it has multiple causes) because of the complex nature of the medium and the intricate way it is involved with society. As all program-makers know, the various factors constantly interact, and a creative decision may be stimulated by a technical or budget problem.

The term '**political economy**' refers to an important tradition of analysis that usefully brings together politics and economics. But such an approach can be strengthened still further by paying attention to textual and cultural complexities. It is a basic assumption of this book that television is best understood by recognising a range of different perspectives and trying to negotiate between them. The medium of television is important in our society culturally, politically, and economically—and it relates to all of these aspects at once. Individual chapters of this book may focus on a single aspect—such as an audience or reception study, an analysis of public policy, an institutional or industrial topic—but it will still keep in mind the com-plex overall situation because that is television's natural environment.

One must also learn to look sceptically at any public statement about television that confines itself to a single factor. It's not that the statement is necessarily untrue, but it is likely to provide only one aspect of the truth. Many groups—political parties, broadcasters, 'concerned citizens', academics —indulge in single-factor explanations when they seek to command the moral high ground or claim to offer a striking new interpretation.

Another useful concept for discussing television is 'the **public sphere**', developed by Jurgen Habermas (1989), referring to the realm of public opinion within any society. In a healthy democracy there is broad partici-pation, freedom of speech, and rational, well-informed debate on the issues of the day, leading to some kind of general consensus. Such debate occurs within society at large, helping to prevent either big business or the govern-ment from simply imposing its own view. This vision of an ideal democratic situation can be used as a measure of our own society. In theory, a medium such as television could do much to assist the workings of the public sphere, but, in practice, television has—according to Habermas's analysis—come under elite forms of control, and is increasingly characterised by emotional-ism and manipulation (such as the work of advertising agencies and political 'spin doctors'). Viewers are treated more often as 'consumers' than as 'citi-zens'. Some New Zealand research into television news and current affairs has documented negative tendencies of this kind (for example, Atkinson 1994a, 1994b, 2001; McGregor and Comrie 2002; and Crofts's chapter in the present book). Our chapter on programming will explore the concept of '**hegemony**' as another way of understanding subtle forms of media control.

It should be emphasised, however, that the idea of the public sphere is meant to encourage activism rather than defeatism. Public debate at the individual level remains lively, fluid, and full of competing views, and at least some of this diversity finds its way into the mass media. Reception studies have confirmed that television viewing is far from passive (Morley 1986; Ang 1991)—we may debate, resist, or re-interpret what we see. Public policy has gone through major shifts over the past twenty years, and in a relatively small country like New Zealand it is possible even for small groups to have some impact on community debate. The TVNZ Charter is one recent example of a policy change that grew out of concern over public sphere issues.

One of the implications for this book is that readers should not be sur-prised or alarmed to find contributors disagreeing with one another. Tele-vision is a rapidly changing field in which (for example) different conceptions of 'New Zealand' are constantly being formed, reformed, and set in competition. It is no longer possible for any individual (or any archive) to keep up with the dozens of channels broadcasting twenty-four hours a day. Our book hopes to offer insights into this hugely energetic, sprawling, contested medium, but can not claim to offer final answers. The concept of the public sphere encourages each of us to become involved, developing our own view of television and how it may be improved, and taking part in the public (or classroom) debate.

If we stress difference and conflict, however, it is important not to forget the other side of the situation, which is inter-connection and inter-dependence. A possible concept here is not 'public sphere' but 'eco-system'. From that perspective, New Zealand television is a small and vulnerable habitat with a number of endangered species. Broadcasters and production companies struggle to survive and grow in a challenging environment, sensitive to any new form of life introduced (such as pay television) or any change of temperature (such as a downturn in advertising revenue). A key aspect of ecology is the awareness that everything is interrelated so that any change has subtle flow-on effects. It is particularly important in a small country such as New Zealand for public policy to take these complex ripples into account, so the trade-offs can be carefully weighed up. Unfortunately this has seldom been the case in the numerous restructurings of the local television system. Governments have tended to ignore warnings from the media industry because they assume that such advice is self-interested. The lesson of history is not that politicians should cease to intervene—after all, taking care of the broadcasting environment is (arguably) as important as taking care of the natural environment, and doing nothing can be the most short-sighted and destructive policy of all—but that those making public policy need to display a greater awareness of the vulnerability and complex dynamics of the field.

The world of television is even more complex than our metaphor since it is an open rather than a closed system—not a pond or a lake but a small part of an ocean, with changing currents and passing predators. Our eco-system metaphor also needs to represent the television environment as active and competitive, stressing the battles and ever-changing alliances. However, this is not to suggest that television is merely a Darwinian struggle for survival of the fittest—many people in the industry are also driven by cultural or creative motives, and every television production requires a high degree of cooperation. In a healthy environment governments and broadcasters will ensure that skills and energies are nurtured rather than exploited or blocked—otherwise a television system cannot adequately represent and contribute to the energies of the culture at large. Like the public sphere, television as an eco-system can function in a more or less healthy, more or less productive way.

For the writers of the present book it is the cultural or creative or textual aspects of the medium that ultimately excite and intrigue us most, but we are also aware that these aspects of television can never be fully understood in isolation from all the other forces in the environment—whether conceived in terms of political economy, public sphere, eco-system, or some other perspective.

References

Anderson, Benedict. 1991. *Imagined Communities: Reflections on the Origin and Spread of Nationalism*. London: Verso.

Ang, Ien. 1991. *Desperately Seeking the Audience*. London: Routledge.

Atkinson, Joe. 1994a. 'The State, the Media, and Thin Democracy'. In A. Sharp (ed.) *Leap into the Dark*. Auckland: Auckland University Press.

Atkinson, Joe. 1994b. 'Structures of Television News'. In P. Ballard (ed.) *Power and Responsibility*. Wellington: Broadcasting Standards Authority.

Atkinson, Joe. 2001. 'Tabloid Democracy'. In R. Miller (ed.) *New Zealand Government and Politics*. Auckland: Oxford University Press.

Dunleavy, Trisha. 1999. New Zealand Drama: The First Thirty Years 1960–1990. Thesis (PhD), University of Auckland.

Habermas, Jurgen. 1989. *The Structural Transformation of the Public Sphere: An Inquiry into a Category of Bourgeois Society*. Cambridge: Polity.

Kelsey, Jane. 1995. *The New Zealand Experiment: A World Model for Structural Adjustment?* Auckland: Auckland University Press & Bridget Williams Books.

Luhmann, Niklas. 2000. *The Reality of the Mass Media*. Cambridge: Polity Press.

McGregor, Judy & Margie Comrie. 2002. *What's News?: Reclaiming Journalism in New Zealand*. Palmerston North: Dunmore Press.

McLuhan, Marshall. 1967. *Understanding Media: The Extensions of Man*. London: Sphere Books.

Morley, David. 1986. *Family Television: Cultural Power and Domestic Leisure*. London: Comedia.

Musgrave, Diane. 2000. Time Shifts: A Comparison of Diversity in New Zealand Television 1984 and 1999. Thesis (MA). University of Auckland.

New Zealand On Air 1999. *Local Content and Diversity: Television in Ten Countries*. Wellington.

New Zealand On Air. 2003. *Local Content 2002: New Zealand Television*. Available at: http://www.nzonair.govt.nz/

Winston, Brian. 1986. *Misunderstanding Media*. London: Routledge and Kegan Paul.

Winston, Brian. 1998. *Media Technology and Society: A History*. London: Routledge.

Notes

1 Television Broadcasters' Council figures for 2001, based on ACNielsen research. See 'Our Eyes are Getting Squarer', *NZ Herald*, 6 March 2001. For waking and sleep, see 'Dying to Sleep' in the *NZ Herald*, 13 May 2000. In terms of audience size, it is estimated that 1 400 000 New Zealanders watched the second race of the America's Cup series on TV ONE in 2003, and even larger New Zealand audiences watched the 2000 Olympic Games on television ('Live Agony for 1.5 Million Viewers', *NZ Herald*, 18 February 2003).

2 Compare, for example, Benedict Anderson (1991).

3 The American/British figures are an educated guess. For some relevant research see Dunleavy (1999) and Musgrave (2000).

2 The History of New Zealand Television:

'An Expensive Medium for a Small Country'

ROGER HORROCKS

While this book focuses on the New Zealand television system today, it is important to have a general understanding of how and why the system evolved into its current form. Laurence Simmons's chapter on the arrival of television in New Zealand will document the particular hopes and fears of the initial phase, attitudes that have continued to colour the public's relationship with television ever since. The present chapter briefly describes the main events and stages through which television has passed over the last forty years, with particular emphasis on the last decade. To begin with a broad overview, what were the challenges that presented themselves to the New Zealand television system from the beginning? It needed to:

1 develop the necessary infrastructure
2 make the best use of technology
3 build a national audience
4 produce a range of local programs
5 represent the country's diversity
6 develop appropriate management and regulatory systems.

These were ambitious challenges for the new system and for the government that initiated it. The local history of television can be seen as a record of changing strategies, driven by forces both from inside the television system and from outside (national and international), to realise and sustain those aims in a small country with limited resources. The six aims (which we shall now consider in detail) were often in direct competition for the available resources.

The first challenge was to *develop the necessary infrastructure*, including studios and offices, camera and editing equipment, a transmission network, and a staff that necessarily encompassed a range of specialised skills (from writers to engineers, sound recordists to presenters). The New Zealand government established such a system in 1960 after a number of delays that reflected worries about the cost. One of the most difficult tasks was achieving national coverage, since the setting up of a system of broadcasting transmitters and repeaters was complicated by New Zealand's extremely uneven terrain and scattered population. In 1969 the four regional stations (which had taken turns to share programs) were combined as one nationwide network, but television reception continued to be a hot political issue in some rural areas.

To *make the best use of technology* involved keeping up with change. New Zealand's small population and the reluctance of governments to spend money for cultural purposes has meant a shortage of capital so that every big change—technological or organisational—has required difficult trade-offs. Colour transmission arrived late in 1973, and television was then hit hard by the costs involved in its coverage of the 1974 Commonwealth Games in Christchurch, and in 1975 by its establishment of a second channel (TV-2, which then became South Pacific Television, before ending up as TV2). These were all popular moves but they led to cutbacks in other areas of television (such as less local production or fewer commissions for independents). Today Television New Zealand (TVNZ) faces another technological and financial challenge in shifting to the digital.

The third aim was to *build a national audience.* Television succeeded in becoming the most popular mass medium in the country. When Neil Armstrong walked on the moon in 1969, an estimated one and a half million New Zealanders watched the event on television, though transmission was not quite simultaneous since the country did not have a direct satellite link for another two years. (Australia already had such a link, an aspect of its television history that provided the basis for the film *The Dish*.) By the 1970s there was a television set in almost every New Zealand household, with huge nationwide audiences for the Melbourne Cup, the Commonwealth Games, the Olympic Games, All Black tests, and the twenty-four-hour Telethons that raised millions for charity.

Today it is estimated that more New Zealanders watch drama programs on television on a single night than attend live theatrical performances over the course of a year (Statistics New Zealand 2002). A book that sells 10 000 copies in New Zealand is a bestseller; an art exhibition visited by 20 000 is exceptional; a film seen by 100 000 viewers is considered a hit; yet an estimated audience of 400 000 viewers would be considered a quiet night for TV ONE. Of course numbers are not the whole story, but for a person or news item to appear in **prime time** on one of the main free-to-air channels means nationwide exposure and the possibility of becoming a topic of dinner-table or morning-tea discussion in every corner of the country. The public's relationship with television has always been passionate, as anyone involved in broadcasting or public policy soon discovers. In the mid 1990s when a TVNZ programmer newly arrived from Australia cut back on the hours of *Coronation Street,* he found that overnight he had become a public enemy. A nationwide petition and other protests forced TVNZ to back down. Networks constantly receive letters from angry viewers describing changes to the broadcast time of a favourite program as a threat to the very fabric of their family life, since household routine and the television schedule have become so interwoven.

One of the most serious aspects of television's popularity has been its role as a national forum. Newspapers in New Zealand tend to be regional, as do radio stations (though there are important exceptions such as the Radio NZ National Program). Television can be a powerful medium for a former colony that is striving to develop an independent cultural and political stance, and struggling to achieve critical mass in a world that seldom notices such a small country. Television has provided an arena for the competing ideas and images of nationhood that New Zealanders have proposed and debated. Current affairs programs (such as *Gallery, Nationwide, Frontline, Holmes,* and *Assignment*) have explored national issues and been the site of famous confrontations. Television has stirred up valuable controversy by its re-interpretations of history, for example in the 1977 drama series *The Governor* and the 1998 documentary series *The New Zealand Wars. The Governor* was, however, fiercely criticised by the government of the time as an extravagance, and large drama and documentary projects are difficult to mount today, only possible as a collaboration between a mainstream broadcaster and the public funding body New Zealand On Air (**NZOA**). Projects on a national scale may become increasingly difficult to fund in the future as channel options multiply and the advertising revenue that sustains the major free-to-air broadcasters is divided up more thinly. Critics would argue that this is healthy as it reduces the possibility of television being misused as a platform for narrow forms of nationalism. From a postcolonial viewpoint, however, there are progressive aspects to the existence of a lively national culture and the availability of a national forum, a function that television has—for all its limitations—played over the years.

Closely related to this issue is the desire to *produce a range of local programs*. Today the forty years of material held in New Zealand's two television archives adds up to an impressively rich heritage. Yet almost everyone who has been associated with local production over that period will see television's success as uneven—not because of the quality of the programs but because of their limited quantity and range.

'Local' is of course a complex term. It can refer to regional as well as national programs, to local readings and adaptations of overseas material, or to our distinctive mixture of British and American programming. But within the production industry the term 'local content' refers to material made by New Zealand-based companies. Such material represents approximately a quarter of the schedule of the main free-to-air channels (and a much smaller proportion of the schedule of other broadcasters), and though it occasionally goes up or down by a few percentage points it has always hovered around this level.

For nearly three decades there was only one New Zealand network and no pressure on prices, and with no quota obligations, the network was happy to fill up most of its schedule with overseas material. At the same time audiences did expect local programs, and some network staff were eager to produce them. The result was a small but steady flow of local material, with news, current affairs, and sport representing the most popular genres. Local documentaries also played a significant part. Broadcasters were more cautious about dramas and comedies, both because these genres were expensive and because public support seemed more fickle. Response has ranged from long-term public enthusiasm for series such as *Close to Home* (1975–83) and *Shortland Street* (from 1992), to the disastrous ratings for series such as *Melody Rules* (1994) and *City Life* (1996). The most successful dramas (such as the 'kidult' or 'family' series of the late 1970s and early 1980s, and the long-running prime-time series produced by South Pacific Pictures in the 1990s) have proved that New Zealand material can achieve both local popularity and overseas sales—although many writers and producers see the local audience as their most important constituency.

In recent years the high ratings and commercial sponsors for 'lifestyle', 'consumer', and 'reality' programs have enabled broadcasters to provide local content relatively cheaply, and other areas of production such as in-depth documentaries and one-off dramas have thinned out (though this change also reflects international trends). Overall, a search through the archives reveals impressive examples of every type of program, yet involvement in some genres has been intermittent, and there are frustrated viewers, writers, and directors who would argue that television has realised only a small part of the potential of New Zealand production. Our book will return to this theme in its chapters on 'local content' and 'television drama'.

A related challenge for television has been to *represent the country's diversity*, and this has been a struggle from the beginning. The small size of New Zealand has meant that not only is it difficult to create large national projects, but it is also difficult for a minority to reach critical mass. Māori language and culture, ethnic and national communities, and 'highbrow' and other specialised interests have not been well served by our television system. Regional coverage—another important aspect of diversity—has been under threat in recent years. In response to these concerns, champions of the free market are inclined to reply: 'Well, what's stopping any group from starting its own channel?' Some resourceful community groups have done exactly this, but there is no public funding earmarked for such ventures and the setting up of even a small channel is likely to cost upwards of a million dollars (to cover the cost of a frequency and the purchase of equipment), to say nothing of the ongoing production of programs and other running costs. Radio has achieved more public access and diversity because it is a much cheaper medium.

The 1989 Broadcasting Act acknowledged the importance of minority interests (though it did not refer specifically to regionalism), and New Zealand On Air, the public funding body for national television, has supported this principle in two ways—by sponsoring specialist minority programs (for ethnic and national groups, religious denominations, the gay and lesbian communities, people with disabilities, etc.) and by '**mainstreaming**' (getting minorities represented in prime-time programs for the general audience). NZOA has successfully championed diversity in the mainstream programs it has funded, but its support for minority programs has been complicated by the reluctance of national networks to make time available. The networks regard their airtime as a precious, saleable commodity, and even when minority programs are offered to them free, they believe that an 'opportunity cost' is at stake. They have been prepared to screen a few such programs but only on Sunday morning (the one part of the schedule they are still required to keep free of advertising) or late at night.

While diversity has increased with the growing number of niche pay channels, most of them deal only in overseas material. New Zealand has had privately owned free-to-air regional television stations since 1991 when Canterbury Television (CTV) appeared—but not being eligible for NZOA funding, these small stations must work hard to stay afloat. A particularly impressive example is Triangle Television, a community access channel that first went to air in Auckland in 1998, carrying programs by a range of ethnic groups (who pay a modest fee for their airtime) and providing a training ground for new and sometimes controversial creative teams (such as *Back of the Y*). There are also some ethnic pay services (such as World TV's package of seven Asian channels on SKY), but few groups in New Zealand have the numbers to sustain their own television service, particularly one with the capacity to produce original material. (The Māori community, with the legal support of the Treaty of Waitangi, is an exceptional case, and Māori broadcasting and program-making will be discussed in a separate chapter.) This difficult situation is one reason why academics writing about television have given so much sympathetic attention to minority programs and interests.

From the first years the government wrestled with the need to *develop appropriate management and regulatory systems*—both for its ownership of TVNZ, and for its regulation of the system as a whole. The professed aim was public policy based on high principles, but unfortunately television soon became a political football. In any situation in which resources are under pressure and a highly popular medium is involved, there is a danger of policy being reduced to party point-scoring. The first of a hectic series of restructurings of broadcasting took place in 1975, and there were no less than seventeen over the next fourteen years, reshaping the relationship between the two television channels and the overall management of the system (Spicer, Powell, and Emanuel 1996, pp. 7–19; Farnsworth 1989, 1992). For example, the NZBS (New Zealand Broadcasting Service) was replaced by the **NZBC** (New Zealand Broadcasting Corporation), then by the BCNZ (Broadcasting Council of New Zealand), and finally by TVNZ (Television New Zealand, as we have known it since 1980). The ceaseless search for cost efficiencies has proved to be an expensive activity in its own right.

Although by 1961 television had gained some autonomy along the lines of the BBC (which operates with an editorial freedom not available to state systems in less democratic countries), prime ministers such as Robert Muldoon still attempted to influence or control it. Similarly, the BBC has had to withstand strong pressure from politicians such as Margaret Thatcher, but its established traditions of independence have given it a few more layers of defence. Muldoon's tactics included the withholding of funding— for example, by refusing to adjust the level of the Public Broadcasting Fee (or 'licence') to keep up with inflation.

Another problem was the tendency for television to develop a self-interested bureaucracy that was stifling both to creative people within the network and to independent program-makers trying to get work screened. Emerging from the creative ferment of the 1960s, the following decade brought the rise of a new film industry in New Zealand, and a range of important political and cultural movements including the Māori renaissance and feminism. Although television made room for some of this innovative work (such as the *Tangata Whenua* series in 1974 and the *Women* series in 1977), it was a narrow door that provided access to only some of the new energies. It gave first priority to its own production departments, and after some of the restructurings there was little funding left to purchase independent work. Thus the young creative people who initiated a New Zealand feature-film industry in 1977 tended to see television as a hidebound institution with a cautious, middle-of-the-road sensibility, apart from a few friends and allies within the organisation who managed to slip them a commission now and then. The belief that television was in urgent need of a shake-up was shared by the neo-liberal politicians who came to power in 1984, but their solution—to fully commercialise TVNZ and to deregulate the system—created a new broadcasting culture that turned out in creative terms to be no less difficult and controlling.

Broadcasting had always been highly regulated. Although some regulations were based on a sound commitment to public welfare and equality, others were paternalistic. When the pirate radio station Hauraki escaped to sea in 1966, many New Zealanders sympathised with this victory by the new youth culture. There were many bids to establish private, commercial television channels but none was authorised until 1987 when TV3 received a warrant, going to air two years later. Whether regulating or deregulating, the governments of New Zealand have been constantly tempted to leave their mark on broadcasting, often with a heavy-handed touch.

Five models of broadcasting

One way to grasp these various political changes is to see the history of New Zealand television as passing through five phases or models of broadcasting:

a government broadcasting (1960–61)
b public service diluted by commercialism (1961–88)
c TVNZ as a commercial broadcaster counter-balanced by NZOA (1989–95)
d dominant commercialism (1995–99)
e attempts to revive public service broadcasting (since 1999).

In 1960 the television system began as a government department. Although this compromised its independence in political terms, its style of operation reflected the values of the British system of public service or non-commercial broadcasting (based on Lord Reith's ideas, which had provided the BBC with its philosophical basis). The most striking aspect was the absence of advertising, but this condition lasted only ten months. Local politicians had always intended the system to be a hybrid of commercialism and public service broadcasting, so the first phase was merely a period of transition.

British public service broadcasting, in its pure form, insists on keeping both commercialism and the government at a distance. The New Zealand version abandoned the first principle but embraced the second at the end of 1961 when the National government gave television more independence by making it a public corporation (the NZBC). The other principles of public service broadcasting were well suited to the prevailing values of the New Zealand welfare state (basically accepted by both of the main political parties), and public funding was the only way to satisfy the nationwide desire for access to the new medium. Free universal access or coverage was a key public service principle, and getting the signal to some parts of New Zealand was so difficult that there would have been no commercial incentive to cover those areas.

The new television service was modelled on the existing public radio network, in the belief (not shared by film-makers) that radio was the medium with the greatest similarity to television. Both radio and television were funded by public licence payments, later combined into one fee, which each household paid annually. According to Reithian principles the government set the level of the fee but was otherwise expected to stay at arm's length, while the licence provided the broadcasters with adequate funding to be used purely for broadcasting purposes in a non-profit environment. But New Zealand politicians saw commercial revenue as necessary to supplement the licence fee because television was such an expensive medium. Their thinking had a pragmatic logic—hybridity or compromise seemed inevitable in a small country—but this had the effect of ruling out the possibility of a pure public service channel (like the UK's BBC, Australia's **ABC**, or Canada's CBC) once and for all.

The New Zealand system retained many links with the Reithian tradition but inevitably there was a dilution and muddying of its philosophy— 'public service' became simply 'public broadcasting'. Radio also developed in a hybrid form, owned by the government but with commercial (ZB) stations alongside non-commercial (YA and YC). However, radio differed from television in that two stations devoted to pure public service broadcasting (the National and Concert Programs) survived intact. Their regular listeners have a clear understanding of non-commercial principles and have always rushed to support the stations whenever they saw such principles threatened. No television channel has been similarly fenced off.

In the second and longest phase, from 1961 to around 1988, New Zealand television operated as a mix of British-style public service and American-style commercialism. For most of this period it still retained a public service ethos in its organisation and its basic approach to programming. First as a single channel and then from 1975 as two channels (which were initially managed by separate public corporations), the network sought to provide something for everyone according to the Reithian belief that broadcasting should 'inform, educate, and entertain'. Key concepts were 'balance' (a particular conception of the term that implied equal amounts of education and entertainment) and 'complementary programming' (providing a distinct choice rather than competing).

Nevertheless, the public service approach was compromised in three ways. First, there was the distraction of advertising. It began as seven minutes an hour (half of today's amount but still substantial). Since advertising was limited to three and a half days per week, this hybrid system was exactly 'half and half'. This was the compromise that the government believed the public would accept, a political calculation that also took into account the amount of the licence fee, the desirable amount of local content, and the basic level of service. When television's finances became perilous, politicians chose to increase advertising rather than the licence fee. After thirteen years at its initial level, advertising expanded to four days in 1974 and five in 1975, and to eight minutes an hour in 1977—an extra minute that brought TV1 an additional $3 million per year (Boyd-Bell 1985; Smith 1996, pp. 151–64; Day 2000, p. 227). Commercial days increased to six in 1985, and six and a half in 1989, leaving Sunday morning the only non-commercial part of the weekly schedule, apart from some restrictions on advertising during children's programs and a few special public holidays. Advertising (and advertisers) became steadily more important to television than licence fee income. In 1976 licence fee funding represented only 43.6 per cent of total income; by 1980 it was down to 29.4 per cent, by 1984 to 18 per cent, and by 1986 to 13 per cent.

The second weakness was the low level of local content. With governments slow to increase the licence fee (for political reasons of one sort or another), television faced fierce budget pressures, and in that situation executives were inclined to see local production as discretionary or optional spending, as an expensive area where savings could be made. Though many local programs were popular, and their production was cheap by international standards, they had to compete with countless overseas programs available at bargain-basement prices.

The third weakness was too much timidity or conservatism, encouraged by the fact that television was often under attack from hostile politicians. Innovation and risk-taking are meant to be special strengths of public service broadcasting but they were tempered in New Zealand by the cautious, bureaucratic atmosphere that developed not only in television but in many other areas of the public sector during the Muldoon era.

The next phase of television history began when the Lange government came to power in 1984 and took its revenge on the bureaucratic and over-regulated style of the previous government. Its program of radical reform was known as 'Rogernomics' (after Finance Minister Roger Douglas). Television was restructured by the 1989 Broadcasting Act, but over the course of the decade television had been getting ready, shifting each year further away from the public service model and closer to the commercial model. This shift was in line with the politics of the new government, which extolled the energies of global capitalism. The government proceeded at breakneck speed to privatise various areas of the public sector, selling them mostly to overseas buyers as part of what it saw as a necessary process of globalisation. It restructured other areas as **SOE**s (state-owned enterprises, required to operate like commercial companies).

When a Royal Commission on Broadcasting delivered a report in 1986 that provided a thoughtful re-assertion of the principles of public service broadcasting, it was out of step with a government that saw public institutions such as TVNZ as lazy and bloated, and was certain that what the sector needed was commercialism, competition, and deregulation. Basically the government ignored the report apart from an eighteen-page addendum by L.A. Cameron, a dissenting member of the Commission, who argued that public service broadcasting needed to be more clearly and narrowly focused. At this time public service broadcasting was also under attack in other countries, as neo-liberal politicians sought to downsize the public sector and give more scope to capitalism and the energies of the 'free market'. The New Zealand government justified its plans to shake up broadcasting on the grounds that the media were about to undergo a digital transformation globally and the only way for the country to reap the benefits was to lift restrictions and encourage commercial enterprise. Accordingly, the 1989 Broadcasting Act restructured TVNZ as an SOE. This was widely assumed to be a method of preparing the network for sale, making it more attractive to potential buyers by demonstrating its profit-making ability.

For supporters of public service broadcasting, the new approach was a calamity. There had been many things wrong with television, but the policies of the new government seemed an extreme over-reaction. Instead of returning to true public service values, the champions of Rogernomics denied that broadcasting had any special cultural importance—they saw it simply as another business, and treated networks and transmission frequencies as assets to be exploited for profit (Easton 1997, pp. 54–70). 'Culture' was a word they seldom used, and in practice the only culture they promoted was that of commerce (seen as a kind of super-culture that encompassed all other values and activities). The new government changed the rules of the broadcasting game in such a way that the commercial always took precedence (Horrocks 1996). The idea of 'public service' was redefined as 'giving the public what it wants', and high ratings and profits were seen as the only reliable proof. There were, however, underlying complications in the fact that television was now primarily in the business of selling audiences to advertisers. Profits confirmed that advertisers were happy, or that the economy was buoyant; and ratings proved that at least a sample of viewers watched certain programs; but neither set of figures adequately measured the level of satisfaction among the public at large. The increased commercialism of television was therefore accompanied by public controversies about audience satisfaction, advertising, ratings, and an alleged 'dumbing down' of standards (Lealand 2000).

Inside TVNZ, the effects of the new model were very much in line with overseas precedents. They included increased advertising and sponsorship, more 'populist' programs (with an emphasis on brisk pacing and emotional impact), a rejection of slow and complex modes of presentation, an increased interest in strategic **scheduling** and the 'branding' of channels, and a huge expansion in ratings, market research, and financial scrutiny of every area of the schedule and every series. There was also increased promotion of the network's stars, whose huge salaries became a hot topic of public debate when scandals occurred (most notoriously in 1999 in the wake of an unsuccessful attempt to shift newsreader John Hawkesby from TV3 to TV ONE). The new approach also involved a shake-up up in the hierarchy of production, with the maker of programs sent to the bottom of the ladder as a mere 'supplier'. He or she had to serve the commissioning editor, who in turn worked for the programmer, who in turn worked for the ultimate 'suits', the financial managers. These changes implied that what was impor- tant about television was the schedule as a whole and the financial success of each slot, not the individual program. Though the makers of programs had never been very high on the ladder, this was clearly a demotion—for them, the new hierarchy was precisely the wrong way round.

The commercial atmosphere was further heightened by the arrival in 1989 of TV3, the first privately owned channel. The introduction of com- petition rippled through every aspect of the system from program-buying to scheduling to marketing, with the conflict between TVNZ and TV3 going to extremes (such as the alleged defacing of billboards and the buying up and stockpiling of more programs than necessary to deny them to the competing network). Nevertheless there were some positive effects, since program-makers for the first time had at least one other possible customer for their ideas. TVNZ was well prepared to face its new rival, having been whipped strenuously into shape during the late 1980s by its Director- General Julian Mounter. TV3 had underestimated the competition, and had already had to spend too much money and energy in its struggle to obtain a broadcasting warrant (with TVNZ fighting a long delaying action). The new network went into receivership after only six months with an estimated deficit of $50 million—a striking example of the risks involved in the small New Zealand television market.

The National government helped TV3 to avoid a fire sale of its assets in 1991 by removing all special restrictions on overseas ownership in broad- casting (creating one of the least regulated broadcasting environments in the world). By the end of the year the Canada-based company CanWest Global

Communications had purchased a 20 per cent stake in TV3, and within six years it owned 100 per cent. TV3 recovered to become a serious competitor of TVNZ, creating its own advertising niche by concentrating on the 19–39 age group, effectively 'driving down the middle' between the audiences of TV ONE and TV2. It also sought to have 'a fresher and edgier feel' than TVNZ. Helping to allay the fears associated with its overseas ownership, it sponsored a wide range of local programs, including ambitious drama series. But in general, while some of its programs were 'appointment viewing', viewers never became as consistently loyal to TV3 as they were to the older network, which had a 'first mover advantage' (the benefits of familiarity enjoyed by the company that had been first to stake out a particular part of the market).

The third phase continued along the same lines despite a change of government in 1990 from Labour to National. Though commercialism was in the ascendant, this phase was still complex or hybrid in some respects. TVNZ never totally shed all its public service associations since they were part of its public image and there were still staff members sympathetic to them. Even the Labour government with its passionate commitment to private enterprise acknowledged that inevitably there were 'market failures' (the inability of the commercial environment to supply certain 'public goods') and so, to cover the gaps, it created a new kind of funding body, the Broadcasting Commission (subsequently NZOA). The government's aim was to pare down TVNZ's former public responsibilities, to focus them more precisely, and to separate 'funder' from 'provider' (or funding body from broadcasters), a division it saw as necessary to keep things transparent. NZOA was urged to obtain the best value for money by shopping around between broadcasters. That was the theory, but in the new cut-throat commercial environment the practice turned out to be more complex. NZOA had to engage in tough negotiation with broadcasters because neither network was prepared to waste valuable airtime on programs that might turn away viewers or advertisers, even when those programs were important for public service reasons and NZOA offered them free (Horrocks 1995, 1996).

NZOA represented a new definition of what public service broadcasting meant for New Zealand and what its priorities were. It was expected to play only a minor role in the new broadcasting environment—as a kind of 'ambulance at the bottom of the cliff', helping to allay public concern over TVNZ's ultra-commercial new approach. Instead, NZOA was able to make a considerable difference by exploiting the fact that so much change was in the air. It had two advantages: it was New Zealand's first single-minded advocate for local content (since that had been only one of TVNZ's interests); and it had additional funds to spend on television thanks to an increase in the Public Broadcasting Fee and the fact that it was a more efficient collector of the Fee than its predecessors. Its emphasis on drama helped drama production to increase from fifty-nine program hours in 1989 to 264 in 1993; and similarly it assisted the increase in documentary hours from thirty-six in 1989 to 190 in 1993. (These figures refer to the main free-to-air channels.) In 1988 TVNZ had started to 'out-source' much of its production—though it kept news, current affairs, sport and children's programs in-house—and NZOA funding helped the independents to take advantage of the situation so the industry grew and diversified. By setting up tenders, NZOA worked to extend the range of local programs, including the creation of the first wholly New Zealand series for pre-school children, *You and Me*, and the first five-days-a-week drama series, *Shortland Street*. (*Close to Home,* the only 'evening soap' made previously, had screened on two nights per week.) Overall, the number of hours of local production more than doubled, from 2112 in 1988 to 5715 in 1992. Obviously some of that increase was due to the arrival of TV3, and production had been at an unusually low level at the end of the 1980s, but NZOA also helped to change the particular mix and range of programs.

NZOA had its critics who did not approve of the reshaping of public service priorities in the 1989 Act. Because of small size and limited funding, public service broadcasting in New Zealand has never been able to satisfy the whole range of needs. NZOA was able to assist with local content (including some minority interests), plus television archiving, subtitling for the hearing-impaired, and non-commercial coverage, but its legislation did not cover regional or access programming (though NZOA gave some assistance), or imported programs for minority or ethnic groups, or imported 'quality' or 'highbrow' material, or a reduction in advertising. It did not subsidise news, current affairs or sports programs because broadcasters appeared willing to pay for those genres of local content. (This policy has become controversial in recent years as free-to-air broadcasters have been unable to afford major sporting events, and the style of news and current affairs has grown more populist.) NZOA had no control over scheduling so that minority programs were not able to obtain convenient time slots. A small market has many 'market failures', and all of the above are valid needs and problems for public service broadcasting to address, but each historical phase has succeeded in satisfying only some of them (Horrocks 1996). Support for public service broadcasting in New Zealand has seldom formed a united front because the various lobby groups argue with one another over their top priorities.

One of the most controversial aspects of NZOA was its support for mainstream as well as minority material. About half of its funding was devoted to prime-time or mainstream programs and the other half to off-peak or minority programs. Initially TVNZ wanted NZOA to restrict itself to the latter, particularly where TV3 was concerned. It sought to rally public support by accusing NZOA of abandoning public service principles. The funding body replied that it had a different interpretation of those principles and saw the low level of local content inside prime time as a relevant problem for public service broadcasting in New Zealand. Its legislation spoke specifically of the need to support dramas and documentaries, and in the post-1987 situation those genres were endangered species. Eventually TVNZ agreed to cooperate, and subsequent years saw a considerable expansion in the number of local programs in prime time (rising from 21–23 per cent of the prime-time schedule in 1988–89 to 37–40 per cent in 1992–93). The 1990s was a great period for popular culture (though a difficult period for high culture), and many of the breakthroughs achieved by local television production—and similarly by New Zealand music, film, and fashion—involved tapping populist energies.

Another distinctive aspect of this phase of television history was the approach taken by Julian Mounter, Director-General of TVNZ from 1986 to 1991 (Smith 1996; Spicer, Powell, and Emanuel 1996). His influence was profound, both in fostering a competitive spirit within the organisation, and in creating an ambitious, long-term strategy, a strategy continued by his successor Brent Harman. Mounter believed that if TVNZ was going to become a commercial operation, it should do so boldly in the spirit of the new global capitalism. He sought to position TVNZ for the digital future by a series of bold initiatives such as taking shares in pay television, establishing a business news service in Asia, and forming alliances with multinational corporations. He was a charismatic but uncompromising leader who clashed with NZOA when its campaign for more local production did not fit with his priorities. Yet, though his vision of TVNZ's role was narrowly focused in cultural terms, it was certainly ambitious and impressive in commercial terms. It was also very much in line with the politics of the day, the ideas and energies promoted by Rogernomics.

But the mood of politics was now about to change, creating a new phase of television history in which the government would turn away both from Mounter's expansive vision for TVNZ and from NZOA's expansive vision for local production.

From a public service point of view, the fourth phase was (apart from some Māori initiatives) the most depressing chapter in New Zealand's television history. NZOA's efforts continued but its effectiveness was undercut in several ways. First, the government refused to increase the licence fee so that NZOA's financial bargaining power was steadily eroded by inflation. Second, the change of culture within TVNZ that began in the late 1980s had by 1995 developed so far that commercialism dominated every aspect of the organisation. Initially promoted in terms of economic and administrative efficiency, the new approach had far-reaching social and cultural implications, widening the gap between TVNZ and NZOA. With rare exceptions, attempts to expand and diversify local production became too difficult. After the departure of Harman in 1995, TVNZ's management style changed to a short-term approach that reflected behind-the-scenes decisions by the government to prepare both channels for sale. The network had to concentrate on cranking up its profits to a record level. It became increasingly loath to take risks such as screening any program that might be regarded as dry, highbrow, or unfriendly—anything that might tempt viewers to reach for the remote and thus reduce ratings. This was a particularly noticeable change for TV ONE, which had retained more links with its public service origins than TV2 (apart from TV2's screening of children's programs). Despite their growing alienation from TVNZ, public service supporters and local program-makers were still alarmed at the idea of the national broadcaster passing once and for all into the hands of an overseas media magnate such as Rupert Murdoch or Kerry Packer.

Since Mounter's long-term growth strategy was no longer relevant to the government's plans, TVNZ sold off its shares in the pay television service SKY, in Asia Business News, and in the telecommunications company Clear Communications. It also sold 80 per cent of its internationally successful Natural History Unit to Twentieth Century Fox (owned by Murdoch's News Media Corporation). In July 1999 the government abolished the Public Broadcasting Fee, overruling the objections of NZOA who described the fee as the bedrock of public service funding because of the arm's-length independence and long-term confidence it provided. Public funding would continue but henceforth NZOA would have to go cap in hand to the government, who would determine the amount each time according to its current priorities.

This fourth phase was also dominated by the ceaseless growth of SKY, the country's only significant pay service. The service started in 1990 but became a major player in 1996 when it purchased major rugby union and league games. (Unlike Britain and Australia, New Zealand has no '**antisiphoning**' laws to prevent the most important sporting events from being sold exclusively to pay television.) Sport plays such an important part in New Zealand culture that SKY's decision to use it as its main selling-point enabled it to build its subscriber base rapidly, among the poor as well as the rich—by February 2003 it had over 520 000 subscribers, representing over a third of New Zealand households. Three quarters of the subscribers received its digital service (Hall 2002; Cleave 2003b). SKY has, however, had to pay such large sums of money for sporting rights—besides having to subsidise subscriber equipment and installations—that it has had difficulty breaking even, despite subscription revenue being complemented by an increasing amount of advertising income. It lost $42 million in the financial year to June 2001, though the deficit has been gradually reducing. Its shareholders—dominated by Rupert Murdoch's News Corp, via Independent Newspapers Ltd. (INL)—are prepared to accept such losses as an investment for the future. For the time being, the losses also have tax benefits for INL.

SKY has led the way in its direct-to-home satellite service (1997), digital service (1998), and interactivity (an email service and games channel in 2002). It can broadcast its programs across the country by satellite because it is not dependent on regional advertising breakouts as free-to-air broadcasters are. The fact that this overseas-owned company has a 'first mover advantage', and essentially a monopoly position, in both pay and **digital television** has created concern that it will become the future powerbroker of New Zealand television. Based as it is on the idea of television for those who can afford it, SKY's pay television and pay-per-view service denies the principle of universal access that is basic to public service broadcasting. SKY also reduces broadcasting to an import business, producing almost no local material outside of its sports channel. For years TVNZ regarded TV3 as its main competitor, but during the course of the 1990s, as the growing number of pay subscribers had a perceptible impact on ratings, TVNZ came to see SKY as the greater threat for the future. The main free-to-air channels still attract about 80 per cent of the audience on a typical night—TV3 captures close to 20 per cent, and TV ONE and TV2 together capture 60 per cent or more—but SKY's audience is increasing and its major sports events create spikes in the ratings.

The most positive aspect of public service broadcasting in the fourth phase was the growth of Māori production. Back in 1989 the government's decision to re-classify TVNZ as an SOE and the prospect of the network being prepared for sale provided the Māori community with an opportunity to take legal action. It mounted a series of brilliantly argued court cases all the way to the British Privy Council, which accused the national broadcasting system of failure to give adequate representation to Māori language and culture. Their campaign focused on the government's obligations under the Treaty of Waitangi, and was part of a larger struggle to safeguard the Māori language, but it also had the effect of delaying attempts to put TVNZ up for sale. In the end the government won the court battles but only by promising to do more for the language. In 1993 it established Te Mangai Paho (TMP), a funding body specifically for Māori language broadcasting, diverting to it 13.4 per cent of the licence fee revenue collected by NZOA (a figure equivalent to the proportion of Māori in the New Zealand population). TMP, which began operations in 1995, has since contributed funding to a variety of projects including animation for young viewers (*Mokotoa*), supernatural thrillers (*Matuku*), and a Māori version of Shakespeare (*The Merchant of Venice*). In addition, NZOA has continued its policy of requiring Māori culture to be represented—where appropriate—in any prime-time series it funds for the general audience. For *Inside NZ* and *Documentary New Zealand,* long-running national documentary series, NZOA introduced an explicit quota to ensure that at least 15 per cent of the individual documentaries had Māori creative control and Māori-related subject-matter. Broadcasters at first resisted the idea of the quota but learned to live with it on the condition that the programs remained accessible to the general audience.

In 1996 the National government funded a Māori television channel, Aotearoa, on a trial basis. Although this Auckland channel produced some interesting programming, its transmission coverage was very limited, and the experiment ended in controversy with allegations of extravagant spending by the channel's managers and poor planning on the part of the government.

The fifth phase began with the defeat of the National-led government in 1999, putting a halt to its plans to privatise TVNZ. Persuaded that broadcasting reforms had gone too far, the new Labour-led government has attempted to resuscitate public service broadcasting. In 2001 it changed the status of TVNZ from an SOE to a Crown Owned Company (CROC), which implied that while the broadcaster was still expected to pursue advertising revenue and make a profit, it needed to balance those aims with service to the community. The idea of cross-subsidising public service activities by commercial ones, regarded as heresy during television's third and fourth phases, was once again seriously considered. The government also announced a Charter for the broadcaster, marking an explicit return to Reithian values as signalled by terms such as 'quality' or the traditional motto 'inform, entertain, and educate'. The Charter sought to remedy some of the major problems of the existing system such as the fact that NZOA was purely a funding body with no leverage at the broadcasting end, or the fact that the 1989 Act had not covered the important genres of news and current affairs or addressed the need for regional coverage.

Ian Fraser, a more expansive chief executive who took office in February 2002, summed up his balancing act in the phrase: 'Deliver the charter but don't screw the business' (Cleave 2003a). Though the broadcaster had maintained a similar mix of objectives through the 1960s and 1970s, some of TVNZ's executives saw the Charter as a confusing mandate. Opposition party politicians were scornful of what they saw as the undermining of a commercially efficient operation that had made an annual profit of $20–40 million. But Fraser conceded there was evidence that audiences were less and less satisfied with the viewing on offer: 'Too much violent and sexual content, too many advertisements, too many repeats, too little quality and educational programs. We know well enough the litany of complaints' (Cleave 2003a). Age was also a factor in this dissatisfaction because of the local advertising industry's emphasis on youth, the age group it regarded as the most important target audience because its brand preferences were still being shaped. The Charter is (among other things) a way to counter advertising's limited interest in the older audience.

Most program-makers and supporters of public service broadcasting have felt encouraged by the government's new approach but some remain sceptical about how much difference it will make. Confirmation of the Charter was delayed until 2003, and the document itself remains aspirational rather than prescriptive. Change inside TVNZ has been extremely gradual, in contrast to the dramatic shake-up in the late 1980s when the organisation was commercialised. For many staff members, and many New Zealanders generally, the philosophy of public service broadcasting is not clearly understood today, having been constantly diluted and muddied.

The government itself is obviously divided between those who see public service television as a high priority and those reluctant to give up the dividend TVNZ has annually handed over to the government for use in other, supposedly more important social areas. The New Zealand situation is very different from that of countries such as Australia where governments are accustomed to putting sizeable sums of money into broadcasting each year for public service reasons. The current New Zealand compromise is the government's offer of an additional $12 million for the first year of the Charter. TVNZ hoped the government would also forgo its usual demand for a dividend, but one was still required. There has been no reduction in the length of ad breaks but TVNZ has agreed to stop screening **infomercials** on TV ONE. With uncertainties about the future of the advertising market (though TVNZ's advertising revenue for 2002–03 was $305 million, $19 million higher than the year before), it is clear that resources for Charter purposes will be limited. An additional pressure is the government's decision to separate TVNZ from its transmission and engineering arm, Broadcast Communications Ltd (BCL), which has long been the corporation's strongest profit centre.

Another point of contention has been the government's delay in introducing the local content quotas that were part of its election policy. There have been campaigns for quotas in New Zealand ever since quotas were introduced in Australia and other countries in the 1960s, but apart from a few specialised examples (such as NZOA's requirements for Māori material) the idea has never been put into practice.[1] Many program-makers remain deeply disappointed that the government has backtracked on its 1999 promise. But New Zealand politicians fear that the introduction of quotas will compromise their support for international free trade agreements, and also that overseas-owned broadcasters may pull out of New Zealand if quotas are introduced. Frustrated by this situation, some larger production companies sought to piggyback on the Closer Economic Relations treaty that New Zealand had signed with Australia by arguing that New Zealand programs should qualify for Australian quotas. In 1998 this 'Blue Skies' campaign won its case in the Australian courts, but since then the number of New Zealand programs sold to Australian broadcasters has remained tiny, despite the deluge predicted by the Australian industry during the court case.

Progress has been made in the development of a permanent, nationwide Māori Television Service, as Tainui Stephens's chapter explains. The Labour government has guaranteed funding for the new channel for its first four years. Some issues remain to be resolved such as whether this will mean the end of a Māori production department within TVNZ (the source of such important series as *Marae* and *Waka Huia*), whether the limited funding available should be used to produce low budget programs in bulk or a few high budget programs, and whether the new channel should restrict itself to Māori language (with or without subtitles, on screen or via Teletext) when only some Māori are fluent speakers. The project has been dogged by controversies such as the dispute over the frequency provided by the government on the **UHF** band (though the Māori Television Service is now hopeful of an alternative arrangement with SKY), or the discovery that John Davy, the Canadian who was initially appointed as Chief Executive, had bogus qualifications. Nevertheless a range of innovative programs are now being created for the new service.

Present and future

New Zealand television history has been shaped by a number of interacting forces, with social needs and cultural ambitions often in conflict with economic pressures, technological changes, and political priorities. There has been a perennial sense of scarcity, and debate over how to make the most of what little is available. In the first and second phases, the majority of the public took it for granted that government ownership and regulation was the answer, that everyone deserved free access to television, and that public service broadcasting was the fairest way to balance different needs and interests. But this approach was compromised by a shortage of public funding, and advertising revenue came to have an increasing importance. In the third phase a new generation of politicians saw the open market as the road to plenitude, as a way to tap the wealth of global capitalism and the power of new technology. By sweeping away the bureaucratic and paternalistic attitudes that had developed during the second phase, the third phase did release a range of new energies, but it opened up new gaps as fast as it closed existing ones. Politicians discovered to their dismay that a small market did not work in the same way as a large market like the USA. The number of channels increased but they created almost no local material, and most of them concentrated on the same mainstream commercial culture. There was also growing public concern that de-regulating and allowing too many assets to pass into overseas hands could create serious problems for the future. Confidence in the ability of commercialism to make the most of broadcasting declined during the fourth phase. The political centre of gravity then shifted again and the fifth phase has seen an attempt to re-introduce public service elements to TVNZ, combining them with commercial elements under the slogan of 'the middle way'. The New Zealand system continues to be a patchwork of public service and commercial elements, though the particular pattern keeps changing.

One of the strongest threads running through this history has been the campaign for more local production—a minority interest, perhaps, but very passionately held. Some periods have been seen as breakthroughs—1975–79, for example, and 1991–95—but even in the strongest periods local material has remained in the minority. Today, when New Zealand television offers a wider range of overseas programs than ever before, the desire to produce original material still tends to involve a sense of mission.

TVNZ and TV3 continue to have substantial in-house production departments for news and current affairs. The private production sector (which makes programs for both networks) contains more than a hundred companies, including some large operations such as South Pacific Pictures (which grew out of the privatising of the TVNZ drama department in 1988 and has been the base for series such as *Shortland Street, Marlin Bay,* and *Being Eve*), the Gibson Group (the home of series such as *The Strip* and *Skitz*), Communicado (source of the *Greenstone* series, the film *Once Were Warriors,* and some related television programs on domestic violence), Greenstone (specialising in documentaries, popular history series such as *Epitaph*, and 'reality and entertainment' series such as *The Zoo*), and Touchdown (successful both locally and internationally in the field of 'reality programs'). Although companies on this scale are needed for large-scale projects aimed at a mixture of local and overseas markets, it is also important that there are plenty of small companies helping to sustain diversity and innovation in the industry. Many consist of a single producer or director who hires freelance staff when a project goes into production.

The shift to outsourcing and employment on a project-by-project basis has involved considerable insecurity for those who freelance, but it has also released new creative energies. Assisted by the arrival of NZOA as an independent funding body, outsourcing was arguably the most beneficial effect of the 1980s restructuring. Growth has brought more people into the freelance industry and over the past decade there have been many more women, for example, and more Māori producers and directors. Most freelancers in the New Zealand industry are specialists but (as in other small countries) they have the versatility to work not only on television programs but also on films, advertisements, industrial or community projects, local or international productions. The infrastructure of editing facilities and equipment rental companies has expanded, and a number of overseas productions have been attracted to New Zealand by the skill and equipment base. The best-known include *Hercules* and *Xena* for the Pacific Renaissance company, and *The Tribe* and *Atlantis High* for Cloud Nine. Such projects tend to reserve key creative roles (producer, director, and writer) for overseas talent, but after such a series has been running for several years there will usually be opportunities for New Zealanders to direct episodes. Overseas productions can give a huge boost to the local economy, but it is always difficult to predict how many there will be or how long they will stay because many volatile factors are involved such as currency exchange rates.

The survival of New Zealand's resourceful production industry will depend on two factors—first, continued opportunities for a variety of large as well as small projects (a situation that will depend on TVNZ remaining under a supportive form of public control and TV3 continuing to take an interest in local production); and second, a healthy balance between local and international projects so that the industry is not narrow and insular on the one hand, nor on the other hand becomes limited to providing cheap crews for overseas companies.

Over the past forty years, television in New Zealand has gone from one to many channels, from broadcasting to a mix of broad- and **narrowcasting** (on specialised or 'niche' channels) (Boyd-Bell 1985; Farnsworth and Hutchinson 2002). A typical viewer today will have access to four free-to-air channels on the VHF band (the two TVNZ channels TV ONE and TV2 and the two CanWest channels TV3 and TV4), and on the UHF band there is the Australian-owned network Prime and a local channel or two (such as Triangle in Auckland). The number of channels continues to increase but the small New Zealand market remains volatile. As noted earlier, all the channels struggle to break even, apart from TV2. For a vivid example of the pressures of the local television market, one has only to consider the history of TV4. Conscious of the strategic advantage that TVNZ gained from its ownership of two channels, CanWest created TV4 in 1997 as a 'youth' channel at a time when there was a dramatic expansion of interest in that market among advertisers. (TVNZ initiated a youth venture in the same year under the MTV brand but it proved not to be viable. The network made itself unpopular at the time by buying out the independent youth channel MAX, apparently to reduce competition. TV4 survived, but instead of helping to expand CanWest's market share it split or 'cannibalised' the TV3 audience.) TV4 continues to lose around $5 million per year and CanWest made unsuccessful attempts in 2002 to sell both TV4 and TV3 (with an estimated asking price of $150 million for the pair). Such moves serve as a reminder of the importance of economics in all aspects of New Zealand television, and the difficulties that have been present from the beginning in developing such an expensive medium in such a small country.

If TVNZ remains under public ownership with Charter responsibilities, it can continue to provide a strong base for New Zealand material (including major local dramas and documentaries). The computer has given us more access to small-scale communication and cheap production, but medium or large-scale communication through a national television channel is no less important. Despite globalising tendencies, the local, the regional, and the national all retain a significant place in our lives. A New Zealand household that subscribes to pay television has access to a growing number of channels but almost none of them offers original local material. In the long run, even if TVNZ's ratings decline (as has happened to the American networks), it can continue to play a respected role along the lines of Radio NZ. Even those New Zealanders who are not regular listeners of Radio NZ tend to agree that such a service should exist. Its core audience is fiercely loyal, and thousands of others tune in often enough to make an impressive '**CUME**' or cumulative audience. At present, however, TVNZ would regard Radio NZ's role as that of a niche service, primarily for older listeners. This is not a fate that TVNZ welcomes—it is prepared to fight hard to hold on to its younger audience, its popular overseas programs, and its centrality in the marketplace.

There has been some talk of a further restructuring that would transfer all NZOA's television funding to TVNZ—in an attempt to return to the second phase of our television history—but the idea is premature until the broadcaster has clearly rebuilt the kind of public service culture it displayed in the 1960s and 1970s. During the competitive environment of the past thirteen years, NZOA's independence, lobbying, and ability to play one broadcaster off against another has produced public service benefits— particularly in the area of local content—that the commercially oriented TVNZ and TV3 would never have arrived at on their own.

Public service broadcasting will need further redefinition in the future. Still an analogue service, TVNZ has not yet found a secure niche for itself in the digital environment. Towards the end of the 1990s TVNZ spent a great deal of time and money trying to find an overseas partner with whom it could create a digital service as an alternative to SKY. Successive governments were not supportive of this attempt, which they saw as too risky and too expensive. In late 2000 TVNZ thought it had found the ideal vehicle, the telecommunications company Telstra-Saturn, but within a year its negotiations with this Australian/American partnership had collapsed, partly due to Saturn's financial problems. TVNZ had no option left but to come to an arrangement with SKY, adding TV ONE and TV2 to the SKY digital platform as TV3 and Prime had previously done—thus further strengthening the appeal of the pay operator. The government has warned SKY to treat TVNZ well or to risk intervention by legislation, but to date its regulatory approach has been very light-handed. TVNZ remains apprehensive that SKY will not allow it to develop the interactive services that could provide new sources of revenue in the future. The working out of this relationship is one of many challenges faced by New Zealand television today as it seeks to sustain national and regional ambitions in an environment increasingly dominated by huge multinational corporations.

References

Boyd-Bell, Robert. 1985. *New Zealand Television: The First 25 Years*. Auckland: Reed Methuen.

Broadcasting Act 1989.

Broadcasting and Related Telecommunications in New Zealand: Report of the Royal Commission of Enquiry. 1986.

Cleave, Louisa. 2003a. 'State TV's Brave New World', *NZ Herald*, 4 January.

Cleave, Louisa. 2003b. 'Sky Signs One in Three Homes', *NZ Herald,* 20 February.

Day, Patrick. 2000. *Voice and Vision: A History of Broadcasting in New Zealand, Volume Two*. Auckland: Auckland University Press.

Easton, Brian. 1997. *The Commercialisation of New Zealand*. Auckland: Auckland University Press.

Farnsworth, John. 1989. Two-channel Television in New Zealand: Ambiguities of Organisation, Profession and Culture. Thesis (PhD), University of Canterbury.

Farnsworth, John. 1992. 'Mainstream or Minority: Ambiguities in State or Market Arrangements for New Zealand Television'. In John Deeks & Nick Perry (eds) *Controlling Interests: Business, the State and Society in New Zealand*. Auckland: Auckland University Press, pp. 191–207.

Farnsworth, John & Ian Hutchison (eds). 2002. *New Zealand Television: A Reader*. Palmerston North: Dunmore Press.

Hall, Terry. 2002. 'Sky's Rising Dollar Bonus', *Sunday Star-Times,* 7 July.

Horrocks, Roger. 1995. 'Strategic Nationalisms: Television Production in New Zealand'. *Sites* 30, pp. 85–107.

Horrocks, Roger. 1996. 'Conflicts and Surprises in New Zealand Television'. *Continuum: The Australian Journal of Media and Culture* 10 (1), pp. 50–63.

Lealand, Geoff. 2000. 'Regulation—What Regulation? Cultural Diversity and Local Content in New Zealand Television'. *Media International Australia incorporating Culture and Policy* 95, pp. 77–90.

New Zealand On Air. 2003. *Annual Report, Local Content Report* (and other policy documents). Available from: http://www.nzoa.govt.nz.

Smith, Paul. 1996. *Revolution in the Air.* Auckland: Longman.

Spicer, Barry, Michael Powell & David Emanuel. 1996. *The Remaking of Television New Zealand 1985–1992.* Auckland: Auckland University Press.

Statistics New Zealand, *The 2002 Cultural Experiences Survey.* Available from: http://www.stats.govt.nz [Accessed 9 February 2003].

TVNZ Charter. 2003. Available from: http://www.tvnz.co.nz [Accessed 1 May 2003].

Notes

1   In July 2003, broadcasters set voluntary targets for themselves. The levels were very modest: 53 per cent local content on TV ONE, 17 per cent on TV2, and 20 per cent on TV3. The targets apply only between 6 am and midnight. Over twenty-four hours, the overall level of local content across the three channels will continue to represent approximately a quarter of the schedule.

Television Then

LAURENCE SIMMONS

'It'll be lovely, it'll be gorgeous. We won't have to go out; we can stay home and be entertained.'

Coffee bar waitress, *New Zealand Listener* poll on the introduction of television, 1960

Imagine a scene. One night in the middle of winter all over the city of Auckland and its suburbs, small groups of people, families and friends, are crowding around a new piece of furniture in the living rooms of their homes, and even larger clusters are gathering together in public areas, some outside shops, and all their eyes are fixed on a new kind of bluish light. Their gazes remain transfixed as the evening's viewing, presented by the hugely-moustached and improbably named Carl Clifford Albert Hexter-Stabbins,[1] runs its course for two hours through *The Adventures of Robin Hood*, an interview with an English ballerina (*On Our Doorstep*), *Halls of Ivy* (a drama in which an American college principal copes with the problems, human and academic, of his daily life), a musical number by the Howard Morrison Jazz Quartet, a short documentary appropriately titled with unconscious irony *Your Children's Eyes*, and finally *The Four Just Men,* a World War II epic starring, among others, Italian film director-actor Vittorio de Sica.

Of course, it wasn't entirely like that. The New Zealand public on whom the phenomenon of television was launched was not completely unsuspecting. Considerable planning and practice and some promotion had gone into the event of this launch. Over the previous months some Auckland viewers had already been 'exposed' to television when they tuned into the transmissions of pirate broadcaster, and soon-to-be television set manufacturer, Al Bell. As the readers of newspapers and magazines, the

Figure 3.1
(*New Zealand Listener*, 20 May 1960, p. 8.)

Figure 3.2 C.C.A. Hexter-Stabbins announcing the first scheduled test programs for the NZBS on 18 May 1959. (NZMA)

7.30 p.m. THE ADVENTURES OF ROBIN HOOD, Episode 1. With Richard Green as Robin, Bernadette O'Farrell as Maid Marian, and Alan Wheatley as the Sheriff of Nottingham.

7.59 ON OUR DOORSTEP (Studio)

8. 7 SUSIE: Episode 1 of a light comedy series, starring Ann Sothern and Don Porter

8.34 STUDIO 2: Howard Morrison Jazz Quartet

8.47 HALLS OF IVY: The first of a series of self-contained dramatic programmes in which an American college principal copes with the problems, human and academic, of his daily life—with the late Ronald Colman and his wife, Benita Hume, as Dr and Mrs Todhunter-Hall, of Ivy College.

9.15 Your Children's Eyes (C.O.I.)

9.35 (approx.) Close down

N.Z. LISTENER, MAY 27, 1960.

Figure 3.3 The first evening's schedule. (*New Zealand Listener*, 27 May 1960, p. 33. Note that this announcement turned out to be incorrect and the advertised program *Susie* was replaced with *The Four Just Men*.)

listeners of radio, and the targets of advertisers they had already been introduced in myriad ways to the new medium they were now experiencing for
the first time. This chapter will attempt an overview of the debates, the
written material, and the advertising around the introduction of television
to New Zealand in the early 1960s. It draws upon a multiplicity of types of
response to the arrival of television: cartoons; advertisements; parliamentary
debates; government papers; individual reports and position papers, like *The
Economics of Television* by Dr William Sutch; the official published histories
of Robert Boyd-Bell and Patrick Day; polls of audience responses by the
New Zealand Listener; letters to the editors of magazines; and personal
predictions and opinions, such as those of the artist Eric Lee-Johnson.[2]

My title deliberately goes two ways: it is both *descriptive* (it indicates that
I will deal with the history of the beginnings of television in New Zealand,
the 'then' being the late 1950s and early 1960s) and *interrogative* (it reflects a
local form of the New Zealand linguistic idiom, a laconic, laid-back
rhetorical questioning that we might paraphrase as 'Well, what's all this fuss
about television then?'). This use of litotes,
in a typically antipodean understatement
of concern, has interestingly been best
represented on New Zealand television by
John Clarke's popular character Fred Dagg
and, as I hope to illustrate, this characteristic of 'playing things down' marked in
many ways the introduction of television,
which seemed to pass, at least on the
surface, almost imperceptibly and without
fanfare.

History of the introduction of television

Let me start with the official historical
details. In the tradition of the lone Kiwi
inventor, such as the early aviator Richard
Pearse, and more recently and notoriously
Peter Jackson's 'mockumented' early film-
maker Colin McKenzie,[3] Dr Robert Jack, a
professor of physics at the University of
Otago, was an early pioneer of television.
He conducted television experiments
beginning in 1924, initially staging a failed

Figure 3.4 John Clarke as Fred
Dagg. (NZMA)

attempt to receive a transmission from the first station in the USA, but within four years was able to transmit legible pictures across his laboratory (Garbutt 1988, p. 3; Sullivan 1998, p. 249). It appears that Jack's work was similar to that carried out by John Logie Baird, the so-called inventor of television, in Scotland at roughly the same time.

During the 1940s, under inaugural director of New Zealand Broadcasting Service (NZBS), Professor James Shelley, a Reithian philosophy of 'public service broadcasting', like that which had been developed at the BBC, was progressively adopted. Shelley was unusual as chief officer in that he was involved hands-on in radio program production and presentation and he believed that the social purpose of broadcasting was the education and cultural elevation of the audience with an aim to promote 'the understanding of life values, and...the emotional discipline of a community' (Day 1994, p. 230). Of course, as Shelley never really acknowledged, there existed a contradiction in that this Reithian philosophy was only of limited relevance to the New Zealand situation, and Shelley's preference for non-commercial public broadcasting, as we shall see, did not match the economic realities of a small dispersed population and a difficult geographical terrain.

Early inklings

In a prescient article written in 1939 entitled 'Television will come to New Zealand', the artist and photographer Eric Lee-Johnson noted that although New Zealanders had so far heard practically nothing of the technical progress concerning television it was no longer a vision but a reality, 'an accomplished fact, a rapidly growing branch of broadcasting which will soon usurp the place of the merely audible type' (Lee-Johnson 1939, p. 1).[4] Lee-Johnson, who had been involved in the design and advertising of television sets for Pye Radio and Television in Britain in the mid 1930s (Turner 1999, p. 23), argued that Britain was ahead of the United States both in technology and programming because television transmission was controlled by a publicly controlled corporation, the BBC, which did not face the problem of competition and was in a position 'to resist the anti-television pressure that is being applied by other interests'. Lee-Johnson foresaw the problems of transmission coverage given New Zealand's terrain and the high cost of producing local television drama and he predicted that 'we in New Zealand, with our small population, will probably be treated to more transmitted films or dramas recorded by special producing companies, than original productions' (Turner 1999, p. 2).

Throughout the 1940s and 1950s there were other sporadic reports on television, in particular from Britain, such as that of J.W. Goodwin in the *New Zealand Listener* on 24 July 1953. He wrote of 'the social revolution [in

Britain] brought about in five years by some two million TV sets' (Goodwin 1953, p. 6). On 23 August 1957 the *New Zealand Listener* carried the account of an NZBS employee, J.H. Hall, who had visited television and radio stations in the USA under the U.S. State Department International Exchange Program. Hall concluded that his 'most favourable impression' of television 'was of its usefulness in bringing news pictures into the home, and this was the element he had found had the biggest pull of all' (Hall 1957 p. 7). In November 1958 the *New Zealand Listener* interviewed another officer of the Broadcasting Service, James Boswell, who had just returned to New Zealand with a Masters in Broadcasting from the University of Southern California. Boswell observed how 'in its development the [American] television industry turned to Hollywood for much of its technique, nomenclature and personalities' (Boswell 1958, p. 9). In the same year James Walshe produced an extended article for *Landfall* entitled 'On the Brink of Television' noting that 'we are not so much choosing television as contracting it like a disease' and arguing for 'control vested in an independent corporation…and programmes devised without recourse to advertising' (Walshe 1959, pp. 359, 363). These and other interventions help confirm, as Patrick Day in his two-volume history of broadcasting in New Zealand claims, that although broadcast transmission remained almost exclusively radio-based during the 1950s 'the introduction of television was the most important issue of the decade' (Day 2000, p. 11).

Parliamentary debates[5]

In 1949 questions were raised in the House by the National Opposition regarding the possible introduction of television and the Labour Minister of Broadcasting, Mr F. Jones, replied that investigations had begun and New Zealand Broadcasting Service officers had been overseas to observe television in operation. In July 1949 the then Labour government set up an Interdepartmental Committee to consider the introduction of television with the Director of the New Zealand Broadcasting Service as chair, the Assistant Director (Administrative), and three engineers of NZBS and The Post and Telegraph Department (Jackson 1960, p. 284). This committee's brief was twofold: first, to study the development of television overseas, and second, to advise on problems of establishing television in New Zealand. Its deliberations were made against a background of postwar economic hardship and it is clear from the committee's composition that the focus was on the technical and economic problems of the introduction of television rather than any extensive considerations of its social impact. Labour lost the election to National at the end of 1949 and the committee went into abeyance until 1958 when Labour came to power again, and at this point representatives from the Treasury and the Department of Trade and Industries were added to its personnel. During its years in opposition Labour had continued to press for action on television claiming that there was no reason for delay. However, despite the fact that a preliminary report of the Inter-Departmental Committee was submitted to the Minister in 1951, at the parliamentary level questions concerning the introduction of television tended to surface only sporadically. The linkage in government minds between radio and television remained a political obstacle in the path of the introduction of television throughout the 1950s and, as Ashley Gorringe notes: 'As long as the transmission of radio remained limited in rural New Zealand, the government remained hamstrung regarding further expenditure on television' (Gorringe 2002, p. 15).

Despite this legislative logjam, the first public display of television was given in 1950 by the Institute of Electronics. In 1951 the NZBS combined forces with an Australian company, Amalgamated Wireless, to present closed-circuit television demonstrations. These lasted ten days each, in Wellington and then Auckland, and on each day six half-hour programs were shown on a closed circuit. The content of the programs included radio personality Aunt Daisy who produced a high speed commercial for a cooking pot, the Ngati Poneke Club performing a Māori stick game, a commentary on a boxing match by sports commentator Winston McCarthy, ballet and tennis demonstrations, a cigarette commercial, and footage of a baboon from the Wellington zoo. (It is worth noting how this early demonstration schedule consisted of a number of what were to later become standard television genres: advertising, lifestyle programs, sports, and wildlife programs, even Māori broadcasting.) These 'public viewings', which were seen by around 3000 viewers in each centre, seemed designed as a promotional exercise to raise public awareness and convince the government to hasten the arrival of television transmission but they were to no avail. In 1953 the government, through the Post and Telegraph Department, issued the first experimental licenses to study technical aspects of television to two radio manufacturers and three tertiary colleges. The first television transmission as such was made over the radius of a few miles in central Christchurch by an experimental station, ZL3XT, at Canterbury University College. However, it apparently produced disappointingly fuzzy and barely legible greenish pictures (Boyd-Bell 1985, p. 63).

By this stage the National government had not yet made anything like a firm commitment to television and in 1955 the Minister in Charge of Broadcasting, R.M. Algie, indicated to the House that the slow progress was deliberate since it was clear, given New Zealand's size and scattered population, that government would have to bear the brunt of the high costs of television (*New Zealand Parliamentary Debates* 1955, p. 1526). During the same year a Labour parliamentarian, Mr Moohan, who had observed television broadcasting in the USA, argued that it was not deleterious to childhood behaviour and that the heavy running costs might be ameliorated in part by advertising revenue. By 1956 it was clear that the Labour Opposition Members of Parliament tended to favour the rapid establishment of television broadcasting, arguing that there were no serious financial, geographical, or technical obstacles to its introduction. Despite this, the National Minister, Algie, stood firm against what he thought might become a potentially large and unnecessary expense.

During these years of parliamentary debate, there were many demonstrations of closed-circuit television at Easter shows in the main centres. These were run by the Pye Company, which was to later manufacture television sets in New Zealand, and included the televising of quiz shows such as that of popular radio, and later television, personality Selwyn Toogood. In 1957 an experimental licence, ZL1XQ, was issued to an Auckland company that manufactured radio sets, Bell Radio and Television. The company director Al Bell desired to manufacture commercial television receivers and it could be argued that he was in fact the first to operate a commercial television station. As Robert Boyd-Bell observes, Bell's operation was 'the first major push by a commercial organization to...pressure the Government to reach a decision on how and when television would be introduced' (Boyd-Bell 1985, p. 64; see also Gorringe 2002, pp. 9–11). Bell's licence for three hours' transmission on three nights a week was restricted to programs of an educational nature and he was specifically barred from showing entertainment. However, Bell got around these restrictions by arguing that everything he transmitted from his Dominion Road factory, including variety shows, was educational since he was training technicians. Bell also made sure that he donated television sets to hospitals and old people's homes in order to ensure his viewership. By 1958 some 200 sets in Auckland were receiving Bell's transmissions and he became in effect a pirate broadcaster who the government could not close down for fear of upsetting his public. In November 1958 The New Zealand Television Society, a lobby group campaigning for the establishment of television services in New Zealand, which included some of Bell's viewers, attempted unsuccessfully to lodge a petition in parliament arguing for the introduction of television (Walshe 1959, p. 360).

In the meantime, Australia had introduced television in 1956 and several New Zealand commentators commented in a similar vein that 'once it's established in Australia no government will be able to withstand popular pressure to get it installed [here]' (Arnold Wall quoted in Day 2000, p. 12). The developments in Australia were widely reported in articles like that of Ian K. Mackay for the *New Zealand Listener* (Mackay 1957, 1958). In Australia the earliest political inclination was to model television on the British example of publicly or state-owned television, with the Labor government in the 1940s regarding it as an opportunity to extend its social and cultural agenda. However when the Menzies conservative government took power in 1949, it quickly favoured a 'dual' or 'mixed' television system. Thus Australian television began in 1956 with what would become the commercial Nine and Seven networks, together with the beginnings of a Government-funded, non-commercial ABC (Australian Broadcasting Corporation) national network. As had happened in Australia, the New Zealand National Government's private enterprise philosophy clashed with Labour's principles of publicly controlled broadcasting. However, unlike its Australian counterpart, and because of dissension in its ranks, the National Party here exhibited a reluctance to address the issue of television over these years. During the 1957 election, National policy was that it was 'not in a hurry to get a television service going', whereas Labour in contrast came out with a policy in favour of the introduction of television and its state control. In 1958 the report of the New Zealand Broadcasting Service, while it acknowledged the public interest in television and its potential, took the view that the economic circumstances regarding its introduction were unfavourable (*Appendices to the Journals of the House of Representatives*, vol. II (1958), F3: 5). Thus, writes Patrick Day, '[d]uring the 1950s New Zealand, historically an early and rapid adopter of communication technologies, became an international laggard with respect to television' (Day 2000, p. 12).

Upon gaining power in 1957, Labour, who inherited an acute balance of payments crisis from the previous government, did not appear to act in any hurry to introduce television. The new Minister in charge of Broadcasting, Mr Boord, appeared to take a similar line as the previous National Government, and the Labour Party strategy was simply to reintroduce the lapsed standing committee. In February 1959, in order to consider public submissions, of which there were over forty, the committee was augmented by the addition of representatives of the Treasury and the Department of Industries and Commerce (Jackson 1960, p. 284).

On 28 July 1959 an influential position paper on television was produced by the Secretary of Industries and Commerce, Dr William Sutch. The paper began as a speech delivered to the Christchurch branch of the Economic Society of Australia and New Zealand, and in his original talk Sutch assumed that it was inevitable that a regular television service would be introduced. The arrival of television was compelling, he said, as it had an appeal beyond any other medium and because it was a visual medium providing a 'window on the world'. The debate, Sutch correctly surmised, was to be over how and in what form television would arrive. His arguments were based on a mixture of economic analysis with a provision of hard statistics as well as an elaboration of what he saw as television's educational role: 'television can help in the spread of knowledge and the arts,' he declared and he reiterated again that it would be able to compensate for 'the lack [of] a full educational background' (Sutch 1959, p. 4). Sutch looked at both the social implications of setting up television—how it might affect reading patterns, newspapers, spectator attendance at sports events, the closure of cinemas—and he considered its economics—arguing that the costs of introduction could be minimised by a £10 a year combined license that would recover £3.4 million over ten years, and he also advocated 'spot advertising', which could ameliorate the costs of introduction even further. Sutch, however, did not advocate private television, which he believed would only serve the main centres and would not be willing to pay for good quality programs. He was also one of the first commentators on the medium to lobby for local content: 'A decision to make television programmes of our own should be a deliberate act of policy and not a course to be adopted only when public pressure demands it…programmes dealing with our social, economic or cultural activities…should enrich the lives of us all,' he declared, adding that 'the main purpose in requiring the production of as large a proportion of New Zealand programmes as is possible, is to ensure that the service provided is especially one suited to our own needs and social requirements. It would give scope for development in the field of film and dramatic production which is essential if television is to contribute to and express our national character' (Sutch 1959, p. 22).

Sutch came to the bold general conclusion that it would not be 'an exaggeration to suggest that in, say fifteen years, the beliefs, tastes and opinion of possibly half of New Zealand will be based mainly on impressions received from television' (Sutch 1959, p. 5). His final proposal was ambitious, with the establishment of four stations at Auckland, Wellington, Christchurch, and Dunedin, each of two channels, plus six single channel stations in regional centres; that is, a locally focused rather than a centrally controlled framework. Despite eventually adopting many of Sutch's recommendations, the Minister of Broadcasting was to consistently deny that Sutch's paper in any way represented or had influenced government policy (Jackson 1960, p. 282).

In November 1959 Prime Minister Walter Nash announced while on a visit to London that New Zealand would have television within twelve months. It was a move that caught many of his government members as well as NZBS bureaucrats and technicians back at home by surprise. Popular satire questioned Nash's motives and pointed to his disregard of government policy; a cartoon in *Truth* depicted the Prime Minister ogling a line of go-go dancers on television and stammering 'I really had no idea… If only I'd known…We…er…must have…um…television…in N.Z.' (*Truth*, 17 November 1959, p. 15, reproduced in Gorringe 2002, p. 12).

Figure 3.5 (*Truth*, 17 November 1959, p. 15.)

The proposed television system was to be state-owned, in association with the existing NZBS, introduced on a staged basis in the four main centres, and would include commercials. Studios were quickly built in Shortland Street, equipment purchased, and the testing of program transmission carried out in early 1959.[6] The first non-experimental program was transmitted on 1 June 1960. In general, the early critical responses were positive. The *Auckland Star* wrote 'Television "arrived" in New Zealand last night… The verdict: A dignified, successful entry' (quoted in Boyd-Bell 1985, p. 75). With more time to reflect, J.C. Reid wrote more circumspectly in the quarterly magazine *Comment* that '[t]he general impression created is of safe, stereotyped, unsensational, consistently mediocre, popular material …it seems likely that we are in for a longish period of adjustment before any programmes of real quality develop here… Whatever government is in power after the elections will have to stand firm against the pressure groups of advertisers, TV set manufacturers, newspaper interests and others with an axe to grind'(Reid 1960, pp. 5–6).

In November 1960 it was in fact National who won the elections and Mr A. Kinsella, the new Minister of Broadcasting, announced that a new Broadcasting Act of 1961, rewriting the Act of 1936, would give effect to National's election policy. Eventually in 1962 a state-owned corporation, the NZBC, which controlled the licensing, programming, and advertising of public radio and television, and supported itself by licence fees and advertising, was set up as the controlling authority for sound and visual broadcasting (Harrison 1962). As already noted, the National Party had been ambivalent about the role that private enterprise should play in the introduction of television and the party caucus was polarised between an exclusive role for private enterprise, a desire for a mixed system of state and private participation, and a third group seeking full governmental control, with the deputy leader J.R. Marshall on the side of private enterprise and the former Minister in Charge of Broadcasting, R.M. Algie, promoting a mixed system (Gregory 1985, p. 39). Not surprisingly perhaps the result was a compromise and it became National Party election policy not to give total control to private enterprise but to utilise its resources and capital thus advancing television quicker and at less cost to the taxpayer than an outright state monopoly might do, as well as speeding up coverage across the nation.

Subsequent to its introduction in Auckland in 1960, three other television stations were started: Wellington and Christchurch in 1961, and Dunedin in 1962. Because national networking was not possible, programs were flown to the four stations and broadcast on separate nights and, although the four stations shared programs, a regional emphasis emerged as each station had its own announcing staff and locally produced programs. This situation, where the four stations retained distinct local identities, continued until 1969 when national networking and centralised programming supplanted the regional emphasis. Private enterprise, in the form of advertisements, first hit Aucklanders on 4 April 1961, when television went commercial and advertising revenue facilitated the increase in transmission hours to twenty-eight per week (Boyd-Bell 1985, pp. 81–2). By the beginning of 1963, television was reaching one-eighth of the total population, with 80 000 licences issued and an audience estimated at 300 000 viewers (Boyd-Bell 1985, p. 87).

In the transition from the mid 1950s to the mid 1960s, the formative decade of New Zealand television, the question of television moved from a focus on its technical aspects to how it might become a consumer good. As television developed program forms and production practices and ran up against regulatory constraints, there was an accumulation of government regulatory reports, as well as the beginnings of a small production industry. It is not difficult, then, to see the introduction of television as the result of a number of debates, marked by the polarised positions of political parties and even within those parties, together with the vested interests of set manufacturers and the advertising and media industries. Indeed, I believe that we can go further to suggest that the important debates over the social applications of television, controversies over technical standards and frequency allocations, the questioning of commercial practices—issues over which much legislative and regulatory ink was spilt through the 1960s and 1970s—all had their roots in struggles and decisions made in the period leading up to the introduction of television in 1960 and immediately after. Let me explore briefly some of those debates and their implications.

Debates over control and regulation

The debates over the forms of television to be introduced were inseparable from questions raised surrounding who would control television programming. In New Zealand these debates were couched in terms of public interest, sheer political expediency, and program aesthetics, but also against the background of radio broadcasting and the recent Australian precedent. As R.L. Gregory suggests, the parliamentary debates 'were based on general party philosophy towards the role of the state in the economy, rather than on consideration of the political functions of public broadcasting in an open society' (Gregory 1985, p. 40). Private enterprise was also determined to have its say: a body entitled the Visual Investigation Syndicate (which later proved to be an association of newspaper proprietors) argued in favour of a dual system which consisted of a state-run, non-commercial channel accompanied by a commercial system controlled by private ownership. However, this intervention of newspaper interests in television broadcasting was seen by the Labour Government as favouring conservative views and free enterprise policies. The New Zealand Motion Picture Exhibitors Association, arguing that there was no evidence that New Zealanders desired television, and that it would affect the motion picture industry (as it certainly did, wreaking havoc on the cinema business), demanded a referendum on whether to introduce television at all. It has been claimed that 'the acceptance of television and the change of status to an independent public corporation, the New Zealand Broadcasting Corporation (NZBC), was the most significant change to New Zealand broadcasting since it was incorporated into the government service in the 1930s' (Day 2000, p. 1). In 1962, 65 000 television licenses were issued and in 1966 the half million mark was reached with income derived from a combination of advertising and the broadcasting license. The requirement to concentrate expenditure on extending television coverage meant an early neglect of local programming, in particular drama (in contrast to the situation in Australia), and during this period '[t]he NZBC became, on a world scale, an abnormally high scheduler of imported programmes' (Day 2000, p. 3). One commentator reflecting on television three years after its introduction remarked: 'The sad truth is that the general pool of "canned" TV material available from overseas sources—on which New Zealand relies for at least 75 per cent of its programme content—is not of a high standard...TV here has not gone out into the streets. It has not brought issues of the day to the viewer in his living-room. It has dodged controversy' (Berry 1963, pp. 68–9).

The degree of independence from government of the new corporation was always a hotly debated topic of contention and there were many calls for a royal commission into broadcasting as had occurred in Australia.[7] There were two issues involved: the first was whether to implement a non-commercial (public service broadcasting) versus a commercial system; the second concerned the amount of government control and direct government intervention in terms of management structure and/or content. The subsequent history of the corporation reflects the strength of state control of broadcasting—virtually a monopoly—as well as the amount of political meddling and influence involved. Under a third Labour government in 1973 the NZBC was replaced with three corporations, one for the publicly owned radio stations, one each for the two television channels, and any further expansion of private broadcasting was curtailed. But this wholesale revision was short-lived and in 1976 a National government reintegrated the three corporations back into a single corporation (BCNZ) in two stages.

Debates over moral issues

As we have seen, television was hailed, by Sutch and others, as a new democratic window on the world. Nevertheless, the other side of the coin also saw television represented as a threatening instrument of social upheaval. In the early 1950s the newspaper *Truth* proclaimed that a generation of television children would become the foundation of a 'decadent nation' and housewives would end up ignoring their chores (*Truth* 10 December 1952, p. 13). And as late as 1962 a *New Zealand Listener* headline trumpeted: 'TV Rivals the Atom Bomb as a Menace to Mankind' (*New Zealand Listener*, 12 October 1962, p. 9). In 1957, one year after its introduction in Australia and three before its New Zealand debut, Sir John Medley, Vice-Chancellor of Melbourne University and a member of the ABC, thundered: 'It's like some malign influence. It'll need an immense amount of family control. I'm not so concerned with the moral implications of TV, for its time-wasting propensities seem to me far more important' (Medley 1957, p. 6). The terms of the debate over the relation of children to television, that television presents an educational opportunity but television violence is an intractable problem, were set down in New Zealand in the 1960s and have regularly reappeared subsequently, the reconfiguration of the same issues suggesting an unresolved social anxiety (see Tichi 1991, pp. 191 ff.; and Weaver 1996). On November 25, 1960, four months after its introduction, the *New Zealand Listener* ran a cautionary article entitled 'Who Should Decide What Children See on TV?' (Hall, 1960, p. 8) and

"He's been seeing too much TV violence"

Figure 3.6 (*New Zealand Listener*, 25 November 1960, p. 26.)

the same issue featured a cartoon that made reference to the connections between television viewing and violence (for more details on the cultural anxiety about children and television in New Zealand see Gorringe 2002, pp. 54–60). Two years later Monte Holcroft, the editor of the *New Zealand Listener*, was arguing for the need to establish a code since 'the need for high standards ha[d] been made urgent by the phenomenal growth of television' (Holcroft 1962, p. 28). As we can see from contemporary cartoons, what John Hartley has referred to as television's paedocratic role as a child minder was already being celebrated at this time (Hartley 1992, pp. 17–18).

"*They play well together, don't they?*"

Figure 3.7 (*New Zealand Listener*, 12 July 1957, p. 19.)

Debate over television as education versus entertainment

In 1960, the Acting Leader of the National Opposition, John Marshall, was adamant that 'TV, while it has limited cultural and educational functions, is largely a medium for popular entertainment' (*Otago Daily Times*, 30 January 1960, quoted in Jackson 1960, p. 293). However, those in the education profession begged to differ. Mr H.W. Sayers, Senior Inspector of Post-Primary Schools, wrote that 'TV in the classroom is one of the most valuable teaching aids ever devised' (quoted in Goodwin 1960, p. 257; see also Reed 1958). Even a conservative magazine like *Church and People* was adamant that '[t]elevision is the greatest educational force since printing was invented and schools were established' (July 1961, p. 18, quoted in Gorringe 2002, p. 69). Political commentator Keith Jackson lamented in *Landfall* that 'it is tragic that virtually no attention appears to have been paid in ministerial statements so far to the problem of what TV can do, in New Zealand conditions, to contribute to the general well-being and political, cultural and social vitality of the nation' (Jackson 1960, p. 293). These poles of television as pure (mindless) entertainment opposed to its educative and nation-building role and cultural power set the grounds for the passion and fury that was to characterise the public debate over television in the subsequent decades.

Debates over aesthetics: live television

The early aesthetics of television is marked by a contrast between filmed and live material; accordingly, for many writers on early television, the essential technological feature of television versus the cinema was its ability to convey simultaneous distant performance visually (see, for example, the comments by J.H. Hall cited above). This was seen as a combination of the immediacy of live theatrical performance and the power of radio to transverse distance, and it is a quality that more contemporary television critics such as McKenzie Wark (1994) have explored as the mass medium's '**vectorality**'. We need to acknowledge as well the constraints of the technical medium: early television had no videotape, so drama had to be live, or be made expensively on film, and even when video arrived it was difficult to edit in a non-linear fashion, so it was desirable to do as much in front of the camera as continuously as possible. In the context of the early 1960s, this aesthetic of immediacy bore an intimate relationship with the conditions of television reception, for the television audience was a mass audience, but it was also an audience, unlike film, of five or six people at a time. This intimacy of viewing was understood to have implications for television directing techniques and a new performance style of acting that emphasised attention to detail and the psychological revelation of character (see Boddy 1990, p. 82). James Boswell, a New Zealander who had one of the first degrees in broadcasting and extensive experience of American television, noted the new performance styles: 'I think that the live play is television in its most creative form. Words, actions and expressions are only a few of the qualities of the complete television actor. Since most of the play is shot in close-up, his timing must be perfect and his position in relation to the set and the camera must be accurate to the nearest fraction of an inch' (Boswell 1958, p. 9).

Another of the first results of television's 'metaphysics of presence' was the polemical linking of immediacy with metaphysical notions of authenticity, depth, and truth. Live television opened up the question of realism and, for many of its early viewers, television's technological immediacy gave the medium an overwhelming feeling of reality. Ian Mackay, reporting on Australian television in the *New Zealand Listener* in 1957, wrote: 'There are indications that the public want local programmes, and stations are beginning to feature those shows which do not require a formal script or lengthy rehearsal preparation. These programmes emphasise speed of production, continuity of appeal and informality of presentation' (Mackay 1957, p. 7).

Debate over local content

As we have seen there was an early importance placed on regional and local production in Sutch's report. This recommendation, however, would not be taken up and an early reviewer of television's progress one year down the line was to remark: 'The New Zealand made programme, the home-product that helped establish television in other countries, plays a Cinderella role…if anyone with imagination had been let loose in television here he would have realized two things. First, New Zealand is too far away to benefit from overseas topical news…Second, New Zealanders, like anyone else, love to peep into other people's lives, especially their own kind' (MacLeod 1961, p. 15).

The essay concluded that 'it is necessary to proceed along a road sign-posted in our language and not in one New Zealanders do not speak'. The call for local content remained unheeded, or was only answered in part, as did the articulation of a coherent overall philosophy surrounding it, for 'broadcasting entered the era of detailed cost and benefit analysis which showed most forms of local production to be uneconomic' (Horrocks 1996, p. 59). Equally, as Roger Horrocks argues, broadcasters could explain away the lack of local production in drama and other genres by being: 'prepared to carry the cost of news, current affairs and sport (in the main codes) as "loss leaders". There were also game shows that paid for themselves. To the broadcasters these genres were the solid core they needed to preserve their identity—this was local content for them' (Horrocks 1996, p. 59).

Installing the television set[8]

As noted above, by 1966 some 500 000 television licences had been issued, with income derived from the combination of advertising and the broadcasting license. The early viewers of television emulated the only other environment for moving images with which they were familiar—the cinema: the lights were turned off, the blinds were drawn, the doors were closed, and talking was taboo. In newspapers and magazines such as the *New Zealand Listener* television viewing was consistently presented as sustained and absorbing and, as Australian commentators have suggested, it is clear that television was 'first watched with a kind of intensity, concentration and lack of conversation that would be unfamiliar today' (Hartley and O'Regan 1992, p. 147). While, as the advertising for television sets indicated, the family unit was seen as the prime audience target, the television set was frequently watched by large groups of friends or relatives, and the family living room was soon transformed into a public space. Television brought with it significant changes in domestic arrangements, as well as the reorganisation of domestic space and of home lives. Magazines like *Home and Building* explained how to rearrange the living room for television viewing (*Home and Building* February 1960, p. 8). With the television set came different accessories such as modular furniture, venetian blinds for reducing glare, and the 'teleglide' used to move a heavy set across the room (see Gorringe 2002, p. 40).

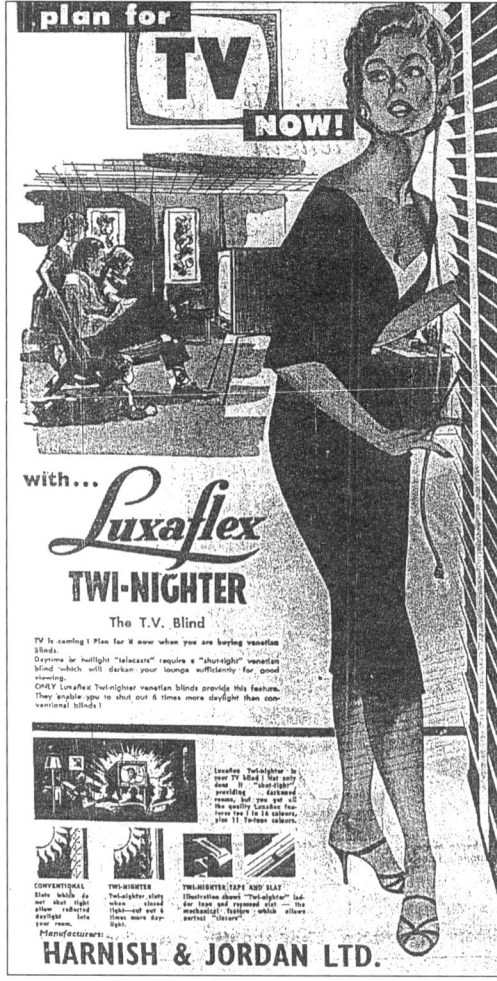

Figure 3.8 'Luxaflex Blinds' (Advertisement) (*NZ Herald*, 11 February 1960, p. 19.)

A number of contemporary cartoons deliberately show the television viewer being manipulated or physically placed under the control of his or her set.

Figure 3.9 (*New Zealand Listener*, 28 November 1958, p. 19.)

"Stanley just won't have TV in the house"

Figure 3.10 (*New Zealand Listener*, 29 April 1960, p. 12.)

Figure 3.11 (*New Zealand Listener*, 20 October 1961, p. 33.)

Several metaphors have been used by subsequent historians to describe the changes initiated by the physical installation of the television set into the domestic environment: these are 'the electronic hearth', 'theatricalisation', and 'the private gaze'. Linked to conservative discourses of the hearth as the centre of family life, the embodiment of traditional values, family cohesiveness, and domesticity is the notion of television as the electronic hearth. 'Lose a Lounge and Gain a Family' was the headline to a page of advice on television printed in the lifestyle magazine *The Mirror* in August 1961.

Figure 3.12 *(New Zealand Listener, 10 March 1961, p. 26.)*

LOSE A LOUNGE AND GAIN A FAMILY

So you've got your set and now you find that life has changed . . . The lounge has become your viewing room, but —

The teenagers stay at home at night now. You don't have to worry about where they are and what they're doing. They're glued in front of your set.

You don't need to spend money on baby-sitters. They queue up for the privilege of minding the baby while they watch TV.

If you're elderly, life takes on more colour, gains interest. You don't need to go out—your set brings the world to your own hearth.

Families find fresh contact with each other in sharing and enjoying TV programmes. At first you want to watch everything—later comes discrimination.

Figure 3.13 *(The Mirror, August 1961, p. 65.)*

Often the new television set was strategically placed alongside the fire-place, resulting in the conflation of the two. Attention was reorganised away from the hearth to a different corner of the room, frequently that where the radio used to be, and with the arrival of central heating the fireplace was to literally disappear in many modern homes (Tichi 1991, p. 42 ff.). In the New Zealand home the television set first took pride of place in the lounge-room, previously a space rarely used for day-to-day living and kept for visitors or special occasions. According to Lynn Spigel, the installation of a TV receiver also brought with it 'a theatricalisation… of domestic space' where the home was literally rearranged as a space of exhibition and an evening's viewing became structured as a quasi-theatrical experience with invited friends and neighbours (Spigel 1992a, p. 12). The television experience was commonly advertised as 'the greatest show on earth' or 'the magic carpet ride', an illusion so compelling that one would be transported out of the domestic environment.

Figure 3.14
(*New Zealand Listener*, 23 March 1962, back cover.)

Television also disrupted the established manners and behavioural norms of the middle-class nuclear family. Television-centred food, in the form of TV dinners, disturbed one of the central rituals of family life, the evening meal. Furthermore, the woman of the household became a hostess, preparing drinks and snacks for the guests invited into her home to sample an evening's viewing. There now existed a conflation of private and public spaces with the private home acquiring traces of public space, the snack bar, theatre, or stadium (Tichi 1991, p. 24).

(C) Punch

Figure 3.15 *(New Zealand Listener, 7 October 1960, p. 9.)*

Paradoxically, as it opened the home up to theatricalisation and shared public viewing, television also offered the possibility of a private gaze that clashed with patterns of communal viewing. Cecelia Tichi has written of 'decentralized television, the one-on-one experience in which television is a private and individualistic act' (Tichi 1991, p. 63) and we might understand 'solo television' as part of the tradition of personal individualism that so strongly marks New Zealand social relations and belies the early advertising images of the social hearth. 'Clearly, at all ages, television is the refuge of the lonely, the unintelligent, and the troubled person' an earlier reviewer announced in the *New Zealand Listener* even before television had arrived (McD 1959, p. 12). Such an emphasis on personal acts and choice in television viewing, setting the individual viewer apart from the family, implied a masking of anxieties relevant to the very traditions television sought to uphold. The 'private gaze' is also linked to the later proliferation of portable TV receivers, shaped like luggage with handles on the top, which could be transported from room to room. Eventually individualistic program preference was to lead to the dissolution of the familial togetherness, a feature of today's multiple-set households.

SMALLEST TV receiver on show at this year's Earl's Court exhibition was this 20 lb. portable model — cost, 49 guineas

Figure 3.16 (*New Zealand Listener*, 11 October 1957, p. 5.)

Neither can we ignore the issue of gender as a structural determinant of early television broadcasting in New Zealand: the limited participation of women in broadcast production and management contrasted with women as one of the primary audiences of broadcasting's commercial address. Television has always looked to women, assumed that they are the primary consumers for their households and, as such, targeted them as a key source of revenue. In the *New Zealand Listener* of 24 April 1959, Prudence Gregory speculated on how women would watch (listen to) television and do their housework (Gregory 1959, p. 9).[9] It was with the introduction of afternoon programming in 1967 that the 'concerns about women and television truly coalesced' and the numbers of shoppers and the usage of public transport fell noticeably as women stayed at home to watch their favourite programs (Gorringe 2002, p. 65). The advertising layouts for new television sets emphasized that they were objects entering a woman's sphere of command but also implied a controlling male gaze: typically they had the male gazing at his family amid his household property, looking upon what he possesses. The presumption was that the provider, the husband-father, controlled the purchase of a major appliance such as the television set.

Figure 3.17 (*New Zealand Listener*, 12 April 1957, p. 2.)

Nevertheless, this still left the television as an object of home décor ultimately to be arranged by the woman of the household. Progressively, the New Zealand suburban home was designed around the television set, and the open-plan design that became increasingly popular during the 1960s emphasized the connection of women's working areas, such as the kitchen, with living areas where one might find the television set.[10] Installing a television set was thus to radically redefine the everyday lives of New Zealanders and the reconfiguration of their domestic living space.

Figure 3.18
(*New Zealand Listener,*
12 May 1961, p. 23.)

Figure 3.19
(*New Zealand Listener,*
30 March 1961, back page.)

Conclusions

I have drawn upon advertisements, cartoon humour, journalism, memoirs, industry promotions, government papers, and parliamentary debate to show how New Zealanders understood the social changes and the cultural continuities brought and represented by television. The central idea behind such an approach is that the acculturation of television proceeds in and from such a public discourse, and these kinds of texts work interpretively to position television in the cultural life of the public. They mediate between the receiver and the on-screen worlds and the individual and the group of viewers that form the nation on the other. They speak about, and on behalf of, the object television, and they represent and enact the cognitive experience of the viewer. As interpretive texts they both shape consciousness and reflect that shaping. Symbiotically, they disclose the social construction of television and they constitute its environment. The argument however, would be that however striking the new technology might be, once introduced it becomes enmeshed in long-term cultural traditions and conflicts that reflect the deep involvement of television in national values: individuality, domesticity, patriotism, sexual politics.

The history of the arrival of television in New Zealand has been conceived of as primarily the history of economic, regulatory, and political struggles. The traditional histories have explained the coming of television into the home through a set of economic determinations, including manufacturer strategies and the postwar climate of consumption. Following the lead of American historians of television such as Lynn Spigel, I have argued here that one must also look at the coming of television in the context of a history of representation and a production of discourses that are centred in popular culture: popular magazines, magazine advertisements, early television narratives, oral histories. As we have seen, the popular discourses surrounding the introduction of television to New Zealand were replete with ambivalence and hesitation. On the one hand, there were Utopian discourses that presented the new medium as the ultimate expression of technological and social progress. On the other, these were matched equally by dystopian discourses that warned of the effects of television on the nuclear family, sport, and recreation, and even dental hygiene.[11]

Television in New Zealand may be seen to arrive among or along with three pre-existing conditions: New Zealand's postcolonial status; the locally existing national broadcasting culture; and the transnational American, British and Australian television cultures. Thus television in New Zealand appeared among an already sedimented structure of broadcasting decisions, definitions, and distinctions and it owes much to the outcomes of the struggles that took place in radio: regulatory structures, organisational practices, notions of scheduling, conceptualisations of the audience. Many contemporary commentators remark upon radio's legacy to television despite what they perceived might be television's threat to radio.[12] Radio had paved the way for local productions and much of the television produced locally through the 1960s tended to use **formats** that were familiar to audiences from radio. Some television shows, such as quiz shows, were literally 'radio with pictures', interestingly enough a phrase first used here by the man who would become Director-General of Broadcasting, Gilbert Stringer (Day 2000, p. 28). Another fundamental link between the two media was that television employed the same dual distribution and exhibition system as radio and the single licence fee helped conflate the two media in the public mind.

At the same time, as we have seen, the earliest reports on television as a phenomenon come from those who had lived or worked in either Britain or the United States and experienced either the public service broadcasting model or the commercial one. The easy conclusion might be that television culture here was simply, and has largely remained, an imitation of British mixed, or overlaid with, American (and to some extent Australian) television culture. However, upon reflection of the popular discourses surrounding television that I have begun to explore here, a wider conclusion might be drawn that New Zealand television culture (its distribution and broadcasting strategies, institutional structures, different activities involved in creating, regulating, screening, criticising—that is, producing and watching television programs) is not simply to be understood as an imitation of transnational forms. As has recently been noted: 'Television in New Zealand has always been characterized by a tension between mixed objectives, such as "public service" versus "commerce", "information" versus "entertainment", "regulation" versus "deregulation" '(Lealand and Martin 2001, p. 22).

It is to be hoped that this examination of the birth of television has disclosed the equivocal nature of New Zealand television with its characteristic uncertainty about issues of originality (how we invent television here) and sameness (how we simply borrow imported programs or more latterly copy their formats). Seen in a wider context of public broadcasting models the paradox emerges that the New Zealand model was conceived of and was reconfigured at a distance from its Anglo-American parents but through its programming (and some of its regulatory structures) it appeared to resemble its British and American counterparts. Given the minimal local contribution to television drama in the 1960s, imports appear to have defined the program categories, but there is another essay to be written about the highly unusual early readings of 'foreign' programs on New Zealand television that can be gleaned from the Letters to the Editor and the regular invited public responses published in the *New Zealand Listener*. While wary of appearing to simply borrow again from the outside, I believe that the notion of 'inter-dependence' proposed by the Australian television historian Tom O'Regan is useful in helping understand how New Zealand television modifies and adapts imported programs and structures (policies, regulatory techniques, program schedules, genres), and how by virtue of its similarities with British, American and Australian television it has generated similar programming responses (O'Regan 1993, p. xxi). The argument would go that New Zealand television functions in an interdependent fashion within the larger transnational system, and so we need to explore exactly how the trans-national forms became indigenised. On the one hand, the transmission of imported programs ensured that the perception of close resemblances between New Zealand and British and American television and culture persisted, but, on the other, the process of indigenisation also made New Zealand television subtly and distinctly different. Methods for obtaining audience coverage were quite different from American and to some extent British models: there was no national simultaneously broadcast schedule; no surrendering of control of advertising to advertisers; a strong regional station emphasis; an indiscriminate mixing of British and American material; and the nature of local television criticism was based strongly in spectator response and letters to the editor. As O'Regan has argued for Australian television, New Zealand television's 'distinctiveness is best understood as a point somewhere between two seemingly opposed positions: …as a particular *invention* of television and…as simply an *imitation* of the transnational form of television' (O'Regan 1993, p. xx). This chapter has been an attempt to understand how that 'distinctiveness' began to mark New Zealand television from the moment of its introduction.

References

Appendices to the Journals of the House of Representatives, 1950–61.

Berry, John. 1963. 'Infant Television.' *Landfall* 17 (1), pp. 67–69.

Boddy, William. 1990. *Fifties Television: The Industry and its Critics*, Urbana and Chicago: University of Illinois Press.

Boswell, James. 1958. 'Hollywood Methods in U.S. Television', *New Zealand Listener*, 7 November, p. 9.

Boyd-Bell, Robert. 1985. *New Zealand Television: The First 25 Years*, Auckland: Reed Methuen.

Day, Patrick. 1994. *The Radio Years: A History of Broadcasting in New Zealand*, Vol. 1. Auckland: Auckland University Press.

Day, Patrick. 2000. *Voice and Vision. A History of Broadcasting in New Zealand*, Vol. 2. Auckland: Auckland University Press.

Garbutt, Russell. 1988. '*It's O.K. Leaving Here*'. *A Brief History of the First Twenty-five Years of Television in Dunedin*. Dunedin: Television New Zealand.

Goodwin, J.W. 1953. 'TV or not TV', *New Zealand Listener* July 24, p. 6.

Goodwin, J.W. 1960. 'TV or not TV. That is the Question for your School', *National Education* 62 (456), pp. 257–8.

Gorringe, Ashley. 2002 'Consol[ing] Vision? Aspects of Early New Zealand Television Audiences 1960–75', thesis (Master of Arts), University of Auckland, 2002.

Gregory, Prudence. 1959. 'Broadcaster Abroad', *New Zealand Listener,* 24 April, p. 9.

Gregory, R.J. 1985. *Politics and Broadcasting; Before and Beyond the NZBC,* Palmerston North, Dunmore.

Hall, J.R. 1957. 'Radio & TV in the U.S.', *New Zealand Listener,* 23 August, p. 7.

Hall, Wendy. 1960. 'Who Should Decide What Children See on TV?', *New Zealand Listener,* 25 November, p. 8.

Harrison, R.J. 1962. 'The Broadcasting Corporation Act', *Landfall* 16 (2), pp. 185–8.

Hartley, John. 1992. *Tele-ology: Studies in Television.* London and New York: Routledge.

Hartley, John & Tom O'Regan. 1992. 'Television in a New Way of Life', in Albert Moran (ed.), *Stay Tuned: The Australian Broadcasting Reader.* Sydney: Allen & Unwin.

Holcroft, Monte. 1957. 'Silent Shadows on the Screen', *New Zealand Listener,* 22 February, p. 4.

Holcroft, Monte. 1962. 'Living Room Murders', *New Zealand Listener* 19 April 19, p. 28.

Horrocks, Roger. 1986. 'Conflicts and Surprises in New Zealand Television', *Continuum: the Australian Journal of Media and Culture* 10 (1), pp. 50–63.

Huyssen, Andreas. 1986. *After the Great Divide: Modernism, Mass Culture and Postmodernism.* London: Macmillan.

Jackson, Keith. 1960. 'TV and Democracy', *Landfall* 14 (3), pp. 281–93.

Lee-Johnson, Eric. 1939. 'Television will come to New Zealand', *Pukeora Review,* 2 (6), pp. 1–2.

Lealand Geoff & Helen Martin. 2001. *It's All Done With Mirrors: About Television.* Palmerston North: Dunmore Press.

McD., J.D. 1959. 'Looking at Television', *New Zealand Listener* 24 April, p. 12.

McIvor, Grant. 1981. The Introduction of Television in New Zealand, Dissertation in History, University of Otago, Dunedin.

Mackay, Ian K. 1957. 'Australian Television', *New Zealand Listener* 12 April 12, pp. 6–7.

Mackay, Ian K. 1958. 'Australian Television—A Second Look', *New Zealand Listener,* 7 February pp. 6–7.

MacLeod, Gabriella. 1961. 'Television in Auckland', *Comment* 2 (3) pp. 14–15.

Medley, John.1957. 'The First Few Years Are Bound to be Hysterical', *New Zealand Listener,* 26 April, p. 6.

New Zealand Listener. 1960. 'Speaking of Television', 19 February, pp. 6–7.

New Zealand Listener. 1999. 'Equipment for NZBS', 13 February, p. 9.

New Zealand Parliamentary Debates, 1949–61.

New Zealand Parliamentary Debates, 1955, Vol. 306.

O'Regan, Tom. 1993. *Australian Television Culture.* Sydney: Allen & Unwin.

Rayson, Cate. 1998. *Glued to the Telly.* Redhill: Elgua Media.

Reed, John. 1958. 'TV and Teaching', *New Zealand Listener* 6 June, p. 9.

Reid, J.C. 1960. 'Television Prospects', *Comment* 2 (1), pp. 5–6.

Roscoe, Jane & Craig Hight. 2001. *Faking It: Mock Documentary and the Subversion of Factuality.* Manchester: Manchester University Press.

Shaw, Peter. 1997. *A History of New Zealand Architecture.* Auckland: Hodder Moa Beckett.

Spigel, Lynn. 1992a. *Make Room for TV: Television and the Family Ideal in Postwar America*. Chicago and London: University of Chicago Press.

Spigel, Lynn. 1992b. 'Installing the Television Set: Popular Discourses on Television and Domestic Space, 1948–1955', in Lynn Spigel and Denise Mann (eds), *Private Screenings: Television and the Female Consumer*. Minneapolis: University of Minnesota Press, pp. 3–39.

Sullivan, Jim. 1987. *A History of Broadcasting News 1921–62*. Timaru: Radio New Zealand Sound Archives.

Sullivan, Jim. 1940. 'Robert Jack', *The Dictionary of New Zealand Biography*, Vol. 4 1921–40. Auckland: Auckland University Press, p. 249.

Sutch, W.B. 1959. *The Economics of Television in New Zealand*. Wellington: Department of Industries & Commerce.

Tichi, Cecelia. 1991. *Electronic Hearth: Creating an American Television Culture*. New York and Oxford: Oxford University Press.

Turner, John B. 1999. *Eric Lee-Johnson: Artist with a Camera*. Auckland: Photoforum.

Walshe, J. 1959. 'On the Brink of Television'. *Landfall* 13 (4), pp. 359–63.

Wark, Mackenzie. 1994. *Virtual Geography: Living with Global Media Events*. Bloomington: Indiana University Press.

Weaver, C. Kay. 1996. 'The Television and Violence Debate in New Zealand: Some Problems of Context', *Continuum: the Australian Journal of Media and Culture* 10 (1), pp. 64–75.

Notes

1 While Hexter-Stabbins seemed improbably named, as did one of his successors Tim Evans-Freke, there was clearly a strong cultural logic to choosing him, because his style was English and because he was 'the nearest thing' that could be found to popular English comedian and media personality Jimmy Edwards (see Day 1994, p. 23).

2 I remain indebted to the efforts of my research assistant Scott Wilson, who helped me track down much of the primary source material that I have used here.

3 For the genre of the mock documentary or '**mockumentary**' of which Peter Jackson's *Forgotten Silver* (1997), containing the imaginary character of Colin McKenzie, is a major example, see Roscoe and Hight (2001).

4 The *Pukeora Review* was the magazine of Pukeora Sanitorium, where Lee-Johnson was treated for tuberculosis in 1939. I am grateful to John Turner for providing me with a transcript of Lee-Johnson's article.

5 For a full account of the parliamentary debates leading up to the introduction of television see McIvor (1981).

6 See 'Equipment for NZBS', (*New Zealand Listener*, 13 February 1959, p. 9) for a full account of the equipment purchased and its installation. Transmission around the world was hampered at this stage by the fact that there was no world standard regarding the number of lines in the television picture. A British system of 405 lines, an American system of 525 lines, and a third option of 625 lines were all available. One of the advantages of the delayed introduction of television was that late in the piece New Zealand opted for 625 lines, which then became more widely used globally.

7   The first calls for a royal commission came in the Letters to the Editor of the *New Zealand Listener,* 13 September 1957, p. 11.

8   In my discussion of the 'installation' of the television set within a New Zealand context, I have been influenced by and drawn upon the work of Lynn Spigel (1992a and 1992b), Cecelia Tichi (1991), and Cate Rayson (1998).

9   It would be possible to make connections here with the historical feminisation of mass culture. Andreas Huyssen explores 'the notion which gained ground during the nineteenth century that mass culture is somehow associated with women while real, authentic culture remains the prerogative of men'. This conception had material consequences for women: 'The universalizing ascription of femininity to mass culture always depended on the very real exclusion of women from high culture and its institutions' (Huyssen 1986, pp. 47, 62).

10 Citing the work of Auckland's Group Architects, but also that of more commercial builders such as Neil Housing, architectural historian Peter Shaw writes that '[b]y the early 1960s, however, a wide variety of exteriors had been introduced and open-plan ideas had begun to influence the way semi-public dining/living/kitchen areas were designed' (Shaw 1997, pp. 162–3).

11 See the account reported in the *New Zealand Listener* 27 February 1959 of the British Dental Association's concerns about the long-term effects on children who watch television with their jaws pressing on their hands.

12 See, for example, Holcroft (1957, p. 4): 'Yet TV has not destroyed radio, and seems unlikely to do so: there are too many functions—especially news and music—which need no visual intervention, in spite of attempts to prove the contrary' and also Hall (1957, p. 7).

'Getting the Picture':

State Regulation,
Market Making, and Cultural
Change in the New Zealand
Television System

NICK PERRY

On maps: Local and global

Two recent images of televised sport provide this chapter's starting point.
Each exemplifies globalisation. The first derives from the emergence in
the late 1990s of that southern hemisphere rugby union sporting competition known as the Super Twelve. The 'Twelve' in question consist of
professional sides drawn from South Africa (three teams), Australia (four
teams), and New Zealand (five teams). The concept of such a competition
forged links between: a) rugby union's development into a commercially
managed and professionalised sport; b) the enormously enhanced financial
and cultural significance of television (as distinct from stadium) audiences
for sporting fixtures; and c) the transnational organisation, ownership, and
control of media interests under the auspices of such figures as Rupert
Murdoch.

One of the distinguishing characteristics of the New Zealand franchises
is that between them they cover the entire country; taken together the
territories they represent map onto and coincide with the spatial boundaries of the nation state; and the teams themselves provide the recruitment
pool for the All Blacks as the national team. The intra-national boundaries
between the franchises do not, however, correspond to any extant administrative or other distinctions on the ground. They are instead a combination
of virtual geographies and imagined markets, the product of branding

strategies and media footprints. As such they are symptomatic of a process of globalisation from above, as it more or less imperfectly articulates with pre-existing social patterns and prior cultural sedimentations. The Super Twelve competition, along with the major All Black games for which it provides the players, are no longer available on terrestrial-based, free-to-air national (albeit commercially driven) television, except in the form of delayed coverage; access to real-time transmission is the prerogative of paying subscribers to the relevant, overseas-owned, satellite channel.

The second image involves a mapping of a different kind. What it points to is less a struggle *over* representation than a struggle *for* it, an attempt to bring it into being. As part of a determined effort to make a predominantly non-spectator sport into a televisual one, the screening of the Auckland-based Louis Vuitton and America's Cup yachting competitions was punctuated by cartoon-like virtual images of the yachts and the courses on which the racing was held. What was distinctive about these simulations, generated through a software program called Virtual Spectator, is that they initiated a novel positioning for viewers, one that made it possible for them to readily grasp the *relative* positions of the yachts in relation to one another no matter what their location on the courses themselves.

Whereas the mapping of New Zealand by Super Twelve franchisees, and the associated construction of 'imagined communities' (cf. Anderson 1991), are signifiers of globalisation from above, the conceptual basis of Virtual Spectator derived from 'watching' the Whitbread Round the World yacht race from a location at the bottom of the world. 'Watching', that is, in the sense that a clustering of Internet-dependent technologies was employed to establish yacht positions. This data was then fed into the relevant programs and the 'movements' of the boats in question were duly traced.

The development of Virtual Spectator might therefore be said to signify globalisation from below, in which a small company in a remote Dunedin location began to construct a hitherto unavailable point of view and an attendant 'imagined world'. The software and its associated applications would subsequently be employed by some 3000 media organisations in their coverage of the many months of competition for yachting's Louis Vuitton and America's Cups.

Each of these contemporary examples serves to indicate the complexity of both the local and the global. They signal that neither the local, nor the global, nor the relations between them are given, permanent essences, but rather they are constructed or reconstructed socially and technologically. Geography is imagined, as is community. And the process of that imagining can take different forms—it can be from above or from below (moving from the global down to the local, or from the local out to the global), or some complex combination of both. Thus in Finland, it is not just the notion of globalisation, but also the term 'Nokiaisation', that has entered their language, in recognition of the planet-wide success of that small country's most famous mobile phone manufacturer.

On windows: Then and now

For many years now, television has played a key part in this process of constructing and imagining. But the conditions of that construction have changed. Both the contemporary examples just cited have a commercial or market context. But when the medium was first introduced in this country it was also influenced by the idea of public service that television was seen to represent—and for which the BBC provided the (globally recognised) model.

It was a model that implied a rather different conception of 'spectatorship'. Almost forty years ago the BBC television series *Panorama* made its first visit to mainland China. The phrase 'A thousand windows on the world' was the result of a translator's imaginative solution to the problem of identifying an approximate Mandarin equivalent to the title of the program. These words were promptly claimed as an apt metaphor and guiding vision for what was destined to become the world's longest-running current affairs series, a series understood to exemplify public service—television's publicly stated mission of educating and informing the citizenry.

At around the same time, the British publishers of New Zealand poet Allen Curnow (1962) produced his *A Small Room with Large Windows*, a selection of poems with a print run that was probably little more than 1000. Yet Curnow's imagery of nation, of building, and of nation-building, was knowingly located between description and aspiration. Hence it too could be said to have signalled an embarkation upon a not dissimilar mission, positioned as it was between a portrayal of the extant cultural meaning of Curnow's homeland and an attempt (with an overseas-based publishing company's support) to bring it into being. In its place of origin, however, the title poem had already proved to be prescient in a way that Curnow had not anticipated. For its first local appearance in print had been in 1957, some three years before the introduction of television into New Zealand. This latter initiative ushered in the beginnings of that subsequent transformation in both the texts and the practices whereby dominant representations of the National and its Other would be achieved. (As the process of becoming digital gathers momentum, that achievement, in its turn, would seem to be destined to be the subject of, and subject to, major changes).

There are obvious differences—in their textual attributes, in the media of their transmission, in the structuring of their practices, and in the composition of their audiences—as between a BBC flagship and Curnow's small craft. It is nevertheless tempting to read the affinities between each of these initiatives as precursors of the current phase of globalisation, as early warning signals for what would subsequently become a flood of media images, of cultural ideas and political ideals, of material resources, technologies and peoples, a flood whose sediments were destined to be spread unevenly across every part of the planet (Appadurai 1990). Moreover, in each case what is also discernible within the associated imagery is not just the purported uniformities of this process, but also the salience and persistence of their respective senses of *place*, made manifest as a differential awareness of the locations from which they speak. And third, thanks in part to Microsoft, a dense cluster of novel associations has subsequently gathered around the term 'windows' as word and as concept.

Thus as a consequence of the circulation of postcolonial discourses it now seems not merely possible, but plausible, to interpret *Panorama*'s 'windows on the world', and the conception of public service television to which it gives expression, as a verbal signifier of panoptic intent.[1] For it can now more easily be read as the presumptively universal and specific encoding of a centralising aspiration, as that wedding of gaze and control, knowledge and power, which is held to be characteristic of globalisation-from-above. This may be contrasted with Curnow's perspective, with its globalisation-from-below imagery of a two-way directional flow, in which 'the window' is at once more ambiguous and yet more transparent than either the mirror or the screen. For it suggests a conception of representation that neither purports to simply reveal nor functions to simply conceal, but rather to frame, to select, to reflect, and to refract both the observer and the world, while incidentally scattering some light onto the processes through which each of them comes to be constituted. And as the poem's stanzas make clear, it also posits a conception of citizenship as plural and multi-perspectival, repudiating a single line of vision (against the notion of one 'true north') in favour of the complexity of 'the whole 360 degrees'[2] (Curnow 1962, pp. 79, 80).

During its forty-odd year history, this country's television system has traversed the spectrum of broadcasting forms. Initially it was based on closely supervised state control under the direct jurisdiction of a government department. By the late 1990s, however, it had become what was arguably the most deregulated broadcasting regime on the planet, in which there were no legal barriers either to 100 per cent overseas ownership of television channels or to new entrants. Responsibility for the maintenance of public service broadcasting, as this is traditionally conceived, was (and is) no longer to be found within a given television channel or channels. Instead what locally remains of that tradition now resides within two commissioning agencies. The first of these is New Zealand On Air, an organisation that for the present, at least, continues to operate at arm's length from the government that now directly funds it (the licence fee, which it had been responsible both for collecting and for spending, having been abolished). Along with Te Māngai Pāho, which is charged with developing Māori programming, New Zealand On Air has effectively redefined public service television as a synonym for, and as the promotion of (a widely defined notion of) local content. There are still two publicly owned channels in New Zealand, notwithstanding that as recently as 1999 one, and possibly both, of these channels seemed destined to be sold off. Whether as SOEs (State Owned Enterprises), or in their most recent manifestation as CROCs (Crown Owned Companies), they are obliged and expected to provide a commercial rate of return for government coffers. Nevertheless a decade-long acceleration of commercialisation—and the associated marginalisation of public service broadcasting has come in for fresh scrutiny—and a measure of re-regulation is currently being implemented.

The first pair of representations/simulations with which this chapter began (of rugby and yachting) are thus manifestations of the continuing pre-eminence of this commercial conception of television in New Zealand and of the kind of entrepreneurial patterns and product initiatives that it fosters. Each of these thoroughly contemporary images reveals how such struggles in and around the representation of the global/national are an aspect of the making of markets. Notwithstanding the differences between them, the implication is that each exemplifies a taken-for-granted congruence between representation and market processes, an implication that is, in turn, symptomatic of New Zealand's thoroughly commercialised television system.

In and of themselves, however, they do not explain how this commercial model came to achieve such a dominant position, or why that dominance is currently subject to interrogation. It is as a preamble to that question that the second pair of (rather different) images (of windows) was invoked. In harking back to the time when New Zealanders were first introduced to the medium, they illustrate that rival conception of broadcasting's cultural mission to which public service television and its supporters have typically laid claim.

The point—both then and now—is not just that the processes of globalisation routinely function so as 'to stir things up'. It is also that the resulting uncertainties extend to whether such processes should be seen as confirming or as confounding the distinction between the idiosyncratic and the abstract, between local particularities and global uniformities, between the postulate of many worlds or of just one (cf. Perry 2000). Hence Roland Robertson (1992, p. 181) has suggested that empirically informed, contemporary theorising about globalisation is distinguished by a 'search for fundamentals [that] brings together in problematic and comprehensible ways the simultaneous advocacy of "totalizing" and "anti-totalizing" positions'.

'Dominant television' as 'seen from a distance'

What this essay has been concerned to emphasise is that in relation to certain tidy sets of binary opposites, New Zealand broadcasting television never quite fits. As Curnow had famously observed of the nation that it constructs and represents, 'It was something different, something / Nobody counted on'- notwithstanding that broadcasting aspires to organise and unify the very concept of a national imaginary (1962, p. 7).[3]

It is the associated uncertainties that provide a warrant for employing *four* images in order to gesture towards *two* contrasting conceptions of cultural production. With respect to both the historical development of television, and the present organisation of free-to-air broadcasting, that contrast is widely interpreted as having been given paradigmatic expression through the American commercial network model, funded by advertising, and the BBC public service model, funded by a licence fee. Such a contrast not only encodes the different principles of legitimation that accompany the distinction between markets and hierarchies, between entrepreneurial and bureaucratic forms, between addressing television audiences as consumers and addressing them as citizens. It has also come to be identified with each system's differential rankings of media formats and the associated distinctions between their characteristic textual modalities (aka their 'look'). Between them, these conceptions of television have both set the terms of debate about how free-to-air versions of the medium *should* be organised in Western societies and have defined the parameters within which they are *in fact* organized.

New Zealand's manifestly geographically distant, but presumptively culturally proximate, television system has thus drawn upon and oscillated between both models. This is made evident in what is variously either an endemic vulnerability to, or an enthusiasm for, the process of making, unmaking, and remaking the system. The result has been a series of hybridised structures that have served to enshrine, but not to resolve, the tensions between both state and market pressures and the imperatives of both consumerism and citizenship.

What is here suggested by the evocation of four cases, however, is that these classic, familiar, and enduringly relevant oppositions are also bisected by a further contrast between 'top-down' and 'bottom-up' organisation. It is thus a contrast that insinuates the presence of a third term. Inasmuch as this latter derives from the diffuse and waywardly ordered networks and dispersed sentiments of civil society, then when it is viewed from within the confines of the two dominant models, it appears as at once the prize that each seeks to capture and the disorder that they are designed to control. Thus the word 'television', which literally means 'seeing from a distance', is not just a condensed description of the medium's main characteristic *as* a medium; it is also symptomatic of its necessary, but necessarily partisan, mode of engagement with this wider social order. And at the same time the forms and content (both organisational and textual) of 'dominant television', i.e. television as it is understood in either Britain or the United States, become in New Zealand both immediately present and yet 'seen as at a distance'.

On making waves with radio[4]

The notion of civil society as both the object of, and the reward for, such controlling practices, helps to clarify just why it is that the structural form through which television would subsequently be introduced into New Zealand is explicable only by reference to the pattern by which radio had developed. For it was with the advent of radio broadcasting in the 1920s, and its extremely rapid growth during the 1930s, that the airwaves provided the terrain on which high and popular cultures would engage not only with one another, but also with a succession of governments determined to closely regulate them both, as well as with emergent commercial interests concerned to amplify their profit-making prospects. At first, radio broadcasting had been based upon a regional and private enterprise format. However, its success with audiences soon prompted government to not only establish commercial and non-commercial variants—and the associated structural tension between them—but to subordinate them both to a system of national coordination and control.

Then, as now, it is representations of sport that provide perhaps the clearest textual indicator of how this variety of interests might be made to assemble together. For example, rugby broadcasts were an early initiative on radio, with a 1927 inter-provincial game representing the very first occasion on which the fledgling medium had organised transmission on a nationwide basis (Day 1994, p. 80). Not unexpectedly, transmissions of rugby and other sports were popular with audiences from the outset. Under a centralised broadcasting regime—and what was to become its attendant (but altogether much less independent) local permutation on a BBC-style Reithian broadcasting project—sport on radio was, however, ad hoc and slow to acquire institutional support. In such a context the medium's endemic and enduring subtext would prove to be the contested and shifting relations between high and popular cultures as they were refracted through realignments within the framing political system.

Thus in 1935 the incoming first Labour government saw in a national radio system a counterweight to a regional and conservative press, and

Colin Scrimgeour, a street-wise, left populist Methodist minister turned broadcaster, was charged with running and developing the entire commercial network. In a characteristic New Zealand reversal, it was therefore precisely the commercial stations that a left-of-centre government was concerned to champion. British ex-patriot James Shelley, an education professor with Reithian but, in context, broadly progressive sensibilities, was recruited to be head of the New Zealand Broadcasting Service. He was given responsibility for integrating the commercial and non-commercial stations and for fostering national loyalties. Shelley (unlike the BBC's Reith) proved reluctant to contest direct governmental control and use of radio for its own ends (Carter 1993), whereas Scrimgeour's rise—and indeed his fall—was actually based upon it (Day 1994). It is also possible to interpret the subsequent Scrimgeour/Shelley relation and its policy consequences as a permutation on the high/popular contrast, as a radio version of what had been rugby's earlier dialogue between the rough and the respectable, albeit at an altogether more 'developed' stage within the civilizing process. If the Reithian-influenced Shelley had envisaged radio as pedagogy in a new key, then for Scrimgeour, it was politics by other means. For both men, however, it was nevertheless recognisably politics as usual, played out on the terrain of the state and with civil society understood as not so much the source, but merely as a resource, for its successful praxis.

It is within such a state-centred and increasingly populist-inflected milieu that the voice of Winston McCarthy came to assume significance, a manifestation of the presence of just that elusive 'third term' to which reference was made earlier. For whereas Scrimgeour had shaped New Zealand broadcasting's representation of politics, the contribution of sports commentator McCarthy was to the politics of representation. Put another way, although McCarthy may not have aspired to speak *for* the (male) working class, he knowingly spoke *from* it. In his autobiography (McCarthy 1973) he indicates that the traditions on which his broadcasts drew were the music hall, workplace humour, and the institution of mateship. Hence 'Listen …' became a kind of catchphrase, with which he was identified as a result of his commentary on a penalty kick during a rugby international in 1945. This was the first occasion on which a sporting fixture was broadcast directly from England to New Zealand. The penalty kick in question seemed unlikely to succeed. McCarthy's (1973, p. 11) own transcript reads:

> Then I added, 'There will be a terrific roar from this vast crowd if it goes over. I'll let you judge for yourselves how he goes. Here he is moving onto the ball. He has kicked it and, LISTEN …' As the ball soared goalwards the roar from the crowd swelled and swelled, and as it crossed the bar I came in again with my piercing voice cutting over the top of the crowd—'It's a goal!'

The effect was to evoke a response that was at once congruent with the traditions of popular culture and drew upon the dramatic and imaginative possibilities of the new medium. The (imagined) action on the field of play, the (hush-to-roar) sound of the crowd, the commentator's own vernacular-informed implication in the occasion, and the listeners at home were thus encouraged to assemble together, a community of response that linked players, crowd, commentators, and culture.

It thereby simulated, yet nevertheless functioned in accordance with what Basil Bernstein (1973) has called the 'sympathetic circularity' of the restricted code. That is, the language acts primarily as a means of consti-tuting or reinforcing a like-minded social collectivity, rather than as a means of constructing or displaying differentiated, individualised subjectivities. One measure of McCarthy's iconic import is that his voice and most famous phrase would reappear in 1990s television commercials for both Ford and Steinlager. 'Listen ...' became McCarthy's call sign and calling card, the signifier of a cultural code that was constructed somewhere between the plain, matter of fact intimacy of Roosevelt's fireside radio talks (an initiative emulated by the contemporaneous New Zealand Labour Prime Minister, Michael Savage) and the call-and-response of the gospel tradition (echoed in ex-preacher Colin Scrimgeour's recognition of radio's rhetorical possibilities). This symptomatic process continued to be grounded in, and to draw its energy from, the direct social relations and representa-tions of civil society, but these were now mediated through the (increasingly obligatory) passage points of a state-controlled broadcasting system.

With the state in play, the state of play was thus transformed: new interests and new players had become involved. The transformation was slow at first, because the broadcasting of sport, although popular, was initially regarded as incidental both to the interests of governments and to the cultural mission of those in charge of the radio medium. No less decisive was that rugby was now being 'played' not just on fields of grass (and mud), but in multiple new locations in living rooms across the country. The changing structure of interests and the novel technology of representation thus acted together. Radio brought men's sport into a domestic setting, where it took up a place among other kinds of programs with other agendas and other sorts of listeners.

McCarthy's mantra had its female counterpart in 'Aunt Daisy' Basham's catchphrase, 'Good Morning, Good Morning, Good Morning'. Daisy Basham rose to national pre-eminence as a star saleswoman, advertiser, and radio announcer on the commercial network, where she introduced an affirmative, personality-based form of consumer-oriented broadcasting to a daytime female audience. It was not just that the accommodations between the high and the popular began to assume somewhat different forms. With the double movement of men's sport into the home and of women's domestic activities into a forum on the airwaves, the traditional contrast between public and private began to blur, as did the distinction between the audience as citizens and as consumers. Women's relationship to rugby (understood both as a sporting activity and as a nation-building forum) had been defined and mediated by and through their relationship to men. What radio programs like Aunt Daisy's offered them as a subject matter was their own socially isolated domestic activity, but what radio as a medium provided was the sense of a shared social condition. No matter whether this is understood as a preamble to, or a substitute for, social action, as a reinforcement of consumerism or as an embryonic politics, what radio therefore represented for women was both a different channel and a channel for difference—and with it came an incidental remaking of that elusive third term.

Rugby had been built from the ground up, on a platform of popular participation, gathering men together in a live drama of their own (Fougere 1989). By comparison, the rituals and rigours of homemaking had been undertaken by women acting in relative isolation from one another. Radio was understood as an aspect of infrastructure and as an instrument of government, perceived as a top-down technology for facilitating centralised state policies. New Zealand rugby, New Zealand domestic labour, and New Zealand radio thus derived from different foundations and were based upon contrasting logics of socio-political representation. Each had its own kind of imperative. If all of these tendencies were to be accommodated, then the dilemma this posed was how to unify their *textual* representation via such a medium. Sport and housekeeping may have only been part of a range of practices through which civil society constituted itself, but they were also widely recognised as especially consequential and therefore as prospectively the object of state regulation. Through what kind of discourse and on what kind of terrain could these matter-of-fact activities of everyday life and broadcasting as a state agency engage with one another?

What emerged was the combination of a commercial form and a vernacular idiom, a pattern that pre-figured a widening of the field of forces and the range of interests that would come to coalesce around sport and the household alike. For although it was a pattern that developed within a hierarchically ordered control structure, it was nonetheless congruent with the operation of a market system. The general process by which radio delivered its listeners to the state could also deliver them to the blandishments of market actors. As radio broadcasting developed it thus became the terrain for the elaboration of conceptions of New Zealandness that derived from the relations of civil society, the policies of the state, and organised economic interests—at the same time as it acted to blur the boundaries between them. This in turn constituted the institutional configuration, discursive matrix, and cultural setting within which television was introduced into New Zealand.

From radio with pictures to the political economy of local content

The terms under which television was developed were thus shaped by the radio broadcasting system from which it grew. National television was first introduced in New Zealand in 1960. As has been hinted at earlier, the system through which it was delivered was a hybrid from the beginning—part state-sponsored, part commercial, yet nevertheless fully owned and regulated by government. Both the type of fully fledged public service model that is exemplified by the BBC and the purely commercial system along the lines of the American networks had been developed in countries with large domestic populations. With a total population (at that time) of less than three million, New Zealand television could not have been funded through a licence fee alone. At the same time, nationwide coverage was regarded as a well nigh absolute political imperative. Yet in such a long, narrow country with a spatially dispersed audience such coverage would not have been achievable—or, at least, not at that time—by way of a purely commercial system. Thus New Zealand's quirky geo-politics, the available level of technological development, the economics of transmission, and the cultural and institutional precedents provided by radio broadcasting all combined to generate a hybridised system whose funding depended upon both advertising revenue and an annual licence fee.

Within such a system, it proved difficult for program-makers (especially, but not exclusively, those with nationalist agendas) to assert occupational autonomy or to aspire to organisational control. Initially, it was the engineering problems associated with achieving national coverage that proved to be pre-eminent. That era (and that technology) have now passed, and with its passing came shifts in the locus of organisational control. Such realignments have been a characteristic of the forty-year history of New Zealand television with—in what is roughly the temporal sequence—government bureaucrats, producers, entrepreneurial managers, accountants, and marketers/program schedulers each having striven for, or been elevated to, positions of professional dominance (cf. Farnsworth 1992; Spicer et al. 1996; Smith 1996).

But irrespective of the proximate structural effects of such occupation-based strategies and struggles, it is the enduring and intractable problems in and around the issue of local content that New Zealand television has above all been obliged to confront. The term 'dismal science' might almost have been invented to describe the economics of producing for the local television market versus the purchasing of imported programs. Because the latter have routinely recovered their costs (and characteristically made their profits) in their own much larger domestic markets (typically Britain, the USA, or Australia), locally oriented programs cannot begin to compete either on price or on production values. Average costs under the pre-SOE, two channel state monopoly system were estimated (in 1988) as just $NZ2000 per hour for overseas material compared with $NZ53 000 for local programming (Farnsworth 1992, p. 200). Post-deregulation (i.e. 1990), and thus immediately after the entry of a new channel, and with it the prospect of competitive bidding, screening costs for an imported overseas program were between $NZ5000 and $NZ10 000 per hour (for programs that may well have cost millions to make). By comparison, Spicer et al. (1996, p. 62) cite the average hourly cost of all locally produced programs as $NZ61 000. Local drama costing was between $NZ120 000 (for a fast **turnaround stripped** 'soap' like *Shortland Street*) and $NZ400–500 000 (for a typical one-episode-per-week drama series).

This basic dilemma is endemic to small nations, but it has been exacerbated by the policies of successive New Zealand governments (Farnsworth 1992). Thus in 1974 the license fee accounted for 42.5 per cent of the state monopoly broadcasters' revenue, and by 1985 it contributed just 16 per cent and was falling (Smith 1996, p. 17). The correlate was, of course, not just a continual expansion in the frequency and duration of commercial breaks. This was accompanied by a normalisation of the notion of advertisers as television's primary clients—a process with far-reaching implications for both program content and program scheduling.

As was noted earlier, New Zealand television has thus become a fully commercial system in all but name, with no restrictions on overseas ownership of television channels and within which the doggedly resourceful but beleaguered public service component has been rendered progressively more marginal over time. Following the entry of privately owned terrestrial broadcasting in 1989 there are now four free-to-air VHF channels (two SOEs, two overseas-owned) with nationwide or near-nationwide coverage. It is therefore symptomatic that in a recent ten-countries' study of small producers, New Zealand television, whose local content hovers around 25 per cent of total transmissions, had the lowest proportion of all (New Zealand On Air 1999). This is a figure that would be lower still were it not for the activities of New Zealand On Air. Locally produced programs often enjoy high ratings, but as a former CEO of the two state-owned channels once made graphically clear to the then Minister of Broadcasting, ratings and revenue do not coincide. Thus in the early 1990s state channel Television One (as it was then known) showed more than twice as much local programming as the second state channel and as a result it regularly won the ratings battle. But not only did Television One cost much, much more to run than the second channel, it also secured less advertising revenue (Smith 1996, p. 103).

Then, as now, it is sport (both in its own right and within the newscasts) and more recently house-and-garden consumer programming that loom large within this local content category, together with low-budget clones of overseas game shows and related formats. During prime time, more than fifteen minutes of every hour is now devoted either to commercials or to station identification. It is above all the commercials and sports programming which, between them, appear to most clearly and to most routinely contest the constraints under which local production is understood to operate. Global branding can and sometimes does mean that 'global' commercials are shown, and the increased integration of the Australian and New Zealand economies can and does mean that Australian commercials are shown. But the most popular commercials are those that have been expressly conceived and designed to catch the attention of local viewers. Hence the commercials on New Zealand television are not only altogether more likely to incorporate local content than the programs that 'interrupt' them, but the best of them are also technically and formally accomplished, incorporating higher production values than many of the locally made programs.

Throughout the 1980s and the 1990s there was an ever widening dependence upon advertising revenue and a continual expansion of television advertising, both as a percentage of screen time and as a proportion of the advertising industry's overall expenditure. Thus Smith (1996, p. 154) cites a total expenditure of $NZ1300 million in 1994, more than a third of it on television, and by the year 2000 television advertising was running at $500 million per annum. One of its effects was to offer funding and opportunities to local film-makers and independent production houses. These latter initially emerged as a response to the rise in advertising, but have subsequently become crucial to local program-making as well. This is because the television channels themselves have responded to commercial pressures by increasing their recourse to outsourcing and commissioning rather than in-house production. Indeed, an important precursor of the Virtual Spectator initiative with which this chapter began was the innovative work on simulation that was first undertaken for an Air New Zealand commercial.

A commercial form of broadcasting with a vernacular idiom had grown inside, but remained subordinate to the state structure of radio. Yet the associated popular nationalism should not be seen as indicative of state capture. Rather it represented an articulation of specific and sectional interests in both state and civil society—an articulation in that it both effected a link between them and spoke from, and for, the cultural position(s) thus constituted. Thus before television was introduced, a popular version of the national imaginary to which both sport and the production and consumption practices of households was integral, and in which commercialism was incipient, was already in place. What was effected through the development of the new medium was the reconstruction and elaboration of that imaginary on new terrain, via a discourse that served to prioritise the hitherto subordinated economy.

The cost structure of local production, combined with the reluctance of governments to provide funding, was such that New Zealand television was driven to at once identify and *confirm* the society's pre-existing centre of cultural gravity (so as to maximise audiences) and yet nevertheless driven to *remake* that centre in a commodified form (so as to secure revenue). If sport and domestic activities between them exemplified the former, then advertising exemplified the latter. Yet by the end of the 1990s the limits of, and limitations to, the elaboration of that project would become evident, dramatised by the migration of the newly globalised, professionalised, and commercialised sport of rugby union on to a satellite subscription channel, where it took up a place alongside earlier defectors such as cricket.

More generally, however, what has confounded both this particular permutation on commercial television strategy and its traditional public service 'other' is not just the departure of rugby but the demise of the centre. Irrespective of whether this latter is understood as simply an exposure of what was always a fiction, or as a reflection of a social order that has become altogether more fractured and more pluralistic, it is a tendency that is fateful for what Graham Murdoch (1997, p. 13) sees as an interest in 'reaching the largest possible number of potential customers at the lowest possible cost'. Put less caustically, this is what John Farnsworth (1998, p. 9) follows Collins and Murroni in identifying as the hotelling effect, in which 'economically rational competitors will crowd in the middle of the spectrum of consumer tastes rather than provide a diverse range of products'. It is precisely such *broad*casting, whether understood in this commercial sense, or in the sense of a paternalist version of public service, that has come to appear vulnerable.

Enter the third term

This interpretation of the New Zealand television system has been filtered through its relation to the more familiar forms of US commercial and UK public service broadcasting. What this incidentally provides and permits is evidential support for resisting any reduction of the unstable and avowedly idiosyncratic features of the New Zealand case to the status of the anecdotal. Herein lies the wider significance of this chapter's sub-textual invocation of the notion of a third term. It's a term that refuses the opposition between state monopoly and market uniformity, between political direction and commercial manipulation, between high culture and mass culture, between global and local, in favour of acknowledging the diversity of civil society, the facilitation of plurality, the complexity of the popular and the cosmopolitanism of the local. As such, it appears within the existing broadcast media as a trickle of resistance rather than a wave. But with the emergence of new media technologies, it is that place where the software of Virtual Spectator and the poetry of Allen Curnow might be made to meet.

Thus rather than seeing New Zealand television as explicable as a more or less exotic, quirky anomaly, a deviant footnote to what are otherwise secure and secured general models, the intention is to begin to bring into question the organisational bases and biases of the general models themselves. In part, this is because when viewed from such a location, there seems to be something peculiarly Euro- or USA-centric about the focus on globalisation as if it were a somehow novel or recent phenomenon. For bit players in the global script, what appears to be novel is not the notion of power flows, but rather their density, their plurality, and the prospect that they are no longer to be interpreted as axiomatically moving in, or from, one direction (cf. Perry 1998). But more generally, it is because when it comes to the implications of globalisation and the consequences of digitisation, then *all of us* are potential antipodeans.

References

Anderson, Benedict. 1991. *Imagined Communities*. Revised ed. London and New York: Verso.

Appadurai, Arjun. 1990. 'Disjuncture and Difference in the Global Cultural Economy' in Mike Featherstone (ed.), *Global Culture*. London: Sage, pp. 295–310.

Bernstein, Basil. 1973. 'A Public Language: Some Sociological Implications of a Linguistic Form', *Class, Codes and Control, Volume 1*. London: Paladin, pp. 62–77.

Bhabha, Homi (ed.). 1990. *Nation and Narration*. London and New York: Routledge.

Carter, Ian. 1993. *Gadfly: The Life and Times of James Shelley*. Auckland: Auckland University Press.

Curnow, Allen. 1962. *A Small Room with Large Windows: Selected Poems*. Oxford: Oxford University Press.

Day, Patrick. 1994. *The Radio Years*. Auckland: Auckland University Press.

Farnsworth, John. 1992. 'Mainstream or Minority: Ambiguities in State or Market Arrangements for New Zealand Television', in John Deeks & Nick Perry (eds), *Controlling Interests: Business, the State and Society in New Zealand*. Auckland: Auckland University Press, pp. 191–207.

Farnsworth, John. 1998. 'Putting a Context to New Zealand Broadcasting Debates', in John Farnsworth & Paul Norris (eds), *The Way Ahead: New Zealand Broadcasting in the Nineties*. Christchurch: Christchurch Polytechnic, pp. 7–18.

Foucault, Michel. 1979. *Discipline and Punish: The Birth of The Prison*. Harmondsworth: Penguin.

Fougere, Geoff. 1989. 'Sport, Culture and Identity: The Case of Rugby Football', in David Novitz & W.E. Willmott (eds), *Culture and Identity in New Zealand*. Wellington: Government Print, pp. 110–22.

McCarthy, Winston. 1973. *Listen…! It's a Goal*. London: Pelham Books.

Murdoch, Graham. 1997. 'Public Broadcasting in Privatised Times: Rethinking the New Zealand Experiment', in Paul Norris & John Farnsworth (eds), *Keeping it Ours:*

Issues of Television Broadcasting in New Zealand. Christchurch: Christchurch Polytechnic, pp. 9–33.

New Zealand On Air. 1999. *Local Content and Diversity: Television in Ten Countries.* Wellington.

Perry, Nick. 1998. *Hyperreality and Global Culture.* London: Routledge.

Perry, Nick. 2000. 'Is the Global Village a Company Town? Was Confucius A Jesuit Cyberpunk?', *Organization* Vol 7(1), pp. 185–200.

Perry, Nick. (c.2003) 'Close Encounters of Another Kind: Nationalism, Media Representations and Advertising in New Zealand Rugby', in Steve Jackson & Dave Andrews (eds), *Sport, Culture and Advertising: Identities, Commodities and the Politics of Representation.* Westport CT, USA: Greenwood Press.

Robertson, Roland. 1992. *Globalization: Social Theory and Global Culture.* London: Sage.

Smith, Paul. 1996. *Revolution in the Air!* Auckland: Longman.

Spicer, Barry, Michael Powell & David Emanuel. 1996. *The Remaking of Television New Zealand 1984–1992.* Auckland: Auckland University Press.

Notes

1   The classic account of the wider significance of the panopticon (a prison design) for the development of techniques of surveillance is by Foucault (1979).

2   Compare this with Curnow's 'The Eye is More or Less Satisfied with Seeing' (1962, p. 62), which begins:

Wholehearted he can't move
From where he is, nor love
Wholehearted that place,
Indigene janus-face,

Half mocking half,
Neither caring to laugh.

Does true or false sun rise?
Do both half eyes tell lies?…

Snap open! He's all eyes, wary,
Darting both ways one query….

3   On the concept of a national imaginary see the collection edited by Homi Bhabha (1990).

4   This discussion of the relevance of radio draws upon Perry (forthcoming, c. 2003).

5

Representing the Country:

Adidas Aotearoa

STEPHEN TURNER

Television seeks to deliver through the product that is programming an audience to advertisers, that is, to deliver consumers to the capital interests that ultimately fund the medium. In New Zealand this function of media economy has a peculiarly self-seeking aspect. This is because a seminal and still primary function of television in Aotearoa New Zealand is to give us our country (constructing the public as nation). Don't ask who 'us' is just yet. Public television policy as much as privately funded advertising subscribes to this agenda (the investment in the nation-place is equally at work, I would argue, in initiatives to increase local content and/or reduce advertising). The idea that television at the superstructural level is in some sense an advertisement, and that its 'product' might be an identity or means of self-recognition, therefore calls for an approach to the medium that is sensitive to its situation, or *setting*. The great urge to provide local content—odd, you might think, in a place where so much has come from somewhere else—makes such an approach prerequisite to media study in the New Zealand context.

The will to self-representation characteristic of television programming in this place is self-colonising, a conjoining of past and present, peoples and place, the nation and international circuits of investment and opportunity. This is to say that producing the local, 'something' called New Zealand, is the not-to-be-questioned agenda of local production. Yet the idea of the nation constrains what we take the public or culture of local television to be, even more so, I would argue, in the post-1980s era of deregulated broadcasting.

That the bundle of interests supporting and supported by this agenda is not merely local (and never has been) may be seen in the use of the New Zealand rugby team by Adidas—or of Adidas by the All Blacks—an arrangement, quite apart from concerns I raise below, which makes for exceptional television advertisements. The location of the widely seen 'haka' advertisement for Adidas, produced by Saatchi and Saatchi New Zealand, is a large part of its appeal. For the greater world watching, the 'location' may be little more than a constitutive association of Māori, rugby, and landscape. Foreign viewers are not simply wrong. Feeding off a mediatised history of just such imagery, television and sport have become integral to the self-projection of this white settler society—a collective that now significantly depends on the technology of mass media and the massing of peoples through sporting interest to identify and unite them. Whether or not you like sport, the imagery is pervasive, shared, and to that extent constitutive of a new common culture. The monopoly of consciousness that results from the interpenetration of television and sport makes it all the easier to equate public, culture, and nation, an untenable reduction given the history and peoples of the place (Māori for instance, so prominent in the haka advert, do not necessarily a nation make, neither for themselves nor for non-Māori).

Yet the more people watch, the more true the image would appear, because this advertisement is not just an image of our making but an image that makes us, or makes us over (the nation and its associated identity, again not true for Māori, long dependent on successful export). Televised sport amounts to a collective performance of a sort (watching) and gains advertisers more profit than most other programming by getting the greatest number of people available in a small place to sit in front of the screen and watch. Television, sport, and advertising, considered together, thus delineate a distinctive economy of representation, an engine of capital interests, which facilitates settler colonialism in its current phase by making New Zealandness itself an object of product placement and site of investment. To grasp the precise nature of this 'location', or equation (of public, culture, and nation), just how the place called New Zealand functions as a representation, requires some preliminary distinctions among different senses of the term 'representation'.[1]

1

'Representation' may be understood: (1) as simple re-presentation, the image of an object in the world, animate or inanimate, re-presented; (2) as 'representative', an image standing in for or on behalf of someone, some group or some thing; and (3) as 'representative-ness' or 'representativity', more than representing someone or something (as a lawyer or politician might do on your behalf) but representing someone, some group or some thing in and of yourself, being an actual instance of what you represent, for example being a sports 'representative'.

The idea of representation as the image of a real-world object has been undermined by the post-Saussurean critique of representation, in particular the attention to representations as elements of a signifying or sign system.[2] But sport is not simply the object of representation, or re-presentation via television in the case of the Adidas advert, therefore subject to a critique of representation; for someone or something is represented in the very activity of sport, instantiated or performed by the action—the attribute of representativeness or representativity. The signification of sport is registered, understood, meaningful, just because the action or doing is shared. Hence the otherwise peculiar value of 'live' transmission. Watching and playing sport are equally part of the non-representational reality, and social value, of *shared doing*. If sport in this participant sense has no representational content— what it signifies lies in the enactment or performance of it—the urge sport satisfies (to run, jump, play) may yet be representative, something shared, commonly practised. That is, the urge is made social, becomes constitutive of a socius, a mode of being together.

Sport, and I will say advertising itself, is better grasped in non-representational, non-cognitive terms—in terms of feelings, or instincts, which are precisely not made transparent, legible, in the act of it, which have a bodily rather than cognitive coding, which work to make the activity inarticulate outside its doing, or the action of its watching (an obscurity, physicality, inarticulacy that marks settler culture). Think of sport not as social text but as culture-in-action, sociality enacted in the New Zealand context, the physical form or embodiment of the psychology of settlement.

I am not so much interested in representation in the second, political sense of the word (representing someone or something in the sense of standing in for or on behalf of them). And this because the idea of the public, which television might be said to represent (or should), is not the same as or may not be understood as such by people who watch. That is, viewers may not take themselves to be the 'public' of public television. In the post-civil society of television, demographic appeal displaces older ideas of representative democracy. On one view, the democracy of television means choosing what you want to watch, which may not be a public television channel (democracy, for better or worse, has gone digital). So the application of this second sense of representation to television misapprehends the nature of the medium, making television a matter of politics—does it represent us (stand in for or on behalf of us)—and if it does not, it makes it a matter of enforcing content, rather than attending to the structure of the medium itself.[3] New Zealand culture, understood in the parochial sense of public—simply as us New Zealanders—is antithetical to a critical public culture, 'public' in the proper sense of the word, where who 'we' are (or where we are) would not simply be presupposed but an object of debate, a question for television rather than an assumption of programming.

I am most interested in representation in the third sense, that of 'representing your country'. In this sense an advertisement is not strictly or simply a social text—an instance of a language or system of signs—nor does it involve standing in for or on behalf of someone or something: representation in the sense of holding political office with connotations of representative democracy. In my third sense you are not simply standing in for or on behalf of New Zealanders or New Zealand but instantiating in and of yourself New Zealandness—a performative quality, or quality of performativity, that I attribute to the sports representative.

Sport, not coincidentally, is the best example of representation in my preferred sense. Sport, locally, has arguably played the most significant role—more than the media, the arts, or war—in establishing the identity of the greater mass of people in New Zealand,[4] shaping the nation-mass or nation-as-mass. The attraction of sport for television, its latent capacity to *amass* audience, not only makes advertising revenue for sport events such as the Olympics, the World Cup (of soccer), and the American Super Bowl the highest in the world, but for that reason is pushing televisual representation towards representativeness or representativity. In the advertising world this leads to 'bonding' rather then branding; bonding describes the distinctive personality or identity of the consumer—the product, like a team badge, articulates a bond—whereas branding describes the distinctive personality or identity of the product.[5]

Televisual representation, ever responsive to advertising revenue, may be understood, historically, as moving through stages: from the realism of a program/product as the image of an actual world with real properties (television as a 'window on the world'); to the program/product as aspirational, an index of a world, or lifestyle, with potential properties; to the program/product as a bond, site of identification or communion without pre-existing reality (the reality of Big Brother or Adidas Aotearoa).

A web site created by the CEO of Saatchi and Saatchi worldwide, advertising guru and erstwhile New Zealander Kevin Roberts, proclaims that simple branding is an outdated way of thinking about advertising.[6] For Roberts a good advert produces a 'trustmark,' or better, a 'lovemark'; the product is a sign of trust or love. Roberts's sincere bond with New Zealand was presumably the basis for a vision of the country that almost won his company the New Zealand tourist board campaign (now '100% Pure').[7] More importantly, the bond Roberts articulates in terms of 'trust' or 'love' is a feeling, a purely affective communion. Quite apart from Roberts's personal advocacy of all things New Zealand I suggest that this communion, collective identification, or (in this new country) will-to-identity, determines the historical trajectory of New Zealand television, ensures the profitability and expansion of the medium, and makes it, today, the pre-eminent tool for the advancement of the nation-mass. The will-to-identity is highlighted by the investment of the medium in sport, apart from its reliance on advertising, to gather audiences in front of the screen, and to consolidate the watching mass of people as a nation. In this place it is not advertising, simply, that underpins the medium: it is, more precisely, self-advertising. Our knowledge of television programming therefore demands that we understand just how advertising works.

2

The representations of advertising are matters of feeling not form, instinct not knowledge, affect not reality—the mood, if you like, of setting (not merely the abstract location of the image, but the actual location of the screen, actual viewers in front of it). This may seem a little grand, but advertising is now arguably the most powerful, certainly the most incessant, conduit of social values (here as much as anywhere). Advertisements are necessarily dense, packed with information about culture and history, an impacted site, in a more pathological sense, of important cultural instincts, anxieties, and desires.

The meaning of an award-winning advert that turns on the word 'bugger', uttered by a string of local characters, including the farm-sheepdog, in response to accidents caused by the surprising power of the new Toyota Hilux, depends on settler history, or more specifically, the good keen man, his travails, endurance, honesty, humour, homeliness. This mythical man-at-home has long been played in local advertising for Toyota by the writer, bushman, and celebrated New Zealander Barry Crump. The 'bugger' ad resurrects a persona blasted by a recent biography in which Crump was alleged to be a wife-beater, depressive, and drunkard (see Colin Hogg 2000). The myth can hardly be believed, yet the charm or affect of the personification floats free, enabling a positive forgetting of a more bitter history of men, women, and land. But such history is not simply representable. The relation of this advert to other adverts (notably Mainland Cheese, Vogels Bread, and Speights beer with another proto-Crump character) is crucial to its success, its resonance. For the social commentary or import of advertising lies in this re-articulation of a fully mediatised history—the history of a place as fully produced, and processed, as its milk. A history that is as subject as anything to the representations of settler economy is necessarily hidden, internal, and affective, never the simple object of an image.

The most successful adverts superimpose or supplant existing popular memory with a memory of adverts, so that the world of advertising itself becomes the stuff of folk memory, a common language ('bugger'), and cultural literacy that defines what is actually common. The inability to remember what the ad was about, that anything was even being advertised, is a kind of forgetting that advertisers calculate. So sayings as common as those of Shakespeare were once advertising campaigns ('diamonds are forever'). More locally, the memory-making capacity of the best advertising depends on a cultural pre-history or preconscious that is also an image-bank. Bigger-budget adverts raid this bank to incorporate the largest audience within the ambit of the product pitch. What makes cultural memory is now the technical capacity to lodge an image in the minds of a great many people; what instigates collective identification is the viewer's knowledge that the image is just so lodged in the consciousness of others. That image is what we share. And that sharing structures a collective, or collective psyche: 'us'.

The allure or appeal of bigger-budget advertising works by enlarging, massifying, an audience, which is not the same as pitching the product to the biggest audience. After all not everyone plays rugby, enjoys yachting and/or drinks beer, prime ingredients of bigger-budget advertising (rugby in particular turns up in advertising for unrelated products from Weet-Bix cereal to Mastercard). Such ads make a claim about the nature or essence or existence of this bigger audience (as people, public, culture, nation, even humanity)[8] as part of the advertiser's appeal to a more local or specific demographic (say, rugby players, sailors, and/or beer drinkers)—a claim to collective identification, to representativity or representativeness. The claim is ideally one that non-target viewers will not find contentious, or at the very least not publicly criticise.

Television programming more generally sustains itself in a small country by appealing to the widest available audience on behalf of advertisers (tending thereby to convert the 'public' of television into the people of the nation). So the country as a large mass of people—the nation-mass or mass-as-nation—whatever its actuality, diversity, consistency, constitutionality, becomes a structural necessity, undergirding the economics of the medium (making quite literal the idea that the settler nation is programmed). The settler nation is in the first instance a concept of *mass*: to succeed as a nation the original idea, and imperative, is that the place must first be filled with settlers. This is the deep psychological or social content of the structure of media (the hard-wiring of transmission, satellite link, underground cables, and so on), ultimately constitutive of an economy of representation.

No doubt people want to see themselves, but for non-Māori that means seeing themselves at home—a place and identity all their own. Who they/ we are has always depended on identifying New Zealanders and New Zealand, precisely because this has not been given, established, obvious. This is why local image-making is overdetermined, charged by a colonial history, and somewhat obsessively predisposed to self-representation. The will-to-identity is an instinct that local advertising knows it can profit most by satisfying.

Historically speaking, representations of New Zealand had one and the same function as advertising (which is to say that from the point of view of the mass media 'New Zealand' was originally an advertisement—a gazette notice, poster, or leaflet). In the first instance any representation of the place was bound up with the desire to get more people to go there, a desire, in the second instance, which ideally became the desire of these same people to stay. The financial investment on the part of, say, the New Zealand Company is also an existential one on the part of its settlers. While this merely describes an emergent economy of settler colonialism it follows that representations of the place and its peoples become self-representations, the media a conduit of investment, desire, and hope. This is not just an 'interest' in the place, such as the financial investment of stockholders, but for settlers a great need to be at home in it (to recover the existential investment), for any representation to also be a self-representation—a logic of representation that does not necessarily follow in other, older countries. The settler economy is underpinned by this psychology; so the best and brightest local advertising plays the identity-card, passport to place, hearth, and home.

If this instinct is consistent the images in which it is manifested are variable, mobile, all the while making the history they would appear merely to reflect (advertisers assume yet will disclaim agency for cultural change).[9] Big-budget, high-production advertising is redolent with imagery of New Zealand from the last century, typically of Māori and spacious if not empty landscape (despite the presence of Māori there appears a whole lot more room). Advertisement series for Air New Zealand, the Bank of New Zealand, as well as Toyota—only the first is a primarily New Zealand-owned company—parlay the same stock imagery: ocean and beach, inland river and bush, Māori and lush, green land, mingled with images of farmers or rural people and suburban families (moving, say, from Toyota landrover to coupe). This landscaping, ever the work of settlers,[10] is significantly making what we see. Arguing with the content, or reality, of such imagery will simply find advertising wanting rather than explaining why it is successful, presumably gratifying to many viewers. Such an advertisement is not exactly a misrepresentation, because it doesn't work as a representation in terms of content or reality. For the real world to which such advertising does or does not correspond, historically, has been made, and made-over, by just such representations.

The timelessness of these adverts—New Zealand was ever thus—is only mitigated by the fact that advertising imagery significantly changes in the expression of this very quality (timelessness). A more recent Toyota advert is filled with obviously diverse people, both country and city, rich and poor, white, brown, Māori, Chinese. While timelessness itself is an ephemeral attribute of advertising imagery, what remains constant is the will-to-place: an old Chinese-looking man in the final shot declares, seemingly unprompted: 'Every day I think this is a great place' (presumably it helps Toyota sell more products for him to allay any doubts about it). BNZ's more deliberate attempt in a notable series by Len Potts to show 'real' New Zealanders now seems painfully chauvinistic, its reflections on 'growing up' here seemingly exclusive of the experience of other New Zealanders, other New Zealands. Potts has explained the turn to New Zealandness in the late 1980s as if his place-making was new, almost a personal discovery.[11] All that is new is the increased value of marketing for capital enterprise since the late 1980s, with the consequent merger of cultural values and production values. That is, the primary expression of cultural values for New Zealanders (too) has been captured by advertising, and the capital available to its image-makers.

3

The Adidas 'haka' advertisement featuring the All Blacks more happily unites corporate capital and settler society (from its origins a corporate-like body). Prominent on global television before the 1999 Rugby World Cup, it features the famed All Black haka, what would be the primal moment of New Zealand-ness, led by Captain Taine Randall and a supporting cast of All Black stars, spotlighting the most well-known, such as Jonah Lomu (used in a further Adidas series featuring world or European-renowned sports stars). The Adidas advert is physical and pulsating, an eye-fest of slapping, moving, and colliding body-parts. The action is unified by the haka, interspersed with fast game action using the shaky or running camera of reality television and recent sports coverage, and with traditional Māori warriors in full-face **moko**. In no time at all the All Blacks leap to a mid-air, slow-mo climax. With a slow turn and hulking walk back to their half of the field, the All Blacks glare over their shoulders at the surely shrinking opposition. Adidas is 'Forever Sport'.

The advertisement captures and magnifies the theatre of the event, making it over or making of it something more with the technical aid of the medium. For a global audience the advertisement is stunning, powerful, picturesque.[12] For a local audience the advert does more than place the All Blacks and New Zealand, full frontal, on the stage of world television, as the country becomes something bigger, more substantial, in the world's reflected gaze. The bowdlerised haka—the entirely un-Māori leap at the end a settler addition for effect—has never held such a stage. The advertisement happily unites past and present, peoples and place, sport and television, and national and multinational interests.

The sentiment of the advert—pride, power, **mana**—is 'real' enough, true to history, place, and people if only because you know others know the advert; the feeling is common, definitive of community, just because it is shared (in the ideal world of advertisers the culture of advertising would thus become culture as such). The sentiment is reducible to a set of expectations, a mediatised history made up of self-advertising of just this kind (i.e. a history of adverts using the All Blacks). A place made in the image of its own promotion is an abstract location—the settler society a simulacrum— not opposed to a real or actual place but opposed by the critical eye of non-target viewers,[13] others who are not excluded yet who exceed the image of the nation-mass. These are viewers, also watching, also included by the claim to representativity or representativeness, who may be New Zealanders but whose experience, disposition, agenda, remain internal to the image, invisible and unspoken (not just Māori).

This internal and affective history (of pain, loss, disrespect, dispossession) may be at odds with the advert but is not at all irrelevant to it. The Adidas ad is notably more Māorified than earlier Steinlager ads using the All Blacks, indicating an increased responsiveness to things Māori, a bedding down of official biculturalism, yet the reconstruction of settler virtues continues unabated. Where Nick Perry reads an earlier Steinlager ad as strikingly camp—the inadvertent effect of trying to make All Blacks attractive to women (Perry 1994, pp. 93–4)—the Māorification of the Adidas ad suggests both a new awareness of other New Zealanders, and ongoing, atavistic, macho-fication (these old-time Māori can't be mistaken as queer). Our patriotism, the resolution and endeavour of our far-flung settlement, is newly stiffened. Other sport-related ads do not simply identify 'us', but more aggressively call us to action, if not to do the haka then to link arms round the island in defence of the hard-won America's Cup (since lost). The jingle for this ad is 'Call me loyal' from Dave Dobbyn's classic song 'Loyal'. In the eyes of this image, New Zealanders who have no interest in the yacht race are lesser New Zealanders.

Entering into the action of sport in settler society is the urge of a true patriot—a physical tribute to the media manufacture of mass, the pumping up of the collective. The settler will-to-identity is all for sport. In a sports-made, sports-mad country, Adidas-like ads enable a partisan amnesia.

More, the Adidas contract, and the sense of identity it helps to promote, is a matter of national security. The All Blacks of Adidas signal the self-recognition of the nation-mass through new multinational funding (for a nation and identity this good, who wouldn't buy the shirt?). Multinationals profit by utilising a known or imagined identity—the identification of rugby with New Zealand—to sell product. Nike has done the same job on soccer and Brazil that Adidas does on the All Blacks. The advertisement trades on the romance of people's passion and history. In the process of this make-over, or merger, of national and multinational interests, the 'identity' of the advertisement's constituency is further secured or tethered to the historically received notion. The audience, say, New Zealanders, is made captive to their own 'best' image: so Adidas is Us (and the wearer of a black Adidas shirt makes a supporter of New Zealand and/or a New Zealander). The manu-facture of nation and identity by big business—the government might be considered in historical terms as New Zealand's biggest business—is not new, but the global power of sporting conglomerates, and the correspond-ingly enhanced effect of their image-making, is new. The nation is not so much a place as a bond, a trustmark, or better, lovemark.

In making the interests of Adidas congruent with the interests of New Zealand there is financial gain and existential loss. If you are interested as a shareholder of the incorporated nation in tabulating historical accounts, what I would call the colonial ledger, identity is a matter of double-entry bookkeeping: the multinational and national interests at stake in advertise-ments write off historical cost as present gain. You get a stronger, more defined identity, at least a more intense experience of self-recognition, at some cost to the advertisement's constituency: being further bound to local history and attendant pathologies (intrinsic contradictions of settler society).[14]

The problem I raise here is patently not sport, or advertising, when con-sidered discrete objects of study, but the pervasiveness of the psychology of the Adidas advert in local television programming more generally. 'New Zealanders' habitually produce themselves precisely by not reflecting on the country's production; what I would call the necessary obliviousness of settler colonial culture to its own instincts. I am not about to wheel in 'history' as the answer—implying a 'false consciousness' of the conditions of production of such imagery—because the kind of colonial or colonising history at issue is not strictly available as positive knowledge, but one that has evolved in and through the process of representation itself (constructing a history in and of the habit of forgetting). This ongoing process makes the representation of place and peoples to an ever greater degree a matter of self-representation, or better, a performance of Team New Zealand—representation understood as representativeness or representativity.

My approach to the problem of the hidden or internal history of the image, the buried history of purposeful forgetting or selective remembering, is to focus on the economics of representation—the demand for a certain reality and its supply by mass media—enabling a settler society to construct an audience for television in the image of its own desires, its own mass, making for a neatly home-spun monopoly (and marking the current phase of settler colonialism). This is not merely the psychological content of local advertising imagery. The larger function of advertising makes the nation-mass the structural condition of New Zealand television. It is the conflicted history of the nation-mass—the needs, demands, anxieties of the majority of the settlers who inhabit it—to which the mass media most deeply respond, a history bound up with the more specific history of television as technology.

The history of settlement suggests a counter-need, if we seek self-knowledge and not merely self-representation, for studying television in its setting—not simply the history of the medium, nor the form, content, or production of the image, but rather the historical (read actual) location of the screen, before which sit actual viewers, drawn to images of themselves. Media studies in the New Zealand context needs to attend to more than matters of industry and technology, that is, more than matters of media, if it is to properly grasp the 'mass' of the mass media. Here I draw attention to a local logic and structure of massification that has as much to do with psychology and history as it does with capital and hard-wiring.

References

Barthes, Roland. 1993. *Mythologies*. London: Vintage.

Baudrillard, Jean. 1994. *Simulacra and Simulation*. Ann Arbor: University of Michigan Press.

Belich, James. 2001. *Paradise Reforged: A History of the New Zealanders from the 1880s to the Year 2000*. Auckland: Allen Lane/Penguin Press.

Davidson, Martin. 1992. *The Consumerist Manifesto: Advertising in Postmodern Times*. London: Routledge.

Hogg, Colin. 2000. *A Life in Loose Strides: The Story of Barry Crump*. Auckland: Hodder Moa Beckett.

Miller, Toby, et al. 2001. *Globalisation and Sport: Playing the World*. London: Sage.

Perry, Nick. 1994. *The Dominion of Signs: Television, Advertising and other New Zealand Fictions*. Auckland: Auckland University Press.

Phillips, Jock. 1987. *A Man's Country: the Image of the Pakeha Male, a History*. Auckland: Penguin.

Pound, Francis. 1983. *Frames on the Land: Early Landscape Painting in New Zealand*. Auckland: Collins.

Notes

1 The attention I pay in the following section to the look and, in particular, the feel of the image distinguishes my approach to the political economy of sport from the

authoritative work of Toby Miller (e.g. Miller et al. 2001). Miller's own interest in the New Zealand All Black rugby team (pp. 26–8) is read as an instance of processes of globalisation, governmentalisation, Americanisation, televisualisation, and commodification, but despite or perhaps due to this totalising rubric (which is designated GGATaC) the book does not address the logic and structure of affective affiliation, or in a local case, the work of representation in promulgating a settler society and promoting its economy, no less an aspect of globalising capital. To even conceive of resistance (p. 5) to the large-scale capital entreprise described in the book, I would argue that we need to understand the psychology and history of affect at the point of local purchase.

2   Roland Barthes's reinvigoration of Saussure's project of **semiology** (a science of signs) has been particularly influential for the study of popular culture (e.g. Barthes 1993).

3   So the ideological drive towards a social charter for New Zealand television, whose agenda appears the production of 'New Zealand', ought to be distinguished from support for local producers and the film-and-television industry. While the need to feed and grow local industry is an obvious good, what remains questionable is state ownership of a commercial channel rather than sponsorship of a fully public service; the former arrangement persists, I suggest, just because television has proved such an effective vehicle for the official self-fashioning of a settler society and young new country.

4   I think the argument is implicit, whether he would agree or not, in James Belich's chapter on sport in his history of New Zealand. See 'Games People Play' in *Paradise Reforged* (Belich 2001, pp. 368–88). In this regard see also Jock Phillips's study of masculinity (1987), in particular 'The Hard Man—Rugby and the Formation of Character' (pp. 81–130).

5   For a useful discussion, amid an extensive literature, of the development of branding, see Martin Davidson (1992), in particular chapter 1, 'Objects of Desire'.

6   'Lovemarks are brands that have evolved from a place in the market to the heart of a culture. With the power of love they create life-long emotional connections.' For more of the same, see www. lovemarks.com—'a Saatchi and Saatchi idea'.

7   A vision that is elaborated through stories, images, and talk of New Zealand and New Zealanders, including Roberts's speeches, is at www. nzedge.com. The thoroughly dehistoricised and de-politicised nature of this web site is suggested by the resemblance between its 'original' concept (the Edge) and the bestselling 'personal power' philosophy of Anthony Robbins, which is sold on the slogan 'get the edge—to transform your life'. Thus Roberts's vision would appear a national version of a highly successful self-help guide.

8   A prime example: the Coca Cola campaign of the early 1970s featuring the hit song 'I'd like to teach the world to sing'.

9   A current advert for the New Zealand Post Office with a beautifully interwoven sequence of images charting the development-through-settlement of the country, as if the place called New Zealand may historically be taken for granted, and has been inevitable, uncontested, and benign, plainly illustrates the point. History in such imagery appears without seams.

10 See Francis Pound's seminal work *Frames on the Land* (1983).

11 See the television documentary *You're Soaking in It*, dir. Bryan Bruce, 1994.

12 This advertisement won awards for Saatchi and Saatchi in several categories at the prestigious Cannes Lions International Advertising Festival (2001).

13 In Jean Baudrillard's coinage, a copy without an original (Baudrillard 1994).

14 A shortlist of 'pathologies' of settlement would include an unresolved Treaty claims process and incoherent constitution, an intransigent monolingualism despite official biculturalism, conflicting claims to rights of more recent immigrants and earlier settlers (how biculturalism even makes sense of de facto multiculturalism), and the settler legacy of severe gender separatism, not unrelated to the prevalence of alcohol abuse, domestic violence, and male suicide.

PART 2

**Between the
Mainstream and
the Margins**

Introduction

Mainstream ('the principal current of a river') is a complex concept, but it offers a way of drawing attention to important conflicts and tensions within any system. What is central, what is marginal, what is completely excluded—and why? There are many television experiences that raise questions of this kind, both for viewers and for program-makers.

One way to apply the concept is to consider the material in 'prime' (or 'peak') time on the major channels as the 'mainstream', in contrast to what is scheduled 'off-peak', or rejected altogether. Each channel regards its airtime as a precious commodity. But 'mainstream' can also be understood more broadly as referring to whichever aspects of television receive the most funding, public attention, or airtime. What is the relevance of this favoured material to New Zealand society at large, to the Treaty of Waitangi, or to the various cultures and subcultures within our community?

Tainui Stephens gives a history (or **whakapapa**) of Māori television. He sees the potential for exciting, unique forms of television culture, but the system has permitted only a small part of this potential to be realised. (Stephens has himself produced such important examples as *Mai Time* and *When Haka Became Boogie*.) Television's reluctance to experiment with such material, particularly in prime time, has meant a loss not only for Māori but for all local viewers. The chapter ends with a reminder (in the Māori language) of our common involvement in the breath of life and the world of light—this is a call to work together in developing some crucial aspects of local television.

Sue Abel makes a thought-provoking contribution to the study of reception. Her ongoing research on the way teenagers relate to advertising looks in this chapter at responses to a television advertisement about a Chinese 'laundry woman'. Abel's sample includes fifteen focus groups of teenagers in New Zealand, and (for comparison) two Chinese groups in Singapore. She investigates the workings of stereotypes, including stereotypes claimed to be 'positive', and demonstrates how individual interpretations are diverse yet still influenced by ethic background. Her research also offers some surprising insights into the effects of 'self-reflexive advertising', the strategic use of 'hip' irony that is currently fashionable.

Shuchi Kothari, Sarina Pearson, and Nabeel Zuberi's chapter draws on their own experiences as Asian New Zealanders, as well as their extensive research into local immigrant or diasporic communities, in analysing the successes and failures of television in coming to terms with social and cultural diversity. This is a thoughtful account of local television as 'a field of competing ideas about race and ethnicity'. In particular, the authors focus on tensions between nationalism and multiculturalism in New Zealand, and explore the difficulties faced by a television series that has the virtually impossible task of representing a wide range of Asian or Pacific Island communities on the margins of the television schedule within a single program.

Geoff Lealand is an academic who has worked as a consultant on children's series. A compelling advocate for more and better children's programming, he is deeply troubled by the ways in which this genre is marginalised in the commercial atmosphere of television today, creating an insecure environment for specialised production teams. His chapter gives us a vivid sense of the complexity of the genre in its need to cater for a range of ages and to respond to rapid shifts in children's taste without losing the support of parents and educators. Like previous contributors, Lealand raises important questions for the new TVNZ Charter.

Margaret Henley's chapter looks at how the mainstream/minority dynamic operates in sport, particularly in television's limited coverage of women's sport. The situation can change dramatically, as shown by Henley's case study of netball, which was able to grasp the opportunities that opened up when major rugby union, rugby league, and cricket events moved to pay television. She follows the action closely and provides many insights into the commercialisation of both sport and television. Her account of the surge in netball's ratings and its changing relationship with broadcasters and sponsors illustrate the rich subject matter that is available to an alert media researcher.

Roger Horrocks's chapter on programming looks at a strategic activity that is a key aspect of television today yet an aspect that remains little understood. Changes of approach in programming serve as a touchstone to how the New Zealand television system has been restructured and redefined over the years. The first half of the chapter looks at programming in terms of broadcasting skills, in an environment increasingly ruled by ratings; the second half looks at broader political implications by using 'the New Zealand experiment' in television to test Antonio Gramsci's theory of 'hegemony' (another way to define and analyse the mainstream).

6

Māori Television

TAINUI STEPHENS

Tuhia te hā o te reo ki te rangi
E kaha ai te mapu o te manawa ora
E rekareka ai te taringa whakarongo
E waiwai ai te karu mātakitaki

Let the language be heard on the airwaves,
Thereby causing the heart to leap with joy,
The ear to appreciate its eloquence,
And the eyes to moisten at its impact.

Te Māngai Pāho mission statement

For myself, and for many of my colleagues who work in Māori Television, Māori choose to see ourselves as the inheritors of a magnificent story-telling tradition. In effect we are the newest branch of a very old family tree. Before the arrival of the Pākehā, and for a good time after, **iwi Māori** received the news of their world and the stories of the times from orators. These **kaikōrero** were highly talented and rigorously trained in the arts of communication. Of course, in those days the means of communication were far simpler than they are today. Without the written word or the benefit of technology, the best way to communicate was to be found in discussion or **kōrero**. As a result, speech-making developed into a highly skilled art form. These tribal orators were veritable storehouses of knowledge and informa-tion. They interpreted the world they knew and observed, for the benefit of their people.

Today, we who work in broadcasting attempt to do the very same thing. Whether we work in news, drama, or in any other of the many areas of television production, we are fashioning stories that we hope will inform and entertain. In the modern Māori world, television may have usurped much of the role originally undertaken by the trained orator. Nonetheless, the need for someone to inform us about the near and distant world we live in remains as necessary as it ever was. More so, in fact. Māori need to have our own media voice so that we can speak to one another. At the moment, and for far too many years past, the ability to speak to ourselves through the medium of television has been controlled by Pākehā. This is not to deprecate Pākehā, it is a simple fact. If the television channels are dominated and controlled by Pākehā, the Māori voice can only be heard if those same Pākehā allow it. It has been like this for a long time.

When I started working for Television New Zealand on April Fool's Day 1984, I was a reporter for the weekly magazine program *Koha*. There was no Māori Programmes Department back then. Our bosses were Pākehā, and they believed that Māori programs should provide a 'window' onto the Māori world. Looking back, I take this to mean that our programs were wanted in order to display and explain ourselves to people who were not Māori. Certainly the earliest Māori programs tended only to be presentations of Māori in performance. During the 1960s, entertainers and the occasional culture group were all that was seen on screen.

There was nothing of real substance until *Tangata Whenua*, the ultimate 'window on the Māori world', was screened. This remarkable series of documentaries captured a Māori way of life that was rapidly disappearing. It also revealed a coming revitalisation of iwi. The 1970s were indeed to become years of political agitation and cultural awakening. I was a teenager in that decade and was profoundly influenced by the *Tangata Whenua* series. I was also caught up in a burgeoning political movement that would eventually lead to the recognition of te reo Māori as an official language of this country.

We are a people who are aware of the power of language. We nearly lost our own tongue and we are determined to reclaim it. Words are vehicles of thought, and stories are vehicles of meaning. It was my own love of language and stories that led me to consider finding a career that would enable me to be with them, every day. By the time I started working in television, *Koha* and the news bulletin *Te Karere* were the only Māori programs being broadcast—a total of just under one hour of Māori programs every week.

We now have many more television channels to choose from. However the amount of Māori television has grown to only about fifteen hours per week (including repeats!). That is a disgracefully small amount of media time for the television needs of a people who are ostensibly equal partners in Aotearoa Te Wai Pounamu. But even those few hours contain a degree of television expertise and philosophy that is dramatic and exciting. Television programs have their own whakapapa—just like the people who make them. *Waka Huia* is virtually a **kaumātua** of Māori programs and has been in constant production since 1987. It is produced entirely in te reo. The series began as a result of the impressive successes of the *Te Māori* exhibition. In the early 1980s our **kuia**, **koroua**, and **kapa haka** had travelled the world alongside the artistic masterpieces of our **tūpuna**. The international community was stunned by the power of *Te Māori*. Television producers Whai Ngata and Ernie Leonard reflected on the disastrous consequences that would result if a plane-load of kaumātua travelling back from exhibitions in the United States happened to drop out of the sky. They were mindful too that the iwi knowledge of our tūpuna was a diminishing resource. Whai then devised *Waka Huia* as a television means to preserve the reo and mātauranga Māori of our tribal elders. In the beginning it was not easy. Kaumātua were suspicious of the presence of cameras. However, through persistence and the fulsome support of Sir James Hēnare, iwi reluctance was overcome. Since its first transmission in 1987, *Waka Huia* has—in about 500 hour-long episodes—captured for all time the faces and voices of many kaumātua who are no longer with us. In the process we have created a vital and important audiovisual archive of iwi and hapū life and history.

The other kaumātua on the television program **paepae** include *Te Karere* and *Marae*. *Te Karere* started life as a daily four-minute broadcast in 1983. It is now a twenty-minute news bulletin screening at 4.40 pm with a repeat the following morning at 6.10. The production of *Te Karere* has weathered many tribulations. The fight for resources has been constant, and the time it is transmitted satisfies very few people. *Marae* is a reincarnation of the previously popular *Koha*. It commenced transmission in 1990 on Sunday mornings. It too is a magazine program and is expected to cover all the social, cultural, sporting, and political interests of Māori of every age and persuasion—clearly a big ask for a single hour of television every week.

For more than a decade the regular Māori programs have only been seen on TVNZ on Sunday mornings. Recent years have also seen the negative impact of specific funding policy decisions. Since 1995 the government funding agency Te Māngai Pāho has taken on the task of supporting programs that are produced in the Māori language. At times their policy was to fund programs that are 100 per cent te reo Māori, and while this may have pleased the language purists, it denied monolingual Māori (and Pākehā) the chance to understand and appreciate what little Māori television was available to them. While this did not affect the kaupapa of *Waka Huia*, the traditional audience for *Marae* that had grown used to a bilingual presentation shrunk immediately. Questions inevitably arose as to whether television has the capacity to teach language, or can it only inspire folk to want to learn te reo?

Until that time, the Sunday morning programming had moved successfully from being a window on the Māori world, to becoming a mirror—a means by which we Māori could reflect ourselves back to ourselves. When 100 per cent reo Māori television became de rigueur, not every Māori could see themselves in that mirror. Non-speakers of the language (at that point, about 75 per cent of Māori and 99 per cent of Pākehā) felt excluded and had to look elsewhere for programs about Māori, but in English. They looked but couldn't find much. Māori programs for the mainstream were specials or one-offs.

In 2000 the traditional reluctance of broadcasters to support mainstream Māori programs was challenged by a general public and industry demand for quotas. This was a strategy to increase the levels of New Zealand production. The government itself was not prepared to introduce a system of quotas, but New Zealand On Air was. Their most significant move was to ensure that long-running documentary series now included a set number of Māori stories, and further that the creative teams making these documentaries be Māori. The key creative positions are considered to be the triumvirate of producer, writer, and director. I believe that this strategy has worked—a little compulsion can be useful!—and there is now a greater sensitivity among funders and broadcasters to ensure that the Māori dimension to national television is catered for and deployed with integrity. Progress has been slow—but it is progress nonetheless.

One of the usual reasons given by broadcasters for their lack of support for Māori television is that it is not commercially viable. It is no accident that most Māori programming is seen on Sunday mornings. This is currently the only non-commercial time on the weekly schedule. This continued relegation to Sunday morning transmission is viewed by many as an insult. But because this period of the week is not expected to generate revenue, the television bosses have not interfered with the making of the programs. The fact that there are no commercials in those Māori programs has meant that experimentation and innovation have been able to take place, with little threat to the broadcaster's 'bottom line'. Extended 'talking heads' sequences, or pithy visual/audio metaphors are examples of the techniques that help to define truly Māori television.

Because of the commercial imperatives most hour-long documentaries in this country are only three quarters of an hour long. On the other hand, for the Māori directors of Sunday morning programs on TVNZ, every hour-long episode really is one hour long. The creative freedom that is therefore available to the director is enormous. This has meant that high quality training of personnel has been able to take place, ambitious programming has been attempted, ideas have been assayed, and the skills base of Māori has increased. The Sunday morning experimentation and the consequent training of scores of Māori professionals have seen vital additions to our television whakapapa.

There has also been educational television. Back in the early 1980s, *Kōrero Mai* and *Te Reo* were designed specifically for teaching te reo Māori to beginners. In 1987, *Te Kōhanga Reo* presented the activities of Kōhanga to viewers who did not have ready access to immersion education. Since then

Kōhanga and **Kura Kaupapa** have sprung up all around the country. A subsequent series *He Kākano* used drama to teach the language.

The popular Saturday afternoon youth program *Mai Time* had been piloted in the *Marae* slot in 1993. Since 1996 it has received regular funding and support from New Zealand On Air. The series presents music videos, celebrity insights, and the happenings of young people in a bi-cultural, bilingual, and bi-funky mix. It is extremely well received by Māori and Pākehā youth who appreciate the simple program philosophy—that it is cool to be Māori. All these programs impress upon their young minds that there is a place for their own language in this world.

Current Māori language programs for youth include the weekly reo Māori series for tamariki, *Tikitiki, Tū Te Puehu,* and TV3's show for teenagers, *Pūkana*. These series use much humour and music in their mix. The respective presenters have become stars and role models for their eager audiences. And these 'screenagers' are avidly scrutinising the world and the opportunities it offers. There is an educational dynamic in most Māori programs that cannot be ignored. Learning stuff *per se* is a significant part of Māori culture. It might be learning how to put down a **hāngi** or cook for a **hui**; it might be learning how to deliver a **karanga** or a **whaikōrero**; it may be immersing yourself in the history and **tikanga** of your hapū. Māori television generally is characterised by the portrayal and observance of tikanga, both on-camera and behind it. Whatever the program format or genre, there is always something to learn about what it means to be a Māori in modern New Zealand.

Obviously enough, this vital medium is not just about education and information. The Māori involvement in entertainment television goes back to the beginning, but stalled soon after. It started with a performance of the Howard Morrison Quartet on New Zealand's inaugural television broadcast in June 1960. There was little else until the action songs of 1970s *Pupuri Rā* and *Taku Toa*. But the skilful presence of Māori musicians in shows like *C'Mon, Happen Inn, 12 Bar Rhythm and Shoes,* and *Sweet Soul Music,* and the enormous popularity of stars like Dame Kiri Te Kanawa, Inia Te Wiata, Sir Howard Morrison, Bunny Walters, Dalvanius, Tina Cross, and many many more was proof positive of the Māori ability to hold and entertain an audience. In 1990, the series *When the Haka Became Boogie* paid respects to the entertainers of the past and showcased new generations of musicians and singers. The popularity of these programs helped to create the environment for the production of *Mai Time. Mai Time* in turn, experimented with a range of youth-oriented documentaries and contemporary music shows. One notable production was concerned with the unique superhero, *Mokotoa*. This semi-dramatic, semi-animated tale featured astonishing design, a futuristic storyline, and battles between the forces of good and evil. And because the language is Māori, this native take on science fiction has become a huge hit with tamariki everywhere.

There are perhaps two fundamental types of Māori programming. There are programs that are made for us, and then there are those that are made for the general audience. This last type has become known as 'mainstream programming', television of a broad appeal that includes some elements of Māori content, character, or language. The most popular Māori mainstream programming can be found in the genre of drama and comedy. Billy T. James has cast a long shadow over comedy in New Zealand. His form of Māori slapstick humour tickled the nation's funny bone like no other. This is a problem for Māori comedians who are finding Billy's footsteps a bit large to step into. Nevertheless, stand-up comic Mike King has established a genuinely funny assured presence on stage and television with his street-smart mouth and his rascal-like character. And, despite the critical pasting, Pio Terei's *Life and Times of Te Tutu* showcases a remarkable talent that is both similar and different to Billy T. Like Billy, Pio possesses a sure touch with the Māori audience, but for the mainstream audience he has moved beyond slapstick into farce and absurdity. His cultural flexibility exemplifies the real skill and talent it takes to make comedy work. And when a country is able to laugh at itself, it is a sure sign of that nation's good health.

To me then, there are probably two significant Māori audiences who deserve acknowledgement and support: those who understand te reo and tikanga—and those who do not yet know. In my view neither audience can be described as being 'more Māori' than the other. In fact the mere presence of Māori television can be a spur for Māori viewers to start to learn their language and the ways of their people. We need to see ourselves on screen because (like it or not) to many people the television speaks the truth. I view therefore I am. When we are bombarded by programs from overseas, we are experiencing in a very passive way an invasion of foreign thought and values. It is only when we can understand the uniqueness of our New Zealandness that we can sort out what is right and relevant for us.

Television and film, at their best, can be a reflection of reality. And in a country like ours where there is so much angst and ignorance about our race relations, a chance to get a clean snapshot of ourselves is a valuable thing. It certainly worked with the movie *Once Were Warriors* and the television series *The New Zealand Wars*. These stories were challenging and a 'hard watch' for very different reasons, but they were also popular with a wide range of viewers.

At present, too much television and film drama tends to highlight Māori themes and content which are generalised at best, and stereotypes at worst. There is much preoccupation with physical conflict, social oppression, or clashes of identity. This is a two-dimensional view of the Māori world, and is ultimately a disservice. However, a growing Māori presence in the ranks of drama producers, directors, and writers gives cause for hope that this limited view of our people will eventually end. Four recent drama projects signal a brave new world for Māori drama. They also highlight the impressive talents of the rapidly burgeoning independent Māori production community.

Feathers of Peace, produced by Don Selwyn and directed by Barry Barclay, is a thoughtful and harrowing account of the depredations suffered by Moriori when Pākehā and Māori colonised the Chatham Islands in the nineteenth century. *Te Tangata Whai Rawa O Wēneti,* produced by Ruth Kaupua and directed by Don Selwyn, is a Māori language version of Shakespeare's *The Merchant of Venice.* The beauty of the original English is matched with a peerless Māori translation by the revered scholar Dr Pei Te Hurinui Jones. *Aroha* is a series of Māori language love stories produced by Joanna Paul, while *Mataku,* produced and written by Rhonda Kite, Carey Carter, and Brad Haami, is a bilingual series that presents truly frightening tales of the supernatural.

These dramas are all superbly crafted. They have received critical and popular acclaim. More importantly however, they possess a tangible '**wairua**'. In part, a Māori wairua is a feeling that is pervasive and reflects a respect for the teachings and beliefs of our culture and lore. It is rooted in spirituality and an understanding that all things are related and interlinked. It is explained beautifully (in my view) by whakapapa. And, when you wed a superb story with a staunch Māori wairua to utterly professional production skills, you give birth to magic!

This surely is the dream that many of us now hold for the forthcoming Māori Television Service. The establishment of an indigenous television channel will be the end result of nearly three decades of agitation by Māori. In 2000 the government agreed to provide basic funding for setting up the service. Unfortunately, the route to the channel's establishment has been fraught because of inadequate resources and political interference. The resulting tensions have been very public and sometimes acrimonious. Nonetheless, progress is now evident and there is an exciting amount of production happening as programs are being prepared for the channel's eventual transmission.

A dedicated, Māori-controlled, and Māori-owned television voice is absolutely essential. For the people charged with the difficult task of establishing the new channel, this is a wonderful creative challenge. In effect they have a blank screen to work with. They must fill that screen with television that not only makes up for too much lost time, but also looks to the future in innovative and creative ways. And looking to the future is what I believe we can do best. Māori custom tells us that we in fact walk into that future backwards, our past is always before us, and our future is behind us. If we orient ourselves to such thinking, one of the benefits has to be simply that we are encouraged to consider our history. Through such observation we acquire an understanding of lessons from the past. We can then enter this data into our hearts and minds. After suitable reflection and cogitation we beam what we've learned through the eyes in the back of our head—illuminating the path we must take.

This then is our way to the future. It is a mixture of rational thought and intuition. A melding of heart, spirit, and mind—knowledge about our past that contributes to a confidence about the future. After my own time as a television producer and director, I can look back with incredible gratitude and pleasure for what I have experienced. I have spent quality time with wonderful people, and I have been privileged to help tell their stories. I am grateful that I have seen the positive impact of the work that we have done over the years. One of the most tangible fruits of our labour is simply the fact that New Zealanders are far more aware of what makes their brown neighbours or brown in-laws tick. The nation is now awake to the idea that Māori are here to stay, and that we are demanding the right to be brown. The fact that we still have to battle for what we believe only serves to make us that much more determined to succeed.

There are many issues still to debate within Māori television. A climate of coming technological **convergence** is but one example indicating the stakes are very high indeed. A digital and actual presence at every level of the telecommunications industry is what we must ultimately have. And the control must be with Māori—the ownership of our resources, our effort, and the fruits thereof, will be ours. That time perhaps, is to be sooner rather than later. But it will assuredly happen during the lifetimes of our children and mokopuna.

As we regard the struggle of our tūpuna of the world of Māori broadcasting, we can only admire the things they achieved in the face of great opposition. There is also much that they have left behind for us to carry on with. While we have achieved some of those goals and more, there remains the knowledge that in time my generation will pass on our own unrealised dreams for the young people to follow up. The importance of Māori television for Māori and Pākehā youth becomes more apparent when we consider the changing shape of the audiences. There is an ageing Pākehā population with a low birth rate, and a young Māori population with a high birth rate. Statistics indicate that by the year 2050, there will be equal numbers of Māori and Pākehā school children.

But the character of the population is changing too. Māori who are now in their teens and early twenties and who have come from a strong Māori educational base, are increasingly 'staunch' about te reo and tikanga. They are fully bi-cultural, and welcome the best of Pacific and Pākehā people and culture into their lives. They are confident and strong, and will imbue these attitudes into their children. The kaupapa will continue with them. I have every confidence that our rangatahi will fulfil our wishes: and more, much more. They really will do stuff that we cannot even begin to dream about!

Tū ki runga, tū ki raro, tū ki wheawhea, tū ka whakaputaina ki te whei ao ki te ao mārama.

Tihe Mauriora!

Kia ora mai.

7

Mrs Lee's Knowing Wink:

Reading Race in New Zealand Advertising

SUE ABEL

How we are seen determines in part how we are treated; how we treat others is based on how we see them; such seeing comes from representation.

Richard Dyer 1993, p. 1

Stereotypes have been granted extraordinary powers by many media critics, as the quotation from Richard Dyer suggests. According to a popular or 'commonsense' view they are seen as inherently simple and narrow in meaning, and always negative. On the other hand, the more extreme forms of **active audience** theory seem to imply that the meaning of stereotypes, as with other representations, is 'up for grabs', with myriad possible readings depending on the life circumstances of individuals (Fiske 1987; Seiter et al. 1989). In negotiating these two positions this chapter argues that stereotypes are not simple and that they are indeed open to a range of readings; but that these tend to cluster in distinct groups according to power relations within the wider society. It also argues that the meanings ascribed to stereotypes are influenced by the social, historical, and/or cultural context within which they are read. The present case history is from a larger reception study in which teenagers aged between 16 and 18 discussed their responses to (or readings of) a range of television advertisements (or ads). On this occasion, the stereotype in question, involving a Chinese woman, appeared in a television advertisement for Drive soap powder made for the New Zealand and Australian market.[1]

In the Drive ad a blond-haired white man in his twenties, dressed in jeans and a blue shirt, with a white T-shirt underneath, goes into a modern laundry with a pile of clothes. Behind the counter is a middle-aged Chinese woman in a neat blue and white uniform, and behind her is a sign: 'Mrs

Lee's Specialist Laundry'. He hands over his laundry and asks: 'Can you help me, Mrs Lee?' She examines his clothes with a little magnifying glass and answers: 'Nasty grime. Grass stains. Greasy food. Specialist clean. Very difficult'. The ad cuts to her looking over her shoulder as she puts some Drive soap powder in the washing machine while the male **voiceover** intones: 'Because all stains aren't the same, Drive has a three-way cleaning action with enzymes that work harder first time'. Cut to the young man returning, and Mrs Lee quickly hides the Drive under the counter. He looks at his clean laundry and exclaims: 'Gee, you're a legend, Mrs Lee! What would we do without you?' The male voiceover enters again with 'Drive out more stains!' as the camera cuts to a close-up of Mrs Lee looking knowingly at the camera.

The social context

The Drive ad was made by J. Walter Thompson (JWT) in Sydney, and screened in Australia as well as in New Zealand in 1996–97. The ad and the response to it can be seen in the context of what became known as the 'Asian Invasion' of the 1990s. In 1984 the New Zealand government, in order to encourage economic recovery, set about attracting overseas entrepreneurs with skill and capital to New Zealand. The emphasis changed from attracting those with skills to fill gaps in the traditional labour market, to the recruiting of those with money to invest. Six years later, the Government increased the annual target to 25 000 new migrants. The closest source of wealth and skill to fill this target was more affluent countries of Asia. In six years the Asian population of New Zealand almost trebled to more than 50 000. In 1991 almost one in two migrants were from Asia, a far cry from 1987 when arrivals from Britain were double those from all of Asia. Nevertheless, according to the 1996 census, Chinese still made up only 2.2 per cent of the population, with Indians 1.2 per cent and other Asian groups too small to record.

The presence of these new Asian immigrants has led to considerable controversy in middle New Zealand, particularly in Auckland, where they have tended to settle. Wealthy Asian immigrants have built large houses in a style that is not seen as attractive or as 'fitting in' by their non-Asian neighbours. Asians driving expensive cars have likewise been an easy target, especially when Auckland BMW dealers say that more than half their sales in recent years have been to Asians (Reid 1998). Asian students have put pressure on the education system in two ways. First, those who arrive at school without much English language have taken up time and resources that might have been used for other students. Second, many have succeeded so well, especially in the fields of maths and sciences, that many Kiwi parents have felt that their children are missing out.

There is more than anecdotal evidence of increasing anti-Asian racism. In 1997 a Time Morgan poll detected 44 per cent opposition to immigration among New Zealanders, but also found that 53 per cent objected specifically to Asian immigrants (Reid 1998). The wealth and status of the new Asian immigrants, together with the work ethic and attitudes to education that they bring with them, have meant that they have in many places been perceived as more of a threat to New Zealand's way of life than previous Asian migrants, most of whom came as lowly paid workers. Letters to newspapers and some newspaper columnists have lambasted the new Asians as being avaricious and materialistic. Dr Manying Ip, of Auckland University's Asian Languages Department, has pointed out however that Chinese have never had an easy time in New Zealand, having attracted discrimination since the early days on the colonial goldfields. New Zealanders in the nineteenth century labelled Chinese as 'undesirable aliens' and the first Anti-Chinese Association was founded in 1856, before there were even any Chinese in the country. Chinese were the only people who had to pay a poll tax to enter New Zealand, and could not obtain citizenship until 1952 (*Southland Times*, 1 May 1993). Dr Ip has also said: 'In the past we were criticised for being ignorant and poor. Now we are satirised for being smart and rich' (Reid 1998).

So where does this position Mrs Lee, screening on New Zealand television sets in 1997? In such an environment it might be supposed that many viewers are more likely to see her as fitting their own (negative) image of Chinese than they are to accept her invitation to laugh with her at the situation portrayed in the ad.

Advertising agencies and their clients are very aware these days of the dangers of creating negative stereotypes of different groups. The records of complaints registered with the Advertising Standards Complaints Board show that in their defence to a complaint the advertising agency concerned will often state that they consulted with members of the group concerned, and this is taken into account in the judgment delivered. This happened with the Mrs Lee ad. Ralf Harding, the Account Director for Drive at JWT Auckland at the time, told me that clients like Unilever (who produce Drive) are very conscious of issues like racial stereotyping.[2] They are multinational companies who do not want to offend groups in the countries they trade in. J. Walter Thompson accordingly consulted with a senior member of the Chinese community in New Zealand, Peter Chang of the Auckland Chinese Community Centre, who said he could see no problem as long as Mrs Lee was shown as a modern day Chinese woman and that she looked like a normal Chinese woman (*Dominion*, 5 May 1997). Personnel I have spoken with at JWT report that they got very little negative feedback. Nevertheless it is clear from my research that the ad was still seen by many viewers, both Asian and non-Asian, as a negative stereotype. At an anecdotal level, the usual reaction when I told people I was researching this ad was a comment about how racist it was. Dr Ip, who often speaks out on matters of concern to the Chinese community, saw the ad as denigrating. She told me:

> I did see the Drive ad and I was very uncomfortable with it, very annoyed about it. The deviousness of an Asian woman who was obviously conning a Pākehā man who looks an innocent, gullible and open New Zealand kid. Mrs Lee spoke in pidgin English—she wasn't speaking grammatical English. And the laundry connotation—the Chinese being in the laundry business. Whoever designed it had this cultural image in mind—I can't say that they had a particular racist thing to push but obviously whoever designed it had got this stereotype of the Chinese as laundry people in mind… I think it was laughing *at* Mrs Lee rather than laughing with her. I see it as a negative cultural image. The same stereotype as the bad Asian driver, the brash Asian banker—they are all accepted and current among the non-Asian New Zealander. Definitely the ad is pandering to popular prejudice, appealing to the lowest common denominator.

The ad became the subject of some public debate, and a complaint was laid with the Advertising Standards Complaints Board. The complaint was rejected on the grounds that '…advertisements often employ stereotypes to simplify the process of creating recognition of both the product offered and the intended consumer. Mrs Lee is sympathetically and humorously portrayed as an acknowledged expert…' The report also states 'Mrs Lee [is] a party to the humour rather than the subject of it'.

Representation and stereotypes

One point in the Drive ad that is open to debate is whether Mrs Lee is a *stereotype* of a Chinese person (and therefore a stereotype of Chinese as a whole), or whether she is a *representation* of a Chinese individual. Definitions of stereotypes differ. One useful definition is that stereotyping is a process of selection, magnification, and reduction; it takes one perceived attribute of a social group, blows that attribute up until it obscures all others, then boils it down until it comes to stand for that group, summarising that group in a kind of cultural shorthand (Medhurst 1998). Andrew Tolson (1996) describes stereotypes as a narrow and restrictive (but also resilient) set of meanings or concepts produced within an ideology—as racism, for example, has produced stereotypes of black people. Most definitions of stereotypes contain the assumptions that they are inherently negative, and that they are created by more powerful groups at the expense of those less powerful.

But Tessa Perkins in her classic essay 'Rethinking Stereotypes' (1979) debunks these arguments. She suggests, among other things, that stereotypes can be positive ('French people are good cooks'), and also that the less powerful can hold stereotypes about the more powerful ('English upper class twits'). The drawback of this argument, it seems to me, lies in the question of who has the power to present or represent which stereotypes in the mass media, and also what is the relative power of the groups being stereotyped. As Shohat and Stam put it: 'while all negative stereotypes are hurtful, they do not all exercise the same power in the world' (1994, p. 183).

In the context of my research, I find the Media Action Network for Asian Americans definition of a stereotype useful—'the incessant recurrence of a limited range of [restrictive] portrayals—coupled with the paucity of compensating images—marks them as stereotypes. A portrayal can act as a stereotype even if its creator doesn't intend it to'. (MANAA 2001) This definition too has its drawbacks—one would still call the 'dumb blonde' a stereotype even though there are many other images of women in the media. Nevertheless it makes two points that are relevant to this case study. There is the assertion that a portrayal can act as a stereotype even if its creator does not intend it to. This is the case in the Drive ad, where Account Director Stephen Whiteway is adamant that JWT did not intend to use a stereotype, and that a Chinese woman was selected because of the positive qualities associated with the Chinese race, which he saw as a dedication to cleanliness and to a job well done.[3] (While some people may read these two statements as a contradiction, Whiteway did not. Like many other people, he apparently sees stereotypes as always negative. The implication of this attitude is that sweeping statements about an ethnic group are unproblematic provided they are positive.)

The second important point in the MANAA definition is that the limited range of representations is coupled with a paucity of compensating images. This connects with the very useful concept of the 'burden of representation' (Shohat and Stam 1994). When there are very few images of a particular group in the media, those that do appear are seen to be typical of all of that group. A young Māori student expressed elements of this concept in his own words: 'About the Asian ad—I think it's because you hardly ever see Asians in ads like that, and I think they [Asians] are so angry because the first ad they see of an Asian is not a good one. But Māoris, we've seen them do it for ages in commercials.'

Shohat and Stam also argue that 'socially empowered groups need not be unduly concerned about "distortions and stereotypes", since even occasionally negative images form part of a wide spectrum of representations.'

This argument is borne out by the responses to the Drive ad from different groups of participants, as I discuss below.

One of the responses of minority groups and others who find stereotypes repressive is to call for more positive images with which to counter the negative misrepresentations. But although well intentioned, the call for positive images has certain problems. First, it merely replaces one stereotype by another. Second, it assumes that all members of the stereotyped group can agree on what might constitute a positive image. In the case of the Drive ad, JWT obtained approval (of the script, at least) from a prominent member of the Auckland Chinese Community Centre, yet the ad met with disapproval from other prominent Chinese New Zealanders.

Stereotypes are an important part of the content of advertisements because advertisers have limited time (in television commercials, usually only thirty seconds and sometimes less) in which to convey a message. Indeed, it has been argued that stereotyping is inevitable in any form of immediate, accessible communication, since there is never enough time or space to describe people in all their complexity. For this reason, short cuts have to be taken, comparisons made, generalisations risked, labels attached. But for advertisers stereotyping can be a double-edged sword. Ralf Harding from JWT, in an interview about the Drive ad, explained that for advertisers 'on the one hand a stereotype says something quickly, on the other it raises the issue of political correctness. If it does one it almost certainly does the other. There is a fine line between being amusing and being offensive.'

To return to the question that opened this section, while not many of my participants used the actual term 'stereotype', a large majority clearly saw Mrs Lee as a representation of Asians/Chinese as a race, in other words, as a stereotype.[4] This bears out Shohat and Stam's point about the burden of representation outlined earlier. As one of very few images of Asians in ads, Mrs Lee was seen as a representative rather than as an individual. Interestingly, the participants who knew the stereotype of the Chinese laundry woman generally saw the ad as less offensive than other participants. They were more likely to see the ad as humorous. On the other hand, these participants tended to be Pākehā and middle class.

Self-reflexive advertising and 'the knowing wink'

One of the key characteristics of what is called 'postmodern' advertising is its self-reflexivity, the way in which ads draw attention to their status as advertisements and to their processes of signification. Self-reflexivity is seen as a way of cutting through the jam and clutter of ads that viewers are exposed to. It offers a means of positioning viewers towards a product name in a way that differs from competing brands. Market research has shown advertisers that more and more viewers object to being 'manipulated' by ads and do not believe much of what ads tell them. Advertisers have therefore tried to become more sophisticated in how they address viewers by suggesting that the ads do not take themselves too seriously.

There are at least two ways in which such an attitude may work in an ad. One is to draw attention to the whole ad as a construction; another is to draw attention to one particular element of the ad as a construction. Goldman and Papson (1991) use the term 'knowing wink' to explain the way a self-reflexive ad, or the character(s) within the ad, draw attention to the whole ad as a construction. They assert that the knowing wink enables characters to visually address the audience, to step outside the narrative and join with the viewer in a wryly speculative commentary on what we have seen. This concept is directly relevant to the Drive ad, where this literally happens, for in the last shot Mrs Lee, in close-up, turns slightly to face the viewing audience directly and widens her eyes. In fact Ralf Harding told me that all ads use an element of hyperbole to make a point and that no reasonable person would say that this ad showed a real situation. The ad, he said, is using hyperbole to make a point, and Mrs Lee is asking you to laugh at the ad itself.

But there are other ways of reading this shot, as my focus groups illustrate. Is Mrs Lee's 'wink' at the audience playful or sly? What is it that Mrs Lee is asking us to go along with? The naïvety of the young man? The Chinese stereotype?

The 'humorous' use of a stereotype is another way in which ads might highlight their construction. Anne Cronin (2000, p. 57) calls reflexive ads 'ironic' ads, and has produced a working definition of such ads as:

> those which incorporate a self-consciousness as to their intertextual composi-
> tion of signifiers… In effect these adverts are explicit about their position in
> popular culture and offer viewers a complicity in this knowledge… This use
> of an ironic or knowing visual address…explicitly signals the *activity* on the part
> of the viewer in producing meanings… Distinctively, a reflexive address refers
> to intertextual popular culture signifiers and actively incorporates an assump-
> tion of the viewer's knowledge and competencies in situating and mobilising
> these signifiers. (Italics in the original.)

Stereotypes are a very commonly used form of 'popular culture **signi-fier**', and many ads use stereotypes in an ironic manner so that they in effect wink at the audience and say 'Don't take us seriously, laugh along with us'. One example of this is the Levis' claymation ad where the hero with strongly chiselled jaw and swished back hair, dressed (of course) in white

T-shirt and Levis jeans, rolls up on his motorbike, swishes a comb through his hair, and then uses self-deprecating ingenuity and courage to rescue the helpless blonde heroine from a fire. The ad is amusing and so hip in its style that it would seem churlish to criticise it in terms of stereotyped gender roles. And in fact Joshua Gamson maintains that since the 1980s much advertising 'has insulated itself from criticism by assuming an audience literate in the manipulative languages of advertising, addressing the charge of hucksterism by acknowledging it and turning it into an ironic joke and a you're-so-hip pitch' (Gamson 1999). In a similar way the Drive ad could be seen as taking the stereotype of a Chinese laundry and a Chinese laundry worker, modernising it, and inviting the audience to laugh along with it.

And yet of course it is not as simple as this. One question that arises is whether or not a stereotype loses its potential negative force if it is presented ironically. Gamson and Cronin point out between them that ironic ads assume that audiences are media literate and aware of the cultural meanings ascribed to the signifiers (in this case the stereotype) used in the ad. Ironic ads also assume that audiences are aware that the stereotype is being used in an ironic sense. This raises several questions for this case study. On a simple level, do viewers see Mrs Lee as a stereotype? If so, do viewers understand the irony and laugh *along with* Mrs Lee? Or do they laugh *at* her, whether or not they see the ad as ironical? Or do they not laugh at all, seeing the representation as a cause for concern?

Then there are more complex questions. To what extent does laughter expose and undermine a potentially racist discourse in the ad, rather than confirm or strengthen it? Can it be seen as politically progressive if viewers feel comfortable enough about minority stereotypes to laugh along with them? Or can such stereotypes, whether ironic or not, serve to reinforce existing prejudice in other racial groups? And of course, which viewers are we talking about? If different viewers react in different ways, what are the ramifications of this? Where and how do issues of power enter the equation? I try to address these questions in the following section in which I present some of the data from my focus groups.

Reading the Drive ad and Mrs Lee

I discussed the Drive ad with fifteen groups of young people in New Zealand, and two in Singapore. Two of the New Zealand groups consisted of Asian students, one of Pacific Islanders, two of Māori, and one of a mixture of Māori and Pacific Islanders. The rest were predominantly Pākehā, but some of these groups also contained new immigrants from non-Asian and non-Pacific countries. Overall the responses ranged from boredom, to disinterest, to mild concern ('It's quite mean', 'It's a bit racist'), to serious concern, to three groups who were incensed by the ad.

Pākehā responses

The dominant Pākehā interpretation of this ad was one of 'now you've mentioned the ad, I do think it is racist' and there were several variations along the line of 'I'd be upset if I were Asian'. In other words, most Pākehā participants saw the ad as racist to some degree or other, but were often not particularly concerned because it did not affect them. It was, however, a common pattern for participants to start off with an acknowledgment that perhaps the ad was racist, and in the process of explaining why, taking up a firmer position.

Surprisingly few argued that the ad was not racist or stereotypical. It is hard to tell how much issues of peer pressure and of saying the 'correct' thing came into these responses. There were participants who chose to remain silent, and this may have been because they did not wish to express a view that might be interpreted as racist. In fact, one group of boys did tell me that they felt uncomfortable discussing the ads because there were things they wanted to say that might lay them open to charges of being sexist or racist. A few students, however, were prepared to argue for their viewpoint. In this excerpt (from a discussion by Pākehā Seventh Form students), D goes on the offensive.

A: *It's a bit racist.*

B: *It's horribly racist!*

C: *Yeah.*

A: *I reckon that in a way it treats the Asian as—cause at the end she's got a look of—um—*

B: *Intentionally ripping him off.*

A: *Yeah, a look of almost evil in her face.*

D: *Huh! If you had a white woman in there, you'd say it's racist against the white woman?*

A: *No I wouldn't, because you've got this thing that Asians are devious—*

B: *I just feel like it's showing that—you always have these ideas that the Chinese are always trying to rip you off and it shows you, it kind of reinforces it, how she uses just a basic laundry cleaner and charges him extra.*

E: *I think it shows that white people are just a bit stupid because he brings in his stuff and pays all this money when he could have done it himself.*

D: *If you see that ad as racist it's all in your mind—you must have*
             some racist ideas yourself. Just because it's got two people both of
             different races it must be racist?

D was one of the few participants who was prepared to say that they did
not see anything racist in the ad, and he argued his case with considerable
passion. Not persuaded, however, both A and B make connections between
the way Mrs Lee is represented and the way Asians/Chinese are perceived by
the wider community. This is an important point—it suggests that this
reading of Mrs Lee as 'devious' and 'evil' comes about precisely because of
racist attitudes in the wider community. To use the terminology that Judith
Williamson might use, Mrs Lee can be seen as an essentially neutral signifier
who only gains meaning through the active connection the reader makes
with a wider referent system (Williamson 1978). It is of interest that, rather
than seeing the ad as therefore 'realistic', both young men see it as racist, thus
dissociating themselves from the racist attitudes of the wider community. The
excerpt also provides an example of an implicit understanding of the
representation of Mrs Lee as a stereotype, although the term itself is not used.

Other students were much more blasé about the ad, for example these
Sixth Form Media Studies students (all female middle or upper middle class
Pākehā):

A: *I don't see anything wrong with it.*
B: *She's such a cute little lady—it makes me think about Chinese*
             people doing that sort of work.
Me: *Do you think it would work as well if she were white?*
B: *She could be a cute little old white lady—but then it wouldn't really*
             be like a Chinese laundry.
Me: *So you're used to the idea of a Chinese laundry?*
Several: *Yes.*
C: *There's also that Levis ad with Bruce Lee where they run into the*
             laundry and it's got clothes everywhere.
D: *Some people say the Mrs Lee ad is racist, but it can't be that racist*
             because the Chinese lady did it and she wouldn't have done it if she
             thought it was racist.

One Pākehā group stood out from the others in its response to the ad.
This was a group of boys who gave the impression of being of lower socioeconomic status.

A (with vehemence): I hate that ad.
Me: *Why do you hate it?*

A: *The lady, Mrs Lee, she makes me angry. She isn't funny—she's such a bitch, fooling all her customers.*

B: *It's just the way they look, it annoys me you know.*

A: *And that dude's so stupid.*

C: *She's evil—Mrs Lee is evil. All she wants is money.*

This group displayed considerable anger not only in their tone of voice and body language (which a transcript does not show) but also in the language chosen, 'evil' and 'bitch' (unusual in this sort of context with an unfamiliar adult). A tentative interpretation here might be that this is the anger of a group that feels threatened. There seems to be evidence here that the participants are drawing on a wider family/community negativity towards and stereotypes of Asians. B doesn't like the way 'they' look—this suggests that 'they all look the same', that Asians have no individuality, that Mrs Lee is in fact representing all Asians. C's reading suggests a drawing on the contemporary stereotype of the new Asian migrants as being (overly) materialistic. His choice of the strong word 'evil' may look back to old stereotypes of evil, scheming Chinese. A's comments ('fooling all her customers') also suggest that he is drawing on a wider discourse about Asians' lack of trustworthiness, with their eye always out for the main chance. While it was relatively common for participants to describe Mrs Lee as 'sly', this was usually in the context of discussing the negativity of the stereotype. These participants seemed to feel personal animosity towards Mrs Lee as a representative of the Asian community.

Māori and Pacific Island responses

Māori and Pacific Island participants, as members of minority groups who also feel that their image in advertising is a negative one, came up with some particularly interesting and often unexpected comments. Sixth and Seventh Form Māori student groups canvassed a range of issues. One young woman (B) raised an important issue that bears directly on the question of whether stereotypes that seem to invite the audience to laugh at their own construction are in fact progressive or regressive.

A (male):   *I think it would have been just as funny if a Māori person had been behind that counter.*

B (female):   *I reckon it depends on who's making the ad. Like with Pio—he's putting down—not putting down but making fun of his own race,[5] where whoever is doing the Fab [sic] ad wasn't Asian—well, from my perspective wasn't—so someone else was putting down the Asian race.*

C (female): It's not putting her down because in the end she's smarter.

B: Well, making her a stereotype of Asians. It depends on who's doing the ad. I think that before you put any other race or culture down you should put your own down.

While many students interpreted Mrs Lee getting the upper hand as a negative representation showing her as sly and as a cheat, others saw this is a positive victory for her, as suggested by C above. The group picked up this point again:

A (male): I think ultimately in the clothes washing ad the Asian lady gets the better of the Pākehā because he just goes 'Oh thank you, Mrs Lee, here's all the money', and all she did was just put in the washing powder.

B (female): But people might see that as Asians ripping people off, and Asians might be offended.

D (male): It can also be seen as she's working for that guy, like slavery again, like 'Wash my clothes' and all that stuff.

The exchange of views in this group also indicates something of the range of readings that are possible. One young Māori man summed up very articulately the polysemic nature of the text: 'What I'm saying is that there's two sides to the coin and it can be taken in a different way. It depends on how a person interprets their version of the ad because there's validity in what the Asian people are saying about how it's putting them down, and you can also see the validity on the other side of the coin which is saying that she gets the better of the other person.'

The group of Pacific Island students felt more strongly than the Māori students about their own comparative invisibility in the media, and about the negativity of the images that did appear. They related this to the Drive ad and Mrs Lee:

A (male): I get sick of just white people in ads.

B (male): But when they show us, it's like Homeward Bound where they go back to her house and it's a state house and they're implying that all Polynesians live in state houses.[6]

C (female): It's like Polynesian people aren't good enough to live in a white society sort of thing

B: And in Skitz as well they mock Polynesians.

D: Yeah, but that's funny.

B: Why are there always white women in ads? Aren't our women beautiful too?

A: *Ads always put us down.*

B: *Like the Drive ad, too—because she's Asian—it's like saying*
            Chinese people rip you off. It's a stereotype.

Me: *What's a stereotype?*

B: *It's a reputation about what people have.*

C: *And what people are—like how they've got—like most white people*
            think 'Brown person—state housing—family's on the benefit' sort of
            thing

A: *Like my family! (General laughter.)*

C: *You know what I mean—like most white people take that for*
            granted—of what that person is.

Me: *Is there anything else you want to say about television advertising?*

C: *What we've been saying about not many brown people—it's not just*
            here—it's also in other countries like Australia.

While the specific discussion of the Drive ad and Mrs Lee is limited here, it is obvious that the group sees Asians (and Aborigines) in the same position as themselves *vis-à-vis* the dominant white population. The discussion in this group was heated, as participants felt strongly about what they saw as the unfairness of media representations of non-white groups.

Asian responses

I had expected that Asian students in New Zealand might be unhappy about the way they saw Asians represented in advertising. I was not, however, prepared for the ferocity of their responses to the Drive ad:

A (male):   *The people who make ads—in their minds they always think about*
             Asian people like barbarians.

B (male):   *The ad with the washing powder gives me the impression that the*
             Chinese woman was trying to cheat someone, and that cheating is a
             way of behaving.

C (male):   *Yes, like the Asian people come here and cheat people.*

Me: *So you don't like it because it's that stereotype about how Chinese*
             are obsessed with money?

B: *Yes, but that is wrong. It's the wrong information to tell everybody.*
             They say Asian people just like money, and people think 'Ah, Asian
             people cheat for money' but we get our money by ourselves.

C: *We work hard and we save hard—they see us drive a big car and*
             have a big house—we work hard by ourselves.

D (male):   *I think it's OK because they use the Chinese woman in that ad to*
             make it more interesting for people to watch than just a white
             woman. It's just an ad anyway.

E (female): I'm just interested in why they choose to have a Chinese or Asian woman to play that character instead of any other European or Kiwi.

Me: Does anyone have anything to say on this?

(Silence.)

Me: I understand that there is a long tradition of Chinese who came to European countries and set up laundries—they earned their money by doing laundry.

E: I don't see many Chinese people doing the washing. That character could be European or Kiwi instead of Asian.

F (female): I agree with E—for a Chinese woman to appear as a washerwoman is not very good. I don't like it. It's not right.

Besides D's dissident voice, there are two arguments going on here. The first is that the ad will reinforce the wider community's prejudices and a belief that Asians cheat. Again we see the burden of representation, carried both by the image and by people who see themselves as being negatively represented by that image. One wonders, however, if these students would have reacted quite so strongly if they had not felt animosity from the wider population—to what extent is their reading and reaction reinforced by their life experiences? The second argument is that it is not appropriate to show a Chinese woman in a working-class position. This highlights the fact that the stereotype is based on earlier waves of Chinese immigrants who were working class—or who were forced to work in working-class jobs—whereas this wave of Asian immigrants are largely wealthy business people and entrepreneurs.

The responses from two groups of Chinese students in Singapore were in some ways similar to those of the New Zealand Asians, but the whole tone of these focus groups was different. The attitude of the participants was largely dispassionately critical, and many comments revealed a detached amusement either at the ad, or at the fact that the stereotype was still being used. From the first group:

A (female): It certainly grabs your attention—I think it's quite funny.

B (female): It's cute.

C (male): The ethnicity came on strong—with a Chinese woman and a Westerner.

D (female): She looks like a typical Chinese woman—well, like Westerners would stereotype a Chinese woman.

C: I can't believe that people are still using stereotypes of Chinese people like that, and of Chinese taking Americans for a ride.

A: The Westerner is stupid.

E (male): I've seen more interesting laundry ads than that.

F (female):   But the stereotype is too strong—the laundrette, her accent—it's a
                sleazy ad.

E: I think it's racist and stereotypical—it makes Chinese people look
                dishonest and obsessed with cleanliness, and inscrutable.

G (male):   It makes Mrs Lee look cunning and crafty, but also stupid—her
                accent does that.

B: She's a cute, sweet old lady.

E: It's the way she sort of looks down—it's sly—it reinforces the
                message.

This group were both amused and indignant about the ad—indignant rather than angry. Although most of their comments about the ad are very critical, they still seemed to remain detached from it, and on the whole did not take the ad personally. They were well aware of the ad as a construction of a common stereotype, and of some of the elements of that stereotype (e.g. 'inscrutable'). It is interesting that one participant took a quality that Steve Whiteway from JWT sees as a positive characteristic—obsession with cleanliness—and decried it as negatively stereotypical. From the second group:

A: It's bad because it seems that they portray Asian people as very
                shrewd and cunning—[mimics ad] 'Oh, nasty grime', 'Specialist
                cleaning'.

B (female):   They are showing Chinese women as inferior, as in lower class
                jobs—it's just laundry.

C (male):   If the young man had been Chinese it wouldn't have mattered.

Me: If they had been in the same culture, you wouldn't have read that
                as a stereotype?

(General assent expressed.)

B: It is very stereotypical that they show Asians as shop owners,
                restaurant owners, tailors, laundry people—why don't they show
                Asians as customers?

As with the New Zealand Asian group, the arguments divide up into a criticism that Mrs Lee is shown as sly and cunning, and a concern that she is shown in what they see as a lower class job. B's last comment ties in with research into the representation of minority groups in American advertising, where both African and Anglo-Americans are shown in jobs such as serving customers at McDonalds, but while African-Americans are often shown serving Anglo-American customers, the situation is never reversed. B and C are also saying in different ways that Asians/Chinese are seen in both this ad and in the wider Western media as being inferior to other races.

The major difference between these two groups and the New Zealand group is that the Singaporeans are not threatened by the ad. They do not fear that they will be judged by it. There are of course issues of power and identity at play here, and I will discuss these in the final section.

Conclusion

The notion of the active reader who creates their own meanings from media products according to their own life circumstances is now an orthodoxy in media studies. It is also commonplace to assume that young media consumers are particularly media savvy (Nava 1997; Nava and Nava 1996). Anderson and Miles state: 'Young consumers of media do not act passively or uncritically but transform, appropriate and recontextualise meanings'. (1999, p. 108) In the case of the Drive ad young consumers recontextualised the meaning(s) in terms of the power dynamics that were relevant in their individual lives. A middle-class Pākehā girl read it as a feminist tract. Pacific Island participants identified with the oppression of being subject to another culture's capacity to define one's culture in negative stereotypes.

Pākehā participants, on the whole comfortable with their position as the majority and power-holding racial group, generally saw the ad as racist, but felt varying degrees of concern over this. An exception was the group of young Pākehā men who expressed considerable hostility to the Mrs Lee character. I have read their remarks as based on prejudice towards Asians, and it is tempting to postulate that a reason for this is that as white working-class or lower middle-class males they see their access to jobs being eroded by females and the new Asian immigrants. But in truth the discussion is far too brief to make such an argument with any real conviction.

The other hostile response was of course that of the New Zealand Asian students who, with one exception, were recent immigrants. Under attack for their big cars and big houses, visible manifestations of a different set of cultural values, participants saw the ad as extremely harmful to them. Like most of the other New Zealand groups,[7] they saw Mrs Lee as standing for Asian/Chinese people, and therefore the attributes they saw constructed for her, those of being sly and cheating, were also constructed for them. Shohat and Stam, in a discussion of the impact negative stereotypes have on oppressed communities, have said 'while all negative stereotypes are hurtful, they do not all exercise the same power in the world' (1994). These participants ascribed considerable power to this stereotype to reinforce existing attitudes towards them. A relatively trivial, but still significant, incident reported by a boys' group shows that there are real-life consequences of media representations:

A: *It doesn't bother me, but an Asian it may.*
B: *Yeah, because they get hassles because they're Asians.*
C: *People start calling them Mrs Lee and that.*

The readings of the Singaporean Chinese are of particular interest because they throw those of the New Zealand Asians into relief. Where the New Zealand Asian response was an extremely emotional one,[8] that of the Singaporean Chinese was almost one of intellectual analysis. Like Pākehā in New Zealand, these participants were also comfortable with their position as the majority and power-holding racial group. They scorned the Chinese stereotype as outdated, although they split between laughing at this and feeling angry that it was still being used, and at what they saw as the crudity of the stereotype. They did not feel threatened by Mrs Lee as a representation, they saw her more as a commentary on Western attitudes towards Chinese people.

In an earlier section I raised several questions, some of which can now be (tentatively) answered. These young adult participants did see Mrs Lee as a stereotype in that they overwhelmingly thought that Mrs Lee had been constructed as a sly, devious and (to quote one of the Singaporean Chinese) 'inscrutable' person whose character could be read as a reflection of the characteristics of the racial group she belonged to. Beyond this basic (but not unanimous) agreement, participants tended to respond to the ad on the basis of the relative power held by the racial group they belonged to. Participants' responses also implied that they thought that stereotypes like Mrs Lee did have some negative consequences for the racial group concerned. Whether or not this is in fact true is of course outside the realm of this paper. Also unclear is whether participants would have felt the same about, say, a negative stereotype of a white man.

It is difficult to answer the very important question about whether laughter exposes and undermines a potentially racist discourse. Despite the intentions of those who made the ad and the Advertising Standards Complaints Board's finding that 'the tone of the advertisement is one of gentle situational humour…with Mrs Lee as party to the humour rather than the subject of it', very few of the participants found the ad humorous. They neither laughed with Mrs Lee nor at her. Mrs Lee's 'knowing wink', then, was seen not as a wink of complicity with the audience over the hyperbole of the ad, but rather as further evidence of her slyness.

One thing that this research does prove is that the emphasis on polysemy in active reader theory remains valuable. Faced with an ad that is supposed to be a positive representation of a Chinese woman, most participants read it as negative to some degree or other. But in almost every group there was somebody whose views on the ad differed. Even in the very hostile New

Zealand Asian group, one participant did not see anything negative about Mrs Lee and said 'It's only an ad'.

References

Anderson, Alison & Steven Miles, 1999. '"Just Do It": Young People, the Global Media and the Construction of Consumer Meanings', in *Youth and the Global Media*. Luton: Luton University Press.

Cronin, Anne. 2000. *Advertising and Consumer Citizenship: Gender, Images and Rights*. London and New York: Routledge.

Dyer, Richard. 1993. *The Matter of Images: Essays on Representation*. London and New York: Routledge.

Fiske, John. 1987. *Television Culture*. London: Routledge.

Gamson, Joshua. 1999. 'Ad Creep', in *The American Prospect Online*, 11 (3), 20 December.

Goldman, Robert & Steve Papson, 1991. 'Levis and the Knowing Wink' in *Current Perspectives in Social Theory*, Vol. 11, pp. 69–95.

MANAA (Media Action Network for Asian Americans). Available at: http://janet.org/~manaa/a/a_stereotypes.html. [Accessed 2001].

Medhurst, Andy. 1998. 'Tracing Desires: Sexuality and Media Texts' in Adam Briggs & Paul Cobley (eds), *The Media: An Introduction*. Essex: Longman.

Nava, Mica. 1997. 'Framing Advertising: Cultural Analysis and the Incrimination of Visual Texts', in M. Nava, A. Blake, I. MacRury & R. Richards (eds), *Buy This Book: Studies in Advertising and Consumption*. London and New York: Routledge.

Nava, M. & O. Nava. 1996. 'Discriminating or Duped? Young People as Consumers of Advertising', in Paul Marris & Sue Thornham (eds), *Media Studies: A Reader*. Edinburgh: Edinburgh University Press.

Perkins, Tessa. 1979. 'Rethinking Stereotypes', in M. Barrett, P. Corrigan, A. Kuhn & V. Wolff (eds), *Ideology and Cultural Production*. Croom Helm.

Reid, Bronwen. 1998. 'Barren Times for Race Relations' in *Time,* 17 May, pp. 40–1.

Seiter, Ellen, Hans Borchers, Gabriele Kreutzner, Eva-Maria Warth (eds). 1989. *Remote Control: Television, Audiences and Cultural Power*. London and New York: Routledge.

Shohat, Ella & Robert Stam. 1994. *Unthinking Eurocentrism: Multiculturalism and the Media*. London and New York: Routledge.

Tolson, Andrew. 1996. *Mediations: Text and Discourse in Media Studies*. London: Arnold.

Williamson, Judith. 1978. *Decoding Advertisements*, London: Marion Boyars.

Notes

1   This paper is a report on work in progress for my PhD, a study of how teenagers in Singapore and New Zealand respond to representations of race and gender in television advertising. As part of my research I have spoken with and listened to focus groups of students aged 16 to 18 in schools in both countries. (My deepest thanks to all the schools and students concerned for their cooperation.) The Drive

soap powder ad that this paper is based on was brought to my attention by a group of Auckland Asian students I interviewed in 1997. I was so struck by how irate they were that if the Drive ad was not brought up by subsequent groups I would introduce it myself as a topic for discussion.

2   My thanks to Ralf Harding, who was Account Director for Drive at the time in J. Walter Thompson in Auckland, for telephone and email conversations (Auckland, March 2001).

3   My thanks to Stephen Whiteway, Account Director for the Drive campaign at J. Walter Thompson in Sydney in 1997, for telephone and email interviews (March 2001).

4   An exception was a middle-class Pākehā female who read the ad as the victory of a woman over a young man.

5   The reference is to well known Māori comedian/entertainer Pio Terei.

6   *Homeward Bound* was a weekly New Zealand television drama in the early 1990s. The fact that B still recalls (or has been told about) a scene involving Pacific Islanders in this show could be seen as an indication of the power of representation.

7   Evidenced by the number of times non-Asian New Zealanders said 'I'd be upset if I was Asian'.

8   This was particularly apparent in the context of the whole interview, as until the point that they raised the Drive ad they had been extremely reticent and cautious about proffering opinions.

8 Television and Multiculturalism in Aotearoa New Zealand

SHUCHI KOTHARI,
SARINA PEARSON, AND
NABEEL ZUBERI

Multiculturalism is the return of the national repressed.

Barnor Hesse, 1999, p. 215

In effect the politics of difference insists that in recognizing my difference, if you wish to treat me equally then you may have to treat me differently.

Charles Husband, 2000, p. 212

Introduction

Television screens the nation, but it does so selectively. Screening has a double meaning; on the one hand it means 'to present', but it can also mean 'to hide'. While television presents images of the national to the citizens of a territory, it 'hides' or marginalises images and stories that are not considered central to national identity. The imagined community of the nation (Anderson 1991) represented on New Zealand television is partial. Non-white/non-Pākehā/non-European minorities are largely absent from the box. When they are present, their visibility is contained by a limited repertory of images that serves to reproduce hegemonic power relations in this settler post-colony. Critical media and television studies need to be sensitive to the continuing racism that pervades local and national institutions, cultural processes, and social experiences.

This chapter argues that television must more adequately represent the diversity of subjects, identities, and communities in an increasingly multi-ethnic Aotearoa New Zealand. First, this involves an engagement with debates about multiculturalism. These are important issues if we want the management of television, its production and programming to become more democratic and inclusive in the future. We argue for television that more thoughtfully addresses the similarities and differences between and within the 'old' and 'new' ethnicities (Hall 1989) that constitute the nation.

In one sense, television is already multicultural; people from various cultural groups occupy different types of programming produced here, in the United States, Australia, Britain, and other locations. Viewers compose their televisual experience from multiple sources. An analysis of how television 'deals with difference' must consider homegrown and imported programming on state-owned television, private 'free-to-air' channels, access and community television, as well as transnational networks like SKY that sell satellite and digital services to subscribers.

Watching television in Auckland, for example, may involve consuming versions of the multicultural from elsewhere together with those constructed in Aotearoa New Zealand. Some of these programs address their national diversity more directly than others. US dramas like *ER* and *The Sopranos*, UK comedies such as *Goodness, Gracious Me* and *The Kumars at No. 42*, US **sitcoms** like *Friends* and *Fresh Prince of Bel Air*, Chinese, Korean, and Indian films and dramas, Australian soaps like *Home and Away*, and Kiwi productions like *Shortland Street* and *Street Legal* all have a place in the television schedule. These shows and other forms of programming, such as news and advertising, project different local, national, and transnational imaginaries. The flows and interruptions of television images and sounds together with other cultural representations and discourses in 'mainstream' and ethnic media constitute a field of competing ideas about race and ethnicity interpreted by viewers in their everyday lives.

Following a general discussion of multiculturalism and television, we focus on one small but significant area of this variegated media landscape. We analyse two magazine programs broadcast on state-owned Television New Zealand (TVNZ) that have been designed specifically to address two minority groups, defined in New Zealand by the racialised/ethnic terms 'Pacific Islander' and 'Asian'. *Tagata Pasifika* and *Asia Down Under* exist on the margins of the 'mainstream' television schedule, but are broadcast on a national platform. Given the importance of public service broadcasting in the articulation of a democratic public sphere and cultural citizenship, the interrogation of these programs can shed some light on the virtues and limits, successes and failures of state-sponsored multicultural television. We hope this critique can contribute to the debate on multiculturalism in relation to the government's TVNZ Charter as it comes to affect national television policy and the diversity represented on screen.

Multiculturalism(s)

'Multiculturalism' is a descriptive term for ethnic diversity as well as a range of different philosophies, political positions, and cultural arguments about how a society organises this diversity. As Augie Fleras (1998, p. 66) points out, the concept 'simultaneously evokes a preference for consensus, but does so along a platform of criticism and reform; of hegemony yet resistance; of conformity yet diversity; of control yet emancipation; of exclusion yet participation; of compliance yet creativity... In short, multiculturalism can mean whatever meaning is assigned to it'. John Downing and Charles Husband (2002) also assert that we should consider multiculturalism as 'disputed terrain' rather than empirical reality. This terrain varies from nation state to nation state, though in all cases multiculturalism has been the focus for arguments about the impact of cultural difference on formulations of individual and group rights. According to Barnor Hesse, multiculturalism has become a 'floating signifier' that 'no longer signifies simply the celebra-tion or problem of cultural diversity, or the limited constitutional recognition of cultural difference; it can also refer to antagonisms between the sacred and the secular, educational pluralism, and the distribution of democratic rights in relation to "race", class, gender and sexuality' (Hesse 1999, p. 207). There is not enough space within this chapter to explore the breadth and depth of arguments around 'multiculturalism'. Here we can only suggest some of the contested and contradictory mobilisations of the term.

Writing in the Canadian context, Charles Taylor (1994) contends that multiculturalism is about 'the politics of recognition' and stages it as a struggle between universalism and particularism. This skates over the fact that the universalism of Western liberal humanism and the Enlightenment was founded on national, colonial, and imperial projects that were quite par-ticular about how certain groups of people were or were not included in the community or commonwealth. Not every individual or subject of empire was part of the 'invented tradition' of the nation (Hobsbawm and Ranger 1983). Critics of Canadian official multiculturalism argue that it has func-tioned as a governmentally devised social engineering project, designed largely to contain ethnic difference by making symbolic concessions to plurality without any substantial motion towards sharing power with Quebecois and First Nations peoples (Fleras 1998). Multiculturalism as a form of diversity management by the state can be a divide-and-rule strategy for the derailment of indigenous claims in many contexts, including Australia and New Zealand.

But multiculturalisms have also emerged from social movements, civil society, and the market, rather than the state. This has been the case in the United States. These multiculturalisms may rest on politically contingent and strategic claims, or on universalist claims to social equality, or on the basis of essentialist or absolute cultural differences. At the same time, discourses about ethnic, religious, and cultural 'tribalism' and apparently 'primordial' ethnicity have functioned to maintain white hegemony and an assimilation-ist paradigm in many Western multi-ethnic states. Considerable criticism has been meted out to subversive multiculturalisms. *Seattle Times* columnist Jerry Large describes America as essentially monocultural with superficial celebra-tions of cultural diversity: 'After we've sampled enchiladas and tofu, we expect to see some good old-fashioned assimilation' (Lange 2002, p. J2). Multiculturalist ideologies and discourses proliferate in the marketplace, sometimes critiquing ethnocentrism but also selling difference and cultural diversity only as far as they can be commodified as burgeoning market category or boutique exotica.

Many notions of multiculturalism also assume the nation and national-ism as the bedrock of identity. As Hesse (1999, p. 221) argues, 'it is only on the basis of this metaphysical conception of origin that the "imagined community" can be imagined systematically as a nation… But the chosen people are not reducible to nationalism; they may be gendered, sexualised, politicised in ways incompatible with its system'. The increased movement of refugees, asylum seekers, exiles, and economic migrants and the forma-tion of transnational diasporas foreground the irreducibility of culture to national origin and territory (Dayan 1999; Braziel and Mannur 2002).

However, the nation state and its institutions remain powerful and influential arbiters in the cultivation of a public sphere. Despite the agonistic plurality of politically conservative, essentialist, radical, and critical multicul-turalisms, the multicultural concept has produced a space in which one can argue about the continuous unfolding of the nation. Multiculturalism has mobilised ethnic minorities towards greater involvement in public and pri-vate institutions, and facilitated the critique of monocultural and essential-ist notions of subjectivity and collective identity.

Multiculturalism in Aotearoa New Zealand manifests aspects of consen-sual and critical multiculturalism but with a key difference in terms of how they are publicly recognised and valued. Oscillating between *de jure* biculturalism and a *de facto* multiculturalism, increasingly emphasised by the growing numbers of ethnic others in New Zealand, debates about diversity and nation have become predictably more fraught.

Biculturalism has been the 'preferred framework for government policy and organizational practice' (Fleras 1998, p. 78) for the last twenty years. Although debated in some form since the 1960s it was not until the mid

1980s that the relationship between the indigenous community (Māori) and colonising British settlers (Pākehā) was placed firmly on the political agenda (Larner 1993, p. 85). Broadly stated by Fleras (1998, p. 81), 'biculturalism emphasizes power sharing between two groups each of which is autonomous in its own right'. Despite official commitments to biculturalism, Māori cultural sovereignty in everyday life is hardly a political reality. In practice, biculturalism 'tends to focus on institutional accommodation by incorporating a Māori dimension into state practices and national symbols' (Fleras 1998, p. 81). Fleras summarises New Zealand's culturalist position (bi or multi) as, 'essentially a society-building exercise that seeks to depoliticize differences through institutional accommodation. In that current use [it] is consistent with Canada's consensus multiculturalism...the goal of...[which] is to make society safe from diversity, safe for diversity' (Fleras 1998, p. 85). Notwithstanding the degree, intensity, and implementation of an actual partnership, official bicultural rhetoric effectively means that Māori bicultural rights supersede the multicultural rights of immigrants. Therefore, New Zealand is a place in which multiculturalism as policy has been explicitly deferred. Nevertheless it lurks in the quotidian shadows as a de facto reality.

Aotearoa New Zealand needs greater public debate on the difficult intersections between biculturalism and multiculturalism. Discussions of Māori sovereignty should incorporate a vigorous conversation between citizens and residents from many communities. The future of a widely variegated national community cannot be deferred until the 'unfinished business' of Māori–Pākehā relations is 'sorted out'. Biculturalism as an ideology cannot become a closed conversation. But neither should multiculturalism be invoked to disable Māori claims and rights. The history of the colonial project and the postcolonial nation has involved the migration and settlement of ethnic others from many locations. This is neither a nation of only indigenous Māori or European settlers, nor simply two nations of these communities in one territory.

The application of a notion of differentiated citizenship rather than the universal citizenship at the heart of Western democracies might be one way towards a more multicultural Aotearoa New Zealand. Will Kymlicka (1995) argues that we can distinguish the historical experience of national minorities who governed themselves in a particular territory and were then incorporated into new nation states (such as Māori) from the experience of ethnic groups who came to those territories through migration. We can recognise specific rights for Māori and then other groups' rights. In a multi-ethnic society, the legal concept of group rights understands individuals as members of social collectives, not isolated subjects. The universalist position based on individual rights has unfortunately been the bulwark of assimilationist policies that have served the majority group, namely whites of European descent. In contrast, the concept of differentiated citizenship recognises what Kymlicka calls polyethnic rights. Downing and Husband point out that in, for example, Norway, Austria, Britain, and Australia, 'principles of polyethnic rights are to be widely found expressed in [media] practice' (Downing and Husband 2002, p. 9). While this is also the case in Aotearoa New Zealand in relation to Māori rights, the group media rights of other non-Pākehā groups have not been made explicit enough in policy or practice.

We acknowledge that Māori have certain foundational rights that have yet to be fully achieved in broadcasting and other cultural institutions and spaces in the nation. In addition, we wish to point to the current racial hierarchy of New Zealand. Within the national culture, apart from Māori, the claim to national belonging has been easier for white Europeans (Pākehā) than Pacific Islanders and Asians, however long they or their families have lived in this territory. In practice, the racism of skin colour determines that recent migrants of European descent, whether they come from Britain, Europe, or other settler nations, often acquire many of the same authorised privileges of national belonging as Pākehā descended from early settlers. Below them in the racial and ethnic order come the Pacific Islanders and in turn the Asians and other groups such as Africans and Arabs. Of course, this racialised order of national belonging does not neatly correspond to the relative economic and social power of particular ethnic communities, but it impacts upon the relative cultural representation of particular groups on television.

Multiculturalism in broadcasting

In many first world liberal democracies, broadcasting is regarded as a power-ful and persuasive technology for nation-building. In addition to the tech-nological advantages of simultaneity and virtually unprecedented scope for distribution, electronic media have supplanted print capitalism in the creation of what Anderson (1991) has called imagined communities. While these electronically mediated imagined communities have been increasingly celebrated as potentially post-national (Appadurai 1997), public broadcast-ing itself reflects the primacy of cultural nationalist agendas, many of which celebrate diversity only to the degree that it can be institutionally accom-modated within the national imaginary. Broadcasting has been a centralising force in nation states. In the New Zealand context, television is regarded as an important dimension of national culture. However, 'official culture' is a contested site, and the limited scope of ethnic television programming reflects ambivalence about the status of multiculturalism in New Zealand.

The Labour government's Charter for TVNZ (May 2001) states that TVNZ shall 'provide shared experiences that contribute to a sense of citizenship and national identity'. It also argues that TVNZ must 'ensure in its programs and program planning the participation of Māori and the presence of a significant Māori voice' and 'in its programming enable all New Zealanders to have access to material that promotes Māori language and culture'. However, the media rights of other non-Pākehā/European ethnic groups are relatively low on the list of priorities and barely hinted at in this document. The network should 'feature programmes that reflect the regions to the nation as a whole [and] promote understanding of the diversity of cultures making up the New Zealand population'. New Zealand On Air describes its financial commitment to 'special interest projects covering a wide variety of audiences including Asian and Pacific Island peoples, Christians, the gay community, rural and mixed ability communities' (http://www.nzonair.govt.nz). The media rights of ethnic minorities might need to be made more explicit in the TVNZ Charter for an increasingly multi-ethnic nation in the twenty-first century.

In the national 'free-to-air' broadcast system, Pacific Islanders and Asians have been accommodated by a very limited selection of programs that purport to address their cultural and social needs. For the most part these have been magazine programs, which cost less than other genres to produce (such as drama and comedy). Their segmented formats are more flexible, allowing them to address a variety of communities, which consist of ethnically, linguistically, and socially distinct national groups. These programs are typically scheduled in off-peak viewing hours (not between 6 and 10 pm) either late at night or early on weekend mornings.

Although deferred and depoliticised, New Zealand's brand of multiculturalism recognises some types of difference more readily than others. Pacific peoples, who constitute just over 6 per cent of the population, have claimed rights to media opportunities in television, as well as in short film and music (Pearson 1999, 2002) more frequently than their Asian counterparts, who make up just over 5 per cent of the national population. In part this is due to the fact that Pacific Island peoples have had a different history of migration to New Zealand. Many arrived between 1950 and the mid 1970s. Their children, who are New Zealand raised or born, tend to participate in New Zealand's culture industries at higher rates than other immigrant groups, the bulk of whom migrated later—in the 1980s and 1990s. There has been a substantial decrease in immigration from Pacific Islands to Aotearoa New Zealand in the last twenty-five years and most of the population increase in the Pacific Islands community is due to internally generated growth (http://www.stats.govt.nz/domino/external/web/prod_serv.nsf/htmldocs/Pacific+peoples). There are also differences in the modes of address used in various programs. *Tagata Pasifika*, which has been on the air for over a decade, is perceived by the Pacific community as a program produced by

Pacific peoples for Pacific peoples, whereas shows designed for the Asian community, such as *Asia Down Under,* have a more explicit mandate to make local Asian cultures accessible and assimilable to the European mainstream.

Tagata Pasifika

Tagata Pasifika is a half-hour weekly program that airs on Sunday mornings at 9.30 am. By government decree, TVNZ provides non-commercial, public service broadcasting on its schedule. The bulk of these programs are scheduled for Sunday morning. In addition to *Tagata Pasifika*, Māori programs *Marae* and *Waka Huia* air on Sunday morning. The show has been on air for over a decade, and receives major funding from New Zealand On Air (NZOA). It has been the most prominent and only national program broadcast for the Pacific Islands community in New Zealand. For the most part, *Tagata Pasifika* is structured as a magazine show. Presenters introduce segments on cultural, community, and educational events, sporting and social achievements, as well as entertainment. In addition to current affairs, the show features a range of other genres. It has aired a number of in-depth documentaries on topics such as tatau and it has broadcast short films such as the *Tala Pasifika* series, as well as Sima Urale's award-winning short film *O Tamaiti*. Music videos by artists such as King Kapisi, Che (Fu), and OMC are often incorporated into the show. And, *Tagata Pasifika* has produced a number of sketch comedies including *Tali's Angels*, a parody of the *Charlie's Angels* franchise, *Uncle Elivisi and Sione*, and the inimitable cooking show *Eaten Alive*, starring fa'afafine performers Buckwheat and Bertha. The program has an eclectic and varied approach in part because it caters to a diverse audience both in terms of ethnicity and age.

The Pacific community in New Zealand is itself multicultural. Some 115 000 Samoans account for a little over half the Pacific Island population, while Cook Islanders constitute 23 per cent, Tongans 18 per cent, and Niueans 9 per cent, followed by Fijians and Tokelauans (http://www.stats. govt.nz/domino/external/pasfull/pasfull.nsf/web/media+release+2001+ Census:+Pacific+Profiles+February+2003?open). As a group, Pacific Islanders tend to be younger than the national average and their numbers are increasing at a faster rate. Most live in and around urban metropolitan areas with high concentrations residing around Auckland and Wellington. By the middle of this century, it is likely that Pacific peoples will make up over 12 per cent of the national population.

The term Pacific Islander has been criticised as a pan-ethnic construct fashioned by 'outsiders—explorers, European colonisers, later anthropologists and archaeologists and now western bureaucrats, policy-makers, and Pacific Island elites' (Anae 1998, p. 108). Pan-ethnic terms such as Pacific Islander, which are imposed upon collections of culturally, socially, and historically distinctive communities have been described as homogenising. When perpetrated by a dominant society, pan-ethnic designations facilitate stereotyping and deny the self-determination of particular groups within nation states (Cornell 1995).

A similar dynamic underpins broadcast multiculturalisms in New Zealand. For example, in order for *Tagata Pasifika* to provide programming for such an ethnically diverse audience, it broadcasts in English. With respect to content, the producers acknowledge that the show occasionally spreads itself thinly to cover as many topics as possible (Stehlin 2001), in effect sacrificing depth for 'representative' coverage.

In addition to ethnic diversity, *Tagata Pasifika* also attempts to address a community that is fragmented in terms of age, experience, and expectation. On the one hand there is an ageing island-born audience, who expect *Tagata Pasifika* to deliver informational programming about traditional cultural events, and would prefer broadcasts delivered in vernacular languages. On the other hand, younger audiences want a show that is entertaining and relevant to their experiences as New Zealand-born-and-raised Pacific peoples. Therefore, *Tagata Pasifika* negotiates a field of proliferating expectations and desires, bearing the brunt of the burden of representation (Shohat and Stam 1994) because of its status as the *only* national program specifically for Pacific peoples. Overall, younger audiences watch the program less frequently, but of those who do, more demonstrate satisfaction with the show's relatively general cultural approach.

Despite some criticism about the linguistic and content constraints within which *Tagata Pasifika* operates, the show is regarded by the community as a significant resource particularly in terms of providing local news and transmitting Pacific cultures to its diasporic audience (NZOA 2001). While community interests are considered paramount, evidence suggests that Pacific communities regard informational broadcasting about Pacific peoples in New Zealand as an important intervention in creating and affirming New Zealand's multicultural society. When asked why programs for Pacific communities in New Zealand were important, 32 per cent of respondents cited news, 29 per cent cited keeping in touch with their culture, and 10 per cent cited multiculturalism (NZOA 2001, p. 25).

Although *Tagata Pasifika* is the only program specifically targeted at Pacific Island communities, New Zealand television features a number of other shows in which Pacific Islanders are represented. Characters appear on prime time including the New Zealand produced daily soap opera *Shortland Street*, dramatic **serials** such as *Street Legal* starring Jay Laga'aia, and figures such as Jonah Lomu appear in sports television. While these representations render Pacific peoples more visible in the national sphere than other ethnic minorities, they are represented in ways that 'mainstream' diversity.

Mainstreaming, the practice whereby ethnic minorities are cast in prime-time programs in ways that are culturally indistinct, allows national broadcasting systems to give the appearance of minority representation without challenging the culturalist status quo. These characters tend to be superficially ethnic; storylines rarely deal with culturally specific material in any consistent manner, and actors speak official languages (in this case English).

In addition to mainstreamed representations, Pacific Islanders have featured prominently in television sketch comedies. The now defunct *Milburn Place,* featuring the dysfunctional Semisi family was perhaps the most successful of this genre. Parodying prevalent stereotypes of Pacific Islanders as naïve, unemployed, addicted to television and gambling, lecherous, and corrupt, *Milburn Place* made fun of, and therefore disempowered those stereotypes for minority audiences. Unfortunately, these parodies may also have entrenched stereotypes for mainstream audiences who failed to recognise the ironic approach at work (Pearson 1999). Representations of Pacific peoples in various forms of mainstream broadcast media tend to reflect a limited and superficial mode of multiculturalism, in which difference is at once celebrated and contained. In the absence of a more varied selection of programs that reflect Pacific interests, various community groups have sought broadcast alternatives.

As has been the case in many multicultural settings, smaller, more specialised forms of broadcasting such as community access and cable have filled the lack of specialised ethnic programming in national broadcasting. Unlike New Zealand-based Asian migrants who can draw upon large, sophisticated media industries in their countries of origin (distributed by cable operators such as SKY), for culturally specific programming in a number of vernaculars, Pacific communities do not have a similar range of cultural products to choose from. Pacific Island nation states produce relatively small quantities of programming and rely upon larger cultural producers such as the United States, Australia, and New Zealand for the bulk of their broadcast content. However, New Zealand-based Pacific communities have initiated their own productions on non-commercial access systems such as Triangle Television, which broadcasts in the metropolitan Auckland area. In this format, Pacific Island communities can produce locally relevant content in relation to their own cultural values and concerns, and most importantly, in their own languages. Smaller communities within the designation Pacific Island, such as Tongans, of whom there are more than 30 000 residing in New Zealand, produce a number of programs for Triangle, including *Fafakitahi Navigator, Friendly Islands Vision, Ko E Pupunga Maama,* and *Le'o'o e Famili* (http://www.tritv.co.nz/local.htm). Despite increases in community access production, Pacific communities have expressed a need for increased programming by and about Pacific communities nationally. The reasons they cite include the establishment of positive role models, the maintenance of Pacific cultures, and the promotion of cultural awareness about Pacific cultures in the general population.

Asians occupy a quite different position in the hegemonic national imaginary of New Zealand. One popular perception constructs these New Zealanders as all recent immigrants, thus ignoring the presence of Asians in New Zealand since the nineteenth century. The times one hears a Pākehā Aucklander express surprise that some Chinese speak English with a Kiwi accent are too numerous to mention. Television and media discourse tend to elide the differences in histories of migration and settlement, social class, and diversity of national origins in resident and passport-holding Asian New Zealanders. Asians appear rarely on television. When they do they are represented stereotypically. In advertising Asians are typically cast as restaurant workers, dairy owners, and laundry owners. In soap operas and dramas, Asians tend to appear as morally corrupt businesspeople or communities that have failed to assimilate into the English-speaking culture of New Zealand. Television has shown little sensitivity to the differences between and within Chinese, Indian, Korean, Filipino, Japanese, Sri Lankan, Cambodian, Malay, Vietnamese, and Thai people. The one state-sponsored program focused on the articulation of New Zealand Asian subjectivities and identities is the magazine show *Asia Down Under* (http://www.nzonair.govt.nz/pag.cfm?i=421).

Asia Dynamic/Down Under

Asia Dynamic was first broadcast on TVNZ in 1994. It was produced by ETV, the educational television branch of TVNZ. In 1996, TVNZ decided to stop in-house production and contract the program out. Asia Vision, a production company formed by Robin Kingsley-Smith and Melissa Lee (who presented *Asia Dynamic* for ETV) successfully applied for the tender. Auckland-based Asia Vision has been producing the program since 1996. New Zealand On Air provides annual funding of $1 million to the company.

Asia Dynamic began its life on air on Sunday mornings as a twenty-nine-minute magazine show in a commercial-free slot. The address of the program was to Asians living in New Zealand. It was then moved to the commercial slot of Saturday morning and became a twenty-four-minute program. In 2001 the program's name was changed to *Asia Down Under* when TVNZ and Asia Vision agreed that the program would move to an 11 pm commercial slot on Thursdays. The hope on the part of the network and the production company was that the show would develop a 'crossover' audience of non-Asian as well as Asian New Zealanders. The new commercial time slot demanded a change of name and image to the more colloquial and local/regional *Down Under*.

When we interviewed the show's producers and director/reporters in July 2002, producer Robin Kingsley-Smith stated that: 'One of the things that the program says is that Asian people might have come from all sorts of different places, they might all look different, they may behave different, they have different religions, but they're all Kiwis'. He emphasised that just as the Southern Man is seen as the quintessential New Zealander, so should the 'Asian community' be seen as typically Kiwi. To say that Asians were now 'down under' was to acknowledge their physical presence and cultural acceptance in the nation.

The change of name and time slot proved successful in capturing a measure of the non-Asian professional audience, but at the cost of the program's Asian viewership. According to Kingsley-Smith, TVNZ was unable to provide a figure for the percentage of Asian viewers on Thursday nights, since it was so miniscule. Older Asian viewers had deserted the program due to its late time. In March 2002 the program moved back to its original non-commercial slot at 8.30 am on Sundays, a time when, according to Kingsley-Smith, most Asian families watch the show. The ratings since then have been the highest since the inception of the program in 1994.

Throughout the history of *Asia Dynamic/Down Under*, TVNZ and Asia Vision have been ambivalent about the show's audience. Who is the show really for? *Asia Dynamic* began as an ETV program largely for and about Asians in New Zealand. Kingsley-Smith said that before Asia Vision took over production, the show was a 'little inward looking'. He decided that it needed to expand its audience to include non-Asian viewers. He sees the purpose of the program as twofold: to serve the Asian community by reflecting it, and to offer the non-Asian viewer a better understanding of Asian people.

This dual agenda for the program might increase intercultural understanding. In fact, Asian television makers and viewers state their desire for a program that will 'explain' Asian communities to the non-Asian viewer. However, this risks representing New Zealand Asian life in an antiseptic and depoliticised way for the 'mainstream' audience. This may avoid 'ghetto-ising' an ethnic television program. But in the absence of any other New Zealand Asian programming, the burden of representation also falls on one show to make a broad range of Asian subjects and communities comprehensible to a largely Pākehā audience. The desire to make the cultural translation for the national community can reproduce the assimilationist imperative of national formation.

Asia Down Under's magazine format opens with a minute-long greeting and preview of the episode by presenter and executive producer Melissa Lee. This opening is usually shot on location in parks and gardens or plush interiors, but rarely in a New Zealand location that is actually peopled by

Asians other than Lee herself. Her introduction is followed by five stories, each four to five minutes long, a short section of community event notices, and a two-minute cooking segment at the end that is the show's most popular feature. On a few occasions, the show has departed from this format with longer stories such as one covering Afghani boys from the Tampa 'refugee ship', now at school in Auckland.

The production team is comprised of three full-time reporter-directors, a few part-time reporter-directors, and an editor. The Asian reporter-directors of each segment research, develop, direct, and present the story on location, then supervise the **post-production** adding voiceover narration. According to one reporter-director, they can suggest stories, but are mainly given assignments by the producer and executive producer.

Every program strongly features 'cultural events' such as festivals, sporting events, awards ceremonies, and felicitations. The reporter-directors confessed that such events were often tedious to cover due to the formulaic nature of these segments. 'Personal stories' of high achieving Asians constitute another segment type and trope of the program. We follow the struggles of an immigrant who has 'made it' in the new country. According to Kingsley-Smith, 'issues' become more palatable when they come tied to a 'human interest' story. But this approach often sacrifices social and political analysis for the narrative of an individual deemed 'representative' of the community. Little attention is paid to 'failure' since this might undermine any analysis of social inequality and racism. One reporter-director told us: 'Since the representation of Asians is very limited and *Asia Down Under* is considered a peripheral program, we are all the more conscious sometimes of not putting out negative representations. I mean the mainstream media does enough of that'. At the same time, this reporter acknowledged that 'we are a peripheral program, because we feel we have to do right by the community. In some ways it's a tunnel vision that keeps us ghettoised'. This reporter added, 'we need to widen the scope of our representation. Very often if you take one week's program and look at it, there are profiles, or stories about festivals or an event that is happening, and even when one of the stories is about something not so pretty, we have to prettify it. I have a strong sense that the program holds back instead of pushing any boundaries'.

Asia Down Under oscillates between its format as a magazine show and the desire of its reporter-directors for investigative journalism and topical current affairs stories. Occasionally segments cover such issues as cultural attitudes to abortion, the health risk incurred and engendered by Asian prostitutes new to New Zealand, human rights in Tibet, and India–Pakistan tensions. Some items deal with important news stories and events in Asian countries, but the emphasis is to affirm the Asian presence in New Zealand, and restate the hospitability of New Zealand as a nation. Reporter-directors also hope for a 'more flexible and organic format' that is less prescriptive and might accommodate aesthetic differences in the various segments.

Community notices about upcoming events, consisting of voiceover narration and graphics, were introduced to the show by Asia Vision to specifically address Asian viewers. The part of *Asia Down Under* with the largest 'crossover' appeal is undoubtedly the cooking segment in which a reporter either cooks an Asian dish, or elicits a recipe from someone's kitchen. One reporter-director noted that the show receives 3000 hits a week for the weekly recipe on its web site. As the recent prime-time documentary *A Taste of Place* (2001) illustrates, food and cooking on television are the safest way of consuming multiculturalism without necessarily engaging directly with different people. Asian identity can come to be defined predominantly by the more easily palatable signs of 'culture' such as food and music.

The program-makers of *Asia Down Under* have to negotiate a varied terrain of institutional and discursive regulations when they represent Asian New Zealand. Asia Vision needs TVNZ's approval for broadcasting and therefore is prone to the state broadcaster's own preferences about the show's format and presenters. From our critical point of view, the program's 'play it safe' tone tends to present Asians as nestling into the New Zealand narrative of an immigrant nation where everyone finds their place, but this place is assigned according to a social hierarchy of ethnic groups. Asian migrants are supposed to be grateful for the warm welcome of the host nation, but have little representation of their political claims in this homeland. In this televisual New Zealand, prejudice and discrimination appear as unusual interruptions within a nation-space marked by secure and (culturally) safe boundaries. The dislocation, relocation, cultural translation, and hybridisation of migrant populations (but never their 'hosts') are visited time and time again in *Asia Down Under* as the banal binary of 'culture clash': apparently age-old, unchanging traditions contrast with the ever mobile modernity of the West. 'How Chinese/Indian/Japanese/Korean/Sri Lankan et cetera, et cetera do you feel and how Kiwi do you feel?' might be the most asked question in *Asia Dynamic/Down Under*'s broadcast history. Rather than point to the cultural hybridity of all New Zealanders, this question ripples with anxiety. Every time we hear it asked, it sounds like a plea to become one of 'us', which means leaving that 'other' behind. 'Asianness' in the orientalist imaginary (Said 1979) has long been considered thoroughly 'alien' to occidental culture. As a settler nation in perpetual crisis about its fragile, postcolonial national identity, New Zealand has relied on a strong assimilationist discourse to support the cultural nationalisms of both right and left political persuasions. This has produced a concept of 'cultural safety' that is not so much about cultural *protection* or keeping New Zealand safe *for* difference, but keeping it safe *from* difference. This pervasive idea

Based round a fictitious North Island timber town, *Pukemanu* (1971) was the first television drama series to give a convincing impression of New Zealand rural life. Characters included Timber Company foremen Angus (Tama Poata) and Charlie (Ernie Leonard). Courtesy of TVNZ.

One of Ian Mune's first screen acting roles was in *Pukemanu* as truck driver Rod. Some viewers were disconcerted by *Pukemanu*'s down-to-earth style and colloquial accents. Courtesy of TVNZ.

Another milestone in the history of New Zealand television drama was *The God Boy* (1976), about a family tragedy seen through the eyes of troubled young Jimmy Sullivan (Jamie Higgins). His new bicycle has just been the subject of a fierce argument between his parents.
Courtesy of TVNZ.

The Governor (1977) was an important drama series based on New Zealand colonial history. Episode one ('The Reverend Traitor') focused on the signing of the Treaty of Waitangi in 1840. The mercurial Hone Heke was played by George Henare. Courtesy of TVNZ.

Shortland Street, a drama serial set in a private medical clinic, first appeared on TV2 in May 1992. Many of the cast quickly became national household names, including Dr Hone Ropata (Temuera Morrison) and Dr Chris Warner (Michael Galvin). © South Pacific Pictures Ltd.

This was the original 'core cast' of *Shortland Street*, New Zealand's first five-episodes-per-week 'soap opera'. © South Pacific Pictures Ltd.

The core cast of *Shortland Street*, photographed in May 2002 to commemorate the tenth birthday of the serial, includes well-known characters such as Rachel McKenna (Angela Bloomfield), Dr Chris Warner (original cast member Michael Galvin), Waverley Wilson (Claire Chitham), and Donna Heka (Stephanie Tauevihi). © South Pacific Pictures Ltd.

The choice of setting is a crucial part of any long-running drama series. Set in a small coastal town, *Jackson's Wharf* (1999-2000, TV2) centred on the sibling rivalry between two brothers – a local country cop and a sports star returning home from the big city. © South Pacific Pictures Ltd.

Marlin Bay (1991-1993, TV ONE) was set in and around a luxury lodge and casino in Northland, and explored the tensions between the down-to-earth local residents and those who worked and played at the lodge. Lucy Lawless (later famous as Xena) appeared in *Marlin Bay* as Chloe Miller. © South Pacific Pictures Ltd.

Since 2001 *Mercy Peak* (TV ONE) has focused on the lives, loves and adventures of the residents of a small town. Here, at the scene of a community tragedy, are (left to right): Dr Nicky Somerville (Sara Wiseman), Dr Alistair Kingsley (Craig Parker), Senior Constable Ken Wilder (Tim Balme, in the foreground), and vicar Wayne (Steven Moore). © South Pacific Pictures Ltd

Urban series include *The Strip* (since 2002), a comedy drama about Melissa Walker (played by Luanne Gordon) who leaves her job as a corporate lawyer to run a strip club. Her club features these 'Man Alive' male strippers. Produced by The Gibson Group for 3.

City Life (1996, TV2) was a relationship drama about the lives, loves and losses of a group of friends living in an apartment building in Auckland. © South Pacific Pictures Ltd

Street Legal (since 2000) centres round an inner-city legal firm. Characters include lawyers James Peabody (Dwayne Cameron), David Silesi (Jay Laga'aia), and Joni Collins (Kathleen Kennard), and Detective Senior Sergeant Kees Van Dam (Charles Mesure). Produced by ScreenWorks for TV2.

Mataku (2001-2002, TV3) was a 13-part anthology of Maori supernatural tales, written, directed, produced, acted and crewed by a predominantly Maori team. Simone Kessell starred in this episode (*The God Child: Tipua*). © South Pacific Pictures Ltd

Warwick Morehu as Te Tako in *The Sands of Time: Te One Tahua*, an episode from the *Mataku* series (2001-2002, TV3). © South Pacific Pictures Ltd

The comedy series *Market Forces* (1997 and 1999, TV ONE), written by popular playwright Roger Hall, revisited the characters of his earlier sitcom *Gliding On* about the public service of the 1970s, to see how John, Jim, Beryl and Hugh were grappling with the brave new world of the market economy. © South Pacific Pictures Ltd

Since 1986 the Topp Twins (Lynda and Jools) have been appearing on television as a popular comic and musical duo. Their many alter-egos include 'the Gingham Sisters', 'Camp Mother and Camp Leader', and 'the two Kens'. (Courtesy of Diva Productions.)

After Mikey Havoc and Newsboy (Jeremy Wells) had become well-known on student radio station 95bFM, they extended their unique brand of comedy to television. Their free-wheeling series for TV2 have included *Havoc Luxury Suites and Conference Facility* and *Havoc and Newsboy's Sell Out Tour*. (Courtesy of TVNZ.)

For its first two years South Pacific Pictures focused on children's and family dramas, including this popular science fiction series *Boy From Andromeda* (1990). © South Pacific Pictures Ltd.

Teen drama *Being Eve* (since 2001, TV3) has been a finalist in the International Emmys and a winner of gold and silver medals at the New York Festivals. Fleur Saville plays lead character Eve, seen here with Jay Bunyan as Sam. © South Pacific Pictures Ltd

House of Sticks (1997, Montana Sunday Theatre, TV ONE) illustrates the emotional intensity that can be produced by a one-off drama. A disturbed 13-year-old girl, played by up-and-coming actress Kate Elliott (left), responds to her unhappy family situation by making false allegations. © South Pacific Pictures Ltd.

The live-to-air, Maori language current affairs programme *Marae* has been appearing weekly on TV ONE since 1992. Its team of researchers and reporters explore social and political events from a Maori perspective. From left: Potaka Maipi, Lynette Amoroa, Lahni Sowter, Tahuru Tumoana, Shane Taurima, and Amomai Pihama. (Photo by Niels Schnipper, courtesy of TVNZ.)

For nearly a decade *Mai Time* has offered 'music videos, celebrity insights, and the happenings of young people in a bi-cultural, bi-lingual, and bi-funky mix'. Its presenters include Fiona Apanui, Patara Berryman and Wiparata Ngatoko. (Photo by Niels Schnipper, courtesy of TVNZ.)

New Zealand's best-known news readers are Richard Long and Judy Bailey who began presenting TV ONE's 6pm news in 1988. Long left in 2003. (Photo Monty Adams, courtesy of TVNZ.)

Paul Holmes began his broadcasting career with the NZBC in Christchurch in the early 1970s, and has gone on to become New Zealand's highest-profile broadcaster on both radio and television. His current affairs program *Holmes* appears on TV ONE. (Photo Monty Adams, courtesy of TVNZ.)

John Campbell and Carol Hirschfeld have been the popular co-anchors of 3 News since 1998. (Photo courtesy of 3.)

Fair Go is one of New Zealand's longest-running and highest rating programs. As a champion of consumer rights it offers a mixture of hard-nosed investigative reporting and more light-hearted stories. Kevin Milne (centre) has led the program for 18 years. (Photo Jae Frew, courtesy of TVNZ.)

Going Straight (2003) is a 'primetime action reality series' presented by Manu Bennett. In competing for a $10,000 prize, the contestants face three challenges that involve moving in a straight line without losing their nerve. (Produced by Touchdown Television for 3.)

Treasure Island (since 2000) is a survival challenge series that has been produced for broadcasters in three countries – New Zealand (TV2), Australia (Seven Network) and Ireland (RTE). The various versions of the series include 'celebrity', 'after dark' and 'extreme'. (Courtesy of Touchdown Television.)

The Zoo is a high-rating documentary/reality series that takes viewers behind the scenes of the Auckland Zoo. There have been five series on TV ONE since 1999. (Courtesy of Greenstone Pictures.)

Carters My House My Castle (2003) is a lifestyle program that covers all aspects of owning a home. Focusing on building and renovation, it is sponsored by a local supplier of building products. The team includes John Cocks, Robert Harle, Hamish Dodd, and Deb Hardy. (Produced by Touchdown Television for TV2.)

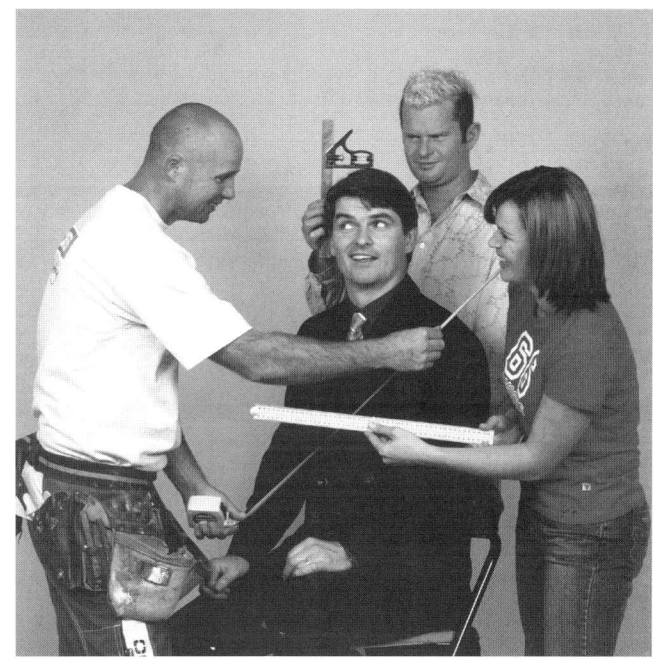

This frame enlargement shows the image of 'Mrs Lee looking knowingly at the camera' that is discussed in Sue Abel's chapter on student responses to a Drive television commercial. (Courtesy of J Walter Thompson.)

For over a decade now, the television magazine program *Tangata Pasifika* (TV ONE) has offered wide-ranging coverage of New Zealand's Pacific Islands communities. Its team, led by producer Stephen Stehlin (front row, left), reports on community events, politics, and the arts, and the program has also included some lively examples of sketch comedy, drama, and music. (Photo by Niels Schnipper, courtesy of TVNZ.)

Since 1996 *Queer Nation* (TV2) has provided an entertaining late night magazine program with a wide range of current affairs and lifestyle items about New Zealand's gay and lesbian communities. Its presenters include (from left): Rebecca Singh, Andrew Whiteside, and Kelly Rice. (Courtesy of Livingstone Productions.)

On the set of *Sticky TV*, a daily, after-school, children's program, presented by Paul Delamere and Anna Hart. (Produced by Pickled Possum Productions for 3.)

For seven years *Squirt*, the Saturday morning children's show, has been bringing together a fascinating mix of computer-animated and human characters. Its games, cartoons and competitions are presented by Matt Gibb with the help of co-hosts Spike T. Penguin and Newt, the Irish fish. (Taylormade Productions for TV2.)

Triangle Television has been broadcasting to the greater Auckland region since August 1998 on UHF channel 41 from a house in Grey Lynn. Led by Jim Blackman, it has become New Zealand's best known regional and community television station. (Courtesy of Triangle Television.)

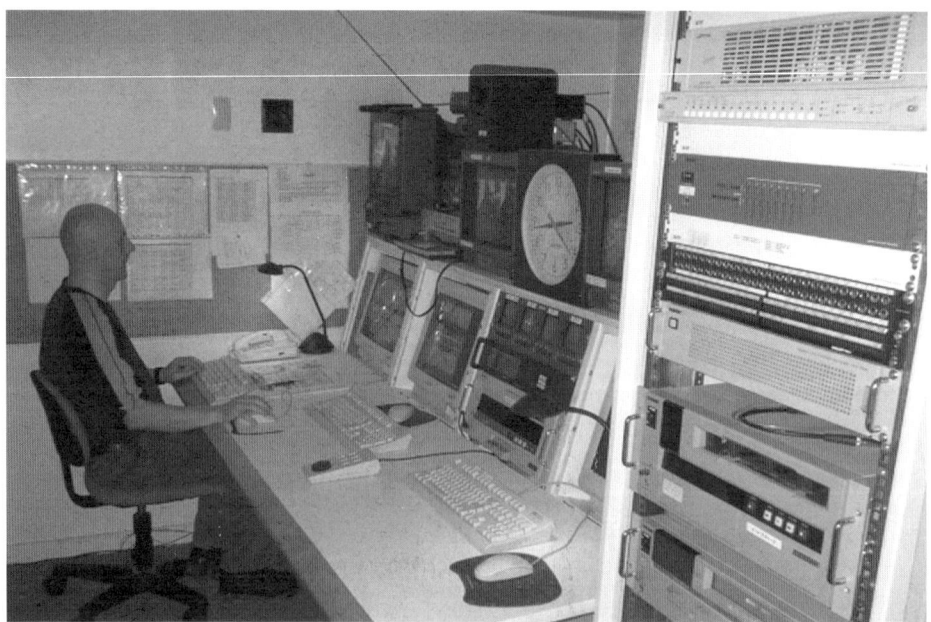

Though the control centre of Triangle Television's operations is tiny by traditional broadcasting standards, its digital system is able to keep the station's 24-hour-a-day program on air, and to record satellite 'feeds' from round the world, including Deutsche Welle German TV and Worldnet Television from the USA. Courtesy of Triangle Television.

implies that cultural difference is something inherently *dangerous*. The current journalistic and academic discourse about 'ethnic cleansing', violence, and apparently primordial propensities to behave 'ethnically' in many contexts has amplified this popular resonance of the term 'cultural safety'. Such an argument, as Downing and Husband (2002, p. 6) state, 'tends to treat ethnicity as though it were in essence a particularly potent kind of dynamite', and obscures the peaceful co-existence of various ethnic communities, even those that have resorted to violent conflict at particular times in their histories.

Conclusion

Television constructs images of the nation selectively. As reflected in state-sponsored multicultural programming, New Zealand regards itself in some limited ways as a Pacific nation, and struggles with the notion that Asian immigrants might be more than permanent guests. These regimes of representation not only reflect the relations of power in New Zealand, but they have a significant effect on the balance of power in the national sphere.

Our national television needs to more actively engage with the historical and everyday interactions between various social groups, and to represent the intercultural and polyethnic reality of life in this nation. This means facing up to both the agonistic and affirmative in our island stories. Race and ethnicity must be discussed in less fearful and more relational terms. Broadcasting can widen and enliven the possibilities of representation for non-Pākehā and non-Māori New Zealanders, behind the scenes, on the screen, and as audiences and active participants in public culture. We hope that in future *Tagata Pasifika* and *Asia Down Under* bear less of a burden to represent their respective minority groups, and that Pacifikan and Asian New Zealanders will appear throughout television programming—not as token symbols of 'inclusion' but on their own terms in sitcoms, dramas, reality television, and so on. Only that way will we engender a richer understanding of the different publics that constitute the national polity. Discussions in academia, the media, parliament, and other public sites routinely centre on the need to examine and articulate New Zealand national identity in and through institutions, texts, and practices. What cannot be taken for granted is that the identity under debate is singular or static.

References

Anae, Melani. 1998. Fofoai-i-vao-'ese: The Identity Journeys of NZ-born Samoans. Thesis (PhD), Department of Anthropology, University of Auckland.

Anderson, Benedict. 1991. *Imagined Communities: Reflections on the Origin and Spread of Nationalism* (Revised Edition). London and New York: Verso.

Appadurai, Arjun. 1997. *Modernity at Large*. Minneapolis: University of Minnesota Press.

Braziel, Jana Evans & Anita Mannur (eds). 2002. *Theorizing Diaspora: A Reader.* Oxford: Blackwell.

Cornell, S. 1995. 'Ethnicity as Narrative: Identity Construction, Pan Ethnicity and American Supatribalism', Paper presented to the *Ethnicity, Multiethnicity Conference*, Brigham Young University, Laie.

Dayan, Daniel. 1999. 'Media and Diasporas', in Jostein Gripsrud (ed.), *Television and Common Knowledge*. London and New York: Routledge, pp. 18–33.

Downing, John & Charles Husband. 2002. 'Intercultural Communication, Multiculturalism and Social Inequality', a discussion paper for the *2002 IAMCR Conference Special Sessions on Intercultural Communication*, Barcelona, 21–26 July, pp. 1–23.

Fleras, Augie. 1998. 'Working Through the Differences: The Politics of "Isms" in Aotearoa', *New Zealand Sociology*, 13(1), pp. 62–96.

Hall, Stuart. 1989. 'New Ethnicities', in David Morley & Kuan-Hsing Chen (eds) *Stuart Hall: Critical Dialogues in Cultural Studies*: London and New York: Routledge, pp. 441–9.

Hesse, Barnor. 1999. 'It's Your World: Discrepant M/multiculturalisms', in Phil Cohen (ed.) *New Ethnicities, Old Racisms*. London: Zed Books.

Hobsbawm, Eric & Terence Ranger. 1983. *The Invention of Tradition*. Cambridge: Cambridge University Press.

Husband, Charles. 2000. 'Media and the Public Sphere in Multi-Ethnic Societies', in Simon Cottle (ed.) *Ethnic Minorities and the Media*. Buckingham, Philadelphia: Open University Press, pp. 199–214.

Kymlicka, Will. 1995. *Multicultural Citizenship.* Oxford: Oxford University Press.

Lange, Jerry. 2002. 'We Like Ethnicity Worn as a Festival Costume', *Seattle Times*, 14 March, p. J2.

Larner, Wendy. 1993. 'Changing Contexts: Globalization, Migration, and Feminism in New Zealand', in Sneja Gunew & Anna Yeatman (eds), *Feminism and the Politics of Difference*. Boulder: Westview Press pp. 85–102.

New Zealand On Air. 2001. *Impressions of* Tagata Pasifika *and Programming Reflecting the Pacific Community: The Pacific Island Community's Perspective. Combined Qualitative and Quantitative Report*. Available from http://www.nzonair.govt.nz/pag.cfm?i=460 [accessed 14 September 2001].

Pearson, Sarina. 1999. 'Subversion and Ambivalence: Pacific Islanders on New Zealand Prime Time', *The Contemporary Pacific*, 11(2), pp. 361–88.

Pearson, Sarina. 2002. 'Moving Image and Photography: Picturing New Zealand as a Pacific Place' in Sean Mallon & Fuli Pereira (eds), *Art Niu Sila*. Wellington: Te Papa Press, pp. 135–49.

Said, Edward. 1979. *Orientalism*, New York: Vintage.

Shohat, Ella & Robert Stam. 1994. *Unthinking Eurocentrism: Multiculturalism and the Media*. New York: Routledge.

Statistics New Zealand, *New Profiles on Pacific Communities*. Available from http://www.stats.govt.nz/domino/external/pasfull/pasfull.nsf/web/media+release+2001+Census:+Pacific+Profiles+February+2003?open [accessed 19 February 2003].

Statistics New Zealand, *Pacific Peoples*. Available from http://www.stats.govt.nz/domino/external/web/prod_serv.nsf/htmldocs/Pacific+peoples [accessed 19 February 2003].

Stehlin, Stephen. 2001. Lecture, Research Methods, Department of Film, Television & Media Studies, University of Auckland.

Taylor, Charles. 1994. 'The Politics of Recognition', in David Theo Goldberg (ed.), *Multiculturalism: A Critical Reader.* Oxford (UK) and Cambridge (USA): Blackwell, pp. 75–106.

Triangle Television, *Locally Provided Or Produced Programmes.* Available from http://www.tritv.co.nz/local.htm [accessed 26 May 2002].

9 Children's and Youth Television:

The Most Important Genre?

GEOFF LEALAND

Children's television, who really cares? Trust me, commercial television stations do!

Cherrie Bottger 1999, p. 90

The metaphors employed by children's marketers [include] 'netting', 'hooking', 'luring', … the 'elusive', 'restless', 'ever shifting', 'changing', 'fickle', 'sophisticated', 'savvy', 'media aware' child audience.

Ruth Zanker, 2001 p. 130

Since the beginnings of television in New Zealand in the early 1960s, there has been children's television, of both the imported and local variety. In the following decades, the 'youth' audience was likewise discovered and provided for. Those who were children in the 1960s are now middle-aged, with children (or even grandchildren) of their own. In their footsteps have followed another three or four generations of children and teenagers.

During these years, television has provided an ever-present and reliable source of entertainment and education for New Zealand children. Television has always regarded young New Zealanders as a special audience, with markedly different needs and wants from adults. Television has undoubtedly been a potent influence in the lives of New Zealand children and teenagers, in the forty years of its existence. Nevertheless, it is probably impossible to measure quite how influential it has been. There is little local research on children's television, and only very recently has there been any significant academic attention to this area of children's lives (Lealand 1995, 2001a, 2001b; Zanker 1999, 2001; Todd and Richardson 2001; Walters and Zwaga 2001). Children's television has always been a significant part of the New Zealand television landscape, but it has always faced considerable barriers on the road to public interest, understanding, and approval. There have been other problems, which will be explored in this chapter. These include problems that can be found in other areas of New Zealand television (the struggle between commercial pressures and public service objectives, for example) but such points of conflict are often more visible and attenuated in children's and youth television.

The absence of close academic scrutiny of children's and youth television is not exclusively a New Zealand trait. Discussions of the child or youth television audience seldom feature in the big books about television—those texts that attempt to take a broad sweep across the terrain. John Fiske's 1987 seminal text *Television Culture* has no index listing for 'child' or 'youth' and the regular updates of the Horace Newcomb-edited collection *Television: The Critical View* include a range of adult genres and perspectives on the adult audience, but very little on young viewers. It is assumed, it seems, that the audiences are all grown up, as are the programs they watch.

Nevertheless, perspectives on the child and youth television audiences can be found in a growing list of specialist titles, including academic work shaped by cultural studies perspectives (such as Buckingham 1993, 1996, 1999, 2000; Davies 1989, 1997, 2002), or more polemical work from North America (such as Winn 1977; Postman 1983, 1985). There are many more articles, monographs, and reports on children and television (it is one of the most vigorous and sustained areas of media research) but there are few occasions when the generational divide between adult interests and children's interests is bridged. Attention to children's television is left to those who specialise in this area, and the arguments tend to be fierce and prolonged.

There are a number of reasons why children's issues and children's television do not get the attention they deserve from other sectors, such as producers, television executives, and policy-makers. This continuing neglect is both unwarranted and unwise, but there are explanations as to why it persists. These include:

- Children's television is regarded as childish by many producers, policy-makers, and academics. This may, in turn, be a reflection of broader attitudes to television as a populist and entertainment-led medium, as John Hartley argues in his *Tele-ology: Studies in Television*: 'For the industry, television is a *paedocratic regime*. The audience is imagined as having child-like qualities and attributes. Television discourse addresses its viewers as children' (1992, p. 108). The desired audience is encouraged to look up, be expectant, open, willing to be guided and gratified, whenever television as an institution exclaims: 'Hi, kids!' (1992, p. 111).

- Funding agencies, producers, schedulers, and politicians are often not familiar with children's television and the complexities of children's culture. There is great dependency on 'commonsense' versions of childhood, dominated by rhetoric of the 'vulnerable child' and the need for 'protection'. For many in the television industry, children's television does not have the cultural standing of the genres of sport, drama, documentaries, and current affairs. At best, children's television is regarded as a training ground, with production dominated by a small cohort of female producers and directors.

- In the case of New Zealand, it is now assumed that New Zealand On Air and Te Mangai Paho (TMP) 'will provide', with broadcasters making little or no effort to produce either in-house or commissioned children's programming. In 2001, for example, the only locally made children's television programs not funded by NZOA were repeats of *Buzz and Poppy* (NZOA 2002, p. 19)

Set against this long-term neglect or intransigence is compelling evidence that, in the case of New Zealand (as elsewhere), a vigorous children's television sector is vital to New Zealand television, in terms of the future health of broadcasters and program-makers, as well as the parents and children of New Zealand (thus the sub-heading of this chapter). The reasons for this include:

- *Audiences for the future*

Children grow up to become adult television viewers. Without vigorous and sustained efforts to provide for them and build their loyalty to television as the most valued leisure choice, there may be no audience for television in the future—and no audience for New Zealand television. Ensuring future audiences is critical as television positions itself in a new environment of rapidly changing technology, media proliferation, and increased global pressures.

- *Children love television*

Even though leisure choices for children are proliferating, television remains so far the preferred medium for New Zealand children. Recent research on New Zealand 8–14 year olds (Lealand 2001a) reports that watching television on a daily basis is the activity shared by the greatest number of children, with the most favoured time for viewing being after school (96 per cent watched television 'usually' or 'sometimes' post-school). We cannot, however, assume that this will always be so. Children are increasingly having access to their own media, most particularly in the private spaces of their bedrooms. Indeed, overseas research is suggesting the rise of a 'bedroom culture', where children (with the assent of parents and caregivers) are developing their own media centres, adding computers and mobile phones to personal TV sets. Their use is frequently removed from the direct scrutiny and intervention of adults. For example, Livingstone and Bovill (1999) report that, in the final year of the last decade, more than two-thirds (63 per cent) of British children had a TV set and 16 per cent had a computer in their bedroom. New Zealand research (Lealand 2001a) produced comparative figures of 30 per cent with a TV set and 29 per cent with a computer in their bedroom.

• *Children's television is a site of controversy*

It is in the world of children's television—most especially in New Zealand—that the tensions and debates about the competing purposes of television are most vividly played out. Television provides the touchstone for critical issues, which embrace both the local and the global. Issues include providing for New Zealand children as members of global communities (fans of imported popular culture, from the dominant cultural production centres of the USA, Europe and Asia), and 'Kiwi kids' (users of locally produced television entertainment).

The relationship between children and television is also a perennial site for various kinds of alarms and accusations, moral grandstanding, and power struggles. Much rhetoric and discussion is generated but less understanding or clarity of thought. It is significant, for example, that a considerable proportion of the *Free-To-Air Television Code of Broadcasting Practice* (August 2001) is devoted to the 'protection' of the child viewer. The 'Preamble' of the *Code* acknowledges New Zealand's compliance with the United Nation's *Convention on the Rights of the Child*, while Standard 9: Children's Interests sets out a lengthy list of guidelines. Standard 9d, for example, instructs broadcasters to 'have regard to the fact that children tend to watch television through to midday on Saturday and Sunday mornings, and during school and public holidays'. This is one of the areas where social objectives and commercial objectives coincide, with 'protection' of the New Zealand child remaining the primary ethos of both legislated regulation (the Broadcasting Standards Authority) and self-regulation (the Television Code). In many respects, the concept of 'protection' persists as an under-interrogated rationale, or reflects a lack of clarity about the nature of contemporary childhood. Does 'protection' mean shielding children from exploitation, or protection from their own base instincts (with young girls preferring the proto-sexual appeal of Britney Spears to the 'innocent' delights of Noddy and Big Ears)? The construction of 'childhood' employed in these circumstances is often rife with class and generational assumptions, centred on competing notions of the purpose of television and 'quality'.

• *Children's concerns are central to public service television*

Children's television remains one of the primary sites for continuing debates about public service provisions in state-owned or state-funded national television systems. In many ways, adequate levels of 'quality' children's programming is regarded as the 'litmus test' of judging whether voluntary or regulated cultural or social objectives have been met. This applies in countries where there is minimal intervention or regulation (the obligations placed on the major US networks by the Federal Communications Commission, for example), and in countries where there are requirements and monitoring, with regard to stipulated levels of children's programming, for both commercial and non-commercial television systems. In Australia, for example, the Australian Broadcasting Authority (ABA) ensures the three commercial networks meet legislated criteria for Australian-produced children's and pre-school programming. In the United Kingdom, the Independent Television Commission (ITC) monitors the efforts of the major commercial networks in this area. Locally, NZOA is specifically required to identify and provide for children and youth, and the *Television New Zealand Charter* (May 2001) states that TVNZ shall

- feature programs that provide for the informational and entertainment needs of children and young people and allow for the participation of children and young people.
- maintain and observe a code of ethics that addresses the level and nature of advertising to which children are exposed.

- *The production base of New Zealand children's television is particularly fragile*
 In New Zealand, children's television is probably the most fragile sector of television production. All sectors of local television production live with levels of uncertainty and doubt but those involved in children's television production never know whether accumulated skills and resources will have any future use, beyond the short-term relief of the annual NZOA funding round. There are few voices to support their cause, with professional groups such as SPADA (Screen Producers and Directors Association) displaying only fitful interest in this area. It is left to NZOA, part-time lobby groups such as the Christchurch-based Children's Television Foundation, and individual producers to champion the cause of children's television. Such constraints and possibilities have always been factors in the production of children's television in New Zealand, an area of cultural production that has had a long and complex history.

Making children's television in New Zealand

TVNZ once had a Children's and Young Person's Department, but it was dispensed with as the network cut costs in the 1980s, with a residual children's production unit operating out of Christchurch until 1998, when it was forcibly moved north to make use of under-utilised production facilities at the Avalon Studios in Lower Hutt. Such moves were one outcome of TVNZ's desire to centralise operations in Wellington and Auckland. The

Avalon facilities continue to produce the long-running magazine program *What Now?*, which screens on weekday afternoons, as a mixture of pre-recorded **interstitials** (segments of presenter chat or continuity) and imported animation, and Sunday mornings, which feature a live studio-based format.

What Now? first appeared on Saturday morning television in 1981, as a thirty-minute program directed by Rex Simpson. By 1995, it had grown into a three-hour magazine program. It remains the primary production site of children's television, supplying TVNZ with a stream of daily and week-end programming. Other production companies, working in the independent sector, provide program strands to both TVNZ and other broadcasters in the specialist pre-school area, such as *Bumble* (Bumble Productions for TVNZ), or in the early primary programs such as *Suzy's World* (Treehut Productions for TV3). In 2002, *Sticky TV* (produced by Mary Phillips) provided direct competition in the form of a similar magazine format to *What Now?* Phillips also produced the pioneering pre-school series *You and Me* (fronted by Suzy Cato), which went to air on TV3 in July 1992. This series, the first all-New Zealand pre-school program, was funded by NZOA and was the outcome of competitive bidding between rival propositions.

Another program strand is Māori-language children's programming such as *Tikitiki* (Te Aratai Productions) or youth programming such as *Pūkana* (Cinco Cine). But, irrespective of their production source, all New Zealand-made children's programming intended for local screening shares a common characteristic. Since 1988 all such programming has been funded from the public purse, either through an annual NZOA funding allocation (for programming in English) or through TMP (for Māori language programming).

This means that a very important genre on New Zealand television has been supplied at minimal cost to television companies, enabling them to fill regular program slots very cheaply while earning significant revenue from the sought-after commercial space associated with such programs. They also acquire assured local content, which serves to fill schedule slots that might not otherwise be filled. This, in effect, suited the commercial imperatives of New Zealand television during the 1990s wherein children's and teen programming did not have a clear remit. It was regarded as still necessary to meet residual public service objectives, but also as a bit of a nuisance in a commercial environment that was profit-driven.

Afternoon programming for under-fives, or the 'pre-school' audience, occupies one of the few remaining commercial-free spaces in the schedules of New Zealand free-to-air broadcasters. This audience is also spared the attentions of ratings measurement as New Zealand viewers are judged to come of age when they turn five. There is also a commercial-free space on Sunday mornings, for *What Now?*, but this has been at some cost to the viability of this long-running magazine program. It chooses, for example, to buy its own prizes for competitions, rather than opting for contra deals which might require further exposure for sponsors or advertisers.

The changing audience

For the purposes of television in New Zealand, the 'child audience' is regarded as comprising the age group five to twelve years. The 'youth audience' is generally regarded as those aged between thirteen and twenty years. But in an argument to be developed shortly, both 'child' and 'youth' are very loose terms and open to interrogation. This is partly a consequence of the questionable age categorisation; most twelve-year-olds, for example, would regard themselves as occupying a very different universe to five-year-olds. It is also a reflection of the slippages between stages of development, as babies grow to adulthood, as well as the emergence of new formations of life stages.

The logic of television scheduling for children and teens in New Zealand is that it mirrors the patterns of daily life. Before school hours provide mainly imported animation, while after-school programming (post–3 pm) starts with pre-school programming (in April 2002, for example, updated series of *Bill and Ben* and *Noddy*), then progressively ages upwards as school-age children begin to arrive home.

One manifestation of the changing audience is the 'ageing-up' or 'aspirational' behaviour of pre-adolescents or 'tweenies'. This new phenomenon refers both to *The Tweenies*, the BBC program designed to appeal to four- to six-year-olds (screening on TV2 in 2002), but also the cohort of boys and girls on the borders of teenage-hood. The editor of the international trade magazine *KidScreen* describes it thus:

> …one over-arching demographic shift that seems to be shaping many a 2001 gameplan is the growing importance of the tween set. A decade-long baby boom means that the bulk of the overall kids demo is now aging into the 10 to 14 age bracket. And while the sheer potential size and spending power of this group is appealing enough on its own…the real dangling carrot is that tweens, more than any other demo, are utterly consumed by the task of carving out their personal identities. And how do they do that? By 'discovering' and latching on to new pop culture entries with a proprietary fierceness that you just don't see with teens (whose responses are requisitely muted by a wash of apathy and detachment), or younger kids and preschoolers (whose moms are still largely guiding their entertainment experiences).
>
> Longworth 2001, p. 10

This is a phenomenon of intense interest to advertisers and marketing, not only restricted to the United States. The New Zealand population, as at 31 December 1999, showed a similar demographic bulge in the ten-to-fourteen age group, with 286 270 at this stage, compared with 271 570 aged fifteen-to-nineteen (Statistics New Zealand 2001). As a consequence, 'tweens' present a similar problem of definition and understanding for New Zealand producers, funders, and schedulers, as childhood seems to be collapsing, and possibly disappearing, with children, 'a generation stuck on fast forward… One minute they're crawling around in the sandbox, the next day they're trawling the internet' (Kantrowitz and Winger 1999, p. 64).

The problem for television producers, funders, and schedulers in New Zealand and abroad, is how to juggle different expectations of children's programming, to meet the desire of its young audience for the latest fashions, while providing material that will satisfy the expectations of parents, educators, and lobbyists who seek the certainty of older styles and imperatives (such as 'educational value'). To put it another way, children want news about the latest pop fad and fart jokes; their parents want polite dramas with well-behaved children, and talking trains or rabbits.

Children's programming, and its potential to shape or encourage consumption, has divided into two camps. On one side there are advertisers, marketers, and commercially oriented television executives who argue that the unfettered celebration of consumption and fashion-following is what should rule. In this argument, there should be a congruency between the interests of advertisers and the desires of children, as in the following assertion from the New Zealand advertising industry newsletter *Fastline:* 'This brings back to us the whole debate about advertising to children and the weighty bureaucracy tied up in ensuring these "vulnerable" people are not exploited. And leads us to observe that advertising and viral marketing are an everyday part of adult life, and the sooner kids learn about this stuff the better they'll be equipped to survive in the real world' (2002, p. 3).

On the other side of the divide are voices such as the Children's Television Foundation and the Commissioner for Children, politicians from the Green Party, concerned parents, and the occasional commentator calling for increased 'protection' of 'these vulnerable people', as in the following criticisms from media columnist John Drinnan: 'One glaring example of the problems at TVNZ is its cynical approach to advertising aimed at small children… You have to wonder about the vision for a public broadcaster that recognizes the need for easy-to-manipulate tiny tot viewers to watch ad-free programming but still targets its most vulnerable viewers' (2002, p. 25).

Despite these divisive versions of children's needs, there is general agreement that there is an identifiable stage of life called 'childhood', with clear parameters of chronological years, and intellectual and emotional indicators. The category of 'youth', however, is more of a problem. According to conventional wisdom (and market research-speak), the age cohort of 'youth' is a sub-set of the age category known as 'Generation X'. Treading on the heels of Generation X is the 'Millennial Generation', which currently includes 'childhood'. According to Walker (2001, p. 7), the attributes of these two generations are:

- Generation X (1965–1985): Much maligned, wanted careers, listened to grunge, and cultivated a sense of ennui.
- Millennial (since 1985): Materialistic, savvy, wise to the world, and technologically literate.

Of course, this urge to categorise and name generations has a long history (from the 'Lost Generation' of the 1920s, to the 'Me Generation' of the 1980s). The labels continue to change and also become rather self-fulfilling. Despite their allure, it is important to continuously examine what (or whose) purpose they serve, and they should never stand in place of deeper, research-based investigations of changes in children's and teen culture.

Funding children's television in New Zealand

It is in the genres of both children's and youth programming that the problems and issues of New Zealand television are most transparent, urgent, and insistent. The slippery nature of the child audience is just another element in a particular sector of television that has always struggled to reach its objectives, to satisfy the competing needs of various constituencies, and to gain a credibility often denied it. It is in children's and youth television that issues and arguments, explored in other contributions to this collection, are most actively played out.

In addition to the problems already alluded to, a number of significant factors shape children's and youth programming in New Zealand. The strategy of funding the bulk of locally produced children's and youth programming through an annual tendering round initiated by NZOA is the major determinant of what gets made and what gets seen. Over the twelve or more years NZOA has intervened in this area, it has had to deal with a set of constraints and considerations. It has, for example, needed to balance the necessity for 'bulk' funding of long-run series, with a desire to fund high-production short-run productions—a balance that is sometimes, and rather simplistically, couched in terms of 'quantity' versus 'quality'. Broadcasters have also regularly come to the annual NZOA funding round with very firm ideas about 'what will work' for the New Zealand child and teen audience, and this has led to a dependence on proven formats and conservative content. Nevertheless, it has also produced programming that is both commercially successful and audacious in content. One example of this is the *Havoc and Newsboy* series (their *Sell-out Tour* and *Convention and Conference Centre* series).

But compatibility between the competing objectives of the broadcaster and NZOA does not always occur. As in other genres, producers of children's programming are constrained by the need to have a scheduling promise from the broadcasters before they turn to NZOA for funding. Neither does NZOA have full freedom to fund everything it desires to see on air. The broadcasters, in turn, have to make certain compromises to ensure they gain largely cost-free programming, to fill pre-determined slots. In this respect, the power to determine what local children's and youth programming is funded, made, and scheduled is diffused across a range of stakeholders. In the last two years, another stakeholder has been added through the intervention of new government policy and the directives of the TVNZ Charter.

As already described, the funding of most locally produced children's and youth programming comes from the public purse, with successful program proposals receiving the bulk of their production costs from the annual (October–November) special funding round conducted by NZOA. Long-running series, such as *What Now?*, look to this annual event for funding for the following year but new proposals are given equal consideration. According to Zanker (2001b, p. 155), during the 1990s 'NZ On Air gave between $6 to $10 million annually to children's genre'. In the 1999–2000 funding year, it provided $10 million of funding for production of around 370 first-run hours in the genre (New Zealand On Air 2002, p. 19). According to their Statement of Intent 2001–02, released in August 2001, NZOA intended to regard children's and youth programming as a 'high priority', with a slight increase in funding of $0.8 million during 2001–02, in addition to a larger one-off allocation of $2.2 million for children's drama.

Even though there most probably would have been little or no locally produced children's and youth programming on New Zealand television screens in the 1990s, if such provision had been left up to the broadcasters, the current structure has led to certain constraints and uncertainties. The production cycles tend to lurch from year to year, with no certainty of on-going funding or production in the coming years. The presence of children's programming, in particular, is swelled by high levels of repeats. Even though this is not necessarily a bad thing (pre-school producers, for example, have always usefully and legitimately recycled their programs to old and new audiences), repeats can sometimes displace the need to provide first-run material, as Zanker argues:

> By 1999 funders found they were locked into a funding pattern dominated by commitments to certain big key daily programs for primary-aged and early childhood. This left little discretionary funding with which to broaden the range and delivery to the children's audience. By 1998 the chair of NZOA expressed the view that children's programming was in danger of being diluted by repeats and cheaper programs. First run children's programs were down 125 hours since 1995 (*New Zealand On Air Content Survey*, 1998). Whilst some of this lowered hours output could be attributed to more expensive genre like computer-generated

Squirt, most was due to the fact that there had been no increase in the licence fee during a decade of rising production costs. After a peak reached in 1992, as a result of the new indigenous early-childhood program (*You and Me*) coming on air, children's broadcast hours during the 1990s were only boosted by early-childhood repeats.

2001, p. 156

In their local content survey of 2000, NZOA reported 'a continuation of the decline in this genre that has followed since the high of 1265 hours recorded in 1992'. They also noted that repeat screenings tended to add significantly to overall totals, especially in respect of TV3, where repeats comprised 80 per cent of its total children's hours. Repeats on TV2 were one-third of total hours. In their local content survey of 2001, they provide a similar message: 'One of NZ On Air's greatest concerns is the continuing decline of locally-made children's programs. The number of children's programming hours dropped again in 2001, continuing a decline that began in 1992' (NZOA Media Release, 15 April 2002). Noting that they were 'the main contributor to Children's and Youth Persons' programming' on New Zealand screens, NZOA made a direct connection between available (or allocated) funds, and program output: 'The overall reduction in children's hours is directly connected to NZ On Air's funding constraints. Broadcasters will not commission this genre without substantial financial assistance' (NZOA 2001, p. 19).

Placed within the broader considerations about the annual funding and future viability of NZOA, children's and youth programming lurches along in a fog of uncertainty. Panic sets in every August or September as bids for funding for the following year are put together. It is not surprising, therefore, that the majority of producers prefer to put their energy into the here-and-now—the daily pragmatics of stretching the money they already have.

The November 2001 round distributed over $11 million to children's television, bestowing the largest amounts on long-established programs (*What Now?*/*WNTV* received $4.25 million and *Squirt 2002* received $1.2 million) but there was also funding for new ventures (such as *Party Animals* $889 438 and *Sticky TV* $964 150). As in previous years, this funding was for one year, with no predictions or promises for the following years.

The complex relationships between the production of children's television, its placement in television schedules, the role advertising plays in such programming, and audience responses to children's television programs are not unique to New Zealand. It is possible to argue, however, that the strains and tensions seem more accentuated here, for a number of important reasons. As with all other genres, New Zealand has been a primary importer of children's programming. The two major sources have been the UK and the USA, with the more recent addition of Asian-produced animation from major production houses such as Saban Entertainment. This has meant that local efforts in this genre have consistently been judged against the exemplars of BBC Children's or Disney Productions, in addition to providing viable New Zealand attractions among such competition. In the last decade or so, the production output from overseas sources has increased, spearheaded by major global successes such as *Rugrats, Teletubbies, Pokemon,* and *Bob the Builder,* as Zanker explains: 'Since 1996, the international children's audio-visual industrial environment has been turbulent. It has seen the global children's market explode… Key public service broadcasters and producers in wealthy, English-speaking countries are adopting strong global "market positions", and transnational media conglomerates, like Nickelodeon, are investing in educational children's products designed to appeal to adults' (2001, p. 121).

In addition to competition from the programming mix on New Zealand free-to-air television, there is further competition from dedicated children's pay channels (Cartoon Network, Nickelodeon) on SKY. Ruth Zanker identifies the primary attraction of these channels as 'the power of animation' (2001, p. 125), whereby animation series with high production values and global appeal, readily cross any cultural or language barriers, and provide draw-cards for the children's zones in the television schedule. Many of these animated series (the pioneer was probably *The Simpsons*) readily cross generational barriers, further blurring the distinctions between 'child', 'youth', and 'adult'.

The imported local content in children's television (primarily animation) serves markedly different purposes for different sector interests. For producers, it provides draw-cards that increase the chances of children seeing the local content sandwiched between imported cartoons. Schedulers use imported children's programming for competitive strategies to win audiences in children's time zones (as TV3 did with *Teletubbies* scheduled against *What Now?* in 1997). Advertisers seek placement with popular imports, in order to reach target audiences and initiate matches between program content and merchandising. Children, and the youth audience, share the enthusiasm of their peers in other countries for breakthrough successes such as *Pokemon* and *Bob the Builder,* and more daring examples such as *The Ali G Show* and *South Park.*

Meantime, the enthusiastic embrace of imported hits frequently attracts the attention—and wrath—of parents and lobby groups. This happens more frequently than any other genre—parents have complained about children and television cartoons (American cartoons in particular) ever since the two were put together. On numerous occasions, imported cartoons are fingered as the primary culprit for a range of undesirable effects, from bad language to imitative violence to unbridled consumption to threats to cultural sovereignty. In a recent Massey University study, parents 'voted *The Simpsons* the worst television programme for its portrayal of negative values' (Middlebrook 2001, p. 2)

It does not seem to matter that there is no local research to substantiate such claims—for many New Zealand parents, imported children's programming is just plain bad. Exceptions are sometimes made for non-American or non-Asian animation (*Noddy, Thomas the Tank Engine*), possibly because they draw adult nostalgia. In this discourse (children's pleasures vs. parent distaste), local children's television production is passed the responsibility of providing less violent, more culturally appropriate, parent-friendly, less commercially oriented alternatives. These objectives also shape, to a considerable extent, the funding decisions of NZOA.

It is vitally important to provide local programming for New Zealand children, and even more importantly, to provide local equivalents of those styles of programming children love best, to provide some counter-balance to the domination of children's time-slots by imports. This strategy would serve two purposes, through appeasing parents while still pleasing children. Nevertheless, this is only *one* possible reason why local children's and youth television production deserves wide public support, and sustained funding.

Children, like their elders, have a right to continue to see programming from other countries but they also have a right to see local stories and faces. Children and teens do have a sense of belonging to a global community of their peers, and television has had a primary role in building this consciousness of shared interests. Locally produced television adds another dimension to this sense of self; young New Zealanders are also able to think of themselves as belonging to a country, and a range of local communities (town, city, country, ethnic group). There are other vitally important reasons why provision should continue to be made for a visible place on New Zealand television screens (across all channels). These reasons include opportunities for participation, opportunities for creative production and employment for New Zealanders, the pleasures of recognition of the familiar, and a locally grounded emphasis on education and information. None of these rationales are confined to children's and youth programming; they are arguments that apply across all genre of contemporary television. Nevertheless, they become more potent and urgent when the focus is on children's and youth television production in this country.

References

Bottger, C. 1999. 'The Challenge of Children's Television', in A. Blonski (ed.), *Shared Visions: Women in Television.* Sydney: Australian Film Commission.

Buckingham, D. 1993. *Children Talking Television: The Making of Television Literacy*. London: Falmer.

Buckingham, D. 1996. *Moving Images: Understanding Children's Emotional Responses to Television*. Manchester: Manchester University Press.

Buckingham, D. 2000. *After the Death of Childhood: Growing Up in the Age of Electronic Media*. Cambridge: Polity Press.

Buckingham, D., et al. 1999. *Children's Television in Britain*. London: BFI Publishing.

Davies, M.M.1989. *Television is Good for Your Kids*. London: Hilary Shipman.

Davies, M.M. 1997. *Fake, Fact and Fantasy: Children's Interpretations of Television Reality*. Mahwah, NJ: Lawrence Erlbaum.

Davies, M.M. 2002. *'Dear BBC': Children, Television Storytelling and the Public Sphere*. Cambridge: Cambridge University Press.

Drinnan, J. 2002. 'Fraser's mission: Stop the Rot and Fix Profit Drain', *National Business Review,* 12 April.

Fastline, (Auckland). 18 April 2002.

Free-To-Air Television Code of Broadcasting Practice, Wellington, Broadcasting Standards Authority, 2001.

Fiske, J. 1987. *Television Culture.* London: Methuen.

Hartley, J. 1992. *Tele-ology: Studies in Television.* London: Routledge.

Kantrowitz, B. & P. Winger. 1999. 'The Truth about Tweens', *Newsweek*, 18 October, pp. 62–4.

Lealand, G. 1995. *Television and New Zealand Preschoolers: A Longitudinal Study* (A research project funded by the Foundation for Research, Science and Technology). Hamilton: Department of Film and Television Studies, University of Waikato.

Lealand, G. 2001a. 'Some Things Change, Some Things Remain the Same: New Zealand Children and Media Use', *Childrenz Issues: Journal of the Children's Issues Centre,* 5(2), pp. 6–11.

Lealand, G. 2001b. 'Children and Youth', in G. Lealand & H. Martin, *It's All Done With Mirrors: About Television*. Palmerston North: Dunmore Press, pp. 202–6.

Livingstone, S. & Bovill, M. 1999. *Young People, New Media: Summary.* London: London School of Economics & Political Science.

Longworth, J. 2001. 'Strap on your Tween Hats', *kidscreen*, January.

Middlebrook, L. 2001. '*Happy Days* for Worried Parents', *NZ Herald*, 29 November.

Newcomb, H. (ed.). 1994., *Television: The Critical View*, 5th edn. New York: Oxford University Press.

New Zealand On Air. 2001. *Local New Zealand Television Content 2000*, Wellington, NZOA.

New Zealand On Air. 2002. *Local New Zealand Television Content 2001*, Wellington, NZOA.

Postman, N. 1983. *The Disappearance of Childhood.* London: W.H. Allen.

Postman, N. 1985. *Amusing Ourselves to Death.* New York: Delacorte Press.

Statistics New Zealand. 2001. *Demographic Trends 2000,* Wellington: Government Print.

Todd, S. & D. Richardson. 2001. 'New Zealand Children Talk about TV advertising', *Childrenz issues: Journal of the Children's Issues Centre*, 5(2), pp. 22–5.

TVNZ Charter. May 2001. Available from: http://www.executive.govt/nz/minister/hobbs/tvnz/charter2.htm [Accessed 28 August 2001].

Walker, V. 2001. 'Last of the Boomers Reaches Middle Age', *The Weekend Australian*, 30 June–1 July.

Walters, R. & W. Zwaga. 2001. *The Younger Audience: Children and Broadcasting in New Zealand*. Palmerston North: Dunmore Press.

Winn, M. 1977. *The Plug-in Drug*. New York: Viking.

Zanker, R. 1999. 'Kumara Kai or the Big Mac Pak? Television for Six-to-12 year-Olds in New Zealand', *Media International Australia* no. 93, November.

Zanker, R. 2001, What Now?: A New Zealand Children's Television Production Case-Study. Thesis (PhD), University of Waikato.

10 Going Mainstream:

Women's Televised Sport Through a Case Study of the 1999 Netball World Championships

MARGARET HENLEY

First, a moment from New Zealand women's sporting history. After the final of the 1927 Inter-Provincial Basketball Tournament,[1] held in the Taranaki Street Harbour Board shed in Wellington, Mrs J.G. Coates, the wife of the Prime Minister, 'at a very pleasant afternoon tea at Kirkaldie and Staines where she received a bouquet of fresias and violets' stated that 'the tournament had produced games of excellent quality' and she saw 'no reason why basketball should not become the national game for girls of New Zealand'. This observation was greeted with a spirited rendition of 'For they are jolly good fellows' and hearty cheers from the players and administrators of the game. The president of the New Zealand Association, Mrs R.S. McInnes, asked all those present 'to help extend the game by arousing public interest and obtaining publicity, for publicity meant money and without money they could not hope to do great things for the game' (*The Dominion* 1927).

Today, as in 1927, sport for many New Zealanders is an integral part of their everyday lives—whether in the role of participant, live-game spectator, television viewer, or knowledgable critic. Following sport, and the 'sports talk' that grows out of it, arguably generates a higher level of participation and analysis from a wider variety of citizens than any other area of popular culture. Sports events regularly feature among the highest rating programs on television. But sport as a social institution also reflects our general social and cultural attitudes where a system of value places some sports at a higher level than others. Traditionally in New Zealand, male sport has occupied the top position, especially rugby which has been considered central to the national character; and this hierarchy has been strongly reflected in media coverage.[2]

Nevertheless, attitudes and preferences can and do change over time. The rise of feminism in New Zealand in the 1970s saw increasing criticism of the sports establishment as male-dominated. However, the biggest changes have come not through political agitation or rational debate but indirectly as a by-product of the commercial ferment of the 1990s. The television environment became increasingly competitive and commercial with the arrival of TV3 and SKY's pay television service, and the government's restructuring of Television New Zealand (TVNZ) as a State-Owned Enterprise; and simultaneously some major sports became commercialised and professionalised. These were changes of seismic proportions in many respects; and one result was to give an unexpected and unintended shake-up to the gender hierarchy in sport.

While rapid change can open new possibilities, traditional attitudes tend to adapt at a slower rate. Netball had developed its game under the guardianship of women's volunteer labour on the margins of mainstream society, overshadowed by the commanding social status of rugby and the resources that were channelled into it. Trying to enter a mainstream dominated by male sports codes was never going to be easy. But now changes in politics, economics, and television broadcasting had transformed the status quo and created opportunities that any code could seek to exploit. Those managing netball were aware that it was imperative to seize the moment.

Such a move was not without risk. Increased coverage, with its associated financial opportunities and access to new audiences, could be potentially beneficial to both television and netball, but it also opened the sport up to pressures as well as opportunities. Changes to the way in which the game is presented may place it on a new evolutionary path that ultimately may serve the needs of commercial partners more than those of the existing netball community. Such exposure means that the sport receives more attention from the mainstream print, radio, television, and entertainment media and is therefore articulated in new ways, such as an increase in commercial hype and celebrity gossip. The populist areas of the media carry their own interests and assumptions, particularly with regard to gender. Traditional notions of gender can more powerfully come into play when increased exposure attracts new sponsors, whose previous associations with sport may have been limited to the main male sporting codes or who have a confining vision of the parameters of female sport. Television may also require changes in the way the game is played in order to make it more televisual. This does not mean that increased commercialisation and increased coverage are necessarily a bad deal—a kind of Faustian pact—but they do imply the need for vigilance on the part of netball as the negotiations take it into less familiar territory. There is an entry fee, so to speak, when one is no longer banished to the back courts.

The 1999 Netball World Championships was the first striking example of the increased media prominence of netball in this country and of the new pressures associated with it. But in order to place this event in context it is necessary first to provide a more detailed historical perspective.

The changing environment of televised sport

Print and broadcast media and sport have been bound together by mutual need. This is evident from early press reports, like the 1927 basketball prize-giving described above, through to television coverage of the Rugby World Cup or the America's Cup. As in Europe and the USA, televised sport has been a central programming genre since the arrival of the medium in New Zealand in 1960. The introduction of major technical developments such as colour transmission were timed to coincide with sporting spectacles of national importance. Up until 1974 New Zealand sports fans' television viewing was confined within shades of black and white (often with a bluish tinge). In that year, however, they were able to watch Dick Taylor's jubilation over his victory in the 10 000 metres at the Christchurch Commonwealth Games in glorious (and for a small country like New Zealand, extremely expensive) colour.[3]

During the 1980s the state-owned Broadcasting Corporation of New Zealand (BCNZ) consolidated its hold over the major sports in New Zealand by contractually creating what amounted to a privileged club known as the 'Big Four': rugby union, rugby league, cricket, and netball. These sports were secured with long-term, renewable contracts that ensured national coverage and, for some, an ongoing income from rights payments. This placed them in an enviable position compared to other sports with lower levels of participation that were assumed to attract less public interest. On the other hand, the security of this privileged position also had its drawbacks. Renewable contracts (some five to eight years in length) had the potential to reward the broadcaster more than the sport as changes in the broadcasting market, commercial sponsorship, and community interest could make the sport increase in value as a television product. Although netball had always been the major sport played by women in New Zealand, it basically considered itself fortunate to be included in this otherwise male group. At the same time, it was still viewed by the media sports establishment as a secondary sport and treated accordingly in financial terms.

Internationally, competition to secure the rights to major sporting events became a major issue for commercial television in the 1960s, particularly in the USA, and grew more intense with the introduction of satellite and cable options in the 1980s. Sports events attract and hold a valuable mass audience that can be on-sold to sponsors and advertisers. They can serve as the life blood of a television network operating in today's competitive environment, and the major building blocks for a pay television service (along with recent release movies). With only one publicly owned network, New Zealand was exempt from this trend until competition arrived in the form of TV3 and SKY. In the intense bidding for sports rights, pay television operators, with their narrower range of program genres, are often able to out-bid free-to-air broadcasters that support a wider range of public entertainment and costly news services. This has resulted in the increasing disappearance of live sport from free-to-air television. In Europe, the USA, and Australia, protective legislation was created to prevent sporting events, considered to be of national cultural importance, from being taken away from the mass free-to-air audience. Such 'anti-siphoning' laws generally require a pay television rights-holder to have a free-to-air partner to ensure that a clearly defined group of sporting events continue to be screened live on free-to-air television. The list of guaranteed events is quite extensive in a country such as Australia, where there seems to be broad agreement that sport is an expression of national culture.[4] No such curb on 'the free market' was seen as desirable during the radical changes to New Zealand broadcasting in the 1990s, a period when the favourite theme was 'deregulation'.

The opening up of the country to more foreign and cross-media ownership provided fertile ground for media change. Although the public funding body New Zealand On Air was created as a counterbalance, its responsibilities did not include sport. In comparison with the needs of local drama, and Māori and children's programming, televised sport was seen as already well represented (even, in the eyes of some critics, as over-represented) and therefore not in need of state funding through the Public Broadcasting Fee. In other words, the lack of gender balance and limited diversity of content in televised sport were not included in the areas of concern defined by the legislation. In practice, NZOA did fund some specialised sports coverage (associated with ethnic communities and disability groups), but for the most part it placed sport with news and current affairs as a genre able to survive without public subsidy, thus leaving it fully exposed to the increasing pressures of commercialism.

While preparing for the arrival of TV3, its first direct competitor in the free-to-air market, TVNZ devoted a great deal of strategic attention to sport (both national and international, but national in particular). In a video presentation to senior staff in 1989, TVNZ's CEO Julian Mounter defined

TVNZ's strategy as totally dominating the New Zealand marketplace in the acquisition and broadcast of sport, since this was of critical importance to the future of the network. His speech drew upon the language of both war and sport, with reference to past bruising encounters between the All Blacks and Australia. TVNZ needed to become tough and aggressive, with no quarter given.

TV3's delayed start date in November 1989 brought it almost immediately into direct collision with TVNZ's exclusive rights to film and broadcast coverage of the 1990 Commonwealth Games. TV3 slumped into receivership a few months later in May 1990. Its inability to compete in the area of high profile national sport had been a significant factor in the demise of the network. One of the claims TV3 made in the ensuing bankruptcy hearings in the High Court was that TVNZ's exclusion of TV3 from broadcasting major New Zealand sports had breached the limits of acceptable commercial behaviour (as defined by the *Commerce Act 1986*).[5] Although not uncommon in other commercial markets, this kind of conflict was relatively new to the New Zealand broadcasting environment, and just a taste of what was to come.

Following the passing of the Radiocommunications Bill in 1989, the way was clear for the introduction into New Zealand of SKY's satellite service. In its first years it was a relatively low-key affair and not without problems as customers and retailers got used to the technical requirements of the UHF delivery system (Smith 1996, p. 90). SKY was founded on assumptions of the sports-oriented taste and viewing preferences of Kiwi males, based on the way Pay TV had grown in the USA and Europe, particularly on Britain's BSkyB. In 1990, SKY went to air with Rugby League, the first of the Big Four codes to move to pay television. League was, however, still available to TVNZ (which had bought shares in the pay service and was so far able to work in partnership).

In comparison to the more spectacular launch and crash of TV3 (prior to its reconstruction under foreign ownership), SKY moved slowly but steadily through the market, waiting for a wind shift. SKY had already achieved a small inroad into the monopoly coverage of rugby by outbidding TVNZ for exclusive rights to the 1992 All Blacks tour of South Africa, but for some time this remained an isolated event (Smith 1996, p. 104). A major break came in 1995 when the international rugby union became professional, based on the recognition that amateurism as 'the central plank on which the game had been built' was 'no longer viable in the modern era' (Fitzsimons 1996, p. 319). The newly professional New Zealand Rugby Football Union (NZRFU) sold the television rights for all big games to SKY in a ten-year contract. Thus TVNZ lost all live rugby coverage of New Zealand, South Africa, and Australian games, including the Super 12 competition and Test matches. SKY also became the major rights holder for rugby league, which it on-sold to TV3. This intense escalation of commercial competition between free-to-air and pay television was moving in tandem with the increased level of open professionalism in the major male sporting codes, which now saw the revenue from television rights as their main source of funding.

In April 1998, TVNZ dropped out of the bidding for the renewal of international cricket rights, which went to SKY.[6] Only two months later there were rumours that TVNZ might also lose its deal with SKY for delayed coverage of top rugby games (Espiner 1998). By September 1999— against the background of the sale of TVNZ's 12.6 per cent stake in SKY to Independent Newspapers Ltd (INL), SKY and TVNZ's bidding duel for the Rugby World Cup, and TVNZ's announcement that it was going to move into digital pay TV as a direct competitor—SKY sold the delayed coverage rights for rugby to TV3. SKY CEO Nate Smith provocatively observed that: 'Rugby, along with news, *Montana Theatre, Coronation Street* and cricket is the fare we associate with TV ONE. Now, with the sports elements of the emotional glue gone, viewers and advertisers may well re-evaluate how they see the channels' (Taylor 1999).

After nine years of competing in the deregulated market, the TVNZ sporting stable was drastically reduced. Sports commentator Murray Deaker noted that 'in the short term, three of the big four sports have slipped from their [TVNZ's] grasp' (Deaker 1999). *NZ Herald* columnist Brian Rudman commented: 'No doubt it's hard for sports-obsessed state television to see the loss of rugby broadcasting rights—coming on the heels of losing cricket—as anything less than the end of civilisation as they have created it for us' (Rudman 1999). In an effort to retain the loyalty of the New Zealand public, TVNZ took out a massive double page advertisement in the *NZ Herald* headed 'WHO'S A GOOD SPORT?' On one page were listed: 'World Netball Champs, Davis Cup Tennis, Rugby World Cup, Formula One World Champs, America's Cup, Heineken Tennis Open, Sydney 2000 Olympics'. These were 'ALL FREE ON TVNZ'. On the other page all the sports events listed under SKY were crossed out, with the explanation: 'SORRY YOU'LL HAVE TO PAY TO VIEW THIS' (*NZ Herald,* 23 September 1999).

Listener editor Findlay MacDonald reinforced the view of TV ONE General Manager Shaun Brown that the dispute was not just about sport and had not been for some time. He added: 'massive commercialisation of the national game has inevitably led to this point'(MacDonald 1999). He quoted Nick Hornby's comment on the commercialisation of football in his novel *Fever Pitch* that 'when the game gets sanitised and commodified and packaged and on-sold and sponsored and branded, something is lost' (MacDonald 1999).

Both Brown and MacDonald's cynicism regarding increasing commercialisation of rugby, such as the rights ownership moving from free-to-air
to pay television, was matched by growing public disenchantment with the
speed at which the All Blacks seemed to be becoming more of a constructed marketing brand, and less of a grass roots expression of 'who we
are'. Despite the hold that rugby as the national game may have had within
New Zealand society in the past as the primary vehicle for expressing
national identity through sport, the slump in popularity following the 1981
Springbok tour had proved that this status was not invulnerable. Many New
Zealanders felt that values had been diluted in the process of professionalisation, values still invoked in the marketing but less often seen in practice.
Therefore the impending Rugby World Cup had a great deal more resting
on it than just the winning of games—the traditional values of national
identity needed to be reaffirmed. Before this was to take place, there were
a few netball games to be played.

Following an extraordinarily turbulent period in media sports during
the first nine months of 1999, New Zealand netball had an exceptional
opportunity to demonstrate what it had to offer to the media and the sporting public. When it took its position in centre court for the Netball World
Championships, it stepped into a tense situation heightened by battles
between broadcasters and by the public's need to recover some of the lost
territory associated with the decline of amateur sport. It would be a long
shot at goal for a women's sport to perform that function within the national
consciousness—a job that had always been done by rugby union, and to a
lesser extent cricket and rugby league. But in netball circles there was
awareness that media interest was increasing, and optimism that the time was
right for the Silver Ferns to topple Australia's impressive record. (Australia
had won six titles to New Zealand's two in the course of the nine World
Championships since 1963.).

Netball World Championships

At 10 pm on Saturday 2 October 1999 with 4.5 seconds remaining on the
clock, the Australian second string Goal Attack, Sharelle McMahon,
faultlessly netted the winning goal, double-checked the scoreboard, and then
threw herself onto a pile of thrashing Aussies in the middle of the court. A
victorious Australian team were incredulous that the Silver Ferns,[7] technically
the superior team on the day, had handed them back the World Championship title yet again. For the New Zealand television audience it was despair
and the deepest anguish. But for TVNZ it was a moment that could warm
the cockles of even the sternest accountant. The last fifteen-minute quarter

contained all the elements of major drama, concluding with another unfor-
gettable sporting tragedy to add to Sylvia Potts's fall just a stride before
crossing the 800m line at the 1970 Commonwealth Games or Jeff Wilson's
juggling act in the dying moments of the 1994 Bledisloe Cup.

This battle between the female siblings of the Australasian section of
the Commonwealth captured over one million New Zealand viewers
(ACNeilsen 1999) over a two-hour period that night, creating a rating spike
that attracted the attention of even the most dedicated denigrators of female
athleticism. The two hours of television coverage provided hard evidence
of the increased potential for the televising of women's team sport in New
Zealand. It was one of the highest-rating programs in New Zealand television history, out-rating the Bledisloe Cup on 24 July the same year by four
points (with the rugby scoring only 873 000 estimated viewers compared to
netball's 1,002,000).

Planned as netball's 'gateway to the millenium, [creating] a platform for
the future of the sport, nationally and internationally' (NNZ 2000, p. 4), the
public interest in the Netball World Championships in Christchurch placed
a solid 'stake in the ground' (Smith 2001) with regard to the sport's relationship with television. This meant that traditional social and commercial
attitudes regarding the game had to be redefined, and perhaps assigned a
new value for sponsors. Television ratings provided the commercially
acceptable evidence for such a re-evaluation.

New Zealand's turn to host the Netball World Championships at
Christchurch in September 1999 was staggered between the four-year cycle
of the Commonwealth Games, within which netball is now an official sport.
Twenty-seven teams competed, mainly from Commonwealth countries,
thereby evoking the reaches of the old British Empire (with a few exceptions, particularly countries where physically active sport has not been traditionally encouraged for women). Netball publicity billed it as 'the largest
single team sporting event for women in the world' (NNZ 2000, p. 4). The
main regions represented were New Zealand and Australia, the United
Kingdom, Africa, the Caribbean Islands, the Pacific Islands, North America
(USA and Canada), as well as a number of Asian countries.

The fortunes and attendance of the lesser known netball nations are
traditionally determined by fluctuating or insufficient funding and in some
cases the availability of Australian or New Zealand coaches willing to work
overseas. The adequacy of funding is a raw indication of the status of the
sport and/or the status of women within a particular culture. The Canadian
and US teams are under-funded because netball is almost unknown in their
countries, and African teams (including South Africa) struggle because of
status problems associated with female sport. Pakistan pulled out before the
tournament began through lack of funding. Botswana's funding was

withdrawn at the very last minute by the military government, which prevented the team from attending.

In a move that was the envy of the representatives of all other nations attending the Championships, TVNZ put together a package that contained an unprecedented thirty-one hours of live television coverage of games over the week of competition and a further eight hours of delayed coverage (thirty-nine hours in total). Ten hours of the live coverage was screened in peak viewing time, between 6.00 and 10.30 at night (the optimum advertising window) and the semi-final between New Zealand and Jamaica and the New Zealand final with Australia were screened on Friday and Saturday night respectively. The televised game coverage on TV2 was backed by items on TV ONE and TV3 in the main news, sports news, and magazine news programs (*Breakfast, Midday, Holmes*) sporadically for the four months leading up to the tournament, and then every day during the competition. There was a combination of live coverage, courtside links, pre-recorded VT items,[8] scoreboard updates, and a noteworthy series of VT items prepared for TV3 by reporter Maryanne Twentyman on location in Africa.

Although the print media were saturated with the lead-up to the impending Rugby World Cup, they nevertheless devoted considerable column space to the tournament as it built towards the final, and even devoted the front page of main sections to reporting the impact of the Silver Ferns' one goal loss to its arch rival Australia. Articles and opinion pieces during the tournament tended to run parallel, in subject matter and angle, to the television news coverage, but frequently they provided slightly more in-depth comment than the 'once over lightly' sound bites.

Almost all the named sports journalists writing about netball in the major metropolitan newspapers were male staff reporters. There were, however, male and female television reporters on both channels and the live links were done by Mary Durham for TVNZ and Maryanne Twentyman for TV3. During actual game coverage, the studio link and presenter, April Ieremia, and commentators Julie Coney and Jo Coleman—all ex-netballers, the first two with international experience—were further backed up by the expert commentary team of Australian international Anne Sergeant and ex-Silver Fern Tanya Cox. The print media, though providing some of the more informed analysis of the game, did not use the talents of ex-internationals for expert opinion pieces for this standout sporting event.

Pre-tournament television coverage occasionally broke the standard mould of 'lead-up to an event' stories. The majority relied heavily on photo-opportunity moments at the airport or training camp, formula crystal-ball-gazing interviews, and historical game footage, particularly of New Zealand–Australia clashes and New Zealand's shock loss to South Africa in the semi-finals of the Birmingham World Champs in 1995. Prime-time rewards for the sponsors were news stories revealing the new Ferns' uniforms and the announcement of the winning chant by the Kaitaia **Kōhanga Reo**. The latter item associated the sport, the competition, the broadcaster, and the sponsor Vodafone with a 'feel-good' story from one of the most under-developed regions in the country.

The coverage by TVNZ up to this point was no more than routine with little variation from stock storylines. Despite a semblance of coverage, enthusiastic sports reporters, and a variety of interviews with key New Zealand and Australian players and coaches, what was missing was any serious discussion of the sport itself. There could have been an informed debate regarding the perceived necessity for netball to be a global game, or an overview of the game's colonial legacy where the skill of the Australasian teams had moved beyond that of the coloniser, England. If these two topics were too serious for sports news items or breakfast television, then a lively analysis by past players on the different styles of netball played by the Anglo, Caribbean, and Pacific nations (supplemented by archival footage available to TVNZ) could have produced some stimulating lead-up discussion for both the casual and the knowledgable viewer. After all, coverage of men's rugby had already established such a pattern.

Throughout all the television news coverage, the impact of Pacific Island teams and individual players was largely overlooked. There were no profiles done on Vanuatu, Niue, the Cooks, Samoa, Papua New Guinea, and only fleeting mention of Fiji, the Pacific Island team with the most outstanding improvement before and during the Championships. Despite strong local interest in the Cook Island, Niue, and Samoan teams, the only Pacific Island profiles before the tournament began were a tribute acknowledging the recent death of ex-Silver Fern and Samoan representative Leilani Read, and a VT item on the problems of breastfeeding mothers in the Cook Island and Tongan teams (*ONE Network News*, 21 September 1999). This made the Pacific Island women at the tournament seem more noteworthy for their reproductive capabilities than for their game skills.

There was almost total marginalisation of the Asian competitors—Hong Kong, Singapore, and Malaysia—who had hosted and competed in netball at the previous Commonwealth Games. The Sri Lankan team got a brief mention because they suffered from the cold. The sports clothing manufacturer, Canterbury, used this opportunity to access non-sponsored prime time by supplying them with jackets. If one judged solely from television coverage it was not clear if the Sri Lankans ever managed to play a game of netball or merely sat around in Canterbury fleecies watching everyone else play.

The exception to the unimaginative and formulaic nature of the coverage during the build-up period were the three African VT items screened on TV3, produced by freelance journalist Maryanne Twentyman on

Malawi, Botswana, and Zambia. With funding from an independent source, Twentyman was able, with TV3 backing, to go to Africa and gather footage before the start of the Championships. Twentyman felt the wealth of stories on offer was likely to receive insufficient recognition, and there was an opportunity for 'colour pieces' to be done that would ignite public interest in the rich variety of cultures coming together in Christchurch. She felt that such items would provide insights into the lives of women playing net-ball in the various countries and help to explain to the casual viewer the obviously huge gap between the leading nations and the black African players (Twentyman 1999).

Once the competition was underway the team that generated the most media interest was Jamaica. Their vigorous on-ball and off-ball play and their feisty courtside interviews and press conferences were selected for sport news coverage, giving an increased public awareness of the passion associated with the way women play this game at the elite level. All games involving Jamaica attracted increased gate attendance and television viewership as it became clear that they were possible contenders to upset the Australian/ New Zealand stranglehold on the final placings. The televised game cover-age, and the vigorous debate in the media regarding their physical style of play, ensured an increased public awareness of the visual spectacle their dynamic skills provided, a stimulating variation on the type of play with which New Zealanders were more familiar.

The semi-final on Friday 1 October between New Zealand and Jamaica, although traditionally a low viewing night, was a ratings grabber, capturing 57 per cent of **channel share** for the evening and averaging an overall (5+) ratings figure of 22 over the two hours of build-up, game coverage, and post-match interviews (AC Nielsen 1999). In the last quarter of the game as the goal difference see-sawed and the chance for the Silver Ferns to be in the final came under threat, the ratings reached 26, pulling most of the available audience from TV ONE and TV3, with men as well as women featuring strongly in all adult **demographics**.

The Friday night game had everything for the experienced netball player and the new viewer. It was not necessary to know the rules of the game to see that the players were stretching the capabilities of some of the umpires, and the physical contest over the ball in the air was the stuff that televised sport thrived on. For the public profile of the game and the commercial interests of TVNZ, this was a perfect curtain-raiser for the final between Australia and New Zealand the next night in prime time. Both print and television media focused on the promotion of the final and the anticipation of a close game whatever the result. Past finals between New Zealand and Australia have nearly always been close, with three finals being decided by one goal. Anecdotal evidence and fervent outpourings in the

Netball New Zealand Internet chat room suggested that the night of the final was one that many New Zealanders were planning their social lives around—this was appointment viewing, not to be missed.

The average viewing rating over the two hours of the final was a massive 30 points (70 per cent of channel share). The only competition on the other channels that managed to nudge a rating over 5 was the teen flick on TV3, *Days of Thunder*. This attracted young males but only achieved a 7 rating towards the end of the movie after the netball had finished. TV ONE was totally denuded of audience. The 55-plus viewers led the charge, a massive 51 per cent of that age group. The male and female viewing figures were close together in all age demographics but there were times when males out-rated females in the twenty-five to fifty-four age group, confirming the television scheduler's popular wisdom that men will watch any sport if it is quality sport, even if played by women—especially if the game is between New Zealand and Australia, and definitely if there is a chance that New Zealand might win. In the latter stages of the game, when it appeared a Ferns victory was within grasp, the ratings soared into television history.

The major sponsor, Vodafone, was delighted. It had come in as a name sponsor of the Silver Ferns in April 1998, but initial market research suggested that its brand association with the Ferns was not sufficiently recognised. The naming rights option for the World Championships had been up for consideration for some time. Sponsors who traditionally only financed male sport were fully committed or considered the package to be overpriced for a women's sport. Vodafone's market research showed that, in contrast to feedback in Australia, the New Zealand public (and the youth market in particular) expressed some dissatisfaction about seeing Vodafone as a male orientated company that only supported male sports (Kirk-Smith 2001). Vodafone therefore decided to pick up sponsorship of the Netball World Championships as a way to change this perception. Based on its previous experience in sponsoring major male sporting codes, the company felt there was potential to improve the branding of the Silver Ferns as an attractive commercial 'product'. The chance to use the Championships as a vehicle through which to increase their own brand awareness in the female market was too good to miss (Kirk-Smith 2001). The association of the game with TV2 also suited Vodafone's marketing strategies as it was interested in being aligned with a younger, more energetic audience where sport was closely linked with entertainment. The association of youth personalities, Havoc and Newsboy, with the Silver Ferns was an added bonus, conveying an element of anti-establishment fun that Vodafone also liked to be associated with (in a safe, commercial way). The results of research soon after the televised finals indicated an increase in 'top of the mind' recall by 6 per cent, which was considered a strategic marketing triumph. By the end of its first year of exposure in the New Zealand market Vodafone had achieved 98 per cent brand awareness, and its sponsorship of netball had contributed significantly to that result (Kirk–Smith 2001).

A new contract

After the World Championships with their proven commercial success for the sponsor, the sport, and the broadcaster, Netball NZ's contract with TVNZ came up for renewal. The support shown to the sport by the broad-caster over a long period of time was not in question and freely acknowl-edged as being unique in the world, particularly in the netball playing countries of the Commonwealth. Netball NZ, mindful of maintaining a strong connection with its player base and in accordance with the wishes of nearly all of its sponsors, was aware that it was important to stay with a free-to-air broadcaster. At the same time, this was a suitable moment to fore-ground the gains that the sport had made in presenting itself in a more professional manner and in adding to its worth for major sponsors, TVNZ being one of those sponsors.

Another element was the need to recognise netball's role in the changing patterns of traditional television viewership and in the control of the female market over the spending of the discretionary dollar. The purchasing power of women in the area of lifestyle products and sports apparel had already been made internationally apparent earlier in the same year with the success of the Women's Soccer World Cup, which had drawn a global television audience of forty million (Campbell 1999).

There has always been a counter-argument that netball is not a global game and that the on-selling of television rights/packages internationally is minimal and therefore limited in the commercial return to the broadcaster.[9] However, in the terms of the contract renewal, TVNZ did accept that some increase in valuation should occur.[10] Although this was a timely recognition for the gains the sport has made, the results still fell short of the fees obtained by New Zealand cricket, rugby union, or rugby league. Granted, those codes are fully professional, whereas netball is not. And ultimately, the most striking aspect of the contract renewal was the fact that netball improved its relative position within the hierarchy of sports, narrowing the traditional gender gap.

Moving into the mainstream under the increased sponsorship of the major free-to-air broadcaster has already provided considerable advantages for the sport. An increasingly attractive visual presentation, extended live and delayed coverage, and placement in prime time have kept the game and its players strongly present in the public mind. Such prominence, coupled with the increased awareness of the commercial importance of the female audience, has allowed the game to attract additional sponsorship. This in turn has opened up opportunities for individual players to capitalise on their media profile, a benefit that has seldom been available to female athletes playing team sports.

Other gains and losses

The recent history of netball serves as a reminder that sport is inevitably involved with and shaped by general social attitudes, including those associated with gender. Clearly these can be re-shaped by economic forces, in association with television as the most powerful mass medium in our society; and where economic change coincides with media change, the result can be a powerful shake-up of social priorities and status. Netball has certainly been able to benefit from the commercial ferment of the last decade, but it has been a volatile situation in which the participants are aware of both gains and losses. This coming of age, or (perhaps more accurately) coming into a new age, has increased both the financial rewards for netball and confronted it with new challenges.

The needs and attitudes embedded in commercial television are starting to alter some aspects of the game, including rule changes, the speeding up of play, the reduction of on-court delays, and a heightened media interest in physical contestation. Going mainstream means increased contact with mainstream stereotypes and assumptions. For example, rule changes designed to speed up the game are in direct response to a perceived need to increase the visual pleasure of the television audience. The netball live audience (the game's most loyal following) know most of the rules, particularly those governing possession, obstruction, and contact. Understanding finer points is not central to the needs of the majority of the netball television audience. Their criticisms of the over-use of the whistle were to some extent justified, and some unnecessary rulings have been eliminated, which were remnants of the time when the game moved at a much slower pace. However, despite television's entertainment demands, a large decrease in the use of the whistle is not achievable for the game in its present form. Essentially it is a game played at speed in restricted spaces with minimal body contact, and it is within those relatively tight restrictions that the skills of the game have been developed.

Physical contact is another area of controversy. Considerable value is placed on physical contestation for the ball in male codes such as rugby union and league, games developed in a settler culture that celebrated and even venerated rugged physicality. It was a very different set of values that shaped the game of netball for women. The expectations of the newly created netball audience, reinforced by the promotional needs of commercial television, are putting pressure on this aspect of the women's game. Replays and channel **promos** have a tendency to reinforce (with the aid of rhythmic editing and music) physical body contact. The 'thrills and spills' entertainment value often overshadows less dramatic but more skilled aspects of play.

This is, however, an argument not to turn back the clock but to remain alert to pressures that are not necessarily always in the best interests of the long-term development of the sport, or in the best interests of women as athletes. Such influences can have a powerful effect on how the game is to be played and how the women players are presented. Netball has to ensure that its legacy from its amateur past, carefully nurtured by generations of New Zealand women, is not being subtly transformed into a mirror version of male sport.

Gary Whannel, in a discussion of media narrativity, identifies sport as an organised and ritualised activity that has the capacity to construct a mythic moment of golden memory within time and place. Historically, these moments have mostly been male achievements that become part of sporting cultural capital that is 'so effortlessly acquired, distributed and used by men' (Whannel 2002). It is noteworthy that, although the 'moment' of the Netball World Championship final was more tragic than golden, it did feed into a wider mythic tradition regarding New Zealand's sporting clashes with Australia. Rather than being totally eclipsed by the All Blacks' failure a few weeks later to achieve a place in the final at the Rugby World Cup, it continued to be remembered and debated as part of the public's soul-searching about the state of national sport.

For some media commentators the amount of attention surrounding a women's sport was unwelcome. Warwick Roger in the *Evening Post* observed: 'That we got ourselves into such a frenzy over the netball is once again evidence of our national insecurity, of our need to be good at something—anything—no matter how inconsequential it is' (Roger 1999). And Richard Boock, the *NZ Herald* netball reporter for the Championships, in his wrap-up of the tournament, 'Netball Misses the Bigger Goal', described netball as a 'bizarre little game' (Boock 1999). But such devaluation of women's sport in the media is nothing new; what was noteworthy was the fact that the national team sport for women had come to be included in mainstream debate about representative performance and national identity. Attention had been almost totally absent four years earlier when the Silver Ferns, with a performance similar to that of the 1999 All Blacks, had failed to make the final at the Birmingham World Championships in 1995.

Just as television viewers new to watching elite netball rethought (or temporarily forgot) some of their traditional prejudices regarding a game for women, a similar shift occurred within the commercial world. Such implications are still unfolding as both netball and the broadcaster seek to shake off restrictive assumptions of the past in forging a closer relationship of mutual benefit. Netball's growing inclusion in public discourse can be seen as progress in constructing the nation along less traditionally gendered lines, but this is admittedly at an early stage.

The effects of the recently established Broadcasting Charter imposed by the Labour government on the national broadcaster are difficult to predict. TVNZ's intention in the Charter to 'reflect the role that sporting and other leisure interests play in New Zealand life and culture' (TVNZ, 2003) could mean increased expenditure to try to return the major male sporting codes to free-to-air television (as many male sports fans have demanded) or it could mean coverage of a greater diversity of sports. The television sports audience may also experience a kind of 'hype burnout' where the talk of snatching a win against impossible odds and the general over-promotion of televised games may come to seem less appropriate to a public service channel. However, the struggle of the underdog playing with national pride against countries with greater resources has always attracted us and this is unlikely to change in the near future. The government's desire for TVNZ to continue to operate at a profit seems certain to maintain the hyperbolic, commercial, competitive environment in which televised sport now operates.

References

ACNeilsen. 1999. *Weekly Television Audience Report*. Week 39, 2 October.

Boock, Richard. 1999. 'Netball Misses the Bigger Goal'. *NZ Herald*. 4 October.

Campbell, Matthew. 1999. *Sunday Star-Times* (reprinted from *The Sunday Times*, London). 11 July.

Deaker, Murray. 1999. *Sunday Star-Times*. 18 September.

The Dominion. 1927. 2 September.

Espiner, Guyon. 1998. 'TVNZ May Lose all Rugby Coverage'. *The Evening Post*. 29 June.

Fitzsimons, Peter. 1996. *The Rugby War*. Sydney: HarperSports.

Kirk-Smith, Lynley (Marketing Manager, Vodafone New Zealand). 2001. Interview. 5 October.

MacDonald, Findlay. 1999. 'Sporting Life' (Editorial). *Listener*. 2 October.

Netball New Zealand. 2000. *Report on 10th World Netball Championships*.

NZ Herald. 1999. 23 September.

One Network News. 1999. TVNZ. 21 September.

Rudman, Brian. 1999. 'TVNZ Moguls Could Discover There Really is Life After Sport.' *NZ Herald*. 28 September.

Roger, Warwick. 1999. 'Netball Hype Made the Fall Greater.' *Evening Post*. 11 October.
Smith, Kereyn (Chairman, Netball New Zealand Board). 2001. Interview. 6 December.
Smith, Paul. 1996. *Revolution in the Air*, Auckland: Longman.
Taylor, Phil. 1999. 'Sky TV Chief Beaming'. *Sunday Star Times*, 26 September.
Twentyman, Maryanne. 1999. Interview. 16 August.
Whannel, Gary. 2002. *Media Sport Stars: Masculinities and Moralities*. London: Routledge.

Notes

1   In 1970 the name change from 'basketball' to 'netball' was made to bring New Zealand into line with the other International Federation member countries. This also avoided the confusion between indoor and outdoor basketball, which were significantly different games, although they evolved from the same origin in the United States, circa 1891.

2   For the purposes of this chapter, press clippings from the major daily and weekend newspapers and the *Listener* were monitored from May to October 1999, along with all the relevant items on television relating to netball and the Netball World Championships (on *ONE Network News and Sport*, the *Breakfast* and *Midday* programs, and TV3 *News and Sport*) over the same period.

3   Because of a lack of technical facilities, only swimming, boxing, and track and field were able to be broadcast in colour at this time.

4   To date Australia's list includes horse racing, Australian Rules football, rugby league, rugby union, cricket, soccer, tennis, netball, basketball, golf, and motorsport.

5   High Court of New Zealand, Auckland Registry, CP No. 929/91.

6   Exclusive coverage of cricket's domestic games in a five-year contract, with a five-year renewal option.

7   Vodafone purchased naming rights to the Silver Ferns in 1999 ('The Vodafone Silver Ferns'). For the purpose of this essay the team will be referred to simply as the 'Silver Ferns'.

8   Video Tape (VT) items are complete, pre-shot and edited news stories that can be voiced over in the edit or by the news presenter at the time of broadcast. They can be constructed well in advance or earlier the same day, and allow a greater editorial control over content and duration than in a live broadcast situation. They can also allow a greater range of opinion to be gathered than is possible in a live location link or a scripted news presentation.

9   Sales from the television coverage of the World Champs only provided:
Australia—sixteen hours Network 10, including ten hours live
South Africa—six hours on SABC, including highlights and delayed coverage
UK—four hours live on BBC, plus highlights
Jamaica—approximately four hours of highlights on JTV
World—finals highlights on TW1 (an Austrian-owned digital sports and weather channel that transmits in German).

10   The precise details of this 2000 contract remain confidential for commercial reasons.

11

Television Programming:

The Dynamics of the Schedule

ROGER HORROCKS

Network strategies

The topic of programming offers us a different way to think about television—not only in terms of separate programs but also in terms of its continuous supply of material throughout the day. Summarised by the television listings printed in newspapers, this stream of words and images has been described by Raymond Williams as a 'planned flow' (1974) and by Nick Browne (1984, 1994) as the 'super-text' of television. Each day's schedule is the result of a number of careful, strategic decisions by specialists in programming (or 'scheduling' as it is also called), who have purchased the programs and then planned the sequence in which to screen them.[1] The study of this process can reveal a great deal about the nature of television, or more precisely, about the ways in which this medium has been conceived or constructed.

Programming has always been part of New Zealand television but its style has changed fundamentally since the days when there was one channel and only half of the week had advertising. In the early days, light entertainment or 'popular' material was seen as particularly appropriate for commercial nights.[2] When the government established a second channel, the main principle was to try to be complementary rather than competitive.[3] Based on the public service broadcasting idea that television should as far as possible offer something for everybody, this meant scheduling programs on the two channels so as to give viewers a definite choice: between documentary and drama, or serious information and entertainment; or between younger and older viewers, male and female, urban and rural. In addition, the programmers also sought to maintain a roughly equal popularity between the channels (they chose not to make one a 'mainstream' or 'populist' channel, and the other a 'minority' or 'highbrow' channel). One other rule of the game was to maintain a balance between British and American material, though this eventually became impossible as the demand for American popular culture increased.

In the course of the 1980s New Zealand television switched gradually to a more commercial approach to programming, in response to changes in government policy, the increasing importance of advertising revenue over public funding, and the arrival of direct competition (in the form of TV3, which began transmission in November 1989). The new theme was competition rather than complementarity, and metaphors of military strategy, warfare, victories, and defeats became common in the talk of broadcasters.

The first priority was to give each channel a distinct 'brand,' focusing it on a particular target audience or market niche. Existing channels received a makeover, consisting of a new station logo, theme song, colour scheme, advertising campaign, and so on (e.g. *Sunday Star-Times* 2003a, 2003b). TV ONE and TV2 were distinguished from each other as 'information' versus 'entertainment,' as 'British' versus 'American,' and as 'older' versus 'younger.' Obviously not all viewers divide up precisely along these lines, but it is still common for many New Zealand viewers to have a 'home' or favourite channel. As an overall strategy the TV ONE/TV2 division was a shrewd way to segment the New Zealand audience. Older viewers tended to prefer British programs, news, and current affairs, and there was a saying in broadcasting circles that 'the knobs on older television sets are all rusted to TV ONE'. In the late 1980s, TV ONE and TV2 were still complementary, but the choice of programs for both became increasingly commercial, and the pair was designed to work as a two-pronged attack in the ratings war with TV3. The theory was that if you didn't find what you wanted on TV ONE, you went to TV2, and there should be no need to look further. Some commentators believed TV3 had made a bad choice of name by implying it was third best.

Once a channel had adopted a particular brand, then certain kinds of programs became unsuitable because they gave the wrong signals to the regular audience—even if those programs were offered free (by New Zealand On Air or a sponsor or a program-maker). Programmers were always concerned about 'the turn-off factor'. Still, if the channel failed to flourish, then its owners were likely to give it an abrupt change of personality. An example was the Prime Network, popular with older viewers for its British programs (such as *Jeeves and Wooster* and BBC documentaries), until its owners decided in 2002 to seek a larger and younger audience by switching to American and Australian material, in association with Australia's Channel 9.

Strategic programming of this kind is as much about finding an advertising niche as it is about identifying an unsatisfied audience. After its initial period of financial disaster, TV3 located such a niche by concentrating precisely on the eighteen to thirty-nine-year-old age group, in the middle of TV ONE and TV2's audiences. TV3's strong focus on 'household shoppers' and families with young children was helpful to a particular group of advertisers. The network was not worried about failing to 'win the slot' (having the largest overall audience for a particular hour of the day) provided its program rated well with a specific group such as household shoppers. That is, it focused on the rating points for its target audience (described by such terms as Target Audience Ratings Points, or TARPs). In 1997, however, TV3 made the mistake of creating TV4 in the hope of tapping the growing interest among advertisers in the youth market. This was a commercial mistake in terms of over-estimating the size of the audience, but since all programming strategies have cultural implications, the mistake was also cultural (that is, a matter of content and style). Since TV3 had already gained a reputation for youthful edginess, its relationship with TV4 could not be as clear-cut as the relationship between the older, more sober TV ONE and the youth-oriented TV2. Thus the creation of TV4 had the effect of dividing the TV3 audience.

Nevertheless, the importance of the youth market has continued to be strongly promoted by the advertising industry and this has influenced the range of broadcasting options. Programming is highly responsive to the interests of advertisers, and the situation today, with many older viewers feeling poorly served in relation to the numerical size of their group, stands in striking contrast to the situation at the end of the 1980s and beginning of the 1990s when a slump put so many young people out of work that interest in youth programs declined among advertisers and broadcasters.

One way to analyse a television program, then, is to seek to identify the target audience by considering the characters and subject matter and comparing them with the kinds of products that turn up in the ad breaks. Television's own method of analysis is based on ratings. In addition to measuring viewers above the age of five, the system breaks the audience down by variables such as age and gender.[4] The adequacy of ratings continues to be fiercely questioned by program-makers and by academics (Ang 1991; Lealand 2002), but the system remains firmly entrenched because advertisers feel they must have some quantitative measurement of audiences, and broadcasters accept the system favoured by advertisers. Broadcasters do supplement this number-crunching with a certain amount of qualitative research involving focus groups, telephone calling, and other feedback methods. Long-running series such as *Shortland Street* are frequently fine-tuned as a result of this audience research.

Not only advertisers but also investors keep an eye on ratings, as shown for example by the ups and downs of TV3's share price during its first year. A *NZ Herald* news item on 30 January 1990 reported that 'TV3 Network's share price dropped to a post-listing low of 170c yesterday as nervous small investors responded to the station's peak-time ratings... The company's chief executive, Mr Trevor Edgerton, attributed the poor ratings performance to the station's decision to screen the early rounds of the Australian tennis open in peak time'. In 1996 it was estimated that 'The loss of 1% [average] primetime rating would be worth around $5 million in advertising revenue' to TVNZ (*National Business Review* 1996). Downturns in advertising can have a rapid impact, as illustrated by a *National Business Review* story that began: 'Competition for the advertising dollar has seen TVNZ slash 154 jobs or 10% of its staff nationwide in a major restructuring'. These are the harsh facts of life that have led broadcasters to attach such great importance to programming.

Advertising dollars and ratings are both crucial but what matters most to the broadcaster is the overall financial performance of each slot, which compares the cost of the program with the revenue it generates, measured against other possible options (the 'opportunity cost'). This kind of analysis became much more complex and sophisticated in the 1980s and it transformed the relative importance of different roles within television. The program-maker was demoted to the bottom rung of the ladder and was now seen as serving the needs of the commissioning editor who worked in turn for the programmer. In the old days a programmer would sometimes be handed the work of an important producer and told 'Here's a program, find a slot for it.' Now the principle was: 'Here's a slot, find a program for it.' In industry terms, the broadcasters expanded their power over the program-makers, the 'suits' over the 'creatives'.

The programmers were accountable in turn to the financial experts or 'beancounters'. Nevertheless programmers did wield new power, and commissions for local programs now had to be based on the precise requirements of channels and time slots. Projects were tailor-made for a desired target audience, with the precise hour determining such details as how 'adult' the content could be. Frustrated program-makers spoke of these constraints on creativity as 'slottism'.

In terms of overseas purchases, the range of material available to a programmer depends on making the best use of available funds on annual shopping trips to various television program markets such as MIP-TV and

MIPCOM (in Cannes). The choice is skewed by the need for 'output deals' with favourite suppliers. A style of purchasing that is frustrating to viewers is the temptation for large broadcasters to buy more than they need to deny the programs to their competitors. There was a controversy over this practice of stocking up in the late 1980s after TVNZ had apparently gone on a massive buying spree to keep programs out of the hands of TV3.

In terms of scheduling, the key principle is to reflect the rhythms of everyday life, though this process is complex because television has not merely mirrored but has itself helped to construct some of those rhythms. There is a basic generic schedule for the week, with advertising rates corresponding to the hour-by-hour rise and fall in viewing numbers. The style and subject matter of programs reflect the fact that each of the 'dayparts' into which the schedule is divided involves different audiences and home activities. For example, an 'evening soap' is different from a 'daytime soap' (which assumes that its viewers are busy with housework or childcare so that a slower, more repetitive style of story-telling is appropriate). Business news may be scheduled at breakfast time, then there are programs for those who stay at home such as older people and mothers looking after preschoolers. As primary and then high school children start to arrive home from school, the target age of the programs correspondingly increases. Something light is appropriate for the period before the family meal, and then more substantial television fare is served up in prime time, from 6 to 10.30 pm. Some 'cult' programs are scheduled for late-night audiences. New Zealanders appear to eat and go to bed early since prime time in the USA, for example, is 8 to11 pm. Friday night has its own atmosphere, as do Saturday and Sunday, public holidays, and anniversaries. There are also seasonal rhythms with more viewing in winter than in summer (the so-called 'silly season', a time for repeats). It is no accident that many series are sold as thirteen weekly episodes, representing one quarter of the year.

Programmers can make mistakes, such as TV ONE's scheduling of *Star of David*, a documentary about a Jewish New Zealander's search for his roots, on a Jewish holy day when devout Jews were not watching television. Since this was the only documentary about this community that had been made for many years, there was a great deal of disappointment at the scheduling, and to TVNZ's credit it agreed to give the documentary another screening (*Sunday Star* 1991). As television became more commercial, such problems became harder to resolve. For example, the weekly Pacific Island magazine program *Tagata Pasifika* continued for years to be screened on Sunday mornings, though the potential audience protested that this was a most unsuitable time because so many members of their community went to church. New Zealand On Air, which funded the program, was also frustrated by the situation but TVNZ's programming lay outside its control.

The broadcaster was adamant that this was the only possible slot because *Tagata Pasifika* was a minority program and Sunday morning was the only remaining non-commercial time. In 2002 (with the Charter approaching), TVNZ introduced a repeat screening at 10.35 pm on Thursday evening. The community welcomed the additional screening though it regarded the new time as still far from ideal.

Programming in the commercial environment involves a range of craft skills based on particular understandings of viewing behaviour. One basic assumption is that people like predictability because this helps them to plan their week, and there is a ritualistic element to viewing. If a program is popular, programmers like to 'strip' it across the week (that is, run it at the same time every day). Sometimes they are disappointed with the initial ratings for a weekly drama and will shift the series several times in the search for the ideal slot. (*Mercy Peak, Being Eve,* and *City Life* are local examples.) There is a huge difference in programming terms between (say) 7, 8, 9 and 10 pm, and the choice of time slot and channel can often tell us a great deal about a program or a broadcaster's perspective on it. Program-makers working within a commercial system know they must familiarise themselves with these broadcasting requirements. Some regard the process of working for a specific audience as a brake on creativity whereas programmers see it as a healthy discipline.

A new series is introduced cautiously since it often takes time for the audience to become attuned to its characters and mood. The program may be 'hammocked' between two established series. 'Block programming' is the strategy of grouping similar shows, for example in the form of 'theme nights'. Hence, a TV3 poster invites us to 'Spend Friday Night with the Boys' while Tuesday offers a night's viewing primarily for women, built around *Sex and the City*. TV4 has similarly offered 'Make-out Mondays', 'Sci-fi Thursdays', and 'British Comedy Wednesdays'. Groupings are based on the idea of 'viewer entropy,' the prediction that most viewers will be happy to stay with the same channel if there is no strong reason to shift. Although some programmers think that too much of the same genre can backfire, they always look for a program that will hold the interest of the audience 'inherited' from, or 'delivered' by, the previous one. Whether or not the programs are similar, there needs to be a flow-on of ratings in the way a baton is passed safely from one runner in a relay race to the next.

A program that provides the 'lead-in to prime time' is particularly important as it strives to establish the channel as home-base for the evening's viewing. Both TV ONE and TV3 attempt to use their 6 pm news program in this way, stripped across the week, and there is a fierce rivalry between the two programs that compete head to head at the same time. In their liking for predictability, viewers demand that virtually all free-to-air broadcasters do their programming in half-hour or one hour units. This places a particular premium on '**junctions**' (the beginnings and ends of programs) and on the four commercial breaks per hour, as moments when viewers may flick to other channels in search of greater satisfaction. Since advertising is the precious life blood of commercial television, programmers must accept these risks, but they make sure the first two minutes of any locally made program provides a strong 'teaser' or '**hook**,' and that the ad breaks are preceded by a cliffhanger or promise of something interesting to come.

To make sense of the ratings a program has received, one needs always to relate them to the surrounding schedule and to what programs the other channels were screening at the same time. Since TV3 arrived in 1989, New Zealand television has seen a constant battle of programming between the two main networks. In April 1991, for example, when TV3 proudly launched *Twin Peaks*, its major drama for the year, TVNZ pulled out the most powerful ratings weapon it had in its armoury, *Crocodile Dundee*, a bestselling film about an Australian crocodile hunter. It scheduled it at short notice but with maximum publicity to coincide with the first episode of David Lynch's critically acclaimed series about the mysterious death of Laura Palmer. Next day large TVNZ advertisements carried the headline 'Laura Palmer Killed by Crocodile' above an image of laughing jaws. Readers were informed that 'The much-touted television ratings battle last night resulted in a decisive victory for Channel 2.' The statement ended with a *Twin Peaks* in-joke: 'Well, at least now we know who did it'.[5] In terms of understanding the series, it helped to have seen the first episode, and *Twin Peaks* never fully recovered from its bad start. Such victories can backfire if viewers blame the rival broadcaster for wrecking their favourite series (which may, in the aftermath, be shifted to a remote time slot or cancelled). Competitive programming has seen many popular series of a similar type scheduled at the same time, causing viewers to plead with broadcasters to back down. In 1993 TV3 switched its Sunday night movies to Monday night, 'claiming that spoiling tactics by TVNZ forced the move' (*NZ Herald* 1993). In 2002 TVNZ resolved a clash between two New Zealand drama series, *Mercy Peak* (TV ONE) and *The Strip* (TV3), by shifting its series to the following night. New Zealand On Air has attempted, by the way it drafts contracts, to avoid clashes of this kind between the dramas it funds, but its powers are limited and ultimately it must rely on the goodwill of broadcasters, as happened in the above case.

The range of tactics described above, when combined with a meticulous study of the ratings day after day, should allow programmers with an adequate budget and the right instincts to steer their channel successfully. But success is never continuous because the television environment is exceptionally fast moving and volatile, with frequent changes in the tactics of competitors, audience interests and fads, deals with suppliers, censorship, advertisers, the weather, management policies and personalities, competition with other forms of entertainment (such as music and sport), and so on. The precision of the schedule represents the programmer's best efforts to negotiate the chaos of the media environment.

Having focused so far on a close-up, short-term view of this search for order, we shall turn in the second section to a more detached study of the schedule over longer periods. In this broader perspective, the most sweeping changes have been the work of politicians rather than programmers.

Political upheavals

Programming can be seen as a basic human activity as we all plan the most strategic use of our time, such as the pattern of our own television viewing. But most people are not eager to spend hours organising their schedule. In the United States new technology in the form of the 'digital personal video recorder' (**PVR**) is allowing an increasing number of owners to 'timeshift' programs to such an extent that some viewers are effectively becoming programmers in their own right, as though creating their own niche channels. But not all owners use the recorders in such an active way, and it seems likely there will continue to be a demand for networks scheduled by programming specialists so that viewers can, in the traditional way, sit back and go with the flow. After all, most viewers have not used the previous generation of off-air video recorders (VCRs) anywhere near as often as the industry had feared.

Expertise in programming is required for any cultural activity in which elements unfolding in time are strategically sequenced, such as the schedule of a cinema, designed to maximise box office revenue. But programming can be informed by different values, so in contrast to a multiplex cinema, a film festival is likely to be scheduled with more emphasis on cultural priorities and it may aim simply to break even, in some cases with the help of public funding. Similarly, complementary programming informed by public service aims produces fundamentally different results from competitive programming with commercial aims. The decision by politicians in the 1980s to transform New Zealand television from a half commercial, half public service type of system to a completely commercial system makes an informative case study. Programming was only one aspect of that shift but it was a particularly revealing aspect because of its strategic importance and the clearly defined limits of what sorts of material were 'in' or 'out'. Yet while the on-screen changes were dramatic, it was not always easy to interpret them because programming choices were influenced (as we have seen) by a variety of factors.

A possible explanatory concept can be borrowed from media studies—'hegemony', a term that draws attention to the limits of any mainstream culture and seeks to explain large-scale changes by relating them to economic and political power struggles. The concept was originally developed by the Italian political theorist Antonio Gramsci, who sought to understand the rise of Fascism. (Gramsci was imprisoned by the Fascists and died in 1937 after eleven years of captivity. His *Prison Notebooks* were published posthumously and became a classic of political thought.) He was a traditional Marxist in his belief that the ultimate power in any society was held by those who controlled its economic 'structure' or its means of production. But he also felt that Marxists needed to pay more attention to the cultural 'superstructure', the less tangible realm of public opinion, political ideology, nationalism, religion, and popular culture. Gramsci wanted to understand why masses of people willingly gave their support to a movement such as Fascism that would ultimately lead them to disaster, a movement that in fact only served the interests of an elite. He sought to analyse the cultural dimension of this movement, particularly the way it offered a world view (or 'hegemony') that was broad, colourful, and coherent—it combined familiar ingredients of culture, national feeling, and religion, and offered a way to make sense of the confusing diversity of the world. The Fascist elite did not simply promote their own tastes but managed to 'impose a general direction on social life', through a hegemonic culture that appeared to champion the national interest. This view was internalised by people en masse and taken for granted as 'commonsense'. There were, however, definite boundaries to such a hegemonic or dominant culture—it encouraged and rewarded some elements and suppressed others, while exerting a collective pressure on ways of thinking and acting.

Gramsci took the term 'hegemony' from *hegemonia*, the Greek word for 'leadership'. Fascism represented a particularly extreme and sinister example of such a world view, but Gramsci saw hegemonic analysis as applicable to any society—there was always a mainstream orthodoxy of some kind, which (according to his theory) served the interests of the elite currently in power. Alternative or counter hegemonies could develop (with the help of their own intellectuals and creative people), but the dominant hegemony did its best to block them by absorbing some of the oppositional elements into its own mix.

Gramsci's theory is not so heavy-handed as to assume there is a conscious conspiracy at work, brainwashing the public with propaganda. The situation is in some respects inevitable as we are all inside some world view or other that provides us with our idea of 'commonsense'. Nevertheless, Gramsci's is a suspicious, anti-establishment approach that encourages us to question the political implications of what we watch, and to think about what is missing as well as what is present.

Even though Gramsci died before the coming of television, his theory is relevant to a mass medium that provides a powerful vehicle for mainstream interests. Some may feel that the Marxist background of the theory rules it out for serious consideration, but the concept of hegemony can still offer a useful starting-point for the analysis of culture and its overall dynamics. It is particularly relevant to the political dimension of culture in any highly politicised situation that involves conflicts of power.

That was the case in New Zealand after 1984, when a new Labour government introduced controversial political changes that meant the promotion of 'free market' capitalism, shifting influence and resources from the traditional business establishment to a group of entrepreneurs representing new industries and new international alliances. This shift was explained in terms of the political philosophy known as neo-liberalism, though popularly it was known as 'Rogernomics', in reference to Finance Minister Roger Douglas. Gramsci's theory would predict that such a shift in economic and political power would inevitably lead to a profound change in the media environment. Sure enough, the government set out to alter the 'general direction' of television by restructuring TVNZ in 1988 as an SOE (State Owned Enterprise), thus requiring it to shed any vestiges of the public service tradition and to become a fully commercial operation. The government also approved the establishment of TV3, a commercial channel under independent ownership, to ensure that TVNZ had direct competition.

Naturally this led to significant changes in the content and style of television. Now the test of Gramsci's theory is whether or not those changes benefited Rogernomics. They were promoted in non-political terms as being 'good for television' and 'more cost-effective'—not as 'in the interests of our new power elite'. When challenged, politicians would insist they had commercialised and deregulated television not in order to impose their own tastes or to promote their own brand of politics but simply to make the medium work better. In their opinion, the commercial model of television with its competitive approach to programming was going to serve its audience more effectively than so-called public service broadcasting. If the government henceforth appointed only business people to the TVNZ board (in contrast to the previous mix of cultural and commercial specialists), this was a matter of efficiency, not ideology. The rule of the ratings system and the pressure on the broadcaster to increase profit would ensure that TVNZ kept in close touch with the likes and dislikes of viewers. From this perspective, programming in the 1990s would offer a truer reflection of what the New Zealand public really wanted to see and not (as in previous decades) what a bunch of bureaucrats and elitists felt that it should.

A Gramscian would reply that these comments ignored a number of complexities. The change of TVNZ culture was not simply a matter of efficiency, it had ideological implications. The viewer who had been regarded (according to the public service tradition) as a fellow citizen was now to be re-conceived (according to the commercial tradition) as a customer or consumer. Television programs were now seen as mere 'products', and program-makers were downgraded to the status of hired hands. Ratings were not a reliable measure of what the public really wanted, and if television had become more efficient, it was in terms of serving advertisers rather than viewers. Advertisers favoured certain audiences at the expense of others, and the small size of the country brought out the worst in the market model because it was difficult in commercial terms for minorities to reach critical mass. Hence, the claim that the market model yielded more choice was spurious because minority tastes (previously sustained by public service broadcasting as a matter of principle) were now marginalised, and all free-to-air channels now served the priorities of advertisers. TV ONE, TV2, TV3, and Prime all converged with a similar mainstream commercial style and ambience.

Yet did this 'style and ambience' amount to a new neo-liberal hegemony? A Gramscian analysis would claim that this was very much the case, pointing to these aspects of the television schedule as circumstantial evidence:

1 There was a huge increase in the amount of advertising, to approximately fourteen minutes per hour. Each ad could be seen as promoting not only a specific product but the general values of consumerism and capitalism.

2 An increase in sponsorship allowed commercialism to spread beyond the ad breaks into the programs themselves. Studio chat, home improvement, travel, and many other types of program incorporated elements of 'advertorial' (marketing that was packaged as information). Government departments promoted controversial political ideas by suggesting projects to documentary-makers (such as the controversial 1997 *Time Bomb* documentaries made by an independent production company in response to suggestions from the Department of Social Welfare). The boundary between information and publicity or propaganda became less clear.

3 Competition for rights had the effect of turning sports events into expensive weapons in the ratings war, and this led to distortions in television coverage. For example, the loss of traditional sporting codes to SKY was clearly one of the reasons why TVNZ became such an enthusiastic sponsor of the America's Cup (a competition closely associated with the commercial elite). This event came to assume such prominence in TVNZ news coverage that some commentators were led to question whether balanced journalism was giving way to self-interested publicity. This is not to deny the fact that some viewers had a genuine interest in

yachting and the Cup, but to note that there is an ongoing debate about whether television basically mirrors the culture or is influential in shaping it. From a Gramscian perspective, TVNZ's decision to shift huge resources to this particular form of elite sport inevitably carried political implications.

4 Investigative reporting that required in-depth research became harder to justify in a commercial environment. There was still a place for the occasional 'loss leader' but it was hard to persuade managers who were already worried about the risk of expensive court cases (such as the litigation that followed the documentary *In The Public Good*) to commit journalists for an extended period of time, particularly as the results of such an investigation were unpredictable.

5 Broadcasters insisted on a populist style of program-making. In the case of documentaries, for example, all topics had to have mainstream interest—they needed to appeal to 'Mr and Mrs Smith', the legendary viewers spoken of by programmers and commissioning editors. Documentaries needed to be personalised (to be structured round individuals rather than ideas), to be as emotional as possible, and to move along briskly. They had to avoid being complicated, 'pointy-headed' (intellectual), or overtly educational. Political issues were regarded as a turn-off unless there were strong personalities, emotions, and conflicts involved. Such requirements were rationalised as being simply a matter of making documentaries more accessible and lively, but cumulatively they had ideological effects by promoting an individualist view of society and making it difficult to ask certain kinds of complex or unconventional questions.

These were some of the post-1984 changes that could be cited as evidence by Gramscians that a new economic and political elite had re-shaped television to reflect their own values and to serve their own interests—subtly, of course, since New Zealanders would have disapproved of any direct political interference in program content. Arguably, the overall effect was to encourage and reward some elements (such as individualism, competitiveness, commercialism, and consumerism—values that featured prominently in the neo-liberal world view) and to suppress others (community access, minority interests, education, intellectual analysis, etc.). Commercial considerations had become the new 'commonsense' of programming and all other aspects of television. Turning TVNZ into a commercial enterprise had changed its contents and style, yet the politicians could insist that this was the result not of politics but simply of consumer choice.

Hegemonic analysis offers a thought-provoking, broad-brush explanation of how and why these changes occurred. Yet there are many complications to the analysis. They do not altogether refute Gramsci's theory but they certainly call for a closer look at the details. To mention a few of the possible counter-arguments:

a   News and current affairs staff would deny that their journalistic ethics and integrity have been compromised. Certainly the situation is complex, particularly as the duty of the journalist to report the facts 'without fear or favour' sometimes coincides with television's belief that conflict is good for ratings. Scandals involving members of the ruling elite arouse strong public interest. In the 1990s politicians were surprised by what they perceived as television's 'tabloid tendency' and unsympathetic coverage, as though their reforms had unintentionally created a monster.

b   Some business leaders were also disturbed by what they saw as 'the dumbing down of television'. The Educational Television (ETV) slot and in-depth local documentaries were not able to survive in the new ultra-commercial environment (with occasional exceptions, mostly funded by New Zealand On Air, such as *The New Zealand Wars*). Television's appetite for 'mindless entertainment' seemed excessive to some politicians and chief executives, particularly in view of the fact that the new business environment urgently required a smart work force. 'Dumbing down' also seemed to contradict the theory that market forces enhanced performance. Some politicians tried to rationalise the situation by arguing that commercialism and deregulation had not gone far enough, and once TVNZ was freed entirely from the shackles of public ownership, it would smarten up its act.

Other media theorists rose to the defence of television by arguing that phrases like 'dumbing down' and 'mindless entertainment' were patronising because they implied that the audience was stupid. Reception studies have highlighted the rich, diverse, and idiosyncratic ways that viewers read and use television programs according to their own needs. Some media theorists were equally suspicious of Marxist talk of hegemony because they saw it as linked to old prejudices about the brainwashing effects of television, and as a kind of conspiracy theory.

Gramscians would, however, deny that theirs was a 'conspiracy theory' since they regarded ideological processes as universal, at work in every society. There was always a dominant hegemony of one sort or another, a particular world view developed by intellectuals associated with the commercial and political elite of the day. The previous phase of public service television could be analysed in the same sceptical terms, as could the new, post-Charter environment.[6] There were differences to the television schedule in each of these three phases, and arguably those differences could be linked to the changing political and economic hegemony.

c   Analysis needs to factor in the effect of New Zealand On Air which continued to fight for public service outcomes in the midst of commercialism. A Gramscian might see its function merely as a safety valve, a way to preserve a few opportunities for dissent and difference with the long-term aim of co-opting or assimilating such elements into the mainstream, yet that sceptical view would overlook some serious conflicts between New Zealand On Air and other state agencies particularly in its early years.

d Perhaps the strongest challenge to a hegemonic interpretation involves drawing attention to the complexity or even chaos of television, the multitude of factors shaping everyday decisions about programming or program-making that makes any single-factor explanation problematic. Gramscian analysis can accommodate this doubt to some extent by arguing that it does not deny the intricacy of individual actions but chooses to concentrate on the big picture—it is not about the everyday tactics of programming but about long-term trends in the culture at large. Yet this bypasses an important dimension of the subject, and does not fully explain the complexity and unpredictability experienced by everyone engaged in the day-to-day turmoil of television (or, for that matter, of politics).

The usefulness of hegemonic analysis will continue to be debated. The on-going changes in the New Zealand television system—as it has shifted from a public service to a mixed model, to a totally commercial model, and lately to a different kind of mixed model—provide a rich body of evidence through which the claims of hegemonic theory can continue to be explored, tested, and argued.

References

Ang, Ien. 1991. *Desperately Seeking the Audience*. London: Routledge.

Browne, Nick. 1984 'The Political Economy of the Television (Super) Text', in Horace Newcomb (ed.), *Television: The Critical View*. New York: Oxford University Press, pp. 585–99.

Browne, Nick (ed.). 1994. *American Television: New Directions in History and Theory*. Langhorne, Pennsylvania: Harwood Academic Publishers.

Dunleavy, Trisha. 1999. New Zealand Drama: The First Thirty Years 1960–1990, Thesis (PhD), University of Auckland.

Gramsci, Antonio. 1991. *Prison Notebooks*. New York: Columbia University Press.

Lealand, Geoff. 2002. 'Ratings and More Damn Ratings: Measuring Television Viewing in New Zealand', in John Farnsworth & Ian Hutchison (eds), *New Zealand Television: A Reader*. Palmerston North: Dunmore.

National Business Review. 1990. 'TVNZ Axes 154 as Ad Revenue Drops,' 25 May.

National Business Review. 1996. 'Here's Andy to Bound Into TV2's Wilting Fortunes'. 16 February.

NZ Herald. 1990. 'Ratings Rebound on TV3 Price'. 30 January.

NZ Herald. 1993. 'Channels Juggle Movies'. 9 October.

Sunday Star. 1991. 'Error Brings Repeat Screening'. 26 April.

Sunday Star-Times. 2003a. 'Six Figure Relaunch for TV2 Next Week'. 26 January, p. A12.

Sunday Star-Times. 2003b. 'New Wave of Brand Identity Has TV2 In Your Neighbourhood'. 26 January, p. F7.

Williams, Raymond. 1974. *Television: Technology and Cultural Form.* London: Fontana.

Notes

1   Nick Browne (1994, p. 71) defines 'scheduling' in his influential essay on the subject as 'the practice of selecting, placing, and coordinating programs with respect to each other for overall maximum competitive business advantage'. This term is also used in New Zealand, though 'programming' is more common. Confusion can arise as the term 'programming' is also sometimes used to describe a group of programs (as in 'children's programming'). Here I am thinking of the activity in terms of many kinds of possible 'advantage', not only the 'business advantage' that Browne associates with American commercial television.

2   See Trish Dunleavy's *New Zealand Drama: The First Thirty Years 1960–1990* (1999) for much valuable information on the history of programming in New Zealand.

3   The pairing is part of what theorists call the 'synchronic' or simultaneous dimension of programming, in contrast to the 'diachronic' dimension or flow of television from hour to hour, day to day.

4   According to the ACNeilsen company: 'A device called a **PeopleMeter** measures ratings. This is a box that sits on top of the television set and electronically records whatever programme is being watched. There are PeopleMeters in 470 households around New Zealand, providing a sample of around 1150 people. As each member of the household comes into the room to watch television, they press a button on the PeopleMeter handset, which tells the PeopleMeter exactly who is watching. Video recording and playback are also monitored. The viewing information is automatically fed down the phone line each night to a central computer within ACNielsen.' Available at: http://www.acnielsen.co.nz/product.asp?ProductID=27#.

5   TVNZ publicity release, 9 April 1991.

6   The Charter officially came into effect in March 2003, but some changes began with the election of the Clark government in 1999.

PART 3

**Between
International
Formats and
Local Meanings**

Introduction

Examining the relationship between global formats and local adaptations, the first four chapters in this Part take a particular genre as a starting point.

Trisha Dunleavy's chapter is based on her PhD thesis, which represented the first detailed history of New Zealand television drama. Her research reminds us of a number of forgotten programs, including those of the 'golden age' that she identifies between 1975 and 1979. Her chapter presents a passionate argument for the importance of local drama and offers a thoughtful perspective on the main theme of this section by tracking the changing relationship between 'localness' and 'exportability'. Too much emphasis on the latter produces bland forms of 'recombinant' (or copycat) drama.

Misha Kavka's rich genre study of 'the reality program' precedes chapters on 'the documentary' and 'the news bulletin' as contrasting approaches to 'reality'. The meteoric growth of reality programming raises provocative questions about how the genre works and why it attracts millions of enthusiastic viewers worldwide. Kavka sees this as a particularly interesting genre for New Zealand. Broadcasters and producers have embraced various versions of it with enthusiasm as relatively cheap forms of local content; but, more importantly, reality programming seems especially well suited to a New Zealand sense of place as it offers up 'Kiwis in their natural habitat'.

Annie Goldson comes to the theme of documentary as an award-winning director with a strong sense of political commitment. She sees television with its commercial priorities and desire for 'fast turnaround' as failing to tap the full potential of the genre. Even 'quality' documentaries on New Zealand television seem to Goldson to be compromised by their nationalist agenda. She links this kind of documentary back to the nation-building approach of New Zealand's National Film Unit, and to the most conservative aspects of the British tradition of film-making associated with John Grierson. In contrast, she traces an alternative tradition of New Zealand documentaries, radical in spirit, more closely linked to indepen-dent film-making than to television, represented by directors such as Merata Mita, Barry Barclay, Alister Barry, and Peter Wells.

Stephen Crofts demonstrates an extremely close reading of a sample news hour, combining **content analysis** (an approach strongly developed in New Zealand by researchers such as Joe Atkinson) with more wide-ranging methods of discourse and cultural analysis. Crofts reveals the under-lying structures, procedures, and priorities of the news genre, and also its typical tactics as it negotiates the 'routine assumptions' and anxieties of New Zealand culture—for example, the way the program generates a cosy 'feelgoodism'.

Roger Horrocks's essay concludes the section by surveying local content across all genres. Strongly committed to the development of New Zealand production (a cause shared by many of the other contributors), he seeks to map the particular field of forces in which local content is created. He examines the complex ways the local and the global interact—through the alleged 'dumping' of overseas programs, the negotiation of international co-productions, the search for overseas sales, and the adaptation of overseas formats. He also looks closely at a theme that crops up frequently in this book—'cultural cringe', or insecure attitudes to the local, a common legacy of societies with a colonial history.

12

Made in New Zealand:

The Genre of Television Drama

TRISHA DUNLEAVY

Introducing the genre

With rich benefits in cultural as well as commercial terms, locally produced drama is a significant contributor to national television culture. A key influence on any area of television production—let alone one as costly and high risk as drama—is the size of the audience market involved,[1] and in large television-producing countries, drama programming has an unquestioned commercial role. But the reconciliation of commercial and cultural justifications for this form of production is necessarily more complex in a small country. New Zealand's legacy as a postcolonial nation, while it has also made it difficult for local television drama to flourish, has kept the genre's cultural role very much in the forefront.

The genre originated in the early 1960s, just a few years after the inception of New Zealand television itself. Although drama's beginnings were far from auspicious (audience responses to the very first dramas were less than enthusiastic) and its development was slow (the genre was confined to one-offs until 1969), it is accurate to claim that New Zealand has never been *without* local television drama.[2] The fact that such a genre was able to develop in New Zealand, has been able to triumph spectacularly at times, and has made such a strong cultural impact (these achievements being against the odds for small countries) is a cause for celebration. Highlighting some of the genre's milestones in the last four decades, this chapter will also outline the perennial problems and conditions of television drama production in New Zealand.

New Zealand television's limited market size and consequent over-reliance on imported programs has made it difficult to sustain expensive forms of television production. Hence, while it has endured through forty years of television, local television drama has remained something of an 'endangered species'. What is endangered is not so much the genre's survival in some form, but its ability to retain both a formal diversity and a strong prime-time presence. Situated very much at the receiving end of international program flow, New Zealand networks have enjoyed ease of access to the best of American and British television exports. While local drama must compete with these for the attention of New Zealanders, it has never done so on an equal footing. Where this competition is driven by commercial logic (as New Zealand television has been since 1990), local drama can seem a relatively dubious investment for nervous commissioning executives, especially because American or British drama imports are relatively cheap to obtain and so often combine a low investment cost with impressive ratings.[3] As New Zealand television has adapted to the addition of new private channels through the 1990s (a chief effect being to fragment audiences and underline the virtues of cheap program forms), the justifications for commissioning new local dramas have increasingly centred on the expected cultural rather than on expected commercial benefits. In certain sub-genres of New Zealand television drama (notably in the short form area) cultural considerations have always prevailed over commercial ones, given that these forms provide much valued diversity.

Within New Zealand television, locally produced drama offers a cultural counterweight to some effects of so-called 'cultural imperialism'.[4] It works both to reinforce a sense of 'cultural identity' and to erode the 'cultural cringe' to which New Zealanders (as one feature of their postcolonial legacy) have been prone. In spite of the genre's ability to contribute to the general culture in such positive ways, it is likely to remain endangered. In any television system, new drama projects are among the greatest financial risks that a network will take in any one season. However, the hope that a drama series may, if a network is fortunate, deliver excellent ratings while generating audience loyalty, makes the risk worth taking. Large television systems (particularly those with secure and diverse export markets) can more readily absorb such risks. In medium-sized and smaller countries, in which imported programs can often dominate prime-time schedules, a proportion of local programming can be ensured via regulation. Although a number of countries employ such regulation, smaller English-speaking countries remain at risk of import dominance in prime-time drama, with Australia being one of the few to apply 'local content' regulations to the genre (New Zealand On Air 1999).

With a population of just four million, New Zealand is too small to manage the commercial dangers of drama production without the 'risk capital' provided by public funding. When New Zealand television was deregulated in 1989 and in the context of the 'strictly commercial' objectives thenceforth imposed on TVNZ, the continuation of Public Broadcasting Fee (**PBF**) support for drama was provided for in the responsibilities given to New Zealand On Air, as the new guardian of New Zealand's public broadcasting purse. Since deregulation, cultural justifications for drama, as written into the statutory responsibilities of NZOA (Bell 1995; Smith 1996), have become the genre's lifeline, particularly in the context of some difficult times for drama series in the 1990s. Moves to re-regulate New Zealand television since 2000 have seen a public service Charter imposed on TVNZ, a change that has helped re-establish local television drama among the public broadcaster's commissioning priorities.[5]

The establishment of a drama production cycle (1965–74)

It is a testament to the determination and resourcefulness of local script-writers, directors, and producers that they have, over forty years of fluctuating fortunes for the genre, remained unfazed by the creative challenges inherent in New Zealand's small market position.[6] From the moment of television's inception in 1960, and incensed by the extent to which British and American dramas were afforded pride of place in New Zealand's prime-time schedule, aspiring New Zealand drama-makers argued for a network commitment to the genre.[7] As early as 1967, the case for a local program quota (involving a range of genres including drama) was being put. For a brief period between 1974 and 1976, a modest quota was even implemented.[8]

Given the many connections between the reflection of 'localness' on television and the rise of New Zealand television drama in the 1970s, it is not surprising that New Zealand's first television drama-makers described themselves as cultural nationalists. The genre's pioneers grew up in the New Zealand of the 1940s, witnessed the inception of television in 1960, and, by 1965, were making moves to initiate a drama production cycle. For them, the ability to tell New Zealand stories, create recognisably local characters, and hear genuine local accents on television, were elements of a much larger cultural project that involved all of the arts and aimed to deliver New Zealand from the doldrums of a 'colonial condition'. While they were greatly inspired by the quality of the imports that New Zealand television screened in the 1960s, they were disappointed at the NZBC's lack of enthusiasm for production. At the same time as providing an enticing 'window on the world' for isolated New Zealanders in the 1960s, NZBC television did surprisingly little to demonstrate its 'localness'. Key manifestations of the NZBC's cultural ambivalence included a paucity of New Zealand programs and the cultivation of pseudo-English accents by local presenters.[9] The NZBC's lack of enthusiasm for drama production in particular (resulting in only intermittent production opportunities and inadequate facilities) meant that the trickle of one-off dramas produced through the 1960s seemed to do as much to encourage as to eliminate 'cultural cringe.'

Pioneer drama-makers understood that their initial success would depend on the pursuit of objectives in three main areas. First, it was important to be able to write drama for television, rather than necessarily adapting literature or theatre as the first dramas had tended to do. Second, local drama would only compete with American and British imports if it could emulate their diversity and achieve an ongoing screen presence. While diversity meant pursuing a range of approaches and sub-genres—including short-form dramas and relatively serious stories—longevity in prime time required the development of long-form popular dramas, including soap operas. Third, to win acceptability for the genre, it would be vital to demonstrate its potential to contribute to the general culture. As was evident in the responses to the earliest drama efforts, the 'localness' of New Zealand television drama was important to audiences, thus drama's cultural expectations would only be met as far as programs could offer what viewers considered to be 'authentic' depictions of New Zealand identity, culture, or history. Accordingly, the creation of successful drama programs entailed, above all, the construction of concepts, characters, and stories that New Zealand viewers could be expected to recognise and accept as their own.

The third and most complex of the above objectives, which can be broadly conceived as the pursuit of 'localness' in New Zealand television drama, warrants more discussion. As 1960s drama-makers were the first (though by no means the last) to discover, the construction of 'localness' in drama concepts, characters, and stories could only be achieved through trial and error. Notwithstanding the many ways 'localness' could be reflected in dramas (these nuanced by TV drama's many 'universal' features), no single concept or program could be expected to distil it to the satisfaction of a broad New Zealand audience. There was also the influence of the New Zealand audience's experience of television drama more generally. Unlike British and American audiences, whose initial expectations of television drama were shaped by domestic productions, New Zealanders first encountered this genre as imported programming. New Zealand audience expectations of drama, formed as they were by frequent exposure to acclaimed British and American products, created a particularly difficult reception climate for locally produced dramas. When the first locally produced TV plays made their humble debuts in the 1960s, audience reactions were often negative. Not only had the dominance of imported programs on New Zealand television contributed to a general sense of 'cultural cringe' among viewers, it had also generated impossible expectations that locally produced dramas should 'represent' New Zealand, and do so favourably. This type of audience response was no better evident than in the 'almost riotous hostility' provoked by early television play, *The Evening Paper* (1965), which inveigled a stinging social critique into an account of white, middle-class family life.[10] As will be outlined below, the first drama series to apparently meet the conceptual challenges of 'localness', and in so doing pioneer a provincial template for New Zealand's 'popular drama series' genre, was *Pukemanu* (1971–72).

New Zealand television drama developed but did not prosper during the NZBC era, which ended in late 1974. While negative influences included an institutional tendency to deride fledgling drama efforts and the absence of sufficient production funding or facilities, one positive outcome of the NZBC era was that New Zealand's first television dramas were offered to a captive audience because there was just one channel. Thus when *Pukemanu* debuted on a Thursday evening in the winter of 1971, New Zealanders found it difficult to avoid.[11] However, as they watched *Pukemanu*'s opening scenes they were anything but disappointed, as Christine Cole Catley has suggested:

> Nostalgia and recognition greeted *Pukemanu*. It's a place and people we know. The people of *Pukemanu* are ordinary people in an ordinary country town… Many of us still see ourselves as simple country people, no matter how long ago the uprooting from childhood farm and little town. We are not yet an urban people. As we learn to live in cities we cling more tenaciously to a romantic, Crump-enhanced picture of open country. The hills are our mythology.

> Cole Catley 1973, pp. 43–4

By contrast with earlier dramas (whose links with mainstream literature and theatre were evident in the predominance of urban, middle-class characters), *Pukemanu* was set in a fictional North Island mill town and depicted a bicultural community of hardy forestry workers. Richly evocative of the 'small town New Zealand' with which New Zealanders have retained a nostalgic identification, *Pukemanu* posited an image of the kind of shared culture and values that viewers recognised and enthusiastically embraced. Achieving national top-ten ratings during its two seasons, *Pukemanu* was the first local drama series to demonstrate the potential of the genre as both a commercial tool and a means to reinforce a sense of cultural identity. Despite *Pukemanu*'s popularity and enduring constructions of 'localness', its achievements were vastly underestimated at the time, and the series was prematurely axed. *Pukemanu* was something of a blip on a barren landscape until 1975, when the drama genre benefited from the advent of a second channel, a PBF increase, and a major restructuring of public television.

By 1975, the genre seemed to be flourishing. Assisted by a short-lived form of local content quota and then by public television's expansion, a drama production cycle was established by 1971 and consolidated by 1976, by which time the genre had achieved an appropriately sustained prime-time presence. Between 1975 and 1979, when two-channel public television involved independent management for the channels and separate drama departments, a number of milestone dramas appeared.[12] The creative innovation, formal diversity, and cultural achievement of these 1970s productions marks the era not only as a watershed in the genre's history, but also one that was facilitated by a convergence of unusually favourable conditions.

1975–79: Golden years for New Zealand television drama?

[T]he idea of a 'Golden Age' of television drama is cloaked in perpetual quotation marks. Golden Ages only exist in retrospect. They are never lived as golden, but can only be constructed in memory from the hindsight of what came after... There is, however, a sense in which the idea of a Golden Age may be meaningful: when it refers to that historical moment when one set of meanings and values is being replaced by another, when the traditions which stabilized a culture are beginning to be questioned and re-written, and when creativity seems to transgress the boundaries of received good taste.

Caughie 2000, p. 57

The above comment by John Caughie refers to British television drama's achievements in the single play heyday of the late 1960s. While Caughie usefully underlines the need for caution around the term 'golden age', he also highlights the way such moments are created by a confluence of favourable social, political, economic, and cultural factors.

In New Zealand, the above kind of questioning and challenging characterised the 1970s. Propelled by a convergence of political, economic, and social forces (common to which were an urge to demonstrate a cultural form of independence from England and a new energy that came into the culture with the 1960s), a new national identity for New Zealand—as a Pacific and bicultural nation—began to emerge and seek expression. Outside of politics and related public forums, the most dynamic outlet for this was the cultural arena—in literature, the performing arts, popular music, and in film and television. Specific outcomes of New Zealand's new-found cultural self-determination were seen in the expansion of television drama (1975–79) and in the establishment of a New Zealand film industry (1977–82) leading to the creation of ongoing feature film production. The burgeoning of television drama production (and of local feature films) was pushed along by, as well as being integral to, New Zealand's journey of cultural self-discovery.

The restructuring of public broadcasting in 1974 coupled with a major licence fee increase set the scene for an expansive period for local television drama from 1975. The establishment of semi-independent corporations for TV ONE and TV2 was part of a new institutional commitment to vastly increase the proportion and quality of local programs. Hence, 'golden' years for drama from 1975–79 were also facilitated by an institutional context in which there was encouragement for higher cost forms of production and sufficient public money for television's 'public service' aspirations to be met. Television funding in these years was characterised by a near 50/50 balance between public and commercial income, which, although it was clearly the ideal for local drama, would not be repeated. Drama flourished in the context of two separate drama departments and the fostering of complementary 'house styles'. Although the two departments would eventually be amalgamated as part of the creation of a unified TVNZ in 1980, their years of competitive independence in the five years prior produced a wealth of drama that ranged across 'popular' and 'serious' approaches and achieved the kind of balance between one-off and long-form output that was rarely seen again.

The genre involved a talented range of contributors, a diversity of form and style, and left equal room for 'serious' and 'popular' types of production. Within the large volume of popular-styled material, for example, were the country's first soap operas—TV ONE's *Close to Home* and TV2's *A Going Concern*. The evident commitment to the creation of 'flagship' dramas for each channel from 1975 did not gobble up production budgets in the way that they would tend to do in later eras. Despite its outlay on several drama series in 1975 (the most successful of which was *Moynihan*), there was still money for TV ONE to commission the television film *The God Boy* and the ambitious historical serial *The Governor*. Underlining the unusual opportunity for innovation in drama was TV2's ability to match TV ONE's output in diversity as well as volume.[13] Yet in an attempt to pinpoint what distinguished this 1970s era from expansive periods for drama in the 1980s and 1990s, it seems fair to generalise that it also involved a more strident pursuit of 'localness' than was possible later.[14]

Although the quality of 'localness' in some ways defies definition, meaning different things to different people, one way to qualify it is to contrast it with another objective within New Zealand television drama—that of 'exportability'. Although, drama scriptwriters and producers were not required to consider 'exportability' in 1975, it would become increasingly important in the 1980s, by which time producers had discovered international interest in New Zealand drama and television's bean-counters were exploring ways to amortise drama's rising production costs. 'Exportability' involves producing drama with overseas viewers in mind, or developing drama in league with foreign investors. As was underlined by the apparent rejection by New Zealanders of popular drama series *City Life* in 1996, 'exportability' has the potential to undermine drama's cultural objectives by necessitating the reduction of local references or details, especially those thought to be inaccessible to foreign audiences. As 'exportability' loomed larger after 1980, the limits on 'localness' that it imposed began to necessitate the avoidance of New Zealand-specific themes such as the bicultural stories in *Pukemanu*, *The Governor*, and *Open House*. The best of the 1974–79 dramas (as exemplified by the *Winners and Losers* anthology, the telefilm *The God Boy*, and the historical drama serial *The Governor*) demonstrated the heights of creative and cultural ambition to which the genre could, under ideal conditions, aspire. Although all three productions were subsequently screened in foreign markets they were nonetheless clear about their role, which was to serve, over and above any other audience, the needs of New Zealanders.

The idea of 'golden' years for local television drama in the 1970s is nonetheless controversial because the prevailing institutional structures limited the participation of the talented independent directors and producers then emerging in the film industry (Horrocks 1977). Two institutional obstacles to the outsourcing of drama prevailed right up to 1989: 1) television was monopolised by public broadcasters, TV ONE and TV2; and 2) drama, as with all other television production, was basically an in-house operation. Independent directors and producers, whose few contributions to television drama were among the most innovative, would have made much more if they had been permitted. Accordingly, the 'golden' glow around drama's achievements from 1975–79 was dulled by the probability that if there had been more commissioning and less monopolisation of production resources by in-house personnel, the potential for innovative, creatively ambitious, and culturally exciting drama would have been that much greater.

Despite the antagonism that film-makers justifiably felt towards television and its closed door attitude, the expansion of local television drama from 1975–79 helped to facilitate the 1977 establishment of a New Zealand film industry in certain ways. First, the diversity and sustained presence of New Zealand television drama programs from 1975 cultivated an audience appetite for local feature films.[15] At the same time as film-makers were lobbying for the creation of a New Zealand film industry in 1975–77, television audiences were enjoying an unprecedented supply of powerful filmed dramas on television. Secondly, although television commissions remained infrequent until 1989, there were more commissions from 1975–79 than in periods either before or immediately after. While these opportunities were still too few to provide an income for aspiring film-makers, they did allow some key personnel to hone their skills while the lobbying for a film industry continued. Producing *Woman at the Store* and *Winners and Losers* for TV ONE, for example, helped prepare Roger Donaldson and Ian Mune for *Sleeping Dogs*, the proficiency and power of which made it a catalyst for a new national cinema. Other future feature film-makers (including Paul Maunder, Geoff Murphy, Barry Barclay, Vincent Ward, Gaylene Preston, and Sam Pillsbury) also developed experience via productions that screened on television between 1974 and 1979. Nevertheless, their frustration at having to struggle so hard for the relatively few opportunities that existed and their irritation at the many compromises involved, fuelled their determination to achieve more appropriate opportunities by building a film industry.

Drama and public funding

Reflecting the blend of 'public service' and commercialism that under-pinned the single-channel NZBC and its two-channel successor TVNZ, a New Zealand tradition of television drama can only remain acceptable (to politicians, administrators, and taxpayers alike) if it can somehow reconcile the different objectives of the system's mixed basis of funding. So, on the one hand, local drama has needed to cultivate broad popular appeal (in pursuit of commercial revenue), and on the other, to foster a sense of local cultural identity (thereby fulfilling elements of public service). The reconciliation between different public and commercial influences—although it was realised in such diverse, successful series as *Hanlon* (1985), *The Fire Raiser* (1986), *Erebus: the Aftermath* (1987), *Shortland Street* (from 1992), *Nga Puna* (1994), and *Tala Pasifika* (1995)—has been no simple feat of creative ingenuity. A balancing act between public and commercial objectives remains a feature of drama's current production environment (as evident in 1999–2002 efforts *Jackson's Wharf, Street Legal, Mercy Peak, Willy Nilly, Being Eve, Love Bites,* and *The Strip*), though it is more complex and difficult in an environment of multi-channel competition and declining public funding.

To the extent that British television drama (a tradition long revered by New Zealanders) is one that has been facilitated both by public service broadcasting objectives and the presence of non-commercial channels

(Bignell, Lacey, and McMurraugh-Kavanagh 2000), the ideal of a mixed public and commercial funding base for New Zealand drama warrants some elaboration. The country's situation of scarce funding for television drama production has been accompanied by a tendency toward political interference in broadcasting, by contrast with the United Kingdom, whose public service commitment to 'creative independence' has worked to keep politicians at a relative arm's length from the operations of television. Political interference has been a general feature of New Zealand television but has strongly affected drama, particularly via fluctuations in the level of the PBF. Reduced PBF input (as characterised the periods 1977–86 and 1993–2000) saw cutbacks in discretionary areas of television's production spending, with drama suffering disproportionately because of its high costs. Future problems in drama's reliance on 'mixed' funding despite a context of declining public funding, were effectively foreshadowed by the furore that emerged in 1977 around *The Governor*, an ambitious historical drama series commissioned by TV ONE. Incensed by rumours of budget over-runs and unnecessary spending, the then Prime Minister, Robert Muldoon, made an example of *The Governor* by initiating a full public inquiry into its costs. Although the inquiry revealed no misuse of public money, it introduced new questions about local television drama production and imposed significant limitations. *The Governor* furore brought equations between production cost and audience size into sharp focus, jeopardising the position of any future drama of proximate ambition. From 1978 on, approval was generally denied to higher-cost drama projects unless they had foreign investment or demonstrable export appeal.

Public funding as 'risk capital' has underpinned virtually all drama productions since 1989 when TVNZ was stripped of Public Broadcasting Fee funding and New Zealand On Air was created. The advantages of 'risk capital' in drama were effectively illustrated early in NZOA's tenure when it commissioned *Shortland Street* in collaboration with TVNZ and Grundy Television. Continuing for the first four years of production, NZOA's PBF input allowed it to exact public service expectations from *Shortland Street*, which have since become important elements of the soap's commercial appeal, both within New Zealand and overseas.[16] *Shortland Street* has highlighted the way in which 'risk capital' can have commercial as well as cultural spin-offs for drama programs (Dunleavy 1995). But a mixed basis of funding for drama seems particularly appropriate given New Zealand's small domestic audience. If it had ever been forced to rely on entirely commercial funding, local television drama would have been in serious trouble. Commercialism left to its own devices would have limited the genre's form, subject matter, and style, in the same way that an increasing reliance on export sales can reduce drama's potential for 'localness'.

NZOA's local content surveys reveal a rise in the number of local television drama hours produced after 1989.[17] While these figures confirm that NZOA has effectively championed drama and that its production was stimulated by the arrival of competition for TVNZ, such surveys underline the way that in a small country television drama's relative health so often comes down to the number of hours on screen. Drawing conclusions about drama's position *only* on the basis of annual volume can be misleading, particularly if 'hours on screen' statistics obscure qualitative indicators, such as drama's representation in different sub-genres or the ambition of particular projects. A related problem is that local content surveys so often use 1988 (a notable 'low' for TVNZ drama) as a point of comparison rather than using figures from earlier, more favourable eras.[18] Applying the hours on screen measurement, one might assume that local television drama enjoyed its best years only after deregulation—an assumption that the 1975–79 era defies in innovation and diversity if not in volume (see Norris and Pauling 2001, p. 125).

More important than comparisons 'before' and 'after' the arrival of NZOA is understanding the optimal conditions for New Zealand television drama. Despite NZOA's significant advantages over earlier systems for allocating public funding to producers, drama's health depends not so much on the existence of NZOA as on the presence of sufficient public funding to limit the influence of purely commercial considerations. While this is but one of several pre-conditions for success in television drama (another being the presence of appropriately talented creative personnel), in New Zealand's case it has seemed extremely important. The genre's greatest opportunities and most innovative output emerged during the following three periods: 1) the early two-channel years, 1975–79; 2) the mid two-channel phase, 1984–87; and 3) the early NZOA era, 1990–93. Common to these periods was a stronger political commitment to public service television, reflected in higher levels of public funding than at other times. Precipitating each of the above periods, PBF increases brought sufficient money into television for its commercial imperatives to be tempered by the pursuit of public service. Thus in the above periods there was relatively more 'risk capital,' providing opportunities for innovation and diversity as well as a certain volume.

Drama and multi-channel television

Safety first is the network rule. There seems safety in numbers: in test results for new and revamped shows, in extrapolations from previous ratings in the case of returning shows. But in the end, the numbers don't suffice to make decisions. To build certainty, the 'science' of numbers has to be joined to the 'art' of hunches—consisting mostly of noting previous hits. The safest, easiest formula is that nothing succeeds like success. Hits are so rare that executives think a blatant imitation stands a good chance of getting bigger numbers than a show that stands on its own. Executives like to say they are looking for something new, but their intuition tells them to hunt up prepackaged trends and then recognise the new as a variant of the old.

Gitlin 1994 p. 63

The above comment introduced Todd Gitlin's exploration of the 'recombinant culture' prevalent in American network television by the early 1980s—a context in which traditional approaches to concept design were threatened by an explosion of cable channels, the rapid take-up of the VCR, and the increasing tendency of remote-wielding viewers to nuke programs that failed to give instant gratification. When Gitlin was writing in the early 1980s, the principle of 'safety first' and its attendant 'recombinant culture' had yet to affect New Zealand to the extent that local executives would automatically reject untested concepts. But, as with many of the processes and considerations described by Gitlin, New Zealand's turn would come.

The local impact of 'recombinant culture' and a network policy of 'safety first' became more obvious after 1988, initially appearing with the advent of TV3 in late 1989 and increasing as other new channels arrived in the early 1990s. Although drama scriptwriters will argue that it has always limited their work, there are greater and lesser degrees of the kind of executive anxiety that Gitlin describes. In New Zealand, 'safety first' has been most obvious as an institutional knee jerk reaction to ratings failure. *Mercy Peak* and *Street Legal* are, in some ways, a response to the ratings failures of *City Life* and *Cover Story*. In *Mercy Peak*, because its concept combines elements from successful local and foreign formats, we can see how 'recombinant culture' works in New Zealand. *Mercy Peak* revisits the kind of provincial New Zealand depicted in *Pukemanu, Jocko, Mortimer's Patch, Marlin Bay,* and *Jackson's Wharf*. However, with an eye to export (by contrast with *Pukemanu* and *Mortimer's Patch*), *Mercy Peak* also draws upon such successful imported precedents as *Peak Practice, Northern Exposure,* and *The Flying Doctors*. What is clear in the conceptual mix at work in *Mercy Peak* is that the New Zealand television drama recombinant involves more than a marriage between *local* drama concepts. Because New Zealand's television viewing diet has always incorporated more imported than local drama (encouraging scriptwriters to graft local 'referents' onto international concepts and vice versa), the New Zealand recombinant has long entailed a complex trade-off between the perceptibly local and the apparently universal.[19]

In the first decade of a new century, New Zealand television drama faces unprecedented challenges given sweeping changes in television's general landscape. Problems in New Zealand are paralleled in the more difficult environment for television drama production overseas and in much larger countries. Internationally, television drama has been obliged to reinvent itself in the context of aggressive multi-channel competition, the rise of 'zap culture' or '**channel surfing**', and an inexplicable fascination with abundance over genuine diversity. In British television, for example, the drama genre is experiencing increasing institutional pressure and inclining steadily toward 'safety first', particularly where the innovative series and lavish costume dramas of tradition fall short of ratings expectations. Disappointing domestic ratings for a diverse trio of British dramas in the year 2000—*Gormenghast, Rebel Heart,* and *Attachments*—highlighted the problems of increasing audience fragmentation and a new type of production economy in the multi-channel era. That British drama (serving a domestic audience of more than 59 million) struggles to maintain the diversity of a decade ago underlines the current predicament of television drama production in New Zealand. The latter is a cottage industry by comparison with the former, and one whose television system is not only challenged by undesirable levels of competition but also by inadequate public funding.[20]

New Zealand audiences (like their international counterparts) are beginning to fragment as newer television channels and services gain market share. The current climate of uncertainty is fuelled by the anticipation of too much 'choice' following the digital switchover, along with personalised viewing technologies (such as TiVo) to further reduce the influence of mainstream channels and traditional scheduling practices. Although a more fragmented audience is the predictable correlate of multi-channel choice, its impact has already begun to be felt in New Zealand. That audience fragmentation would emerge as a particular problem in this country is hardly surprising when we consider that its entire population amounts to under half of the ten million viewers considered the ratings target for the domestic success of a British drama series (Ansorge 1997, p. 137). Audience fragmentation had raised the risks for New Zealand series drama more noticeably by the mid 1990s, when other channels were competing with TVNZ and TV3 for the eyeballs of New Zealanders. Although there were additional contributing factors, the disappointing ratings of mid 1990s drama series *Cover Story* and *City Life* owed something to the expanded line-up of channels available. The irony of this situation is that even though New Zealand television drama's domestic audiences are destined to be more fragmented in the future than they have ever been in the past, the pressure on local drama to justify its investment by returning acceptable ratings has become one of the two most influential features of the genre's post-deregulatory environment.[21]

As television systems begin to realise the multi-channel potential offered by new and converging technologies, the prospects for expensive or innovative drama projects seem increasingly uncertain (Moran 1998). The worst news is that the aggressive competition driving these changes can only increase when analogue transmission is switched off, leaving all viewers with equal access to multi-channel menus.[22] In British as in New Zealand television, network anxieties about new drama series and serials have centred on those that seem particularly expensive (like costume drama *Rebel Heart*), involve innovative concepts (like the dot.com series *Attachments*), or have a mix of both traits (as exemplified by the lavish *Gormenghast*). In New Zealand, producers of long-form drama have minimised both cost and risk in order to survive. They have learned to avoid the untested and to divine the most robust recombinants possible.

Drama today

As the millennium year approached, marking both the end of a decade of deregulation and New Zealand television's entry into an era of relative 'abundance', there were concerns about the future of locally produced drama.[23] Despite the optimism generated by NZOA's many early achievements, television's deregulated and highly commercial environment did not auger well for expensive, risky forms of production. From 1995–99, anxieties about local drama were renewed in an uncertain environment for television that was characterised by: 1) declining levels of New Zealand programming overall; 2) government moves to privatise TVNZ; 3) a shrinking total budget for NZOA as PBF funding lost value due to inflation; and 4) the increasing realisation within NZOA that, because of continuing funding pressures, it could no longer support drama in all desired areas.[24]

Despite the above difficulties, collaboration between NZOA and leading broadcasters TVNZ and TV3 has continued to deliver some notable successes and innovations for the genre. As a long-running soap stripped at 7 pm on five nights, *Shortland Street* has assisted the development of New Zealand television drama in four ways, by: 1) sustaining a prime-time profile and effective 'showcase' for local talent and stories; 2) offering regular work or training for television drama personnel; 3) claiming prime-time schedule space that would otherwise be given to imported drama; and 4) fostering, particularly among impressionable youth demographics, a viewing appetite for domestic drama (Dunleavy 2003). *Shortland Street*'s achievements in the long-form area have been effectively complemented by NZOA/network collaborations on successive anthology drama series. Among these series, *Nga Puna, Tala Pasifika,* and *Mataku* have profiled the work of Māori and Pacific Island drama-makers and helped to maintain the genre's cultural diversity.

In New Zealand's 1999 general election, the re-regulation of public television and expansion of local television content were part of Labour's winning manifesto. By 2003 (following Labour's re-election in the previous year), the 'strictly commercial' remit given to TVNZ in November 1988 had been replaced with a public service Charter, with both TVNZ and NZOA receiving some additional funding to help support quality and diversity in local television programming. Although there has yet been no move to impose a New Zealand content quota on television broadcasters, the mere presence of a TVNZ Charter, coupled with increased funding for NZOA, is helping to revitalise local television drama and assuage the network anxieties that inhibited the genre's growth through the late 1990s. The first years of the twenty-first century have seen stronger, more consistent ratings achieved by local television dramas in a range of sub-genres. The blend of commercial and critical success achieved by new prime-time series in recent years (including *Mercy Peak*, *Street Legal*, *Willy Nilly*, *Being Eve,* and *The Strip*), has helped renew confidence in the genre's value as a ratings weapon for leading networks.

Conclusions

In the concepts, stories, characters, and settings they have constructed, the writers, producers, and directors of drama have pursued 'localness', inventively reconciling drama's prized cultural objectives with necessary elements of 'universality' and 'exportability'. In an age of global and **postmodern** television, the achievement of 'localness' may seem obsolete. However, in a small country swamped by foreign culture, the perceived 'localness' of New Zealand culture and its cultural products will remain important. It is through television drama's presumed ability to reflect a sense of 'cultural identity' (this expectation being overt in current broadcasting legislation) that the genre claims enough public funding support, not only to survive in New Zealand's commercialised TV system, but also to conduct necessary experimentation and reinvention.

Drama has so far managed to perform this difficult balancing act between cultural relevance and commercial success (including 'exportability'). Apart from fluctuations in the level of public funding, the most significant problem for the genre has been television's inundation by an unrestricted flow of quality imports. Being at the end of the line in international television flow has meant that New Zealand networks can purchase quality imports at cheaper rates than those charged in more significant markets. Thus when a television broadcaster invests in a local production, as opposed to purchasing an American or British drama, it takes a sizeable commercial risk.

Especially in periods of institutional uncertainty or funding pressure, the low-risk option for broadcasters has been to step up their imported drama purchases and reduce their investment in local drama. In these periods the most vulnerable areas of local dramas have included: 1) one-offs and anthology series; 2) series and serials with relatively expensive or untested concepts; and 3) dramas produced for minority audiences, notably children. The fact that locally produced drama has remained such a strong contributor to New Zealand television (and has survived the new challenges of a multi-channel environment), is a testament to the mix of cultural/commercial value it is believed to have. In the 'localness' of this drama, public broadcasting agencies have recognised a vital cultural good, while broadcasters have found a way to foster audience loyalty.

References

Ansorge, Peter. 1997. *From Liverpool to Los Angeles: On Writing For Film and Television*. London: Faber & Faber.

Bell, Avril. 1995. 'An Endangered Species: Local programming in the New Zealand Television Market'. *Media, Culture and Society*. 17, pp. 181–200.

Bignell, Jonathan, Stephen Lacey & Madeleine McMurraugh-Kavanagh (eds). 2000. *British Television Drama: Past, Present and Future*. London: Palgrave.

Boyd-Bell, Robert. 1985. New *Zealand Television: The First 25 Years*. Auckland: Reed Methuen.

Broadcasting and Related Telecommunications in New Zealand: Report of the Royal Commission of Inquiry. 1986. Wellington: Government Printer.

Caughie, John. 2000. *Television Drama, Realism, Modernism and British Culture*. Oxford: Oxford University Press.

Cole Catley, Christine. 1973. 'TV Drama in New Zealand'. *Landfall*. 27 (1), pp. 43–54.

Dunleavy, Trisha. 1995. *Marlin Bay* and *Shortland Street*: Aspects of 'Localness' in Popular Television Drama. Thesis (MA). University of Auckland.

Dunleavy, Trisha. 1999. New Zealand Television Drama: The First Thirty Years (1960–90). Thesis (PhD). University of Auckland.

Dunleavy, Trisha. 2003. 'A Soap of Our Own: New Zealand's *Shortland Street*'. *Media International Australia*. 106. February, pp. 18–34.

Ellis, John. 2000. *Seeing Things: Television in the Age of Uncertainty*. London: I.B. Tauris.

Gitlin, Todd. 1994. *Inside Prime Time*. New York: Pantheon Books.

Horrocks, Roger. 1977. 'Surviving in New Zealand Films'. *Islands*. 20 (6), pp. 136–60.

Moran, Albert. 1998. *Copycat TV: Globalisation, Program Formats and Cultural Identity*. Luton: University of Luton Press.

New Zealand On Air. 1999. *Local Content and Diversity: Television in Ten Countries*. Wellington: New Zealand On Air.

New Zealand On Air. 2001. *Local Content Survey 2000*. Wellington: New Zealand On Air.

Norris, Paul & Brian Pauling. 2001. *New Technologies and the Digital Future: The Impact on New Zealand Local Content and New Zealand On Air Funded Programmes.* Wellington: New Zealand On Air.

O'Regan, Tom. 1993. *Australian Television Culture.* Sydney: Allen & Unwin.

Smith, Paul. 1996. *Revolution in the Air!* Auckland: Longman.

Tomlinson, John. 1991. *Cultural Imperialism.* Baltimore: John Hopkins University Press.

Notes

1   When exploring Australia's position relative to that of much larger television-producing countries (like the USA, Japan, France, Germany, and Italy), Tom O'Regan suggested that Australia was not large enough either to 'support local programming across the schedule' or to approximate the scale of production in a range of television genres. O'Regan's assertions about how national television production is limited first and foremost by market size apply even more strongly to New Zealand which, with a population of around four million, is five times smaller than Australia (O'Regan 1993, pp. 11–12).

2   The first play to be produced for New Zealand television was *All Earth To Love* (1963), its achievements being eclipsed by *The Evening Paper* (1965). Genre groundbreakers to follow included the first drama anthology *The New Zealand Actor's Workshop Series* (1967), first comedy sketch series *In View of the Circumstances* (1969), first drama serial *The Alpha Plan* (1969), first drama to depict colonial events *The Killing of Kane* (1971), first docudrama, *Gone Up North for a While* (1972), first drama in Māori language *Uenuku* (1974), first sitcom *Buck House* (1974) and first children's serial *The Games Affair* (1975).

3   The 'bargain basement' prices at which New Zealand networks can purchase imported television dramas is a major influence on the sense of risk surrounding new local drama projects. The high production values of imported dramas are undoubtedly part of their attraction to New Zealand viewers. But drama imports can also be purchased at a fraction of their production cost. From a New Zealand network perspective then, a local series has two disadvantages relative to an imported series. First the local series entails many times the investment cost. Second the local series, despite its high cost, cannot approximate the budget (and therefore the production values) of its genre equivalent from the USA or UK.

4   According to John Tomlinson, cultural imperialism (and the 'cultural imperialism thesis') centres upon the claim that 'authentic, traditional and local culture in many parts of the world is being battered out of existence by the indiscriminate dumping of large quantities of slick commercial and media products, mainly from the United States' (Tomlinson 1991, p. 8).

5   For details of the Charter refer to TVNZ's web site (http://www.tvnz.co.nz) and also to the 2003 *Television New Zealand Act*, Part 2, Section 12, pages 5–7.

6   Pioneers of local television drama (either as early network executives, or drama producers, directors. and scriptwriters) included Bill Austin, Roy Melford, Brian Bell, Douglas Drury, Tahu Shankland, Tony Isaac, Michael Noonan, Michael Scott-Smith, Des Monaghan, Kevan Moore, Keith Aberdein, Chris Thomson, John

McRae, Ian Mune, John Barnett, Murray Reece, Ross Jennings, Roy Hope, Julian Dickon, Hamish Keith, and Jane Galletly (see Dunleavy 1999).

7   Such a commitment was not forthcoming until 1974, at which point New Zealand's first network (the government-owned NZBC) was being restructured to effect an institutional split from public radio and television's expansion to two channels.

8   Pressure both inside the NZBC and from organisations of independent screen writers and directors led to the formation of a New Zealand Content Quota Committee that lobbied for regulation from the late 1960s to the early 1970s. Initial content regulations appeared in the NZBA annual report for the year ended March 1974, to be imposed from April 1974. These set a weekly local content figure of 30 per cent, stipulating that it must be broadcast between 7 and 10 pm, and establishing a minimum annual drama output of thirteen hours. (See Appendix to the *Journals of the House of Representatives of New Zealand: Report of the New Zealand Broadcasting Corporation* for the year ended 31 March 1974, p. 5.)

9   The effects of 'cultural cringe' were not only evident on NZBC television and radio but equally evident in the continuing dominance of English and European theatre over New Zealand theatre.

10   Michael Noonan, 'A Preliminary Report—Proposed Review of New Zealand Television Drama 1963–1970' (unpublished paper, 1995).

11   While *Pukemanu* warrants particular attention because of its evident popularity and because its concept has been so influential (*Jocko, Mortimer's Patch, Roche, Marlin Bay, Jackson's Wharf, Mercy Peak*), there were a few other drama series prior to 1975. Achieving varying degrees of success were thriller serial *The Alpha Plan, Section 7,* a series about the probation service, and the urban sitcom, *Buck House.*

12   Milestone productions from 1975–79 included soap operas *Close to Home* and *A Going Concern*, anthology series *Winners and Losers* and *Ngaio Marsh Theatre*, tele-films *The God Boy* and *The Park Terrace Murder*, drama series *Moynihan, Jocko,* and *Mortimer's Patch*, historic drama serials *The Governor* and *The MacKenzie Affair*, initial 'kidult' serials *The Games Affair, Hunter's Gold* and *Children of Fire Mountain* and children's one-off *The Mad Dog Gang Meets Rotten Fred and Ratsguts.*

13   These included successive costume dramas, such as telefeature *The Park Terrace Murder*, anthology series *Ngaio Marsh Theatre* and children's serials *Hunter's Gold* and *The Children of Fire Mountain.*

14   One of the reasons why 'localness' was able to be pursued more stridently at this stage was that television drama was not yet considered to be an 'export product,' nor did the requirement of 'exportability' necessarily feature in concept design. 'Export appeal' began to loom larger in 1979, following the fuss over *The Governor's* budget and the impressive export earnings returned by children's serial *Hunter's Gold.*

15   In this sense the 1970s was a considerably more suitable moment for the launch of the kind of feature film industry that New Zealand feature pioneer John O'Shea had struggled to establish in earlier decades.

16   In exchange for its PBF funding input through the first years of *Shortland Street*, NZOA exacted two particular 'public service' oriented provisions. These were: 1) that the soap reflect, in its core cast, the cultural diversity of New Zealand's population; and 2) that it maintain a proportion of issues-based stories with particular relevance to teenagers.

17   See, for example, New Zealand On Air 2001, p. 29.

18   TVNZ's drama production from mid 1987 was deliberately wound down, in anticipation of the disestablishment of its in-house department by the end of 1988.

19   NZBC drama series *Section 7* (1972) was an early example of recombinant programming in New Zealand television. Apparently 'British' in influence where *Pukemanu* seemed overtly 'Kiwi', *Section 7* was the first of successive prime-time New Zealand drama series to demonstrate the difficulty for drama-makers in successfully reconciling 'localness' with 'universality'.

20   As noted by Paul Norris and Brian Pauling (2001): '[The] amount of public money New Zealand spends on television is also one of the lowest per capita in the western world—NZ$12 in New Zealand, compared with NZ$45 in Australia and NZ$144 in the UK' (p. 129).

21   The other most influential feature, as already suggested, is declining public funding.

22   In homes that have access to satellite, cable, or digital services, there is clear evidence of declining audience participation in traditional TV channels and program fare. In American homes currently receiving these extra services (and where the availability of such services has existed the longest), terrestrial audience share has fallen to 50 per cent. In equivalent British homes, terrestrial audience share has fallen to 57 per cent (Norris and Pauling 2001, p. 122).

23   Television's eras of 'scarcity', 'availability', and 'abundance' are usefully explored and contrasted in Ellis (2000).

24   PBF funding remained fixed at its 1989 level through to May 1999, at which point the National government announced its intention to replace the PBF with a system of direct funding. NZOA responded by highlighting what it now considered to be a crisis for the ability of New Zealand television to continue to deliver quality and diversity in local programming. Underlining the 1999 situation, local content surveys revealed 'an alarming decrease in hours of locally produced children's programmes and confirmed the fragility of local drama' (David Beatson, NZOA Press Release, 20 May 1999).

13

Reality Estate:

Locating New Zealand Reality Television

MISHA KAVKA

R eality TV is a favourite topic of critical and even viewer disdain, but this does not keep people from watching it or New Zealand channels from showing it. In fact, each channel since at least 1998 has had its own particular brand of reality programming: British-format programs on TV ONE, American-format and homegrown programs on TV2, the American thrill-clip shows on TV3, and MTV's 'Real World' and American blooper/stunt shows on TV4. Indeed, what sets New Zealand markedly apart from television programming in other Western countries is the sheer bulk of reality television programs shown not just on one but on all of its main channels. Whereas in the US reality television was largely the property of the little-brother Fox channel before CBS became the first of the major networks to wade in with *Survivor* and *Big Brother* (in 2000), and in Europe reality television has been restricted to fledgling private broadcasters, in New Zealand it has developed with equal pace across the public as well as private channels.[1] Though TV2 may be the hands-down leader in home-grown product development,[2] TV ONE has given us shows such as *Pioneer House* and *Location, Location, Location*, while TV3 has fronted up with the ironic *Survivor* spin-off *Rafted* and the garden makeover program *Firth Ground Force* (not to mention that both channels reveal a penchant for so-called 'documentary series' with suspiciously strong RTV characteristics). Reality television, in other words, is all over the show in this country.

This undoubtedly has to do with the fact that New Zealand is a small country with a financially limited television industry and a strong penchant for seeing Kiwi faces on the small screen. After all, reality television is, or at least can be, cheap programming. Compared to the huge studio, crew, and actors' costs of making a drama series, a reality show basically requires a producer/director, a cameraman, and an editor (or a few of each), plus perhaps some prize money or minimal appearance fees. Yet if it were only a matter of securing cheap programming, we would be seeing a lot more BBC wildlife documentaries and syndicated US sitcoms in the early-evening slots. Unlike such filler programming, ratings for most reality television shows are high, with new series gaining media attention to boot.[3] The point is that reality television does not just fill the airwaves, or even the spectre of New Zealand production quotas, but rather gives something back to local viewers. I would claim that this is true of all reality television, no matter where it is shown or how global the format: reality television is a ratings success because it offers something valuable to local viewers, namely a strong sense of cultural place. One could argue that the history and size of New Zealand make this sense of place especially wanted here.

I. What is reality television?

Given that 'reality' television is all too obviously constructed, let's dispense right away with the urge to lambast the term as false advertising or a misnomer. Reality television gets its name not for being true to everyday conditions but for the fact that it uses 'real' people, albeit in exceptional situations, and focuses on their personalities and individual dramas. The point of the constructed formats of reality television is a simple one: to heighten the impact of unscripted drama and make it 'good television', at least in terms of entertainment values. The definition of 'real' in this context is naturally loaded with difficulties. On the one hand, we must take it literally: real people are not fictional characters, and hence have lives that stretch beyond the time spent in front of the camera. On the other hand, we must take it more metaphorically: actors may be real people, too, but in the mobile categories created by media culture 'real people' refers to anyone who has never been before a cinema or television camera (i.e., most of us), and therefore has no name- or face-recognition from viewers (at least at the *start* of a reality tele-vision program). In the rhetoric of reality television programs, the participants are 'ordinary' people, sharing with viewers the crucial characteristic of never having been picked out by the camera. These people are ordinary because they're like us, television watchers who, given the good fortune of opportu-nity and casting, have momentarily moved to the other side of the screen.

The definition of ordinariness, however, has a more basic meaning, for reality television breaks with the time-honoured television tradition that only people who are already in some way 'special' are deserving of being on television, either because they are actors or authorities or celebrities or presenters with household faces. Reality television, by contrast, is the only genre which deliberately seeks out 'ordinary' or 'normal' people, and emphasises this ordinariness by placing them in at-home or on-the-job settings.[4] The effect on the viewer is that we feel as though we potentially know the people we see on screen, as though they could be unmet neighbours from down the street.[5] This itself reflects not reality (they are almost never our neighbours, and what would it matter to the show if they were?) but rather produces an *effect* of authenticity. We watch reality television because real people, especially those whose roles or personalities we recognise, matter more than fictional characters.

The raw material of reality television consists of filming how such people act and interact without a script. The very phrase for the genre used by *Survivor* producer Mark Burnett, 'unscripted drama', suggests that the emphasis of reality television is on the unpredictability of what real people—as opposed to fictional characters, celebrities, or household faces—say and do in particular situations. There is thus a level of curiosity and experiment built into reality television, and its appeal lies in promising to take us behind the scenes, to what lies beyond the usual on-screen characterisation, which is much the same thing as saying that reality television appeals to us by promising to show us what people are *really* like. For our curiosity to be answered—and the promise must be answered if the ratings are to stay high—the camera must indeed reveal something about these people that is not available to the public eye. It must turn out that people in private collusion with a camera, or people caught by the camera in a private moment, do indeed make for good drama. The constructed situations of reality television (also known broadly as formats) have the single purpose of ensuring that conflictual, difficult, or extraordinary situations arise.[6] Even where the set-up is relatively normal, as in the New Zealand series *Flatmates* (1996),[7] the initial casting choices endeavour to create conflict or romance or at least a healthy dose of dramatic frisson. Once the material is on tape, this is edited to highlight conflict and to create recognisable story arcs (one person will have trouble with another, for instance, and we will see this brewing, exploding, and moving toward resolution). Editing is so important to reality programs that, after the producer (who either creates or buys the format), the editor has the most important function on the team. Whereas fictional programming relies heavily on a good script and watchable actors, reality television is highly dependent for its success on the three technical aspects that produce dramatic heightening: formats, casting, and editing.

There is little danger of confusing reality television with fictional programming (note that you can always tell when dialogue has the pace and tone of a script, not least because there is no rhetorical waste). The dividing line that tends to be blurred lies rather between reality television and documentary (see Corner 2002). But while many, if not most, documentaries strive to erase the presence of the camera in order to heighten the effect of actuality,[8] reality television programs are shameless about the cameras, often asking participants to speak to them directly or advertising the number of cameras used in the show (e.g., the graphics of *Big Brother* and *Life on Tape*). In more general terms, documentary tends to reflect on a socio-historical context that both makes sense of the individual documentary subjects and provides the educational or consciousness-raising impetus that defines documentary. Where documentary is about society and history, though, reality television is about individuals. While individuals often play an important role in documentaries, they tend to have a representative function; they stand in for a larger group of which they are but one particular, albeit interesting, facet. By contrast, participants in reality programming represent no one. We learn the participants' names, try to make sense of their personalities, predict how they will act, and strive to know them as individuals. This holds true even of programs such as *The Real World* or *Survivor*, which inevitably cast one black guy, one gay guy, one party girl, etc.; such casting decisions in reality shows are a function of the format rather than of the participants' representativity (the gay guy is not a 'study' in gay people, for instance, but usually a bait to potential conflict). And since these individuals do not belong to a larger group, they also do not have historical subjectivity; that is, we are not asked to reflect on their place in society or history. Rather, reality television is played out in an ever-present moment. In *Survivor* we know which day it is, down to the hour, while in police programs such as *Police* or *Motorway Patrol* we are witness to incidents that have neither a past nor a future, though they usually have an hour and minute designation. Reality television is thus not so much a slice of life as a slice of the present, lived out by a group of individuals brought together in a constructed situation. These characteristics—that reality television is personalised, presentist, and constructed—separate it from documentary, and ultimately separate entertainment values from political or educational ones. Let us not, however, underestimate the value of entertainment.

Reality television certainly lacks the didactic impact and political consciousness of documentary,[9] and in New Zealand, which has a very strong documentary tradition and faith in the value of realism, reality television comes in for a great deal of antipathy and even contempt.[10] Other than complaining about it not really being real, detractors of the genre regularly focus on two particular criticisms of reality television, both with moral implications. The fact that these shows are so heavily constructed and edited for dramatic tension and/or emotional appeal gives rise to accusations of manipulation—of the participants as well as of the viewers. In certain cases, ex-participants have even sued the broadcaster for false representation (such as the ex-*Castaway* member who sued the BBC for making him look argumentative and aggressive), while most big shows have their publicised litany of participants who claim that that was not 'really me'.[11] Moreover, because the results of editing are largely invisible, we as viewers have no way of knowing what the rest of the footage consists of, and often do not see the temporal or spatial seams between shots; this means that viewers can end up feeling manipulated, too. The other major criticism of reality television is precisely the opposite; rather than bemoan our lack of direct access to what *really* went on in front of the camera, critics rail against this genre because it invites voyeurism in the first place, offering us 24/7 access to what should be lived behind closed doors. Savour the irony: in the first criticism, we don't get to see enough; in the second criticism, the fact that we want to see this at all underlines our perversity as viewers.

Both of these criticisms combat the basic, broad appeal of a genre that promises access to something real and even heightens the moment so that we can feel it happening (let's face it, making the bed is also perfectly real but lacks the frisson to make it matter). This description is not so far off from what television, since its earliest days, has always promised: to let us see something up close but from a distance. With the advent of the sitcom, what we were allowed to see was precisely into the privacy of people's living rooms. Thus, rather than write off reality television as bad entertainment or trash television, it is worth noting that this genre is a logical extension of the televisual medium itself. Television, after all, always promised to be a 'window' through which we may peer, in particular into the domestic lives of people behind closed doors—even though these doors have, until recently, been fictional. Moreover, because reality television is so much in the present, always seeming to coincide with the moment of our viewing, it offers a simulation of 'live' television, with its uncanny ability to collapse space and multiply time frames (as famously promoted by Walter Cronkite's weekly intonation '… and you are there' at the start of the 1950s TV series of the same name) (see Kavka and West c.2004). In this sense, reality programming is not the sorry debris but rather the *sine qua non* of television as a medium. No wonder people are watching.

In the last few years there has been much tussle in the press, especially in the US, over whether reality television will replace scripted television as the favoured form of the medium. Though the glut of copycat programs and even the attacks of September 11 have suddenly made this seem highly unlikely,[12] the debate goes well beyond any conventional wisdom about cheap programming for a cheap-date viewership. Why is reality television so attractive in comparison to the standard forms of fictional television? On the one hand, as I have suggested, the appearance of real people makes it matter, giving us grounds to care. (Gossip works on the very same principle: something happening to a friend of a friend of a friend, no matter how distant, is still more interesting than a crisis in the life of a character in a novel.) There is, however, another crucial element. I have talked about the two interlinking characteristics of reality television—personalisation and presentism—but I have so far left out the element of *place*.

Importantly, in reality television participants are either sought out in their 'natural' habitat (e.g., *Service with a Smile*, following students at the Auckland University of Technology's Hotel School) or, if they are sent to an artificial habitat (as on *Treasure Island* or even *Trading Places*) then they always recognisably *come from* somewhere. In either case, what we see on the screen are not just 'real' people, but people who bear the markers of a particular place, who carry the stamp, as it were, of a neighbourhood. We barely notice this part of reality television because these places are so familiar, but the programs in this way consolidate what it is we know about our own country and the kinds of people in it. Reality television, in other words, rewards our hours of watching with cultural (self-)recognition. It is not that viewers directly identify with the participants or find themselves reflected in these programs, but rather that what we might 'know' in the abstract about our place is given texture through the way such cultural knowledge is enacted by program participants. This turns out to be particularly important in a small country like New Zealand, whose sense of place is too apt to be pushed off the screen—both on television and in the cinema—by products with greater global cultural capital. Though Kiwis may be proud of New Zealand actors and directors who make it big (even if they call themselves Australian—damn you, Russ), such cases are few and far between. What reality television offers—and to which audiences respond— is a regular flow that gives viewers a more particularised sense than other programming of who we are, in the place where we live.

II. A short history of NZ reality television

In 1995—before the days of TV4, Prime, or the brief sojourn of MTV— real-people programs consisted of consumer shows, talent shows, and the perennial run of *The Great Kiwi Video Show*. A quick look at a sample week of programming in September 1995 reveals a penchant for consumer information (*Fair Go*, a program that has aired consistently ever since) as well as shows for the armchair traveller, gardener, or chef (in this period, *Air New*

Zealand Holiday airs consistently and *Palmer's Garden Show* begins, soon to be renamed *Maggie's Garden Show*). Notably, all of these shows focus on presenters, familiar faces who act as the point of mediation between our living room and the exotic destination or garden on view. More in keeping with the range of what is now called reality programming is the talent show, represented by programs such as *Star Factory*. Nonetheless, the talent show fails to count as reality television in one important sense: each person's talent serves as a justification for being on television. The unknown faces belonging to anybody's neighbours were on screen because they had the potential to be 'special' and thus worthy of broadcast. Presenter-led consumer and DIY programs were also bastions of 'specialness'; they balanced the small-celebrity faces of the presenters with various experts who knew more than the viewer and were in charge of divulging information. The program that made this penchant for specialness most clear was a show called *Success* (early 1995), in which a set of presenters interview New Zealanders who had made it big in some way. These were New Zealanders *worthy* of being on television.

By contrast, non-celebrities do appear in the 'caught-on-tape' show, whose granddaddy is undoubtedly *Candid Camera* and which aired in 1995 in the triple format of *The Great Kiwi Video Show* (a spin-off of *America's Funniest Home Videos*), 'bloopers' programs and practical-joke shows (such as *Just Kidding* or *Joke's on You*). Such shows required ordinary, on-the-street people to make them work, but the emphasis lay on the joke or test itself, never on the personality of the individual involved. Ordinary people caught on tape came and went every few minutes, while it was the presenter's job to have all the personality and link together the comic foibles. The idea of putting ordinary people on prime-time television for the very fact of their normativity had not yet struck anyone as making for watchable television.[13]

Overseas during the first half of the 1990s, dating back to the initial seasons of *America's Most Wanted* (1988) and *Cops* (1989–90) on the US Fox channel, the popularity of caught-on-tape programs was giving over to crime/disaster programming. Though this form was developed in the USA, it was soon exported to the UK, France, and Germany.[14] In New Zealand, these programs initially appeared in the original US version, but in 1995 they only aired in the 'dead hours' between midnight and 6 am when cheap programming was needed (e.g., *Top Cops* at 3:55 am, *Rescue 911* at 5 am, and *Cops* at 11:55 pm). Interestingly, all of these night-owl shows aired on TV2, a channel already carving out its reality programming niche. By 1996 NZ broadcasters decided to edge such programs into greater visibility, showing *Rescue* (TV2) and *Police Stop!* (TV3) in prime time. By 1997, New Zealand was producing its own call-in police program (*NZI Crimescene*, which, like *America's Most Wanted*, used dramatic reconstructions to spur the

viewing public to call in with tips), its own behind-the-scenes hospital programs (*Hospital*, set in Wellington, and *Middlemore*, set in Auckland), as well
as its own thrill-clip show (*Real TV*, which, though it collects clips from
around the world, is New Zealand-presented). What holds all of these programs together is the focus on a disaster or climactic moment, which allows
the viewer to engage in the thrill of being out of control—a victim at the
hands of fate—while exerting some control in the very choice of watching
and interacting with the program. In this sense, caught-on-tape and crime/
disaster programs lie along a single spectrum, moving from the home-video
show through call-in and ride-along police programs,[15] to emergency
services programming, and even natural-disaster and *Wackiest Videos*
shows—all of which give the viewer access to controlled engagement with
a fateful, possibly comic but increasingly life-or-death moment.

Just as this first-generation genre of reality television was peaking overseas, sample New Zealand programming from 1997 reveals that now reality
programming was becoming a turf for battles over audience share. The 1995
favourites are still there on the family-oriented weekend nights, but TV2 is
beginning to vie for an audience more interested in thrills, with programs
such as *Great Escapes* ('unbelievable rescues and death-defying heroics') and
the natural-disaster genre (my favourite title: *Wow! The Most Awesome Acts
on Earth II*).[16] TV3 also enters the ratings battle with TV ONE and TV2
respectively by increasing the number of presenter-led travel programs on
the one hand and adding the medical and thrill-clip shows on the other
(*Hospital* and *Real TV*). Most importantly, this is the period in which New
Zealand broadcasting begins to draw on the growing number of small
production companies to develop its own brands of reality television. Prime
among these is the 'challenge' show, consisting of some combination of
adventure, sport, and local orientation. Such programs are still fronted by
well-known faces (this is the beginning of those seemingly countless years
of Matthew Ridge and Marc Ellis), but now there is a more sophisticated
sense of marketing and cultural appeal. Shows like *Mountain Dew on the Edge*
(TV2), *Fresh Up in the Deep End* (TV3), and *Powerade Blood, Sweat and Tears*
(TV3) point to what will become the effective New Zealand reality mix of
product-placement, cultural devotion to the sportsman, and 'getting to
know you, New Zealand' style.

Of all these, it is the need to 'get to know you, New Zealand' that will
carry locally produced programming into the reality television age with a
bang. Though the nation-making project is as old as New Zealand itself,
the need for national self-assertion had steadily intensified in the 1990s era
of globalisation, threats to national sovereignty, increased Asian immigration, and Māori demands for greater political and cultural capital. One
response, especially in the face of global sales of American television shows,

was to demand a greater degree of the local on screen, not just in the form of New Zealand-produced programs but also a wider range and concentration of Kiwi faces on air. And this is precisely what reality television can deliver, at affordable cost.

By 1999 reality programming was booming on New Zealand television, and it's by no means over yet. In the first full week of January 1999, there was a reality show, challenge show, or people-based lifestyle show on each of the three major channels five nights out of the week. Though in the lazy summer days of January this meant, for the most part, screening US- or UK-produced programs (with *The Best of Trading Places* being the only New Zealand-produced offering), it nonetheless indicates a surge in the production and especially the ratings of reality television since 1997. During the course of 1999, one could tune in to at least five New Zealand-produced crime/disaster programs and any number of renovation or redecoration shows.[17,18] For the animal lover there was *The Zoo* and *Pet Vet*, for the sentimentalist *Arnott's Dreams Come True*, *Make or Break*, and *April's Angels*, and for the romantic sentimentalist *Weddings*. The travel-based gameshow *Wish You Were Here* offered a surprise destination combined with a challenge, while the British-derived *Love Thy Neighbour* highlighted neighbourly feuds. There were also home-produced shows that fitted no pre-existing categories, such as *Guess Who's Coming to Dinner?*, *Behind the Wheel*, *Get Your Act Together,* and the by now famous *Popstars*, an original format produced here and sold overseas. In addition to new 1999 series of *Trading Places* and *Middlemore*, what all of these shows have in common is the focus on real people, real dramas, and real reactions—where 'real' means your as-yet-unmet neighbour in an unscripted moment. What they also have in common is the search for the everyperson: the couples in *Mitre 10 Changing Rooms* are in their way as much a normative Mr and Mrs New Zealander as the participants in *Garage Sale* or the nabbed drivers on *Motorway Patrol.* Yet the ordinary person, crucially, is always to be found in an extraordinary or heightened situation. In this lies the secret of how to put viewers 'like us' on the television screen without losing the dramatic heightening that makes television watchable.

The programs that achieved the greatest audience share and media attention—perhaps unexpectedly, given New Zealand's strong documentary tradition and perceived British bias—prove to be American-influenced; they embrace the contrivances built into reality television through American-style seamless editing, thus allowing us to become caught up in the lives of individuals whom we 'know' in mediated form, and they are aggressively personalised and presentist.[19] Where we might locate the particular features of the New Zealand reality television boom in relation to foreign streams (themselves now in any case sharing the most marketable formats) has to do with *habitats*. Reality television programming operates on two axes: the axis of participants, who may be either found on site or selected for the show, and the axis of habitat, which may be natural or constructed. All reality television shows combine these axes in some way, with participants who are found in their natural habitat most resembling the documentary, while people selected to appear in an artificial habitat (such as *Big Brother*) make up the most contrived—and hence perhaps the truest—mode of reality television. In New Zealand-produced programs, what is striking is the insistence on retaining the natural habitat, even where the participants are carefully selected. Of course, this has to do with a financial bottom line: artificial habitats are simply more expensive to create and run (cf. the expense of putting up four women in an inner-city apartment and encouraging them to date and throw parties, as was the premise of *Single Girls*). But the difference between the critical outcry against *Single Girls* and the more muted response to *Flatmates*—the former located in an artificial and the latter in a more natural habitat[20]—suggests that this has to do with more than just production funds. The criticism that *Single Girls* was heavily manipulated by the production team and hence 'false', as though somehow this were cheating the viewers, implies that the will to natural habitat in New Zealand reality television is ideological, and psychological, as much as financial.[21]

If we look for ways to characterise the 1990s, aside from the broad term 'globalisation', one way to do so might be to focus on loss of habitat—in terms of ecology, communities, migration, political refugeeism, etc. Reality television is important because, through the modality of entertainment, it registers this loss of habitat and has the power to reconstruct it. New Zealand can be said to suffer from loss of habitat in all of the ways mentioned above, but it is also important to realise that the New Zealand habitat, in a historical sense, never was 'natural', that is, never was inhabited by a proto-historical tribe of New Zealanders. As latecomers to their own country, non-Māori New Zealanders have a deep investment in naturalising this habitat as their own, which explains in part why the loss of habitat through globalisation is such an impacted zone in the cultural psyche (see chapter 5). On New Zealand reality television, Māori and Pacific Islanders (as well as Asians) are strikingly absent, despite their strong presence elsewhere on screen (e.g., in advertising, as news readers, or on the local soap drama *Shortland Street*). This fact, that reality television here rarely makes use of and is not screened for minority populations, deeply implicates reality television in the white reconstruction of nation, and the naturalisation of habitat. Pākehā New Zealanders' interest in place and in their own place in particular is registered through the form and content of television programming. Significantly, the strongest genre of reality television in New Zealand—both in terms of the number of homegrown variants and in the sheer number of series produced—is the property genre. New Zealand reality shows prefer to foreground ordinary Kiwis in possession of their own place.

III. Bringing it all home

In locally produced television, the nation-making project is played out in and around the home. This is more than a comment about television as an apparatus that mediates between the domestic setting of characters and the domestic space in which viewers watch television. As a rule, New Zealand does not produce sitcoms, the television genre that traditionally centres on a domestic setting, and its longest-running soap opera is set in the community of the workplace, the hospital on *Shortland Street*. The home, so absent from fictional programming in New Zealand, is rampant in reality programming: renovating, rebuilding, decorating, selling, buying, even barging in just to see what people's homes look like, are all tried and true reality television themes in New Zealand. As a country with a settler history, this makes a great deal of sense. Like any new world nation, New Zealand was settled after Māori by those drawn here by the promise of land and a homestead. But in this country the promise of owning a quarter acre and your own home still lingers as the felt basis of settlement, of cultural rootedness. Real estate here *is* heightened reality—it is a dramatic enactment of identity and place; as such, it is in and around their homes that New Zealand reality television goes looking for ordinary people who will facilitate cultural (self-)recognition.

The range of real-estate programs and their spin-offs is sizeable. Britain's *Changing Rooms* and *Ground Force* were adapted for New Zealand production in 1998, adding Mitre 10 and Firth as named commercial sponsors and filling the equivalent format with a Kiwi presenter and participants. This was then extended to numerous series, including *Mitre 10 Dream Home*, where two teams compete to gut and renovate a house under pressure of time and aesthetics, and the more recent *Mitre 10 DIY Rescue*, which sends builders and designers to help people whose own renovation projects have become hopelessly stalled, and even a program like *Hot Property,* where the requisite experts prepare a house for sale on a limited budget. These programs are New Zealand versions of 'classic' reality television in that they are fully personalised and played out in an uncompromising present, often with a clock running on and money running out. Though viewers do pick up some information about renovation and design, and though the sponsors are sure to advertise the cost of their wares at the end of each episode, ultimately we watch because of the individuals who are highlighted, the sense of a clock always ticking, and the dramatic arc created by the competition between the teams and the sometimes boisterous conflict among themselves. This is admittedly different from the more cross-generic real-estate programs—the lifestyle show such as *Homefront*, the consumer program *My House, My Castle*, or the gameshow *Whose House Is it Anyway?*—but even in such programs two basic elements remain: the personalisation, and hence realisation, of people through the medium of their homes, and the malleability for the purposes of television of the home itself, the ultimate natural habitat.

The program that most adroitly realises a range of Kiwi faces through their attachment to the home is *Location, Location, Location* (1999). As the title suggests, this show is about the real estate trade, the buying and selling of houses, but it offers only minimal information about house prices and sales routines; rather, the focus is first and foremost on the people involved, and the emotions and conflicts generated by the sale of property. The opening credits make clear that this will be a show about ordinary people in a particular place: at the start of the 1999 series, the camera panned across Auckland suburbs against a backdrop of the Sky Tower, eventually highlighting one house from above, while the 2000 series used colour-filtered suburbs as a backdrop for close-ups of people's faces moving across the screen. Following the tripartite episodic structure developed by *Cops*, each episode tells three stories of an individual, couple, or family trying to sell a house. Integrated into the line-up of characters are the agents, the sellers, the (potential) buyers, and even the house itself (as well as, less visibly, the sponsor, Westpac Trust). As the voiceover in the credits reminds us, the program highlights the home as the site that generates personal narrative: 'every house is a home, and every home tells the story of someone's life'. This story is then packaged through interviews and intercutting into a dramatic arc of viewings and waiting, setbacks and anxiety, gaps between offers received on an old house and those made on a new one, before a successful resolution is reached. In some cases, indeed, a house is not sold at the end of the episode, but rather rides over into the coming episode as a narrative '**cliffhanger**'. In all cases, the interviews focus on those 'ordinary' people who have the greatest emotional investment in a house and whose lives take the most dramatic turn, even if it turns out to be someone who happened into the filming by coming to the right house at the wrong time (such as the man who had already sold his own home, but then had his co-offer on the televised house refused and his partner decide against living with him—he warranted a long interview).

What we see at work here are the basic elements of reality television, congealed through the emotions that accompany the buying and selling of homes: the focus on individuals in a particular place, a selectively heightened reality, a seamlessly defined story arc, and a sense of time being played out to the minute, as auction gavels hover or offers are signed, discussed, and countersigned. *Location, Location, Location* also shares in one other element common to reality television, which is the propensity of this televisual mode to create national celebrities out of its 'ordinary' participants. In the case of this program, which devotes less than ten minutes' air time to each pending sale, this was unlikely to happen to any of the sellers or buyers. It did, however, happen for the agent who showed up most regularly in the 1999 series and whose job it was to orchestrate the sale of the most expensive houses, Michael Boulgaris. The line between ordinary person and celebrity in reality television is notoriously fluid, as any *Big Brother* housemate-turned-late-night-presenter can attest; in New Zealand, this once-ordinary estate agent of 1999 shows up two years later as the celebrity element of a *Quest for Success* episode.

Though reality television may lure us into thinking that we, too, can become household faces through the celebrity-making machinery of the camera, it does not set up a simple relationship of identification between viewer and character on screen. When the New Zealand viewer watches *Location, Location, Location*, he or she neither identifies the particular house on display nor identifies with the individuals involved in the sale. Rather, he or she recognizes the kind of house it is, without any less appreciating (or condemning) its particular features; the house is like any house in the area, the suburb, the town, while retaining its individual attributes. The same goes for the people in front of the camera: the viewer does not identify with them but rather *recognises* them as belonging to an area, a class, a kind of Kiwi. This ordinary person in front of the camera simultaneously resists typification by providing his/her personal narrative. Like Suzanne Paul barging into someone's home and digging through their closet (in *Woman's Day Style Challenge*), the viewer of reality TV is allowed to barge through the doors of a house and find out who are the people in the neighbourhood. Of course, we know the neighbourhood to begin with, so the person we find comes as no surprise. Rather, the result is comforting, for these programs situate us in the culture, enacting for us a more detailed, visualised sense of place. In this modality of television, individuals serve the double purpose of performing the culture while adding details to the face of the place. Unlike fictional programming, where we are encouraged to identify with the main character, in reality programming we identify with the situation, and are rewarded with a feeling of situatedness. In New Zealand, where there is an ongoing struggle to keep a sense of place alive in the global mediascape, reality television adds its weight to the project of identity construction. Like the Kiwi bird in the zoo, drawing crowds peering through the dim light of its habitat to catch a glimpse of the living national icon, home-produced reality TV offers up a stream of Kiwis in their natural habitat—the renovated house on a diminishing quarter acre.

References

Corner, John. 2002. 'Performing the Real: Documentary Diversions'. In: *Television & New Media* 3 (3), pp. 255–70.

Glynn, Kevin. 2001. *Tabloid Culture*. Durham, NC: Duke University Press.

Kavka, Misha & Amy West. Forthcoming, c.2004. 'Temporalities of the Real: Conceptualising Time in Reality TV', in Deborah Jermyn & Susan Holmes (eds) *Understanding Reality Television*. London: Routledge.

Nichols, Bill. 1991. *Representing Reality*. Bloomington: Indiana University Press.

Nichols, Bill. 1994. *Blurred Boundaries: Questions of Meaning in Contemporary Culture*. Bloomington: Indiana University Press.

Roscoe, Jane. 2001. '*Big Brother* Australia: Performing the "Real" Twenty-four-seven'. In: *International Journal of Cultural Studies* 4 (4), pp. 473–88.

Appendix

An extensive but not exhaustive typology of New Zealand-produced reality television. Dates indicate the year of the first series.

Consumer (with reality television elements)
Target (1999)
Money Doctor (2000)

Caught-on-tape
The Great Kiwi Video Show (1995)
Real TV (1997)
Behind the Wheel (1998)

Challenge
In the Face of Fear (1998)
Across the Ditch (1998)
Wish You Were Here (1999)
I Dare You (2000)
Can You Hackett? (2000)
The Money Game (2000)
The $20-a-Day Challenge (2001)
Adventure Central (2001)

Opportunity/philanthropy
Caltex/Arnott's Dreams Come True (1998)
Guess Who's Coming to Dinner? (1998)
April's Angels (1998)
Make or Break (1999)
Kev Can Do (2000)
Mucking In (2000)
Together Again (2000)
Quest for Success (2001)

Crime/disaster
Police Stop! (1996)

Rescue (1996)
NZ Insurance Crimescene (1997)
Great Escapes (1997)
Real Emergency (1997)
Police (1998)
Emergency Heroes (1998)
Street Stories (1998)
Without Warning (1998)
AA Insurance Police Alert (1999)
Motorway Patrol (1999)
Against the Odds (1999)
Towies (2000)
Rescue One (2000)
Priority 1: Middlemore (2000)
Choppers (2001)

Talent (with reality television elements)
Get Your Act Together (1999)
Popstars (1999)
The Big Time (2000)
Stripsearch (2001)

Institutions/professions
Middlemore (1997)
Hospital (1997)
Driving School New Zealand (1998)
Trading Places (1998)
Pet Vet (1999)
The Zoo (1999)
Private Investigators (2000)
Service with a Smile (2000)
Going, Going, Gone (2000)

Real estate/makeover
Mitre 10 Changing Rooms (1998)
Firth Ground Force (1998)
Garage Sale (1998)
Woman's Day Style Challenge (1998)
Mitre 10 Dream Home (1999)
My House, My Castle (1999)
Bayley's Home Front (1999)
Location, Location, Location (1999)
Whose House Is It Anyway? (2000)
Hot Property (2001)
Mitre 10 DIY Rescue (2001)

Life stories/natural habitat
The Street (1998)
Modern Love (1998)
Love thy Neighbour (1999)

Weddings (1999)
Life on Tape (2000)
Get a Life (2001)
Second Honeymoon (2001)
NZ's Richest (2001)

Historical habitat
Pioneer House (2001)

Intimate strangers
Flatmates (1996)
More Flatmates (1998)
The Big OE (2000)
Single Girls (2000)
High Country Dance (2001)
Adventures in Wonderland (2001)

Intimate strangers subcategory: Survival games
Treasure Island (2000)
Rafted (2000)
The Bounty Hunters (2000)
Internet Island (2001)
The Mole (2001)
Celebrity Treasure Island (2001)

Notes

1 This has occurred in part because of the precedent established by UK broadcasters, which in the mid 1990s began to show pseudo-documentary series on the one hand—the documentary that 'follows' a certain group of people or those attached to a workplace, also known as the 'docu-soap'—and social-experiment programs like *Castaway* (BBC) on the other. By the end of 1998, TV ONE began showing a raft of such British series like *Vets in Practice, The Cruise, Hotel, Airport, The Shop*, etc. Since then, it has shifted more to locally produced versions.

2 This has been largely due to the decisions of Geoff Steven, who took control of TVNZ commissioning (for TV ONE and TV2 in the mid 90s, and then for TV2 solely from 1999).

3 Ratings are high in part because locally produced programs tend, worldwide, to attract viewers more than imported programs. Notably, in 1999 TV2 reported that five of their top six programs were locally produced (the American sitcom *Veronica's Closet* being the one exception). However, it is not just the local that rates well, but locally produced reality television shows; of TV2's five top-rated local programs in 1999, four were reality television series: *Dream Home, My House, My Castle, Motorway Patrol* and *Weddings* (with *Shortland Street* being the single non-reality-television show in the top ratings).

4 I am thinking here of programs like *Big Brother* or *Trading Places*, but this is in some way true of all RTV. Ride-along police programs emphasise ordinary people in set roles, where the selected police officers are 'ordinary' authority figures and the

people whom they interrogate/chase/arrest are 'ordinary' criminals. Crime-reconstruction shows, on the other hand (like *America's Most Wanted*), shift the focus to the victim as ordinary person while the viewer becomes the agent of crime prevention. (See Kevin Glynn 2001, pp. 5–6.)

5   Note that a very early version of New Zealand reality television, originally shown in 1973 and then revived in 1998, was called *The Street*.

6   Interestingly, many critics attributed the ratings failure of the first American series of *Big Brother* to the lack of conflict among the majority of the participants. In a more subtle version of this argument, Bill Wyman has claimed that the television audience of *Big Brother* didn't like conflict, thereby voting out the most aggressive participants, but then found the show unbearable to watch ('Reality Flops: Who Screwed Up *Big Brother*?', http://www.salon.com/ent/tv/feature/2000/09/29/bb_final/index.html).

7   This early New Zealand-produced reality television show is a homegrown, more down-to-earth, and less dramatic version of 'The Real World.'

8   For a categorisation of documentary in terms of the relation between camera and actuality, see Bill Nichols (1991, pp. 32–75).

9   Bill Nichols phrases this criticism in terms of the following analogy: 'Reality TV is to the documentary tradition as sexual 'perversion' was to 'normal' sexuality for Freud. The biological purpose of sexuality—reproduction—is no longer served by perversions that have purposes of their own. Similarly, representations whose purpose is to absorb and neutralize all questions of magnitude no longer serve the ostensible purpose of news: to facilitate collective action based on fresh information' (1994, 51). Though Freud is careful not to hierarchise or moralise the distinction between 'normal' and 'perverse' sexuality, the tone of rebuke here makes it clear that Nichols is using this analogy precisely for the moral overtones.

10   As one *Listener* reader wrote in when *More Flatmates* began to air: '*Flatmates* is an almost perfect example of the low-brow crap that passes for documentary these days. It seems that, in about 1993, somebody decided that any film that wasn't fiction must be documentary. In the process we lost almost all watchable documentaries. Instead, we get a kind of real-life "issues" TV in which any remotely appealing subject is fair game for a couple of self-trained camera operators and a director or producer who doesn't really understand anything except the "market"' (*Listener*, 7 February 1998).

11   Interestingly, this is more true of the early runs in various countries of *Big Brother* and other high-ratings formats; later participants have been less likely to complain about misrepresentation. It is as though the participants from later series learn from watching the earlier series, and accordingly have different expectations of the experience and after-effects of being constantly on camera.

12   The terrorist attacks on America in September were followed, among other reactions of shock and mourning, by a drop in ratings for reality television programs and much speculation that after the potent images of collapsing WTC towers television-produced reality could only ever be trivial and offensive. See 'Love Cruise Sank: Can Networks Keep "Reality" Shows Afloat?' by Lisa de Moraes (http://www.washingtonpost.com/wp-dyn/articles/A32409-2001Sep26.html) and 'Whither Reality TV?' by Andy Dehnart (http://www.salon.com/ent/tv/feature/2001/10/03/wtc_tv/index.html).

13   The exception, of course, is MTV's *The Real World*, which began airing in 1992. It did not appear on New Zealand television until 1997, however, with the launch of TV4, and it is important to recall that even in America it was a cult rather than a mainstream program.

14   For instance, *Rescue 911*, a dramatic-reconstruction show, moved to the UK as *Emergency 999 and Crimewatch UK*, to Germany as *Notruf* and to France as *Témoin No. 1*.

15   *America's Funniest Home Videos*, like *The Great Kiwi Video Show*, focuses on the comic mishap, while the ethos driving the crime/disaster genre is to focus on the serious mishap. These very different shows can thus be thought of as representing two sides of the same coin.

16   Interestingly, *Fair Go* temporarily moves to TV2 in this time period, leading directly into *NZI Crimescene* as a way of indicating that both of these programs are about consumer/citizen responsibility, and not just victims.

17   Such as *Police, Emergency Heroes, Against the Odds, AA Insurance Police Alert,* and *Motorway Patrol.*

18   Such as *Firth Ground Force, Location, Location, Location, Mitre 10 Changing Rooms, My House, My Castle, Bayley's Homefront, Jude's House,* and *Garage Sale.*

19   *Life on Tape* is a good example of how these elements are combined in New Zealand reality television. Interestingly, the US cable channel A&E also bought a reality series in 2001 to be titled *Real People TV,* in which 'ten everyday people' would be armed with hand-held digital cameras, allowing them 'to share their wildest adventures' (http://www.boston.com/dailynews/114/variety/A_E_to_hand_over_to_rea:.shtml; 26 April 2001).

20   The show *Single Girls* placed four women into a high-rise, inner-city apartment for six weeks while they were encouraged to actively seek men; *Flatmates* placed six young people (three men and three women) in a run-of-the-mill suburban house, much like the sort in which students and school-leavers would go flatting, and asked them to do nothing but live together.

21   I am not suggesting that *Single Girls* was free of pre- and post-production manipulation; I wish rather to draw attention to how much perceived manipulation matters in this particular cultural context.

A Look In:

Documentary on New Zealand Television

ANNIE GOLDSON

Two things written by Bill Nichols, a well-known documentary theorist, resonate with me. The first is that documentary has long offered its audiences a particular pleasure, that of epistephilia, or the 'love of knowing' (Nichols 1994, p. 180). The second is that, in providing a source of knowledge, documentary makes the difference between representation and historical reality available for consideration, describing, and interpreting the world of collective experience (Nichols 1991, p. 31). One powerful manifestation of collectivity is, of course, national identity.

Recognising the pleasures and challenges presented by documentary, there seems reason to offer up some reflections on the state of the genre in New Zealand today. In fact, in a collection on national identity the inclusion of documentary is critical. The genre was consolidated here during World War II, the historical moment that national identity became a preoccupation. Documentary was introduced deliberately to represent the nation and in fact continues in this purpose.[1] Its alignment to the national project is thus amplified; not only was it conceived at the moment of the emergence of national identity, it now shows almost exclusively on television, which has itself become the central cultural apparatus through which and from which the nation is broadly styled and understood.

But, to paraphrase Nichols again, what 'epistephilic' urges—needs, demands, desires—is documentary in fact satisfying? What world of apparent collective experience is it interpreting and describing, and what are the consequences, if any, of its interpretation?

Documentary has always been popular here, and it is certainly true that the scenic beauty of these islands was captured on film by both local and international film-makers at a time before 'documentary'—or even the dramatic feature for that matter—was named as a genre. 'Documentary' as such was only consolidated after the visit of John Grierson, the British film producer and writer. Grierson's influence on documentary worldwide was extensive. It is commonly believed (although also contested) that he coined the term 'documentary'.[2] He defined documentary as 'the creative treatment of actuality' as well as founding and leading various film units that forged the prestigious British Documentary Movement (Rotha 1952, p. 70). Finally, Grierson spelled out, in a series of books and articles, what he considered to be documentary's purpose and function in social life (Hardy 1979, 1981).

Grierson visited New Zealand in 1939, as part of a tour of Commonwealth countries. The British government clearly understood the value of documentary in shoring up the war effort of its allies and possibly undermining the 'creeping Americanisation' that they feared would engulf the Western world. Wartime chaos and shifting allegiances in fact had seen the 'Kiwi'—New Zealand's war-time identity—emerge as the romance of Empire faded. The task facing documentary was complex: to attract young men to fight, it was necessary for documentary to keep alive the idea of Empire, yet at the same time, it was equally important to build a sense of national war purpose, if but to show the Empire that the small far-flung Nation was prepared to do its bit. Documentary then was seen as a vital tool, maintaining this dual sense of Empire and Nation.[3]

Grierson's idea of the documentary film varied during his career. By the time he reached New Zealand, he had shed his earlier concerns with experimentation and was emphasising documentary's role in providing a creed of social interconnection and 'good propaganda'. The type of documentary he favoured by this stage can only be described as functional and instrumental, explicitly opposed to categories such as art and authorship. The role of the mass media, Grierson argued, was to foster national unity and should result from a 'clericy' of intellectuals cooperating with politicians, communicating national objectives to people at large, regulating and administering social life for the national good. The overall tone of the Griersonian-style documentary was not one of critical enquiry, but of an optimistic exposition of faith in the ability of the nation to surmount its problems. His prescription offered little room for social critique or any challenge to the existing establishment and indeed, his practice at 'home' and throughout the Commonwealth could be seen as an attempt to contain and diminish the democratic potential unleashed by the war (Aitken 1998, pp. 35–52).

Grierson was derisory about New Zealand's documentary efforts thus far, complaining about New Zealand film's touristic tendencies—nobody, he said, would recognise 'the face of a New Zealander' in our early screen efforts (Sowry 1981, p. 22). His recommendations led somewhat indirectly to the establishment of a National Film Unit and to the production of a popular series of cinema shorts called *The Weekly Review* (McCartney 1994). Made up of newsreels and the occasional short documentary, *The Weekly Review* ran for the decade of the 1940s, showing before features in local cinemas throughout the country.

The Weekly Review was intended exactly to fulfil Grierson's goal of 'civic education'. The film-makers, as civil servants themselves, were to work in tandem with other government departments. During the war, the *Weekly Reviews* concentrated on the New Zealand war effort at home and abroad. In the postwar period, the spirit of nation-building took over. Indeed, according to one government list, suitable subjects for *Weekly Reviews* included: the current activities of ministers; a 'meet the worker' series designed to build pride in occupation; sport; scouts and guides; community service; education subjects; the dental service; health; forestry; and selected industrial subjects.[4]

In fact, a number of the young film-makers at the NFU, often left-wing and somewhat feisty, attempted to circumvent the rules and regulations of film-making laid out by the Labour government, their immediate employer.[5] This resistance was difficult to maintain, however, and ultimately, the majority of the *Weekly Reviews* offered a white, masculine, and moral-ising vision of the country. New Zealand appeared bland and homogeneous, peopled by Pākehā men toiling hard, in tandem with the government of the day, to build the new nation. There was little sense of the cultural differ-ences among Pākehā. Indeed, significant numbers of non-British peoples—Dutch, Croatian, and Chinese—were, where possible, presented under the homogenous Pākehā label, and where impossible, largely ignored. Women, when they did appear, were shown as the grateful recipients of the efforts of state and man. Whether attending Plunket to weigh their babies, moving into a new state home, or taking advantage of the new mod-cons, their par-ticipation was confined to the domestic sphere. Māori were also rarely glimpsed, often treated in a patronising fashion according to the assimila-tionist philosophy of the day.

On the whole, then, the *Weekly Reviews* present a harmonious, hardwork-ing model of the incipient New Zealand nation, as—to use Benedict Anderson's famous phrase—an 'imagined community' comprising Mum, Dad, and the kids, who combined their efforts to restore calm to a culture disrupted by war (Anderson 1983). The litany of subject matter of the *Reviews* would have pleased Grierson of the 1940s and 1950s. By this point in his career, he lauded 'realism' and had an apparent distrust of 'fancy' film-making; hence his proposals had fallen on fertile ground, in that they paralleled the predominant aesthetic already at play in this country. In summary then, at the moment of the apparent consolidation of national identity, we see Griersonian documentary championed as the preferred form, providing an image of New Zealanders at work, at play, and at war. This was the prevailing image of public culture, an image that audiences found deeply satisfying; it was a vision that fulfilled a desire, a felt need to shore up the sense of collective unity and nationhood. Critically, this vision was prescriptive rather than reflective. As Graeme Turner has suggested, our nationalist stories are not 'unmediated reflections of history but transformations of it', and thus work 'to construct a very specific way of seeing the nation' (Turner 1986).

The *Weekly Reviews* were followed by various other newsreel series that continued to screen in cinemas, but in the early 1960s, with the introduction of television, documentary found its new home. A television documentary department was set up within the New Zealand Broadcasting Corporation (NZBC) and produced some well-crafted serious documentaries similar in genre and style to those established by the BBC, which itself was influenced by the Grierson model.[6] By the 1970s, however, a new wave of independent film-makers, aligned with the counter-culture and political movements internationally, began to attack the in-house producers, labelling their work conservative, viewing their budgets and salaries as bloated. Although some were able to penetrate the state broadcaster, most agitated from the margins, producing and screening their work in any way they could.

The next radical shift in the broadcasting context occurred in mid 1980s, part and parcel of a massive restructuring of the New Zealand economy. The country had traditionally followed a highly protectionist economic structure, based on tariffs, subsidies, and a large public service. This was to be rapidly dismantled, replaced by an extreme monetarist regime, one that stressed individualism, competition, and commercialisation. Along with the shift in the economic base, there was concomitant change in the cultural superstructure. One clear result was the commercialisation of television, a process that was rapidly accelerated in 1988 when the government turned that state-broadcaster, renamed Television New Zealand, into a 'state-owned enterprise', forcing it to operate as a successful business, each year delivering a sizeable dividend to its owner (the government itself). In addition, a new, privately owned channel—TV3—was allowed to go to air. Commercial, competitive tendencies were rife through the cultural sector and were manifest on television through the increased reliance on, and presence of, advertising; the branding of channels; the battle for rights for major sporting events; and an increased emphasis on ratings and strategic scheduling. By the end of the 1980s, TVNZ had closed its in-house documentary unit and such work was outsourced. Continuing to face community support for the idea of public service broadcasting however, the government created a television body, the Broadcasting Commission, dubbed 'New Zealand On Air', which had a mandate to support various priorities within broadcasting—in summary 'local content, coverage, Māori culture, children, and minority programmes' (Horrocks 1996, p. 54). Although there was concern about the apparent overall 'Americanisation' of New Zealand television, particularly from those makers who had belonged 'in-house', the documentary sector grew and diversified, as aspiring film-makers took advantage of the development within the state arena. Although the diversification was welcome and the establishment of NZOA did lead to a boom in both local drama and documentary production, there was a catch. Commissioners from the highly commercial broadcasters, both TVNZ and TV3, had to give broadcast approval prior to any project receiving funding from NZOA. This led to significant tensions among those involved in production, that is, the funders, broadcasters, and documentary-makers. Increasingly, through the mid to late 1990s, the National government pressured TVNZ to increase its profits to make it a more attractive candidate for sale and the focus and range of acceptable documentaries narrowed, reflecting the ratings-driven culture of the state broadcaster. With the election of Labour in 1999, however, the rampant commercialisation has been tempered. The government has pledged to continue ownership of TVNZ, and in fact, has instituted a Charter that attempts to reintroduce more public service content into the TVNZ system. However, the tensions continue today, many of them pivoting around the state of documentary.[7]

I want to turn now to an examination of the two major traditions of documentary as they exist in broadcasting today. These strands, one described as 'quality,' the second as 'fast turnaround,' are frequently seen as polarised. However, although they have their distinctions, they both continue to promote an idea of national identity, aligning themselves with the Griersonian tradition. Given that the images of the *Weekly Review* will hardly suffice today, the prevailing idea of nationhood as represented through broadcast documentary has had to be reconstituted in the face of new historical developments and demands. In the following segment, I will attempt to trace what the new vision of national identity, contained within the two competing documentary tendencies, might be.

The 'quality' series

The most direct and obvious antecedent of the Griersonian tradition is the serious civic-minded series on a weighty subject. *Landmarks,* a geography series produced in the early 1980s, prior to the commercialisation of television, has been followed by *Heartland, The New Zealand Wars, Our People Our Century, Immigrant Nation, New Zealand Sex* (yes, even that was weighty and serious), all made in the 1990s. Alongside these series was a related strand of programming, the quality 'one-offs', some of them somewhat more lighthearted, others focused on a major artist or public figure. Continuing to engage with ideas of nationhood, they tended to be structured by the use of either a voice-of-god narration or the presence of a public figure as a substitute authority (who nevertheless remains authoritative rather than interactive or self-reflexive), and they used interviews with participants and experts that supported the rhetorical line or 'voice' of the documentary (Nichols 1986). A mix of archival material and cutaways provided visual illustration, with the meaning of the images fixed firmly by the soundtrack. As the titles of the works testified, these documentaries were often presented as significant interventions in the expression of culture, and often connote nation-building, the consolidation of national identity, the character of our populace, and so on.

Two of the series listed above stand out in this regard, the first being *The New Zealand Wars* (Landmark 1998). This five-part series, directed by Tainui Stephens, first aired in 1998, and was based on a book by historian James Belich (1986). This form of expositional documentary is in the classic nation-building mode and represents a bold revisiting of a traumatic period in this country's history, one suppressed during the assimilationist period of race relations, dominant through the 1970s. Belich's emphasis is on the skill and warriorship of the Māori. He claims that Māori invented 'trench' warfare through their use of the *pa,* providing British troops with a method of defence that proved vital in World War I. He also undoes the myths in the mould of British ideology that implied that these conflicts constituted an honourable war, and points out that Britain only 'won' through deceit and sheer numbers. The series was popular, watched avidly by Māori and non-Māori alike. A certain constituency of Pākehā, already embittered by treaty settlements and what they saw as a culture of 'hand-outs' to Māori, began a campaign of letter writing, denying Belich's interpretations and reasserting their own understanding of the past.

It is possible to understand *The New Zealand Wars* simply as a positive progressive force that was intent on liberalising the views of the majority audience, but there are other interpretations. The traditional denial of racism and colonialism in this country was not challenged by Pākehā goodness, but by the rise of Maoritanga, reclaimed through the Māori land marches, the revival of the Māori language, and through the explosive events surrounding the Springbok tour in 1981.[8] The introduction of the Treaty of Waitangi as a semi-constitutional document and the establishment of the Waitangi Tribunal to arbitrate land disputes, instituted a bi-culturalist ideology, condoned by successive governments. Biculturalism is understood as a recognition of the Treaty and an acceptance that the two peoples, Māori and Pākehā, have had a 'special relationship' in founding this country.

But as vital as the restitution process is, biculturalism can also be understood as potentially staving off Māori sovereignty (tino rangatiratanga), allowing the 'nation' to survive rather than to splinter. Hence, rather than being simply a liberal force, *The New Zealand Wars* can be seen as part of the Griersonian tradition, as reformist, an attempt to contain and diminish Māori anger and, importantly, their claims for sovereignty. It also offers a view produced, as Stephen Turner has pointed out, 'through a triangle of discourses—the University, the media and the state—all invested in the continuation of...a settler economy' (Turner 2000, conference paper). Indeed, the mode of production of *The New Zealand Wars* fulfils Grierson's dictate, cited above in this article, that is, that documentaries should be produced by a 'clericy' of intellectuals cooperating with politicians in communicating national objectives to people. Or as John Langer cites in his study of Australian television, nationhood is continuously restyled and 'enduring myths and cultural reference points' are always in process, 'if not undermined, at least reconstituted' (Langer 1994, p. 264).

The second Griersonian style series *Our People, Our Century* is the story of New Zealand's last 100 years, produced for the Millennium (Ninox 2000). Structured around the oral histories of the elderly and interlaced with archives, it is closely modelled on the BBC series of a similar name. As with *The New Zealand Wars,* however, this series reconstructs nationhood, complicating Pākehā-ness through its acknowledgment of other cultural groups. The distinct histories of Dutch, Scottish, Māori, and English families are presented, and emphasis is placed on the cultural specificity of their experiences. Thus, it offers a more diverse picture of New Zealand nationhood than previously permitted. But, as with the Belich series, it is necessary to see beyond what might be understood as a progressive liberal vision of a society. Cultural groups have asserted enough pressure to ensure some acknowledgment, some representation of 'multiculturalism', that challenges the white masculine majority vision of old and engages with the bicultural ideology of today; but the double use of the word 'our' inter-pellates viewers into a unified national body, one that marches together, in all its cultural richness and diversity. By acknowledging the pain and dis-crimination of the past, but emphasising the idea that all peoples forged 'our' history, the dissension, class differences, and conflicts that continue to exist among our shifting population groups can be more readily contained.

'Fast turnaround' documentaries

'Quality' documentaries, such as those described above, struggled in the highly commercial period of the mid to late 1990s, and a series of more ephemeral 'fast turnarounds' hit the airwaves. Documentary began to be subsumed into reality and lifestyle television, which proliferated across the two state-owned channels and the privately owned channel, TV3. As a term, documentary began to be collected under the umbrella of 'factual programming.' The broadcaster opted for more and more personal, intimate, and sensationalist topics, which some saw as 'tabloid' or 'light and fluffy' (Horrocks 2003). These programs, which continue to enjoy broadcaster support today, have prime-time weekday schedules and attract large, mainstream audiences. Currently, they comprise approximately forty-five minutes per broadcast hour and are structured to allow for frequent commercial breaks. Limited budgets restrict research, travel, and purchase of archival footage. As a consequence, they are mostly shot in modified 'direct cinema' fashion, blending some expositional features (they are usually very reliant on narration) into a more observational style of documentary. The footage is frequently gathered by following one or more characters as they move through their respective days or experiences. The desire, it would seem, is to capture or observe something of 'reality' as it unfolds, something that is hopefully arresting or sensational. The 'fast turnarounds' are gathered into two weekly series, *Documentary New Zealand* (aired on the state broadcaster TV ONE) and *Inside New Zealand* (shown on the Canadian-owned station, TV3).

Interestingly though, as with the 'quality' series, the 'fast turnarounds', at least on the state broadcaster TV ONE, also tend to focus on nationhood, but in a rather more modest fashion. Rather than defining and redefining nationalism, many such programmes take what are already its 'proven' characteristics and explore them. For example, as a random example, in the two weeks I have written this paper, two documentaries have aired on TV ONE: *Getting Away from it All* (LV Films 2001).which shows a range of New Zealanders going on holiday, and the second, *Inventions from the Shed* (Frame Up Films 2000), a look at New Zealand inventors and inventions. Rather than offering an exhaustive bibliography of the documentaries of this genre, I have selected these two, not because they are exceptional but rather, because they are representative. Other 'fast turnaround' works may display an unanticipated level of craft, or may have sufficient impact to migrate into the territory of television 'event'. But my argument here is predicated on what is ordinary rather than extraordinary and, although these two examples may be at the less sensationalist end of the spectrum, they display typical characteristics.

Getting Away from it All takes what is understood as a necessary New Zealand tradition—going on holiday. It profiles three different families as they go about this business, the camera following them on their respective trips. An affluent, established Pākehā family returns (again and again) to their bach at Waipu Cove. A Chinese family, evidently recent migrants to New Zealand, are 'shouted' a trip on an ocean liner by the woman's father. And a single mother with three children stays at a nondescript motel.

The documentary points to the differences among the family groupings, which are in fact far greater than any apparent similarities they share as 'New Zealanders'. The Waipu Cove family appears to have an established circle and it would seem, a sense of ownership passed down through the generations. The bach is in fact an icon of national identity, an asset that was reputedly available to all New Zealanders, regardless of class or income, in a more 'egalitarian' age. Possibly never true, this myth is exploded in the documentary. The evident and quiet affluence of the Waipu Cove family, steeped in apparent tradition, contrasts sharply with the more 'showy' wealth surrounding the Chinese family on the cruise. The latter show a diligence, too, that differs from the relaxed attitude of the beachcombers. The children on the cruise, budding musicians, are required to do hours of music practice every day despite it being a holiday. Meanwhile, the single mother, interviewed in the depressing interiors of the motel or watching her children swing on the monkey bars at the local playground, seems determined to go on holiday just to say she has. The economic strain, the austere motel, the youth of her children (who would barely remember the holiday), make the experience appear more stressful than relaxing.

Whereas once the tradition would have shown all New Zealanders going on holiday to the beach or baches in roughly the same fashion, the class and cultural differences among the families are now made evident. It is as if the documentary acknowledges New Zealand is 'not what it was' and shows a greater diversity, but fails to challenge a fundamental certainty—that going on holiday is a necessary national tradition. This may seem a trivial example, but is indicative of a process that has significant cultural ramifications.

Inventions from the Shed is an exploration of the 'number eight fencing wire' tradition; the masculine domain of Do It Yourself, Kiwi ingenuity born out of the colonial experience where commodities were in short supply. It too is structured around 'case studies' and individual personalities. Most inventors profiled were in fact men, their products designed to assist on the farm (a special feeder made from recycling plastic milk containers; a gate closer; a shearing platform that saves backache) or in sports of some kind (a kind of hovercraft that runs on land and water; a model aeroplane; motorbike accessories). Again, however, the exceptions are shown. A young woman of Indian or Arab descent proudly displays her 'eco-brick' manufactured from waste newspaper, while an older Pākehā woman displays the Tozzo, her rat-catcher. While maintaining the general mythology of New Zealand practicality, *Inventions* expands out to represent a slightly more diverse population base.

Within these two major strands of documentary, the 'quality' and the 'fast turnaround', television's historical representation of the nation is in the process of formulating a new kind of 'imagined community'. To control anger and resentment, it has had to update, projecting a society that includes those who, in past representations of the nation, have been simply absent. The nation as a coherent unit, in fact, is in trouble and appears increasingly vulnerable. The rise of identity politics, clustered around gender, ethnicity, sexuality, and the environment has undermined older nationalist formulations, a position further complicated by pressures such as major economic shifts, such as restructuring and deregulation, the dismantling of state organisations, and a new international mobility of capital and culture. Nation as imagined community, seen through the documentary vision of the *Weekly Reviews*, could not simply be reproduced—it had to be transformed. Hence, New Zealand television documentary today, with its re-stylisation of nationhood, can be labelled reformist. Like Grierson's prescriptions of fifty years ago, the role of documentary continues in its attempts to foster national unity, contain dissent, and administer social life for the national good.

Alternatives

Although I have argued that both the two dominant styles of documentary share characteristics of representing 'nationhood', they are generally understood as not just distinct, but opposed. In fact, the proponents of each stream tend to be locked into something of a rhetorical war. The former 'quality series' are accused of being elitist, pointy-headed, and enjoyed only by academics; the latter more populist work is accused of being ratings-driven and advertising soaked, overly focused on trivia. The degree of polarity has tended to force people into one camp or the other. If one rejects one style of documentary, one is seen to embrace its opposite. What then is squeezed out in this debate is any sense of an alternative that rarely, as a result, gets a 'look in'.

In fact, there has been an alternative tradition here, albeit a small one, which continues a certain vital and defining third strand of documentary that works against the reformist model proffered by John Grierson. Although there is insufficient room to do more than list these works, they were evident from the beginnings of documentary. Cecil Holmes's *Mail Run* (1947) used the newsreel format of the National Film Unit to present an anti-colonial polemic, consistent with his Communist beliefs and at absolute odds with the government policy of the day (NFU 1947). After he was fired from the NFU, largely because he was a Communist, Holmes produced *Fighting Back*, a militant interpretation of a union lock-out. In the

1970s, the rise of Maoritanga and a reaction against the uniformity of the Holyoake era generated more documentaries including the *Tangata Whenua* series, produced by John O'Shea's Pacific Films, written by historian Michael King and directed by Māori film-maker Barry Barclay (Pacific Films 1975). In embarking on a Māori series, the film-makers wished to explore in part why Māori called themselves Māori rather than New Zealanders (King 1985 p. 108). This break with the assimilationist tendencies that had predominated involved pitting Māori culture against New Zealand's national history in order to celebrate Māori difference. The *Survey* series, which showed on television through this same period, included the experimental work of Tony Williams, whose documentary *Deciding* was a parodic meditation on the labyrinthine workings of the public service (Pacific Films 1972).

By the late 1970s, a new wave of political documentaries broke into the cinemas and, belatedly, on television. *Bastion Point: Day 506* (Mita, Narbey, Pohlman Production 1978) and *Patu!* (Awatea Film Productions 1983) drew on historical materialist and Marxist traditions but, with Merata Mita taking a leading role as director, had a distinctly Māori orientation. *Patu!* finally had its first screening on TVNZ in 1991, ten years after the events it documented. *The Bridge* (Merger Productions 1982); *Someone Else's Country* (Vanguard Films 1995); and the more recent *In a Land of Plenty* (Vanguard Films 2002) represented union struggles and perspectives. They have been unable as yet to obtain a mainstream television screening, though *Someone Else's Country* was picked up by Triangle TV, an Auckland-based channel committed to community access. Gaylene Preston's *War Stories My Mother Never Told Me* (Gaylene Preston Productions 1995) acted as a counterpoint to *The Weekly Review's* optimistic depiction of the 1940s. An oral history that is minimally edited, the documentary speaks of the pain, disruption, and disillusionment that New Zealand women experienced during the war and its aftermath. It was screened on TV ONE. Finally, Stewart Main and Peter Wells have produced formally innovative and, at times, overtly gay documentaries since the 1980s. Wells's *The Mighty Civic*, for example, a decorative and fantastical piece, celebrates the Auckland Civic Theatre's 'queer' architectural sensibility, which almost led to its destruction at the hands of New Zealand's conventional no-frills building tradition (James Wallace Productions 1989).

This strand of alternative documentary has had varying relations to broadcast television. Some works make it to prime time, despite what could be seen as their 'subversive' tendencies, others are assigned to 'ethnic' and 'cultural' slots at the margins of the television schedule. Some fail to make it altogether. But one thing these documentaries have in common is their sense of kinship with the film tradition. This association of more political documentary with film is something of an anachronism that has emerged from New Zealand institutional history. An impediment to the development of an alternative moving image culture was New Zealand's failure in the late 1970s to make the transition from film to video that occurred in other countries. During this period the Sony Portapak, the first relatively portable video system, was seized upon by independent documentary makers within the larger metropolitan centres—London, New York, Berlin, San Francisco—and, interestingly enough, by political and guerrilla movements in the Third World. The relative ease and cheapness of video made it a deeply attractive alternative to film, and it was embraced. Dissociating video from television (while formally and politically critiquing it), these artistic and political movements relied on a network of museums, galleries, community centres, and political networks for distribution. In New Zealand, video failed to take off in this way. The country's small population and its lack of alternative infrastructure made this mode of distribution difficult: the relative scarcity of video art and 'independent video' testifies to that. In addition, draconian importation regulations of the 1970s and 1980s made it difficult or costly to import the new, potentially liberating technology of video. Hence film, despite its expense, remained the focus of a tradition in which 'resistant' practices continued. The fact that New Zealand television became more commercial in the 1990s strengthened the distinction. It is no longer simply a matter of the physical medium used, for today there are independent documentaries, made for budget reasons on video or digital video, which strongly align themselves with this film tradition and deliberately reject what have become the dominant conventions of the television documentary.

In my overview of New Zealand's television documentary, I have related the nation-building tendencies of both current major strands to the influences of John Grierson. Although the two traditions, which I have labelled 'quality' and 'fast turnaround,' are frequently seen as polar opposites, their remaking of nationhood is remarkably similar. Of course, their representations have to be continuously updated, if they are to satisfy the changing demands of their viewership, the New Zealand population. However, despite the more contemporary images of New Zealand on offer, the documentaries largely continue to contain difference and dissent, recuperating them back into the fold of nationhood in true Griersonian style. Meanwhile there has always been a lively alternative type of documentary, only occasionally accepted by television. Rather than recuperating 'difference' under reconfigured structures of nationhood, documentaries of this third type tend to offer real social critique or aesthetic experimentation that emphasises, rather than conceals, disruption and dissension. Despite their evident marginalisation, these documentaries, which call nationhood and identity into question, and suggest other visions that are not state-sanctioned, are often the ones that are destined to endure.

References

Aitken, Ian. 1998. 'Grierson's Theory of Documentary Film' and 'the Critical Debates on the Documentary Film Movement', in *The Documentary Film Movement*. Edinburgh: Edinburgh University Press, pp. 35–52.

Anderson, Benedict. 1983. *Imagined Communities: Reflection on the Origins and Spread of Nationalism*. London: Verso.

Belich, James. 1986. *The New Zealand Wars and the Victorian Interpretation of Racial Conflict*. Auckland: Auckland University Press.

Corner, John. 1996. *The Art of Record: a Critical Introduction to Documentary*. Manchester and New York: Manchester University Press.

Goldson, Annie. 2001. 'Home and Away: National Identity and Documentary in the 1940s' in *English in Aotearoa: English and New Zealand Cultural Identity*, No. 41 (NZATE), pp. 51–61.

Grierson, John. 1926. 'Flaherty's Poetic *Moana*', *New York Sun*, 8 February; reprinted in: Lewis Jacobs, (ed.). 1979. *The Documentary Tradition*, 2nd edn. New York: W.W Norton & Co., pp. 25–6.

Hardy, Forsyth. 1979. *John Grierson: A Documentary Biography*. London: Faber.

Hardy, Forsyth (ed.) 1981. *Grierson on the Movies*. London: Faber.

Holmes, Cecil. 1986. *One Man's Way*. Ringwood, Victoria: Penguin.

Horrocks, Roger. 1995. 'Strategic Nationalisms: Television Production in New Zealand'. *Sites*, 30, pp. 85–107.

Horrocks, Roger. 1996 'Conflicts and Surprises in New Zealand Television'. *Continuum*, 10 (1), p. 50.

Horrocks, Roger. 2003. 'The Documentary on Television'. Paper delivered at a documentary symposium, organized by NZOA, at the University of Auckland. Available from: www.nzonair.govt.nz/pag.cfm?i=671

Jacobs, Lewis (ed.) 1979. *The Documentary Tradition*, 2nd edn. New York: W.W. Norton & Co.

Kilbourn, Richard & John Izod. 1998. *An Introduction to Television Documentary: Confronting Reality*. Manchester and London: Manchester University Press.

King, Michael. 1985. *Being Pakeha*. Auckland: Hodder & Stoughton

Langer, John. 1994. 'Videation of a Nation', in P. Fuery (ed.) *Representation, Discourse, Desire*. Melbourne: Longman Cheshire.

McCartney, Jane. 1994. Weekly Review: Backbone, Mainspring, Heart, Soul, and Bread and Butter. Thesis (MA). University of Auckland.

New Zealand On Air. Available from: www.nzonair.govt.nz

Nichols, Bill (ed.) 1985. *Movies and Methods, Vol.2*. Berkeley: University of California Press

Nichols, Bill. 1991. *Representing Reality*. Bloomington: Indiana University Press.

Nichols, Bill. 1994. *Blurred Boundaries: Questions of Meaning in Contemporary Culture*. NewYork: Routledge.

Rotha, Paul.1952. *Documentary Film*, 2nd edn. London: Faber & Faber.

Sowry, Clive. 1981. *The Tin Shed*. Wellington: The New Zealand Film Archive.

Turner, Graeme. 1986. *National Fictions: Literature, Film and the Construction of Australian Narrative*. St Leonards, NSW: Allen & Unwin.

Turner, Stephen. 2000. 'Making History: The New Zealand Wars on Television.' Conference paper (unpublished). *Documentary Sites: The Third International New Zealand Documentary Conference*. University of Auckland.

Williams, Deane. 1999. 'Between Empire to Nation'. *Screening the Past: An International Refereed Electronic Journal of Visual Media and History*. Available from: www.latrobe.edu.au/www/screeningthepast.

Winston, Brian. 1995. *Claiming the Real: Documentary Film Revisited*. London: BFI.

Filmography

Bastion Point, Day 507. 1980. Mita, Narbey, Pohlman Production.

The Bridge. 1982. Merger Films.

Deciding. 1972. Pacific Films (for the NZBC).

Fighting Back. 1949. Cecil Holmes.

Getting Away from it All, 2001, LV Films.

In a Land of Plenty: The Story of Unemployment in New Zealand, 2002, Community Media Trust in association with Vanguard Films.

Inventions from the Shed. 2000. Frame Up Films.

Landmarks, 1981. TVNZ documentary unit.

Mail Run: Weekly Review 310. 1947. National Film Unit.

The Mighty Civic. 1949. James Wallace Productions.

The New Zealand Wars. 1998. Landmark.

Our People, Our Century. 2000. Ninox Films.

Patu!, 1983. Awatea Films.

Seeing Red, 1994. A James Wallace Production.

Someone Else's Country. 1996. Vanguard Films.

Tangata Whenua. 1974. Pacific Films.

War Stories My Mother Never Told Me. 1995. Gaylene Preston Productions.

Notes

1   The first listed mission statement on the web site of the primary funding agency of documentary, New Zealand On Air, is: 'To fund programming on radio and television about New Zealand and New Zealand interests': www.nzonair.govt.nz.

2   In his review of Robert Flaherty's film, *Moana*, Grierson wrote that 'of course, *Moana* being a visual account of events in the daily life of a Polynesian youth and his family, has documentary value' (Grierson 1926). For an alternative interpretation of the genre's origins, see Brian Winston (1995, p. 11).

3   I draw here on research carried out by Deane Williams (1999), who studied Grierson's influences in Australia.

4   List quoted in unpublished essay by David Newman, Victoria University, 1984. The quote is from an undated memo for Walter Nash, the Acting Prime Minister, by J.T. Paul, the Director of Publicity of the time (Tourist and Publicity File 49/87/10). It refers to production from the Mirimar Film Studios.

5   One such film-maker, Cecil Holmes, a member of the Communist Party, was in fact fired after a scandal known as the 'satchel snatch', where his political affiliations were widely aired and blamed for political unrest. See his own book (Holmes 1986), my film *Seeing Red* (1994), and my article, Goldson (2001) for an overview of film-makers at the NFU and the Holmes case.

6   For discussions about the influence of the Documentary Film Movement on British television documentary, see Corner (1996) and Kilbourn and Izod (1998).

7   I refer here to a recent keynote speech by Roger Horrocks (2003).

8   The Springbok tour of 1981 led to deep civil unrest. Its initial focus on racism and apartheid in South Africa shifted to include an analysis of racism against Māori in New Zealand.

Introduction and methodology

This chapter has three aims. First, it seeks to demonstrate the importance of textual analysis to the understanding of television news. Second, it argues the importance of critically examining this most widely consumed form of news. Third, it wishes to answer the question of how a sample of television news in New Zealand constructs this nation state, the sample being a bulletin screened by Television New Zealand (TVNZ), whose remit as the national broadcaster underwrites its self-conscious address to viewer-members of the nation state.

What follows is a non-formalist textual analysis, one informed by awareness of the placement of the television news bulletin within the history of New Zealand society, economics, and politics. It is based on content description. It is not content analysis in the customary sense, which tends to flatten out the text's discursive and narrative constructions in the service of quantified generalisations. The undoubted worth of content analysis in the present context is well illustrated in Joe Atkinson's and Daniel Cook's longitudinal studies of changes in television news coverage respectively in 1985–92 and 1984–96 (Atkinson 1994; Cook 2002), work that can be seen as complementary to that undertaken here. The current analysis attends carefully to content description as a protection against selective rendering and impressionism.

In other words, what actually appears on screen needs to be analysed in detail. This is to acknowledge three factors. First, there are the huge number of person-hours and the occupational ideologies that inform the production of each news bulletin. Sue Abel has valuably detailed these processes:

> The news that finally gets to air has been filtered though a series of 'gates' as dictated by news selection, gathering and editing routines. At each stage—the foreign and home desks, the news executives' meetings, the commissioning of reporters and crews, the reporting and filming process, the editing, the final selection of items for the bulletin, the writing of intros and final presentation— news is selected and shaped not only by organisational requirements, but also by 'news values', the traditional criteria by which news workers make professional judgements about what is newsworthy and what is not.

Abel 1997, p. 15

Second, these **news values** are themselves framed by the complex network of discourses obtaining within the nation state—routine assumptions about what constitutes success, constructions of gender, ethnicity, and so on—which each bulletin mobilises and recirculates. Another set of news values informs the third factor, namely the generic assumptions about television news that are operative for both news producers and news consumers. These news values, disengaged by early research into television news, include such criteria as the recency of the events reported and news's attention to the non-routine or the exceptional, as well as considerations like the preponderantly domestic address of television and the increasing precedence taken by the verbal over the visual (Galtung and Ruge 1965; Gans 1980; Ellis 1982; Bell, Boehringer, and Crofts 1982). Other generic conventions include the mystique of 'live' coverage ('direct from our reporter at the scene', 'updating now'), verbal forms of continuity covering visual 'gaps' with reporters' voices, and the hierarchies of studio presenter/reporter/ interviewee that have become stabilised over so long a period as to appear perfectly 'natural'. Television news, after all, has an extraordinary capacity to pass itself off for most viewers as a transparent window on the world. The density and complexity of the construction of individual bulletins thus justifies detailed textual analysis, in this chapter, of just one bulletin.

As I have argued more fully elsewhere, textual analysis disengages the reading positions offered by the text; and these may or may not be taken up by individual readings of it (Crofts 1993, pp. 79–88). Such a textual analysis does not assert a textual determinism to the effect that texts are *necessarily* read in a given way, positing rather a preferred reader, who makes sense of the text concerned in accordance with the conscious intentions and unconscious assumptions of the producer(s) of the text, as well as allowing for discrepant readings, including critically oppositional ones. As will be seen below, there is one point at which the news bulletin analysed here adopts a dual address to different reading constituencies. Overall, however, the reading positions offered by this national news bulletin are decidedly unambivalent/homogeneous. While attending in detail to the preferred reader posited by the bulletin, this textual analysis will also propose some oppositional readings of its constructions of dominant discourses.

It therefore attends not just to generic, narrative, verbal, and visual constructions of dominant discourses, but also to the ways in which these *address* the television news viewer, offering us various forms of identification: i.e., who does the bulletin think we are as it talks to us? As a New Zealand news bulletin with predominantly locally produced items unlikely to be shown elsewhere in the world, it assumes its viewers are New Zealanders, that is, its address is national. We can hypothesise that the address extends beyond such familiar discourses of national identity as sporting nationalism and Māori/Pākehā biculturalism. For in addressing all in the population who have a television and wish to see the news bulletin, it mobilises and recirculates other discourses within the nation state. These may not only be concerned with 'official' national identities and nationalisms, but also with the specificities of the cultural formation, e.g. particular conceptions of the individual or the nation state *vis-à-vis* the rest of the world, or specific con-figurations of class, gender, ethnicity, region, and so on. The word 'national' is used below to indicate news stories based in New Zealand, even if their focus may be decidedly local or regional.

ONE Network News regularly figures very highly in the ratings, and is thus treated rather than *TV3 News*, the other New Zealand-produced news program. Given its national remit, it has a particular role in generating unifying notions of the nation state by presenting stories sourced across its length and breadth. By the same token, however, it should be stressed that this is clearly not an overtly propagandistic or nationalistically coercive strategy: it is one that simultaneously reflects existing discursive assumptions about the unity of the nation state and also reinforces them, as well as dis-charging the responsibilities of a national broadcaster.

Description

The bulletin selected for detailed analysis is that of TVNZ's *ONE Network News* on Tuesday 11 May 1999. The particular bulletin is both randomly chosen but also typical of *ONE Network News*. As a Tuesday bulletin, it carries rather more crime items—crime tends to peak at weekends—and reports fewer sports results than do some other days of the week. It includes some major items of foreign news alongside many national items. In terms of historical placement, it may be helpful to recall that this was the time of the Kosovo War and growing international protest against Indonesia's treatment of East Timor, while in New Zealand tourist preparations for the Auckland meeting of the Asia Pacific Economic Cooperation forum (APEC), the America's Cup defence and the Millennium celebrations were making big news. (On the question of the sample, my vouching for the typicality of this bulletin is necessarily impressionistic; a proper—and massively larger—analysis would need to examine many more bulletins in similar detail.)

Channel ONE, **ONE Network News**, *11 May 1999*

0'33		*Teasers and Introduction*
		[A: National 1]
5'23	1.	Light aircraft crashes
2'14	2.	Government issues Contact Energy shares
1'36	3.	Hukerenui murder
0'22	4.	Hamilton death
0'22	5.	Campaign for harsher crime penalties
1'20	6.	Media cat goes missing
0'19		*Teasers*
4'00		*Ads*
		[B: Overseas, including foreign policy]
1'51	7.	PM Shipley visits Peru
0'37	8.	MPs call for Indonesian disarmament in East Timor
1'48	9.	Yugoslav troop withdrawal offer; NATO bombs Chinese Embassy
0'51	10.	President Clinton apologises
1'33	11.	False hail damage claims in Sydney
0'18		*Teasers*
4'00		*Ads*
		[C: National 2]
2'23	12.	Gisborne cancer pathologist
1'46	13.	Wellington schoolboy beaten to death
0'49	14.	Christchurch child molester not yet pardoned
0'19	15.	Alcohol tax increase due in budget
0'48	16.	Share, currency, debt markets
0'25	17.	Wellington traffic proposal
0'38		*'Updating our top stories tonight'*
1'51	18.	Plans to celebrate the dawn of the Millennium at Gisborne
0'21		*Teasers*
3'45		*Ads*
		[D: Sport]
1'55	19.	All Blacks selection possibilities

1'23	20.	Rumours of players/coach split in Auckland Blues
0'50	21.	Manu Samoa team arrives for Pacific Rim rugby
1'35	22.	Touch rugby dispute
1'32	23.	'Black Caps could win' cricket against England
0'35	24.	Chelsea beat Spurs in UK soccer
1'08	25.	New Zealand hockey hopes to beat Australia
0'18	26.	Auckland Warriors' new Australian player
0'15	*Teasers*	
4'25	*Ads*	
	[E: National 3— 'Extra']	
1'41	27.	Emphysema operable
4'15	28.	Window cleaner climbs to safety; Weather
0'49	29.	Car-kissing competition
	End	

Formal analysis of structure

The advertising breaks divide the bulletin into five brackets (A to E above; square parentheses indicate my own titles), whose alternating rhythm returns the viewer to events in New Zealand (Sections A, C, E), with intervening excursions overseas (Section B) and to sport (Section D). The national, in other words, opens the bulletin, closes it, and figures as a point of return in the middle. This suggests the safe comfort of the nationally familiar common to the domestic address of television (Ellis 1982). In the same way, the reliability of the weather report at or near the end of the bulletin performs a reassuring role. Sports items figure at the less 'serious' end of the bulletin, structurally echoing the traditional division of the day into 'real world' work followed by leisure.

The overall timing is sixty-one minutes, of which advertisements, teasers, sport, and weather consume thirty-one minutes, nineteen seconds. Thus the time dedicated to news—defined as public service information about the world, and excluding sport—is twenty-nine minutes, forty-one seconds: rather less than half of the television news 'hour'.

Analysis of major news categories and the identifications they offer

The following analysis is largely ordered in sections treating the national and the overseas. Within each section, where appropriate, news items are grouped by content category (e.g. sport, crime; the categories are based on Bell, Boehringer, and Crofts 1982, pp. 148–51). These categories are sequenced by the number of items in each category, i.e. the importance

accorded by the bulletin to particular kinds of news, and by their prominence in the narrative of the bulletin. Some, less important, items are not
discussed in detail.

The national

Eight items on sport (items 19–26)

These include four on rugby union, and one each on rugby league, cricket,
hockey, and soccer. Six of the eight involve New Zealand teams. The other
two represent something approaching opposite poles of global power chains.
One, a report on British soccer, suggests more perhaps than just the global
popularity of soccer. Its inclusion points to the strong ongoing influence of
British culture in New Zealand. It is one of only two sports items with no
New Zealand team involved. The other concerns the Manu Samoa rugby
team training in New Zealand. As a Pacific Island nation state, Samoa's relative
economic weakness enables New Zealand to attract many major Samoan
players, an operation partly naturalised by the blurring of national boundaries
effected by the significant Samoan diaspora in New Zealand. Thus the
bulletin shows and speaks of 'former All Black, Viaga Tuigamala' as well as
Pat Lam and Steve Bachop, with the result that Samoa is constructed as
something of a client-state and no threat to New Zealand rugby superiority.

Six of the eight sports items involve international competition, i.e. a
team playing a non-New Zealand team, and so focus nationalist sentiment.
This is obvious with the national teams of rugby, touch rugby, cricket, and
hockey (items 19, 22, 23, and 25), and a little less obvious with regional
teams: the Auckland Blues' competitors in Super 12 rugby are largely South
African and Australian teams, while the Auckland Warriors are the only
New Zealand team in the Australian National Rugby League (items 20 and
26). The sports category, then, carries a heavy burden of national pride
found nowhere else in the bulletin. The only other items with so explicit a
focus on the nation state as such are items 7 and 8, reporting Prime Minister
Jenny Shipley's visit to Peru and MPs petitioning on East Timor. The force
of sport as definer of the nation state—here outweighing international
affairs and all else by a factor of something like three to one—indicates the
centrality of sport to discourses of national self-definition. Rugby union
plays a crucial role here. It accounts for three of the sports items, and is the
sport in which over many years more national psychic energy has been
invested than any other in New Zealand, to the extent of one university
offering grief counselling to its students after the All Blacks' loss to France
in the semi-final of the 1999 Rugby World Cup.

With no items on any female sports teams, national sporting identity is
defined overwhelmingly through male sport, and so plainly illustrates a

central thesis of Jock Phillips's *A Man's Country?* (1987). It should be noted that the rest of the bulletin, both in terms of its presenters and reporters, and in its selection and treatment of stories, works to substantially correct this gender imbalance.

The kinds of identification predominantly offered to viewers in these sports items are evident: collective identifications, in a nationalist mode. These nationalist identifications are, however, somewhat undercut by a frequently voiced anxiety about losing. Item 19, on possible team changes in the All Blacks' preparations for the World Cup, is underpinned by their indifferent performances at the end of the 1998 season, an anxiety referred to in the item and evidenced a few weeks after this bulletin in the lavish praise heaped by coach and media commentators on the All Blacks' success in beating its own New Zealand A team. In item 20, Jed Rowlands, coach of the Auckland Blues, once dominant in Super 12, reflects on the team's return from what the sports news anchor, Peter Williams, calls 'a dismal South African campaign': 'We need a bit longer to get back to the strength of Blues teams in the past'. In item 22, on the over-30s touch rugby won by Australia, 'a bureaucratic bungle cost one of New Zealand's top teams the chance of claiming the ultimate prize' (Williams). Here a dispute over the eligibility of a Samoan playing for New Zealand resulted in the team being disqualified. The item concludes on a note of literal and metaphorical disability, speaking of the forthcoming token, non-competition game against Australia as maybe 'eras[ing] some of the injuries the likes of one-armed star Brad Zia have endured' (reporter), with footage of the player named.

Item 23 continues to speak of potential international success—'Well, the Kiwi cricketers are on their own World Cup quest'—and is pleased to note the team's 'receiving surprising support from a prominent section of the English media' (Williams). The London-based reporter reveals this to be the Murdoch-owned tabloid, *The Sun*, which, she says, 'thinks the Black Caps could win'. Captain Stephen Fleming remains professionally 'cautious'. The reporter's commentary on the warm-up match against county side Surrey casts the English as untrustworthy, describing the taking of a New Zealand wicket as a 'trick', before showing the Black Caps scoring with considerable ease and winning by a substantial margin. (Commentaries and footage in international sports items from most nation states are routinely less than respectful of protocols of bipartisan reporting, leaving no doubt as to which team the national viewer is expected to support.) Item 25 opens similarly: 'New Zealand hockey's hoping to strike it rich' (Williams) playing Australia in the Commonwealth Championships. The reporter amplifies: 'New Zealand must win this three-test series to gain automatic entry to next year's Sydney Olympics.' This item deploys the same trope of success-against-minor-side-before-the-real-test as does the Black Caps item: 'After last night defeating a Queensland selection 3–0, the first real test is on Thursday night' (reporter).

Typically of dominion settler nation states with pioneer founding mythologies, sport takes on a major and muscular, if anxious, role in national self-definition. And much of this news bulletin bespeaks an arguably insecure nationalism, a nation state anxious to prove itself on the world sports stage, and particularly to 'move on from' the All Blacks' weak late 1998 season.

Six items on crime (items 3–5, 11, 13–14)

The first grouping consists of a Northland murder, a 'suspicious' death in Hamilton, and a campaign for tougher penalties (items 3–5). Both violent crime events reported here are introduced by the newsreaders set against studio graphics reading 'Police' and 'Police Emergency'. The news reporting likewise overwhelmingly accords agency to the police, who are routinely described in the active voice and the present tense, as dealing as effectively as they can with the crimes, while the deaths and criminals are presented in the passive voice and past tense. Witness the opening sentences of the Hukerenui item: 'A sixteen year-old *has been* charged with murder after a fatal shooting in the far North last night. Thirty-four year-old Steve Mitchell *was found* dead in a house in Hukerenui, north of Whangarei. Leigh Taylor *reports*. [Female anchor Judy Bailey hands over to reporter.] Detectives *are* still *trying* to piece together the last hours of Steve Mitchell's life. His body *was discovered* last night by close friends who owned the farm he worked on. He died of a single gunshot wound to the head. [Reporter. An interview with a detective follows.] Police *say* Steve Mitchell knew the sixteen-year-old now charged with his murder [reporter].' (my italics). Immediately following the two violent crime items is one introduced by a scales of justice graphic, on a campaign for a referendum for harsher penalties for violent crime, with the news that 'the government has introduced legislation that aims to crack down on violent offenders' (Bailey). In this cluster of three items, studio graphics, interviews with police, recurrent footage of police vehicles and bright yellow crime barriers, grammatical voice and tense, and narrative structure cast police, democratic process, and government as protectors of our safety. At the same time, however, the agency accorded to the police tends to cast crime victims as powerless, while the immediacy of news reporting and the interviews with ordinary people 'just like us'—publican, neighbour, eyewitness, and in item 13 grieving friends and relatives— underscores the immediacy of violent threat to our everyday lives, and leaves us ample space to identify as fearful victims of crime ourselves or as closely connected to victims. This connectedness holds particular resonance in a fairly urbanised nation state with a small population, often characterised as a country with only two degrees of separation.

Items 13 and 14 adopt a similar narrative pattern. Another 'Police' studio graphic sits behind the anchor, who introduces item 13 on the fatal beating of a 14 year-old Wellington schoolboy. His consumption of alcohol and a hallucinogenic drug before the beating in a city lane is not treated censoriously. Rather, the bulletin attends to the loss of a young life: 'Friends today overwhelmed. [….] Geoff's friends say he loved music, art and colour, which is why he dyed his hair purple two weeks ago' (reporter). The descriptor 'purple' is the basis of the bulletin's one use of dual address. Indicating gayness and marking the event as a gay-bashing, it enables the station to address gays and lesbians as significant market sectors, while not offending unsympathetic viewers lacking the sub-cultural linguistic codes to read the item in this way. The item offers reassurance (of a kind) in noting the establishment of grief counselling at the boy's school. The following item reasserts faith in the justice system: 'There'll be no pardon for convicted child molester, Peter Ellis—at least not until his case has been dealt with by the Court of Appeal' (Bailey). Interviews with his QC and his mother support his appeal for release after six years in prison. The sequencing of a story on violent crime and one on justice offers similar narrative palliatives to those in items 3–5 treated above. And the return to the safely governmental is bolstered somewhat by the next item, on an increase in alcohol tax.

The kinds of identification offered by these crime items, then, are individual and familial. Since it would be very hard to read these items as a guide on how to commit crime, we are addressed centrally as potential crime victims and empathisers with crime victims, and secondarily as supporters of the police and legal system, thus with some (rather fragile) reassurances about the powers of law and justice. It is worth noting, too, though, that the prevailing conventions of news reporting afford even less analysis of the socioeconomic reasons for most such crime—as being responses to poverty or exploitation—than do most politicians.

One item on accidents (item 1)

Much the longest item in the bulletin—at 5'23', longer even than the weather or any ad break—is that on a light airplane crash. It is also the first item. It mobilises two discourses in particular: a pioneer discourse of the vulnerability of humans and their technologies to the bush—the reporter asyntactically describes the wreckage of the plane as 'Barely visible. The littered remains of a Piper Cherokee hidden in dense bushland'—and a neo-liberal discourse of go-getting success. Thus the crash story per se licenses ancillary reports on the pilot, an 81-year-old 'who wanted even more, to fly faster machines and further afield' (reporter), a live update report from the crash site, and a capsule history of the twenty-four people [in a population of 3.8 million] who had died so far that year in plane crashes. The identifications on offer in this main item of the bulletin are with wealthy individuals who, like this owner, can afford a new V8 car and a plane, which the reporter describes as 'the $70 000 baby he bought'. His death is presented to us as a 'tragedy' (reporter) with which we are urged to empathise. While the bulletin accords this rich man sustained attention as tragic victim, it might equally be argued that he was foolhardy, taking a big risk, and bringing on his own death. One might pause to consider how typical is the tiny percentage of the population who own planes, and ask, for instance, how many industrial accidents, which manifestly affect far more of the population, are reported on television news?

Two items on health and safety (items 12 and 27)

Item 12's report on a Gisborne cancer (principally cervical) pathologist draws attention to *ONE Network News*'s own investigation as well as to concern about the victims of his incompetence: 'And *tonight ONE Network News has learnt* that senior medical professionals have been worried about the pathologist's work for several years. Some also fear that the incidence of misdiagnoses could be more widespread' (Bailey; my emphases). The report concludes quite forcefully with the remark that 'the women of Gisborne are still waiting for answers' (reporter). A similar, humanely concerned mode of address emerges from item 27, on a new form of surgery that could relieve emphysema, even though it would not be available in the public health sector. Severe anxiety on the one hand (the pathologist's apparent gross incompetence) is scarcely eased on the other by the emphysema treatment available only to the wealthy. It is worth noting additionally that *ONE Network News*'s older demographic may explain its larger proportion of health items than that aired by *TV3 News*.

Three and a bit items of 'light' news (items 6, 18, 29 and part of 28)

This grouping cuts across more traditional content categorisations of animals (a media-famous cat, which appeared in ads for a computer company, goes missing in item 6), human interest (a car-kissing competition in item 29), leisure and entertainment (preparations for celebrations of the Millennial dawn at Gisborne in item 18) and a tiny accident report, the near-fall of a window-cleaner, which follows the emphysema item and is tucked in at the beginning of weather (item 28). The significance of these items lies less in their content than in their narrative placement and their feelgood, upbeat entertainment role at the end of a bracket of items and/or after a grimmer item like that on emphysema. In Sue Abel's gloss, '[t]he end story (or 'kicker') is usually aimed at the viewer's emotions and designed to leave them smiling' (Abel 1997, p. 11).

These items' upbeat address to the viewer might offer some happy respite from the (largely gloomy) main news, as well as encouraging a more receptive attitude to the news items announced in the teasers following, and to the goods and services advertised thereafter. The tone is epitomised in the teaser to the media cat story, full of snappy alliterations, puns, and colloquialisms: 'The missing moggie with the television pedigree. What's happened to the frisky feline?' (male anchor, Richard Long, almost loses his *gravitas* on that one). Needless to say, there is no analysis here as to what socioeconomic circumstances might drive people to spend seventy hours kissing a car in order to win it. Rather, the item's humorous tone resolutely distances the likelihood of any such critical framework of thinking.

These items represent a kind of nationalistic good news. But what kind of news is this? It arguably represents a triumph of tone over substance. The jokey media cat story would hardly affect public affairs or the quality of life of more than a handful of New Zealanders. The car-kissing, though actually serious, is trivialised (and examined in more detail below). The Millennial celebrations instance a growing category of news, like the sports items 23 and 25, which adopt what grammarians call the optative mood (that which it is desired will happen) rather than the indicative mood (that which empirically has happened or is happening): it was surely obvious that the impoverished, small township of Gisborne would never be able to build the infrastructure necessary to support a huge international event starring Dame Kiri Te Kanawa and David Bowie; and indeed, it did not. The address in these items is national and collective, in a chattily optimistic, downhome, and cosily feelgood register that just possibly deflects attention from their less than serious attention to real world events.

Overseas

Two items on international relations, two items on war, one on crime (items 7–11)
Most items in this block demonstrate New Zealand concern about major world news. This works firstly in terms of *ONE Network News* showing the then current state of Yugoslavia's war against Kosovo, courtesy of a CBS feed which (surely disingenuously?) describes the NATO bombing of the Chinese Embassy in Belgrade as 'mistaken', and shows President Clinton apologising (items 9–10). New Zealand concern about major world issues is registered also in terms of MPs from all parties, 103 out of a total of 120, calling for the disarmament of the Indonesian militia in East Timor (item 8). (It might be observed that the attention paid by the fourth largest country in the world—and one run by the military—to a petition from a small democracy is likely to be negligible.) Leading this bracket of overseas items is Prime Minister Shipley's visit to Peru to drum up support for the forthcoming free-market APEC Conference, reported by *ONE Network News*'s political editor, Duncan Garner, accompanying the Prime Minister

(item 7). This item acutely focuses two issues. First, *ONE Network News* at this time was responding to *TV3 News*'s less than reverential reporting of the Prime Minister by itself engaging in some similar reporting. Second, this manifests itself here in a critique of the value of APEC's neo-liberal agenda—at least for Peruvians. Coupled with shots contrasting President Fujimora's opulent palace ('clearly more upmarket than the Beehive') with beggars and slums ('Peru's poverty stands out') is a criticism voiced both by Long and Garner that the Prime Minister refuses to visit 'any of the poorer parts of South America. Yet it's these people who need to be convinced the most that the benefits of APEC will flow through' (Garner). This evocation of class difference is indeed unusual for a television news bulletin, yet it is interestingly qualified. Not only is the focus of criticism principally on the Prime Minister's distance from (Peruvian) poverty, but the implied comment on the modesty of the Beehive and the shots of extreme poverty in Peru refer back to New Zealand, addressing national viewers as enjoying a more egalitarian polity than Peru. Further, one might note, the reporter's apparent assumption that Peru's poor might be consulted or allowed to express a view about APEC betrays either an ignorance of the nature of that police state and/or a projection of a New Zealand-like social democracy as the global norm. One might also ask what consultation with its local poor the more democratic New Zealand government made in the preparations for APEC. This item, then, is less an invitation to read New Zealand in class terms than a reading of Peru through New Zealand lenses, which endorses New Zealand's less class-divided society.

The viewer address in these items is to the New Zealand viewer as concerned with major events in distant parts of the world, who at the same time may very well be glad to be far removed from Balkan bombing and ethnic cleansing, a brutal war in East Timor, and the extremes of Peruvian poverty. Not surprisingly then, concern could be argued to be tempered by a certain domestic self-congratulation. Again, typically of international news reporting in many nation states, the East Timor petition could be seen as endorsing a national moral (not political) superiority over the Indonesian regime.

Item 11's report on false hail damage claims in Sydney differs from the preceding items in this overseas bracket in being hardly major international news, in thus having a lighter tone than its predecessors, and in that Australia is relatively familiar to New Zealanders. Its account of trans-Tasman insurance scams plays on anti-Australian discourses common in New Zealand. It also offers a familiarising, New Zealand angle of address by noting Sydney's need to employ twenty-five New Zealand roofing contractors: 'With emergency repairs to roofs expected to take up to ten months to complete, the Kiwis could be in for a long stay' (reporter).

Two items on finance (items 2 and 16)

In addition to the regular daily report on shares and currency markets (item 16), this bulletin devotes the second item in its running order to the government's release of Contact Energy shares. 'For the thousands of Kiwi and big overseas investors who chose to sell [the same day], it meant a quick profit' (Long). The bulletin presents this as a triumph for consumer sovereignty. Along with a montage of anxious male faces scrutinising share price displays at the Wellington Stock Exchange, brokers speaking into phones and looking earnestly at computer screens, there are interviews with brokers as experts, statistics, and a graph showing the day's sale prices. Vox pops here are limited to two small investors. The bulletin invites us to note that even a schoolboy can profit from shares. Sporting the tie of a Wellington private school, he is both named and given far more screen time than the other investor: 'Trading screens for blackboards is high school student Chris Blore, an investor choosing a quick sale' (reporter). Striking here is how ingeniously this characterisation naturalises share ownership and notions of consumer sovereignty, as if to say: 'Even a schoolboy can trade shares!' Leaving aside the trivial question of whether his school punished him for playing truant, this construction does gloss over some serious questions: most obviously, what percentage of the New Zealand population—or indeed of *ONE Network News*'s demographic—can afford shares? The bulletin's use of expert insider voices, images, and statistics mystifies rather than clarifies how shares actually work not so much *for* most viewers, but *against* them. For higher share profits correlate directly with higher charges for customers, which are easily enforced when government-licensed private companies monopolise essential utilities such as energy and phones. And the major shareholder beneficiaries of shares in small neo-liberal economies like New Zealand or Australia are routinely foreign, mostly US and mostly very big corporate investors. The identifications proposed by this item differ from those of all other serious items in the bulletin. We are invited to identify with both success and agency—of the New Zealand share-owning class, that is—identifications that may well traduce the actual everyday experience of the majority of viewers angry at high power and phone bills. We are here *not* invited to identify with victims, namely *ourselves* as over-charged consumers (there is a similar populist sleight-of-class-hand noted by Nick Perry in his analysis of America's Cup campaign commercials (Perry 1994, pp. 27–33)). The schoolboy profiteer not only diverts attention from the *non-New Zealand* nationality of the majority foreign shareholders benefitting from the Contact Energy shares sell-off, but also, very dubiously, individualises this world controlled by massive finance corporations. And this individualisation transforms a loss for the majority into a personal triumph for the profiteer.

It is time to return to the car-kissers. This item provides the bulletin's only success story aside from that of the share profiteers and Chelsea beating Spurs (item 24). Significantly, it shows one of few routes to wealth available to poor people (other, equally unreliable ones would include gambling). Significantly too, one of the winners, a Māori male, talks with justified pride of the qualities enabling his success, qualities not evident in the schoolboy profiteer: 'It's mentally hard. And physically hard. Never do that again.' In this final item of the bulletin, class difference comes home to New Zealand, having been repressed by the shares item's invitation to most viewers to identify against their own experience, and having been displaced in the APEC item by Peru's being so obviously *more* class-divided than New Zealand. Yet, the flip, humorous tone discourages any serious attention to the socioeconomic issues underpinning the desperation of kissing a car for seventy hours—the action itself a remarkable metaphor of post-industrial consumer capitalism! One could draw the conclusion that in this bulletin the victims of class exploitation figure either as foreigners or as jokes.

Conclusions

The major groupings of the bulletin's news items propose to the viewer a predominantly anxious sense of being in the nation state. (Compare the curiously titled local social geography textbook, Harvey Franklin's [1978] *Trade, Growth and Anxiety*.) The sports grouping identifies this in terms of a nationalist collectivity, with a fear of sporting losses, the crime grouping in terms of potential individual victimhood, and the health stories in similar terms. Such anxieties find marginal consolation in two areas: the law and order discourse promoting the police and legal process; and in the overseas items, which imply that we live in a better, safer place than the world's troublespots, which—typically of international television news worldwide—constitute the bulk of overseas news. This notion is reinforced by the bulletin's constant rhythmic returns to the national.

The sole examples of successful agency in New Zealand are those of the share profiteers, with whom the bulletin urges viewers to identify against their own majority interests, and the car-kissers, whose real strengths are undercut by the item's trivialising tone. Where New Zealand class differences are at all visible—though not marked as such by the bulletin—the bulletin accords seven minutes, thirty-seven seconds to the rich (share profiteers and aircraft owner) and only forty-nine seconds to the poor, the car-kissers. Overall, and especially in the crime items and their elision of factors of unequal distributions of wealth, socioeconomic causality is never invoked. Perry well notes of television's institutional position: 'Television is too intent on maximising audiences to ignore popular sentiment, too important to the powerful for them to ignore it, and too interested in developing a measure of institutional autonomy to unambiguously subordinate itself to the expectations of either of these constituencies' (Perry 1994, p. 17). In this bulletin, tensions between corporate capital and popular address are resolved not in terms of class or unequal distributions of wealth, access, and opportunity, but in terms of neo-liberal, populist fantasies of consumer democracy. If the bulletin references any unqualified winners besides the share profiteers, it would be the two groups who actually benefit from the upbeat, 'light' news items: first, the television station that advertises its forthcoming attractions in its teasers, which 'soften' viewers for the adverts; and then the advertisers who advertise their various goods and services, and finance the television station. Viewers, then, are addressed as lacking agency except in the form of 'consumer sovereignty', consumer purchases, and lifestyle fantasies. Certainly, New Zealanders are not addressed as thinking critical agents—even in the (safely overseas) critique of the APEC agenda.

Here the 'light' news items return to our analysis. As the jokers in the pack of traditional content categorisations, their grammatical mood is more optative than indicative (for such categorisations presuppose a referential relationship between news and the real world of public affairs). Operating more in the realm of the fanciful and the frivolous, the 'light' items occlude questions of socioeconomic causality: what kind of media-saturated culture are we living in that seeks to make a cat a celebrity? What would drive people to kiss a car for seventy hours? How could an impoverished region of a poorish nation state raise the money for a huge infrastructure, and so quickly? Instead, the mode of identification proposed in the media cat and car-kissing items is a light-hearted nationalistic community of laughter and feelgoodism. That urged by coverage of the plans for the Millennial celebrations, as by two of the sports items, is wishful rather than substantial, nationalistically fanciful rather than nationalistically realistic. These oddball departures from traditional news categories surely mark a recognition that—particularly in an increasingly ratings-sensitive environment—the predominant gloom of the news and constructions of insecure national identities need a cheery, upbeat entertainment gloss.

Given that national identity is a form of collective identification, how much are viewers of this bulletin addressed in collective terms? Collective identifications are offered only in two groupings of the traditional content categories: in the uneasy national identifications of sports, and in the thinking New Zealand person-of-the-world invoked by international relations and war. In all these items collective identifications are *externally* defined, underwritten by nation states outside New Zealand: by the overseas sporting enemy or the distinctly different geo-political entity (Australia's relative closeness enables its construction in New Zealand to oscillate between same and different). In traditional content categories based *within* the nation state, the bulletin offers no collective identifications any larger than the family and friendship networks invoked by the crime items. Thus the bulk of the internal national identifications the bulletin proposes to the viewer are individual. Only the 'light' items offer any internal collective national identifications, but then in an escapist (post-modern?) manner. The absence of internal collective national identifications offered by news items in the *indicative* mood points towards national insecurities, people's limited social agency and the anxious and victim-oriented identifications already mentioned. Two arguments flow from this: one about historical developments in individual/collective address in New Zealand television news, the other concerning the importance of acknowledging the institutional factors mediating between dominant national discourses and individual texts.

A reflectionist account of this stress on the individual might construe this bulletin's representations as a *direct* effect on television news of national shifts in political economy and ideology engaged in New Zealand since 1984, globally recognised as the world's limit-case experiment in neo-liberalism, whose cause here finds a shining exemplar in the schoolboy shares profiteer. The individualist modes of address would thus find their explanation in the atomised individualism promoted by this political philosophy and practice, and in its associated promotion of (individualist) consumer over (collective-thinking) citizen. While this is surely a major cause, it is not a direct one. The reflectionist account overlooks factors that *mediate* between text and discourses. One such factor is the commercialisation of television in New Zealand from 1987 onwards, and specifically of *ONE Network News*. This is the cause ascribed by Cook in his content analysis of changes in *ONE Network News* between 1984 and 1996. In conclusions that endorse the present analysis of this 1999 bulletin, he argues that declining percentages of news items about labour and public policy and growing percentages on crime, economics, and consumerism lead to a 'lessening conception of the audience as collectives, and more as individuals' (Cook 2002, p. 144).

Another mediating factor would be the preponderantly domestic mode of address of the increasingly commercialised television institution. This would—in part, but not wholly—explain not just the dominant individualism, but also the anxious, victim-oriented modes of address in this bulletin, and even the rarity of social agency. For television's domestic mode of address targets individual and family in the putative cosy security of the living-room. Dedicated to keeping the viewer at home, enthralled to the flow of television scheduling and blithely delivered to advertisers, this domestic address, it may not surprise us, will likely stress the dangers and fearfulness of the outside world, and reliance on agents of law and order for our protection.

These institutional factors, then, mediate between society's dominant discourses and text. Television and television news have undoubted power, but are not omnipotent. They are beholden to dominant discourses, and also exercise considerable influence on them. So the foregoing account should not be read as suggesting that the news bulletin's constructions of an anxious, victim-oriented nation state are directly *expressive* of same. They are, precisely, *constructions* that both draw on national discourses and are products of the television institution. However, given the influence of television news, they can powerfully affect viewers' conceptions of the nation state.

How anxious, passive, and victim-oriented are New Zealand conceptions of national identities? Internationally comparative analyses would reveal the extent to which in other nation states similar constructions are evidenced. With some experience of work on overseas news, though not directly comparable ones (Bell, Boehringer, and Crofts 1982), I can suggest that there are similar constructions at work, but that there *are* differences of degree, and that these may relate to New Zealand's serious economic decline since the 1980s and its unsettled cultural confusions about its colonial past and present.

References

Abel, Sue. 1997. *Shaping the News: Waitangi Day on Television*. Auckland: AUP.

Atkinson, Joe. 1994. 'The State, the Media and Thin Democracy', in Andrew Sharp (ed.), *Leap into the Dark*. Auckland: AUP.

Bell, Philip, Kathe Boehringer & Stephen Crofts. 1982. *Programmed Politics: A Study of Australian Television*. Sydney: Sable.

Cook, Daniel. 2002. 'Deregulation and Broadcast News Content: ONE Network News 1984 to 1996', in John Farnsworth & Ian Hutchinson (eds), *New Zealand Television: A Reader*. Palmerston North: Dunmore Press.

Crofts, Stephen. 1993. *Identification, Gender and Genre in Film: the Case of Shame*. Melbourne: Australian Film Institute.

Ellis, John. 1982. *Visible Fictions*. London: RKP.

Franklin Harvey. 1978. *Trade, Growth and Anxiety*. Wellington: Methuen.

Galtung, Johan & Mari Ruge.1965. 'The Structure of Foreign News'. *Journal of International Peace Research*, 1.

Gans, Herbert. 1980. *Deciding What's News*. New York: Vintage.

Perry, Nick. 1994. *The Dominion of Signs*. Auckland: Auckland University Press.

Phillips, Jock. 1987. *A Man's Country?* Auckland: Penguin.

Construction Site:

Local Content on Television

ROGER HORROCKS

16

The circumstances in which New Zealand material is made, broadcast, and viewed are much more complex and challenging than most viewers realise. The first thing to note is the relatively small amount of local (New Zealand-made) material on the main free-to-air channels, representing approximately one quarter of the schedule. Apart from repeats and some sports coverage there is virtually nothing on the pay channels (New Zealand On Air 1999, 2002). In other parts of the English-speaking world, audiences can take it for granted that the majority of free-to-air programs will be produced locally (i.e. within the same country), and there are strong production industries because populations are larger and a taste for local programs has been built up over generations. Furthermore, countries such as Australia and Canada have quotas to make sure that broadcasters give a central place to national production.

Besides the lack of quotas and the small size of its market, there is another reason for the low level of New Zealand production—the extent to which the industry is disadvantaged by competition from cheap imports. This is an economic fact of life that no discussion of local content can afford to ignore (though many do so). Television programs that have already proven their popularity with American or British audiences can be purchased by New Zealand broadcasters for only a fraction of their production cost. To take a typical case, a one-hour episode of a popular American or British drama series that has cost, say, $3 000 000 to make will be available for $25 000 (and often less). New Zealand prime-time drama will be made on a much lower budget—say, for $500 000 per hour—but this is still twenty times more expensive than buying an overseas product. There is a similar price differential for other genres such as documentary (where an hour of New Zealand documentary made for $125 000 must compete with overseas documentaries with million-dollar budgets on sale for a few thousand dollars). The reason overseas programs are sold so cheaply is that their producers have already recovered their costs in their own countries, then made some profits in large overseas markets, and now regard a sale to a small market like New Zealand simply as a little extra income. For overseas producers it's the end of the line, and New Zealand broadcasters are relieved to be able to fill their schedules cheaply. Local producers have been very enterprising in developing low-budget methods of production but they resent having to compete with what they see as 'dumping'. Broadcasters dispute that term because their own margins are so tight. The arrival of competition in the form of TV3 increased free-to-air prices for TVNZ by a factor of 400 per cent or more, and broadcasters have the worry of dealing with fluctuations in the value of the New Zealand dollar and an inevitable share of dud programs. Nevertheless, local production has always had to compete on an uneven playing field.

New Zealand On Air has been created essentially as a subsidy mechanism to go some way towards remedying this imbalance. In terms of the amount of the subsidy, it is difficult to generalise as each project has unique aspects and needs to be analysed individually; but it is not unusual for NZOA to provide 50 per cent or more of the budget of a drama series, 75 per cent of the budget of a documentary, and 100 per cent of the budget of a special interest program (a program for children, say, or for an ethnic community, or for some other special interest group—material that broadcasters see as having little or no commercial value). NZOA does not assist news, current affairs, sport, entertainment, lifestyle, or 'reality' programs. (There are occasional exceptions, such as a program about sports for the disabled, which may help the funding body to meet its obligations to minority groups under Section 34 of the Broadcasting Act.) From the experience of programs being dropped by the broadcaster, it is clear that many genres would disappear almost entirely without NZOA's support. Yet its available funding of approximately $50 million per year for television is very limited when we consider that it is equivalent to the budget of a single medium-sized Hollywood feature film, or one or two thirteen-part television drama series made by the BBC or an American network.

NZOA judges the level of subsidy in terms of the minimum amount required to realise the project. To make the most of its limited funding, it operates close to the point at which a broadcaster will cancel the project.

The funding body has had many years of experience in making such calculations as it plays an ongoing game of brinkmanship with the broadcasters. An additional strategy for adjusting the subsidy is the fact that NZOA operates as an investor rather than a grant-giver, so it shares in any income from the program. Naturally such an approach is not popular with producers, and critics of NZOA have accused it of becoming too commercial in its thinking; however, its main aim is not to invest for profit but to make sure it pitches its funding at the right level. Few New Zealand programs have significant sales potential (apart from drama), and if any income is produced, NZOA simply puts the money back into the production pool. In the case of *Shortland Street* NZOA ceased to be involved once the series was established. It sees that as the ideal funding model—to provide the risk capital required to initiate a series that otherwise could not happen. It should be added, however, that in the current environment an ambitious project like *Shortland Street* will happen seldom, if ever, even with NZOA's potential support. That particular series was the result of more than a year of lobbying by NZOA, a huge creative commitment by the production team, and a series of happy accidents (including an ideal conjunction of people in positions of authority at TVNZ).

Those who have not had direct experience of the industry since television was restructured in 1989 are inclined to underestimate the harsh economic realities that production companies, funders, and broadcasters have to live with. The term 'commercial' is often used broadly and disparagingly, without a specific understanding of what is or is not commercially viable in the New Zealand situation. For example, a standard history of New Zealand broadcasting published in 2000 declared: 'The [NZOA] legislation does not offer a coherent programming philosophy or purpose other than to support New Zealand programming, much of which would have been purchased or programmed anyway by competing commercial broadcasters'.[1] In fact, the commercial pressures of television since the 1980s have been so harsh that most if not all of this local production would definitely not have happened without NZOA's funding and behind-the-scenes negotiations.

New Zealand's culture is still in many respects under construction, and the primary aim of a funding body like NZOA (or its cinema equivalent, the New Zealand Film Commission) is to keep the construction process alive. As the contributors to this book have stressed, the local and the global today are intermeshed in complex ways, as we can see in the television schedule, and (as we shall discuss presently) in international co-productions. Yet while the local is often a complex hybrid, and program-makers are among the most restless and itinerant of New Zealanders, the practical realities of production are much more sharply defined. The classic situation for those who work in a complex medium such as television—particularly in a small country like New Zealand—is that one can continue to ply one's craft only so long as adequate funding is available and a broadcaster is willing to screen the results.

Overseas sales and co-productions

Why do New Zealand producers not follow the example of the British and American industries and use international sales to finance their program-making? To some extent they do, but there are complications. Many countries have (as we noted earlier) local quotas to give an advantage to their own producers. A smaller population can create problems because it is difficult to earn enough in the home market to cover costs, which is standard industry practice overseas. Also, a number of New Zealand projects are necessarily one-offs, and many overseas broadcasters cannot be bothered purchasing material on such a small scale—they prefer the packages and 'output deals' available from large Anglo-American production companies. New Zealand networks share the overseas preference for series, since it is more economical for them to publicise a series than individual programs, yet from a cultural point of view one-off dramas and documentaries have always played an important role in our television culture in terms of diversity and innovation.

In recent years a new market has opened up for program ideas, with the enterprising producer Julie Christie selling the concept of *High Country Dance* (about a match-making train trip introducing urban women to rural men) to an American network, and Bill Toepfer and Jonathan Dowling's idea for the New Zealand series *Popstars* (about wannabes groomed to become a hit band) has been used in twenty-five countries. The problem New Zealanders have encountered is that ideas are hard to protect and receiving fair payment from a large overseas corporation may in some cases involve an expensive legal battle.

Also, while New Zealanders have grown up with British and American programs and have a basic familiarity with their accents and cultural references, overseas knowledge of New Zealand is minimal. Though New Zealand production displays a strong British and American influence, there is still a local flavour or inflection that strikes overseas audiences as unfamiliar. Accents can be a problem, and many of the documentary topics that fascinate New Zealand audiences have no relevance to people overseas. An exception is natural history material, which requires no knowledge of social contexts and has no 'lip-sync' (synchronised dialogue). Its voiceover commentaries can easily be dubbed into other languages. While it is also possible to re-voice and recontextualise social documentaries, any '**versioning**' tends to be an expensive process, only justified when large overseas sales are likely.

These industry complexities remind us that while the meaning of terms like 'local' or 'national' has today become very fluid, the experience of local relevance is still a powerful force that is hard to argue with. There is much talk about the ability of sophisticated viewers to enjoy cultural difference from around the world, and overseas there are channels such as SBS in Australia that specialise in multiculturalism, but most audiences are comfortable with only a small amount of difference. Makers of drama series have to walk a fine line between 'being too New Zealand' for the overseas market and 'not being New Zealand enough' for the home market. For example, *City Life* was one of the most successful recent series in terms of overseas sales but had a disastrous reception locally because New Zealand audiences could not relate to it because they found it too American.[2] They might have accepted a similar style and similar characters in *Melrose Place* but could not do so in familiar Auckland settings.

While *Shortland Street* has satisfied the local audience, and has been sold to England as an afternoon soap, Australian viewers rejected the program when it screened briefly on SBS. Whereas thousands of hours of Australian programming are purchased by New Zealand television each year, there are only a few sales in the other direction—the Australian market is resistant to New Zealand material, to such an extent that some New Zealand producers waste no time on it but head straight for European markets, which seem better attuned to New Zealand television programs and films.

To maximise the possibility of overseas sales, it is a common procedure to make stories more generic, less specifically local, and to restrain accents. The international television industry regards this as a necessary process of 'making a story universal'. New Zealand producers are increasingly well-informed about international requirements and happy to try to satisfy them, but there are limits. Some creative people are strongly motivated by the desire to tell local stories, stories of a different kind from those told by British or American films, and there is a point at which they see scripts becoming too generic and bland. Such tensions can occur in co-productions. Most New Zealand drama series need an overseas investor or two—a television channel, say, or a distributor—to join the New Zealand investors, who usually consist of the local broadcaster, the production company, and NZOA. Every investor has particular needs and priorities. For NZOA, for example, the project must have a local dimension, add to the range of existing drama, and satisfy its quality and 'public service' expectations. For each broadcaster, the series must satisfy a desired target audience and suit a particular slot in the schedule. If characters are immigrants to New Zealand, the overseas investor may welcome the idea of an initial episode set in their home country. It is customary to include at least one overseas actor in the principal cast, and sometimes also an overseas writer, director, and some crew members. Conditions of employment have to be reconciled between different countries. There can be financial problems and artistic differences in the early stages of a project, as illustrated by the drama series *Greenstone*, set in colonial New Zealand. The BBC was ready to invest in this project alongside TVNZ, NZOA, and the production company Screentime Communicado, when two things happened to stop the deal—a new person took over the job of commissioning editor, and the BBC was disappointed by the ratings for its colonial drama *Rhodes*. Alternative investors were eventually found—including a New Zealand Māori tribe—but changes were necessary, including a reduction in the number of episodes. *Greenstone* still emerged as an impressive drama series with a strong bicultural spirit. In contrast, there have been co-productions where overseas investors insisted on the removal of Māori characters and other elements that specifically identified the country as New Zealand.

Co-productions are complex and time-consuming, and are best suited to large companies that can specialise in them and develop long-term international partnerships. In addition to Screentime Communicado, successful companies of this kind include the Gibson Group, who collaborated with Millenium Pictures (Australia) to produce the award-winning children's drama series *Mirror, Mirror*, and South Pacific Pictures, which has worked with a number of overseas partners to produce popular drama series such as *Jacksons Wharf, Marlin Bay, Mercy Peak, Plainclothes*, and *Shortland Street*.

In contrast to dramas, with their larger budgets and greater international appeal, most New Zealand documentaries are made purely for local consumption. The main exceptions are projects about natural history or travel themes of interest to international broadcasters such as the Discovery Channel.

Local content and the culture of broadcasting

If overseas programs are available so cheaply, why do New Zealand broadcasters bother with local ones at all? It is because local programs that click with the audience create a special sense of relevance and loyalty. The examples include news and current affairs programs, major sporting events, the most popular dramas, documentary series such as *Country Calendar* and *Heartland*, and some lifestyle or consumer programs (such as *Fair Go*, now in its twenty-fifth year). Even if NZOA helps to fund some genres, those programs will still cost the broadcaster more than comparable material from overseas. The broadcaster accepts this situation—including the need to cover the total cost of news and current affairs programs—because the network needs some local content as a 'loss leader'. (This is a newspaper term referring to lead stories that are expensive because of the research involved, but are needed as a strong and exclusive selling point for the particular newspaper.) Similarly, a channel will screen some programs that cost more than the advertising revenue they generate. This is particularly important early in the evening, for many of the viewers drawn to the six o'clock news on TV ONE will stay tuned to that channel for the rest of the evening. *Shortland Street* (now in its 12th year) holds a similar strategic value for TV2. But broadcasters cannot indulge in too many loss leaders because they involve an 'opportunity cost'. (The opportunity is the greater profit the network could potentially have made by screening something cheaper.) Such calculations illustrate the fact that ratings are not always the most important criterion for a broadcaster. In the case of TVNZ, TV ONE tends to gain higher ratings than TV2 but is less profitable because TV2 screens more overseas material. Although TV ONE may also attract more advertising revenue, the cost of local programs, even with the help of NZOA subsidies, makes TV ONE a more costly channel to run. Hence, even though New Zealanders may be eager for more local content, there are financial disincentives to providing it.

A further disincentive is the element of risk in creating something from scratch. An overseas program arrives in a tidy plastic box, complete with a proven track record. Its local equivalent requires the broadcaster to negotiate with a group of creative people over a project that could run behind schedule or over budget, wander away from its original brief, create censorship problems, or end up being less impressive than its pitch. Production companies tend to be generally reliable, however, because they have a lot at stake—personal reputations and future commissions are at risk, and the company carries the financial responsibility for delivering the program it has contracted to make. When problems do arise, their source often lies elsewhere, for example in the failure of a network to communicate in practical terms what it really wanted.

Particularly in the last twenty years, the culture of broadcasting has been different from that of the production industry in terms of priorities and personal styles, and the interaction between the two cultures is a complex, intriguing business. At present TVNZ's Chief Executive is a New Zealander with extensive production and broadcasting experience, but this is untypical. Production is only one aspect of broadcasting, and during the era of Rogernomics it tended to be assumed by politicians that a complete outsider was the best person to run an SOE because he or she would not be 'captured' by interest groups, would be more likely to come up with fresh perspectives, and would not be distracted from the most important aspect of the business, which was to make money. It was also widely assumed that executives should be hired from overseas because they offered a broader viewpoint and useful overseas connections. Some overseas executives have taken a genuine interest in the local production industry and in the cultural and creative energies of the society at large, but there have been times when new arrivals were too narrowly focused and out of touch.

Cultural cringe?

When broadcasters are criticised for being grudging in their support for local content, there is another issue they can raise in their defence. This is the fickle, hard-to-predict response of the New Zealand public to local programs. There is even a hard core of viewers who believe that local programs are a complete waste of time because they can never match the excellence of overseas programs. This lack of consistent support in the public has not helped campaigns for local content quotas or increased funding. What produces such mixed attitudes? The fact that New Zealand is primarily an English-speaking country is both a curse and a blessing—on the one hand it gives its programs potential access to a large overseas market, but on the other hand the local market is already awash with imported material. Speaking a language other than English fuels the eagerness of a national audience to see and hear local programs rather than dubbed or subtitled imports. Apart from those who speak Māori, or recent immigrants, New Zealanders do not have that kind of motivation. Nevertheless, the issue of language offers only a partial explanation.

Another potential reason for mixed feelings about local material is the fact that New Zealand programs are generally made on lower budgets. Broadcasters can seldom afford to 'pilot' a new series (that is, make a trial episode which may never be made public). In recent years there has been a trend towards low-budget lifestyle and 'reality' programs, and though these have continued to rate well, they have polarised audiences and given local content a reputation in some circles for cheapness and superficiality. Although the distinction between 'high' and 'popular' culture has become more fluid, most production in the current television environment focuses on the popular end of the spectrum. A few projects that may be described as 'high culture' in the traditional sense are produced with special funding from NZOA, usually screened by TV ONE and distinguished by such terms as 'auteur' or 'festival'. But broadcasters generally encourage local producers to take a populist approach, and when they want 'high end' dramas or documentaries they turn to overseas sources such as the BBC. Television has developed strong and productive links with some areas of

New Zealand culture—such as entertainers and sports people—but it has largely ignored other groups such as artists and intellectuals. The local production industry, which has to depend on what the networks are prepared to buy or commission, is sometimes unfairly blamed for what critics see as 'the dumbing down of television' over the past decade.

Comedy has for some reason been the riskiest of all local genres. Successful examples have become a permanent part of the national culture, such as programs involving Billy T. James, John Clark (as Fred Dagg), Ginette McDonald (as 'Lynn of Tawa'), David McPhail and Jon Gadsby, and Roger Hall (*Glide Time* and *Market Forces*). Some types of humour polarise the audience, such as the folksy style of *Willy Nilly* or *Letter from Blanchy* (which have received good ratings but mixed reviews), or the youth-oriented comedy of *Skitz* or *Havoc*. These did succeed in attracting loyal followings, but many other television comedies have flopped and broadcasters have become nervous about the genre. Market research suggests that New Zealanders are more mixed in their attitudes to New Zealand comedy and drama than to news, sport, or documentary. For the creative teams involved, this is not a reason to stop searching for the magic formula, but the fact remains that New Zealand broadcasters wish they could count on a higher level of audience support. As a local comedy series is perceived by some viewers as interrupting the flow of dependable American or British material, it has to work hard to gain acceptance.

One way to explain this phenomenon is to see it as another of the many aspects of New Zealand life that are coloured by what is known as 'cultural cringe', an insecure attitude to local culture expressed either as embarrassment or as over-assertiveness. This kind of thinking turns up in countries that are or have been colonies, particularly small countries. Frantz Fanon wrote about similar forms of psychology in Algeria, Africa, and the Caribbean (1967a, 1967b). This is not to deny that some local programs are badly made, but it is to ask whether our judgment may be subtly influenced by traditional expectations and imported values. Consider the history of accents in the New Zealand media, which has been well documented by linguists.[3] Until recently many New Zealanders felt a sense of embarrassment when they heard 'New Zealand English' in films, television dramas, or on stage. Broadcasters insisted on announcers and presenters using 'Oxbridge' or 'BBC' accents (also known as Received Pronunciation). A colloquial New Zealand accent was simply not appropriate, it lacked authority and seriousness. As recently as 1982 the *NZ Herald* reviewer confessed that the accents in local television drama made him uncomfortable: 'In the manner of the shock that most people get when hearing themselves recorded on tape, television viewers are not used to hearing themselves in a dramatic situation. And at first it sounds incongruous' (*NZ Herald* 1982, p. 21). Many viewers felt more at home with the language of *Coronation Street* than with Kiwi slang, which first penetrated television in 1972 in the innovative drama series *Pukemanu*.

As recently as 1992, when program makers and actors were creating *Shortland Street*, New Zealand's first daily soap, they worried if the audience was ready for it. Elizabeth McRae (one of the core cast) commented subsequently: '[All those] involved with the show were biting their nails… We were so used to hearing [overseas] accents on television, and we were recording *Shortland Street* for two months before it went to air with its kiwi accents, so that was a tense time' (*Shortland Street* 1995, p. 42). Research conducted in the previous year by NZOA had shown that many young people were not expecting to like the results. As one teacher reported: 'The students quite like the idea of a New Zealand drama, provided it doesn't have New Zealand actors'! Suspicion of local culture tends to be particularly strong among teenagers who derive a special excitement and sense of expanded horizons from overseas cultures. This attitude is strong in music and New Zealand's popular singers tend instinctively to imitate British or American accents, unless (like Don McGlashan) they are aware of the cultural politics and consciously resist. The particular choice of British or American is also significant as New Zealand culture has always been shaped by the conflict or negotiation between those two extremely strong influences. The pendulum has swung back and forth—from British punk to American disco, from American grunge and hip-hop to Britpop and rave music, etc. A similar competition between the two influences can be seen in many other areas of New Zealand culture, including television.

If American and British material has always been 'the default setting' for television, is it any wonder that some New Zealanders see local material as the odd man out? In terms of cultural cringe, the television medium has been both problem and solution. Television has often reinforced derivative, colonial attitudes, but when a local program has succeeded in breaking through—such as *Pukemanu*, or *Radio with Pictures* with its down-to-earth presenters such as Karen Hay—the medium has become a powerful promoter of local culture. Inevitably as the years went by, television helped to accustom viewers to the New Zealand voices and faces that had previously seemed out of place on the television or cinema screen. Today, colloquial Kiwi accents are so widely accepted on television that it is hard to imagine how strong the prejudice against them in broadcasting used to be—until we come across recordings from the 1960s. The history of accents serves to illustrate the power of deeply embedded colonial attitudes, and it would be reckless for us to assume that attitudes of this kind were not still deeply embedded in our social thinking.

TVCs and interstitials

If the New Zealand production industry has grown in recent years, this has been mainly due to overseas films and drama series being made in New Zealand. The total hours of local production for television have increased slowly but steadily (from 4249 total hours of local content on the main free-to-air channels in 1990, to 5018 in 1995, to 6190 in 2001), but there has not been any dramatic increase since the start of the decade, when the hours jumped from 2112 in 1988 to 4249 in 1990 after the arrival of NZOA and TV3 (NZOA 2001). Over the last few years growth has been mainly in what the industry calls the 'cheap and cheerful' category. The general attitude to local material on television remains complex. As we have suggested, the public has not entirely overcome a certain self-consciousness and ambivalence towards the local, resulting from a particular set of histori- cal circumstances that has enshrined overseas programs as the norm. Australia offers a striking contrast in this respect, thanks to its larger market and early establishment of quotas.

Broadcasters in New Zealand tend to believe that the best way to ease viewers into local material is to employ familiar overseas formats so its 'New Zealandness' will be a matter of quiet nuance or local colour, avoiding the common accusation that a program is trying too hard. Compare the way singers add a local inflection to an overseas genre (South Auckland hip hop, say, or South Island versions of country-and-western music). Over time, inflection may produce a local combination or hybrid that will be seen by the world as original. This gradual approach seems realistic in terms of the local audience, and it is interesting now to recall the initial criticisms of *Shortland Street* for being 'too American' and 'too Australian'. As part of the TV2 line-up, alongside so many American and Australian programs, *Shortland Street* did come to be seen as a series with local relevance, a dramatic universe with a comfortable familiarity, something that was 'ours'; yet that acceptance took time, and its similarity to the surrounding pro- grams helped to overcome the initial resistance from young viewers. Ironically, recent (unpublished) research by NZOA suggests that the young have come to accept the series so totally that they no longer think of it consciously as a 'New Zealand' drama, which means that subsequent local drama series cannot benefit by association—they have to walk the same gauntlet before being accepted.

Has New Zealand yet produced forms of television that are original? Culturally the most distinctive are to be found in the growing field of Māori production. Yet even Māori projects have a strong tendency to use popular overseas genres—for example, *Makutu*, a series of 'ghost' or 'horror' tales that is able to function both as generic television entertainment (in the tradition of *Ray Bradbury Mystery Theatre*) and as an ingenious way to tell Māori stories and to present Māori cultural and supernatural elements. Across the general range of production, 'New Zealandness' tends to be a matter of detail, accent, and nuance rather than genre or style. Local audiences, local broadcasters, and overseas buyers seem to agree that the ideal New Zealand program should offer a little difference but not too much. It is therefore one of the tasks of the good critic to become as finely attuned as possible to such nuances. The subtle and ever-changing flavour of New Zealandness—or the way in which a New Zealand product is distinctive in comparison with its overseas counterparts—can provide a rich dimension of analysis (alongside generic, authorial, and production aspects).

Broadcasters tend to see the 'local' differently from producers. To them a channel is 'local' if it is successful in providing its viewers with what they want to see—the particular mix of British, American, and Australian programs that represents the country's or the region's taste. Since there has been talk over the years of beaming in various Australian channels by satellite as a cheap way to operate, it is interesting that no broadcaster has ever picked up the idea. The time difference between the two countries would be a complication since television scheduling is closely linked with the rhythms of domestic life; but more importantly New Zealand audiences would find it difficult to bond with such a channel, despite familiarity with many of its American or Australian programs. Though New Zealanders have a complex attitude to the local, they need at least some local connections to feel comfortable. Eventually, computerised television recorders and channel surfing may destroy the kind of personal relationship that viewers have with their favourite channels, but the country is a long way from that situation yet.

Broadcasters seek to give their channels a clear brand identity and to build brand loyalty in the audience. Local content is only one ingredient of the brand, and broadcasters prefer not to spend too much on production, so they have developed strategies to make a little go a long way. One strategy involves the use of 'interstitials' or 'links,' small bursts of local content such as presenters interacting from time to time—as in the children's series *What Now?* or the teenagers' series *Ice TV* (subsequently *Ice As*)—to create a sense of localness around the overseas items. News programs are a classic example of such packaging, with studio presenters and re-editing of satellite footage evoking a national perspective on world events. It is also a common practice to repackage overseas current affairs material, and in the old days TVNZ's figures for local content were inflated by the practice of counting such programs as a whole. Such presenting or packaging is still minimal on pay television, but the local content on SKY's popular sports channel does provide the network with a New Zealand connection. Its movie channels presumably rely on the fact that New Zealanders expect little local content when they go to the cinema.

The genre of local material that broadcasters have worked hardest to develop is not interstitials but television commercials (**TVCs**). If we include station 'promos' in this genre, TVCs occupy almost a quarter of the free-to-air television schedule. Some are imports, some are local, and some are adaptations of overseas originals (adding a New Zealand voiceover, for example). Tiresome as they may be, commercial breaks do provide viewers with a certain sense of local orientation. In the early days of television they represented virtually the only forms of New Zealand drama and comedy. It is not surprising then that advertising has been, for better or worse, a strong part of what New Zealanders think of as their shared culture.

In addition to these influential but limited forms of local content, full-scale programs continue to get made and can be among the highest-rating programs of the week, adding weight to the argument that local material is one of a broadcaster's most powerful weapons, particularly as it is possible to shape it specifically for a particular channel, time slot, and target audience. Broadcasters have come to acknowledge that New Zealand mainstream taste is distinctive in some respects, such as its huge appetite for documentaries (a television genre elsewhere in decline). High ratings continue to provide the commercial broadcaster with a rationale for commissioning at least some local programs. For the program-maker, and the broadcaster whose interests are not confined to the commercial, local content is essential for other reasons, particularly social and cultural reasons. In their view it is self-evident that a society should be active and creative, that its children should grow up with programs that reflect and validate their everyday lives, that Māori and Pacific Islanders and other groups should have the opportunity to see and express themselves on screen, and that the news of our community and the new energies of our culture should be regularly shared—both with local audiences and with overseas ones.

References

Day, Patrick. 2000. *Voice and Vision: A History of Broadcasting in New Zealand*, Vol.2. Auckland: AUP.

Fanon, Frantz. 1967a. *The Wretched of the Earth*. Harmondsworth: Penguin.

Fanon, Frantz. 1967b. *Black Skin, White Masks*. New York: Grove.

Gordon, Elizabeth & Tony Deverson. 1989. *Finding a New Zealand Voice: Attitudes Towards English Used in New Zealand*. Auckland: New House.

Jean, Rachel. 1998. City Life: A Case Study in the Production of a Television Drama. Thesis (MA). University of Auckland.

New Zealand On Air. 1999. *Local Content and Diversity: Television in Ten Countries*.

New Zealand On Air. 2001. *Local Content Survey*. Available at: http://www.nzonair. govt.nz/ [Accessed 20 February 2003]

NZ Herald. 1982. 1 March.

Shortland Street: The Official Magazine. 1995. Autumn.

Notes

1   Patrick Day's *Voice and Vision: A History of Broadcasting in New Zealand, Vol.2* (2000, p. 421) is not strong on production or commercial broadcasting, but this history remains very useful in other areas, particularly in its political and institutional coverage.

2   There is an important study by Rachel Jean (1998) that offers a range of interpretations of what went wrong with this series.

3   See the work of Donn Bayard, Allan Bell, and Elizabeth Gordon, among others (e.g. Gordon and Deverson 1989). Also see Shirley Horrocks's television documentary *Kiwi As* (Point of View Productions 1998).

PART 4

**Between the Past
and the Future**

Introduction

The final Part, 'Between the Past and the Future', picks up many of the threads of the book. It sees the present moment as a turning point for New Zealand, as globalisation and digitisation move to a quantitatively and qualitatively new stage. The medium of television itself is now in question, as is the medium of the book, at least in the forms we know them today. (Perhaps it is ironic that we are using one of these media to discuss the other at a moment of change for both.) Yet from another perspective the tensions of the immediate future seem merely a continuation of the same issues we have seen throughout the history of television in New Zealand—the problems associated with smallness as a nation and as a market, the shortage of capital, the limited political support for the funding of culture, and the conflict between commercial and public service values. Once again a new technology confronts us with both threats and opportunities. Our final two chapters identify trends and offer suggestions for the future.

Nick Perry returns to sport—acknowledged by many contributors to be central to our culture—but poses a new question. How will New Zealand sport, which has been so intimately linked with the regional and the national, evolve in an age of global capitalism and digital media? Perry offers two case studies, New Zealand rugby and the America's Cup (with its Virtual Spectator technology). They illustrate two very different ways that our culture may evolve, summed up as 'globalisation from above' and 'globalisation from below'.

Luke Goode and James Littlewood offer a broad perspective on the many changes now in progress that are adding new complications to the idea of the 'local' and the 'nation'. These are global changes but, as always, there are still some distinctive local inflections. 'As a small population economy at the furthest reaches of the planet,' New Zealand must negotiate and create its own arrangements. The overseas ownership of SKY is a key issue for the future. Goode and Littlewood have a strong commitment to public service broadcasting and raise thoughtful questions about New Zealand's continuing reluctance to adequately fund 'the public sphere' or to protect it by legislation.

17

Boots, Boats, and Bytes:

Novel Technologies of Representation, Changing Media Organisation, and the Globalisation of New Zealand Sport

NICK PERRY

Introduction

Sport *really* matters in New Zealand—economically, politically, and culturally—and the sports that are routinely identified as mattering the most are rugby and yachting. Thus in the media imagery and national imaginary of All Black rugby, and of the yacht and yachtsmen of Team New Zealand, which won the America's Cup, the processes of textual and political representation are combined. The sports from which they derive do, however, have very different genealogies. These latter offer a starting point from which to interpret, compare, and contrast some of the recent technical initiatives (e.g. Virtual Spectator software) and organisational developments (e.g. New Zealand Rugby Football Union franchising) by and through which such representations have been accomplished. In this chapter, these patterns and their products are plotted in relation to local cultural meanings and institutional characteristics, and in relation to the processes of constituting and positioning them within global markets.

What this serves to illustrate is Manuel Castells's (1989) maxim that although we may now live in a world in which power moves in global flows, people nevertheless continue to live in, and to form attachments to, particular places. Such flows are enormously facilitated by a dense infrastructure of technological developments, technologies that at the same time may be understood and employed as resources for fashioning conceptions of local identity. One of the best-known cheerleaders for such transformations, Nicholas Negroponte (1995), has even claimed that the process of going digital will not only bring the notion of *broad*casting to an end, but that it will also threaten the oft projected era of narrow casting and niche marketing. What his vision of the digital future purportedly promises instead is an audience of one(s), in which each of us will be able to so customise our media reception and interactivity as to render it wholly in accordance with individual preferences. The emphasis of this chapter, however, is that our engagements with the media in the future will continue to be social and cultural in character—and that a sense of place will continue to matter and make a difference.

From boots to boats

Under the shadow of globalisation, All Black rugby and America's Cup yachting are presently gathering together. This is notwithstanding their otherwise very different histories. Thus the America's Cup is the oldest international sporting trophy on the planet, whereas rugby union's World Cup is one of the most recent. New Zealand participation in the America's Cup dates from the mid 1980s; the history of involvement in international rugby competition reaches back to the nineteenth century. From the outset, entry into America's Cup competition has been the prerogative of very wealthy men, corporate interests, and those they were willing to bankroll; for most of its history New Zealand rugby has been an amateur sporting code enjoying the widespread support and participation of ordinary New Zealand boys and men. Thus the former has always been an elite activity organised from above, whereas the social foundations of rugby's appeal and popularity have been understood to derive from its organisation from below. Under globalisation, however, these (admittedly stylised) contrasts can be seen to unravel, as each of these competitions move into new relations with modes of governance, corporate practices, commodification, and popular culture that are themselves subject to internal and external processes of realignment.

So does such globalisation mean that everything is made different, or that everything is made the same? Is the world being made more uniform, or is it becoming ever more fractured and fragmented? Does it mean one world or many? Are the processes of globalisation to be understood as the multiple manifestations of a single underlying logic of development, or are they everywhere a complex combination of particular characteristics that defy attempts at generalisation? Roland Robertson (1992, p. 181) has suggested that empirically informed, contemporary theorising about globalisation is distinguished by a 'search for fundamentals [that] brings together in problematic and comprehensible ways the simultaneous advocacy of "totalizing" and "anti-totalizing" positions'. This observation is, moreover, accompanied by an approving nod towards what he calls the 'conversion' of Clifford Geertz. For Geertz's (1983) eloquent and influential advocacy of the merits of 'thick description' and the pertinence of local knowledge has yielded to a concern with how to 'enlarge the possibility of intelligible discourse between people quite different from one another in interest, outlook, wealth and power and yet…tumbled together…in endless connection…[In such] a gradual spectrum of mixed up differences…something new having emerged both in "the field" and in "the academy", something new must appear on the pages' (Geertz 1988, pp. 147–8).

The form of bi-focal vision and framing device that Robertson points to—at once close-up and particular and distant and general—would seem to be an appropriate means by which such a hitherto improbable sporting twosome and the associated changes in the process of representation can be put into perspective.

National television/rugby nation

As has been noted in Roger Horrocks's discussion of local content, a recent ten countries' study of small producers showed that New Zealand television had the lowest proportion of local programs (New Zealand On Air 1999). Sport looms large within this latter (both in its own right and within the newscasts), and it is sports programming, together with commercials, that appears to most clearly and most routinely contest the constraints under which local production is understood to operate. A recurring theme of this book, and of the television system that is its subject, is the intractable problems that derive from the cost structure of local television production in such a small country. These difficulties, combined with the reluctance of governments to provide funding, have been such that New Zealand television has been concerned to at once identify and *confirm* the society's pre-existing centre of cultural gravity (so as to maximise audiences) and yet nevertheless continually driven to *remake* that centre in a commodified form (so as secure revenue).

If sport has long exemplified the former, then advertising has come to exemplify the latter. By 1980 the engine of sport was a (by now thoroughly mediated) pattern of popular participation and spectatorship; the engine of advertising was the large companies of the local corporate system. An institutional imperative for television was how to construct a discourse that might somehow bring the differing priorities of these two constituencies together. Rugby, especially rugby at test match level, televised live and duly bracketed by match preambles and post-mortems, generated the audience. The large firm advertisers that it attracted provided the revenue. In such a small economy the large company system was not that large. It consisted of that handful of economically significant local enterprises and subsidiaries of overseas multinationals that had emerged and grown inside the shield provided by the import substitution strategy of the New Zealand state (Perry 1992, pp. 45–9).

During the two decades following the introduction of television in 1960 there had been both a decisive enhancement in the structural power of these large companies and a gradual, but no less decisive, erosion of rugby's hitherto taken-for-granted claim to occupy and to exemplify a nation-defining position. Rugby's problems were administrative, political, economic, and cultural. Administratively, there were the first signs of a challenge to a tradition of amateur and gerontocratic control by advocates of professional management. This contrast imperfectly mapped onto another—that between the priorities of assertive, younger players and the policies pursued by the game's officials. Politically, the maintenance of a sporting connection with an apartheid-based, rugby-loving South Africa had led to increasing pressures at home and abroad (Thompson 1975). Other New Zealand sports teams and individuals were subject to international sporting boycotts, and a once marginal protest movement within New Zealand had gathered broad-based support. Economically, the persistence of this South African connection began to induce a measure of publicly expressed anxiety among exporters. Within the game, exposés of 'shamateurism', the increasingly transparent fiction that top level rugby was an entirely amateur code, signalled the build up of pressures to extend the professionalisation of the sport to include players and coaches as well as administrators. The existence, and attractions of, rugby league reinforced these pressures. This profes-sionalised version of the game was popular in Australia. In New Zealand it had a developing social base amongst the various Polynesian communities in particular and the working class in general. Culturally, the diffusion of aspects of second wave feminism, the political and cultural resurgence of Māoridom, and the expansion of an urban, purportedly more urbane (and hence explicitly more consumerist) middle class were all indications of an ever more visible gap between rugby's social base and the characteristics of the society that it claimed to represent.

This latter became all too apparent in 1981. The scale and intensity of the protests that accompanied the 1981 tour by South Africa's national side indicated how deeply and how evenly the country was divided. For week after week the imagery of a society in turmoil appeared in streets and stadiums throughout New Zealand—and on its television screens (Chapple 1984). Far from symbolising national unity, rugby had come to signify social division.

Its subsequent reconstruction during the 1980s was based on the forging of a more direct alliance between the interests of some of New Zealand's larger corporations and the game's administrators, with television providing the terrain on which this new union would (eventually) be textually consummated. In 1986, the corporations had seen the economic benefits that derived from aligning themselves with New Zealand's challenge for the Australian-held America's Cup, an international yachting competition wholly dependent upon corporate sponsorship and deeply congruent with corporate interests. Yet it had not only proved possible to orchestrate something like the kind of popular enthusiasm that had once been reserved for All Black rugby, but also to extend it beyond the sectional appeal with which the latter sport had come to be identified (Perry 1994, pp. 27–33).

Like the yachtsmen, the All Blacks had proved to be an internationally competitive team—but rugby had problems. Given the extent of the realignments in the field of social forces from which it had developed, then if All Black rugby was to be made (once again) to represent the nation, it would have to be made over. Only now 'representing a nation' was to be subordinated to 'building a market', and hence a possible or incidental effect rather than an intrinsic objective. Whether or not the furtherance of the economic goal shared an envisaged common referent with the practice of nation-making was a matter of contingency. Inasmuch as the nation as an 'imagined community moving through time' (Anderson 1991) had derived from the policies of the state and the relations of civil society, then the state (axiomatically) and civil society (conventionally) were understood as spatially delimited and territorially defined. Economic activity was not subject to any such formal limitation. Indeed, with the demise of the import substitution strategy and the ascendancy of large corporations, the removal of such constraints was positively valorised in theory and powerfully supported in practice.

Reconstructing rugby so as to render it congruent with such interests depended upon combining the textual possibilities made available by television as a medium with the material extension of commodification as a process. Telecasts of important games had always been, and would no doubt continue to be, relied upon to deliver audiences to advertisers. Nevertheless, up until the 1980s the relation between the representations of televised rugby and the content of those television commercials with which they alternated was one of, at best, affinity rather than necessity. Any similarities between them were explicable as a by-product of their appeal to, or targeting of, a common demographic category. But beginning with the build-up to, and screening of the first Rugby World Cup competition in 1987, the television commercials for Steinlager as sponsor and the televised contests themselves, each moved into more explicitly symbiotic formats, into close encounters of a different kind. The commercials initiated a trend of knowingly eroticising and stylising the bodies of All Black players and of dramatising the action of the game so as to broaden the demographic to which both the game and the product would appeal (Perry 1994, pp. 91–5). Incremental changes in the narrative emphases and visual imagery employed in telecasts of games (cf. Star 1992), the trailers for forthcoming transmissions, the discussion programs, even the feature stories in women's magazines, all signalled the growth of intertextuality and of representations that were compatible with this emergent commodity aesthetic. The audiences were intrigued, enchanted even. But the (economic) genie was now out of the (state-sponsored) bottle—and about to go global.

The sky's the limit: rugby goes global

Up until the early 1990s All Black rugby was screened on free-to-air television in real time. The associated sponsors and advertisers were either New Zealand's own fledgling multinationals or local branches of overseas-based companies that were prepared to play the nationalist card as an indicator of their good corporate citizenship. But with the development of cross-media and planetwide communications companies such as Rupert Murdoch's News Corporation, All Black rugby's traditional sponsors, such as the aforementioned Steinlager, literally began to look like small beer. No less significant was the fact that the scale of the rewards available to players in the fully professionalised, and hence more clearly commercialised, league code was accelerating dramatically and drawing an increasing number of top players into changing codes. Thus in 1995 the officialdom of New Zealand rugby narrowly averted a crisis when the entire All Black team seemed set to jettison their links with the national administration in order to participate in the development of a lucrative, global rugby circuit that was expressly oriented towards television audiences. Hence by 1996 the game's administrators had been obliged to transform the All Blacks—and the game's upper reaches—into a sport that was as fully professionalised as rugby league (Fitzsimons 1996). Transmission rights had been sold to Murdoch, who onsold them to a local (but US-owned) pay network called SKY (in which INL, another Murdoch company, subsequently bought a dominant interest).

A SKY commercial on the free-to-air channels served to signify the resulting newly preferred relationship between rugby and its supporters. The establishing shot showed what looked like a stage set containing half a dozen rooms on two levels. Each room contained a small group of people who seemed to be settling in (and looking towards the camera) as if about to watch television. Both the rooms and the 'viewers' clothing were highly stylised and distinctively colour-coded. As the commercial began to build a sense of occasion and excitement, one or two group members succeeded in establishing contact with those on the other side of the partitions that divided them. The camera started to pull back and we now saw that they were surrounded by many more such similar sized rooms, each of which contained would-be viewers. As the camera pulled yet further back, the rooms dissolved into the simulated shape of television sets that seemed to be moving up and down in an excited fashion. Before going to the SKY logo/pack shot the sequence concluded with a simulated long-distance view of a packed sports stadium in which the stands were filled with these self-same 'excited' television sets.

Technically, this dance of technological artefacts in an imaginary space might thus appear to be a kind of reversed version of the famous docking sequence in Stanley Kubrick's *2001: A Space Odyssey*. Culturally, however, it pointed to a close encounter of another kind, one that was fully within the realm of simulation. As such it signalled that the merchandising of rugby as a global game and the All Blacks as a global brand overrode and conditioned the terms under which a national team may now act in relation to the very national imaginary (cf. Bhabha 1990) that they helped to constitute.

The All Blacks' role as agent and symbol of national identity formation had initially been grounded in direct relations as mediated by social and linguistic rules (with print occupying a subordinate role). The early history of the game in this country is a history of popular participation by men and boys, both as players and as spectators. This foundation in face-to-face social relations provided the platform for those subsequent processes of cultural sedimentation, layering, elaboration, and mediation that derived from the encounters with national radio and television respectively. As such, All Black rugby has followed a trajectory that is an antipodal confounding of the sequence identified in Steven Spielberg's *Close Encounters of the Third Kind*, in which the first encounter is an auditory signal, the second a visual sighting, and the third face-to-face (sic) social contact. And whereas in the Spielberg movie, it was making music *together* that had provided the basis for communication and social exchange, in the All Black drama the introduction of music as a sound track for the commercials might better be seen as an indicator of, and substitute for, the progressive closing down of any such reciprocal relation. Put another way, such differences might be said to signify a distinction between communicating with aliens and the alienation of communication.

The All Blacks, together with the top layer of New Zealand provincial teams who compete in the recently established 'Super 12' (a twelve team, tri-nation competition between South African, Australian, and New Zealand-based sides), are now globalising. The All Black team is recruited from within the ranks of the five New Zealand sides involved in the Super 12, and taken together these five franchises cover the whole country. As we saw in my earlier chapter, however, they are the product of a market driven mapping that is based upon a 'virtual' media footprint rather than corresponding to any pre-existing political or administrative boundaries 'on the ground'. The decisive determinant of such mapping is prospective market size rather than historically grounded local loyalties. More recently still, the original city-derived or regional prefixes have been deliberately muted; what was previously the Auckland Blues and the Wellington Hurricanes are now marketed as the Blues and the Hurricanes. This is a process whose logic extends to, and weakens, the traditional pattern of the All Blacks/national nexus. Is this process to be interpreted as 'de-territorialising' or as 're-territorialising', as indicative of the dark underside to Mackenzie Wark's (1994) notion of virtual geography, or as a movement towards a bright spotlight on a global stage?

What this form of globalisation certainly seems to mean for a small nation is that—like the past—it is now another country. Moreover, with such a shift from the sociopolitical to the virtual-simulated, there is the prospect that such a national icon will become someone else's. For where Rupert Murdoch goes has been a pointer to the path that All Black rugby has followed since 1995. And Murdoch, in order to better compete as a global player in his chosen game of media control, had shown himself willing to forgo his initial citizenship and national affiliation.

From Steinlager to Whitbread

My other case study is the America's Cup, perhaps the most striking example of the new forms taken by 'national sport' in the new phase of global capitalism and digital media. This example was introduced in my previous chapter but will here receive more detailed treatment. From the beginning, very rich men and their toys have been obviously and deeply implicated in the history of the America's Cup. One might therefore expect that whereas for rugby a narrative of corporate dominance is a relatively recent phenomenon, it has long been the central thread of the America's Cup plot. It is, to be sure, not difficult to read New Zealand television coverage of the racing, in which TVNZ is involved not just as a broadcaster but as a sponsor of the defending syndicate, as in accordance with such a narrative. What makes it of interest for present purposes, however, is not so much the expected continuity and explicit commercialism of such corporate concerns, but rather how the altogether more recent struggle to make them new translates into making America's Cup yachting available for representation in a popular medium. In this respect the problem should not be seen as deriving from a historical connection with privilege and social exclusivity (for, as the playwright Dennis Potter once caustically observed of royalty, it could be commercialised without being democratised). Rather, the struggle was to bring it into representation at all, since the location of its practice seemed almost incompatible with the very idea of spectators. Hence in Auckland, these screenings depended upon skilled production teams, state-of-the-art microphones, sophisticated editing facilities, and a technologically refined, nomadological thicket of more than thirty television cameras—at sea, in the air, and on the ground. As was noted previously this wickedly expensive but aesthetically orthodox effort to make a predominantly non-spectator sport into a televisual one is punctuated by charming, cartoon-like virtual images. These latter simulate a maritime course and the yachts racing across it as if these contests were taking place on a precisely marked and clearly demarcated field of play. The relevant software was inspired by PlayStation and rests upon a combination of the technologies of CD-ROM, global positioning via satellite, tactical yachting software and the Internet. The associated programs make it possible to produce simulations of these (and subsequently other) actual sporting events that may be viewed either in real time or in delayed form.

What is evident here is an emergent subtext that I am concerned to amplify. The Virtual Spectator software in question was an initiative that received its initial impetus from the making of an Air New Zealand tele-vision commercial and the Whitbread Round the World yacht race. It was, however, within the US and subsequently Auckland-based television screenings of the Louis Vuitton and America's Cup yachting competitions that it assumed local pre-eminence (aka world famous in New Zealand). As Ian Taylor, one of the principals of Virtual Spectator Ltd, explains:[1]

> The idea basically came from the Whitbread (round the world yachting race)—we were doing that from Dunedin, so here were these yachts thousands of miles away and we were using the Internet to get their positions. They were coming to us, the stuff would feed into our machines and we'd sit there and watch the boats move. And we had the best view in the world for what was going on, we had the earliest view of what was going on—we had better views than the other yachts had because they didn't know where the other boats were. And we thought, wouldn't this be fantastic if you could do it from home?—and we thought one day everybody *will* be able to do this. And then I went home and a couple of weeks later I walk in and the boys are sitting on a machine, with a CD Rom, some kind of air combat game and they were playing it over the Internet with someone else. And I looked at it, looked at the graphics and thought, It's not the future, it's happening now, these guys are using it for something else.

This software package was developed by two companies that are headed by, respectively, a one-time children's television presenter for whom redundancy loomed, but who nonetheless wanted to stay in his beloved Dunedin, and an art school dropout and passionate sports fan who joined the wrong queue at the Auckland dole office. Their business premises were located at opposite ends of the country (i.e. in Dunedin and in Auckland), but there is surely something appropriately symbolic about the fact that the resulting Virtual Spectator company that they formed in 1999 has no physical headquarters of its own. Thus by contrast with the globalising from above of the All Blacks, the development of Virtual Spectator might be said to signify globalising from below, in which a small company in a remote Dunedin location began to construct a hitherto unavailable point of view, a novel subject positioning, and an attendant imagined world.[2]

Read one way, this chapter returns to, and reaffirms, the theme of my earlier chapter, namely that the different versions of globalisation that Virtual Spectator's yacht simulations and today's All Blacks (can be made to) represent are windows onto the world. But read another way, they are also windows onto ourselves. And what this glance through these windows confirms is that our sporting culture should not be thought of as fixed, but rather as an ongoing struggle over meanings. It is a struggle in which traditional concerns may well be made new again in and through novel technologies and modes of representation.

References

Anderson, Benedict. 1991. *Imagined Communities*, revised edition. London and New York: Verso.

Bhabha, Homi (ed.). 1990. *Nation and Narration*. London: Routledge.

Castells, Manuel. 1989. *The Informational City*. Oxford: Blackwell.

Chapple, Greg. 1984. *1981: The Tour*. Wellington: Reed.

Fitzsimons, Peter. 1996. *The Rugby War*. Sydney: Harper Collins.

Geertz, Clifford. 1983. *Local Knowledge*. New York: Basic Books.

Geertz, Clifford. 1988. *Works and Lives: The Anthropologist as Author*. Stanford, CA: Stanford University Press.

Negroponte, Nicholas. 1995. *Being Digital*. New York: Knopf.

Norris, Paul & Brian Pauling. 1999. *Local Content and Diversity: Television in Ten Countries*. Wellington: Report for New Zealand On Air.

Perry, Nick. 1992. '"Upside Down or Downside Up?": Sectoral Interests, Structural Change and Public Policy', in J. Deeks & N. Perry (eds) *Controlling Interests: Business, the State and Society in New Zealand*. Auckland: Auckland University Press, pp. 36–58.

Perry, Nick. 1994. *The Dominion of Signs: Television, Advertising and Other New Zealand Fictions*. Auckland: Auckland University Press.

Perry, Nick. Forthcoming, c.2003. 'Close Encounters of Another Kind: Nationalism, Media Representations and Advertising In New Zealand Rugby', in Steve Jackson & Dave Andrews (eds), *Sport, Culture and Advertising: Identities, Commodities and the Politics of Representation*. Westport CT: Greenwood Press.

Robertson, Roland. 1992. *Globalisation: Social Theory and Global Culture*. London: Sage.

Star, Lynne. 1992. 'Undying Love, Resisting Pleasures: Women Watch Telerugby' in R. du Plessis et al. (eds), *Feminist Voices: Women's Studies Texts for Aotearoa/New Zealand*. Auckland: Oxford University Press, pp. 124–40.

Thompson, Richard. 1975. *Retreat from Apartheid: New Zealand's Sporting Contacts with South Africa*. Wellington: Oxford University Press.

Wark, Mackenzie. 1994. *Virtual Geography: Living With Global Media Events*. Bloomington and Indianapolis, IN: Indiana University Press.

Notes

1   From an interview undertaken by Auckland postgraduate student, Katrina Chandra.

2   Such representations are also, of course, an aspect of the making of markets. The software and some of its applications would subsequently be employed by some three thousand media organisations in their coverage of the many months of competition for the Louis Vuitton and America's Cups. Efforts to market this and various other sporting applications of the software (such as car rallies and golf) to individual sports fans through the Internet have thus far proved less successful.

18 Digitising the Land of the Long White Cloud:
The Future of Television in Aotearoa New Zealand

LUKE GOODE AND JAMES LITTLEWOOD

Digital television arrived in New Zealand in 1998. Today policy debates are getting underway although there is, as yet, no coherent government strategy designed to address the implications of digitisation for consumers, public service broadcasting, and the media environment at large. The 'road ahead', to borrow a hackneyed digital cliché, is at the very least uncharted. Nevertheless, by attempting to document (and to some extent speculate on) the issues it raises for this country, we hope to show that the advent of digital television illuminates some aspects of the nation and its political, economic, and cultural situation, while a study of the New Zealand case makes some contribution to a wider understanding of the issues surrounding the digitisation of broadcasting.

We begin this discussion by sketching out the main contours of the political–economic context that is greeting the arrival of digital television in New Zealand. In particular, we discuss the rather troubled and unstable interface between commercial and public service models of broadcasting and pose some questions about its future under the impact of digitisation. We then move on to question some of the ways in which issues of political economy connect with issues of culture. In particular, we look forward to the development of a digital environment in which issues of 'local' content and culture may be called into question in new and interesting ways. Most of the issues we raise in relation to the digitisation of television are not unique to New Zealand; to that extent, they have a relevance beyond the shores of this small island nation. At the same time, however, we aim to show how the broader themes associated with digitisation (including technological and economic convergence, bandwidth management and interactivity, for example) are currently and may in future be played out in ways that are inflected by some of New Zealand's peculiar characteristics.

TV in New Zealand: The backdrop for digitisation

The heavy dependence of electronic media industries, including television, upon economies of scale derived from network effects is heavily documented (for example Owen 1999; Noam 1996), and it comes as no surprise that electronic media have tended to originate and develop most rapidly within populous societies. Although Britain and the United States adopted opposing strategies in establishing national radio networks (a state-managed monopoly and a largely free market model, respectively), both strategies were predicated upon the capacity of large, robust consumer economies to drive the development of transmission networks, production equipment, reception devices, and content production (see, for example Briggs 1985; Cain 1992; Douglass 1987; Jarvick 1996; Ledbetter 1997).

With a population of less than four million (spread out across a land mass comparable with Britain's), the New Zealand broadcasting environment is lacking in such economies of scale. Geographic isolation exacerbates the problem since it limits the extent to which New Zealand can share in a transnational media space.[1] The emergence of television in New Zealand in 1960 rapidly exposed problems associated with funding mechanisms whose viability had become taken for granted in other locations. The commercial market, the Public Broadcasting Fee (PBF), direct government subsidy, and pay subscriptions have variously failed to produce healthy and dependable revenue streams for either free-to-air (**FTA**) or pay television. Notwithstanding (or perhaps because of) such detriments to electronic media development, New Zealanders on average demonstrate a high level of demand for new media products. By various measures, New Zealand currently ranks alongside Sweden, Canada, Australia, The Netherlands, and Denmark in the uptake of Internet services, for example (see, for example MED 2001).

Since the arrival of TV in New Zealand, there has been a frustrated body of opinion wanting to see it used for a variety of public services that are variously rejected, ostensibly at least, on grounds of cost. Roger Horrocks (1996) identifies 'at least nine competing conceptions of…"public broadcasting", encompassing: local content;[2] universal coverage/access; 'highbrow' and 'informative' programs; children's programs; news and current affairs coverage; less advertising; more Māori programs; more programs for minority interests; more coverage of nationally significant sporting events'.[3] In practice, policy-makers have tended to blur the boundaries between commercial and public service broadcasting agendas. Within a year of the country's first TV transmissions, for example the government paved the way for the New Zealand Broadcasting Corporation (the state-owned broadcaster) to subsidise its government grant with advertising revenue. Since then, various governments (under both main parties) have seen fit to reinvent the national television broadcaster, as well as the rules under which it operates. Within this long sequence of changes, advertising revenue emerges as the most constant component of public broadcasting.

Political support for public service media has been less than stable in New Zealand. Between 1984 and 1999, the television industry was subject to far-reaching policies of rationalisation and commercialisation. This period began with the election of New Zealand's fourth Labour government, which surprised both its traditional centre-left supporters as well as its right-wing opponents with a string of neo-liberal reforms across many aspects of society. This trend was equally embraced by the right-wing National party when it came to power in 1990. During these years of neo-liberal rationalisation, the electronic media environment in New Zealand underwent a string of regulatory and commercial changes that added up to the progressive commercialisation (albeit politicised) of the television industry. They do not, it must be stated, spell the outright elimination of public service broadcasting as is made clear by the threefold increase in local content broadcast during prime time, for example.[4] However, the commercial system that emerged now faces further uncertainty and upheaval on at least two related fronts.

First, TVNZ now faces a Labour party-dominated government (elected in 1999, re-elected in 2002) that wishes to stem the tide of commercialisation and turn the organisation more strongly towards public service goals. Second, the technological convergence (particularly between the broadcasting and telecommunications sectors) that is integral to digitisation raises thorny questions about the capacity for a television-centred policy to guarantee public service broadcasting, including local content. And because technological convergence is associated with economic convergence (witness the global flurry of mergers and alliances between previously disparate entities such as Time Warner/AOL, for example), it is unclear how compatible the lack of foreign ownership restrictions will be with the commitment to local content. Currently, for example, Television New Zealand's (TVNZ) move towards digitisation is dependent upon access to the 'digital gateway' granted by SKY (on its terms) that controls the only digital (satellite) platform in New Zealand to date. Moreover, the prospect of further convergence between broadcasting and the Internet renders the organisation's longer-term digital strategy dependent on a telecommunications and information technology infrastructure beyond its control.

TVNZ's first serious attempt to forge a digital strategy (after being rebuffed in talks with SKY) involved a proposed alliance with British cable operator NTL in 1999. The deal, however, was blocked by the newly elected Labour government on the grounds that the high costs ($200m) were not in the public interest. The same government appeared self-congratulatory when TVNZ announced some months later an alliance with the Australian-owned **cable television** and telecom provider Telstra Saturn, at a cost of about $10–14 million. While TVNZ brought to the deal a large audience reach and established content library, and Telstra brought its network expertise, the deal did not progress to the stage of finalising details. Telstra decided instead that its commercial fortunes would be better served by an alliance with SKY.

The trend in the digital era towards strategic alliances and consolidation between hitherto disparate media companies (particularly in the form of **vertical integration**) is well documented (see, for example, Schiller 1999). Digitisation has scarcely yielded the reduction in barriers to entry or the arrival of 'friction-free capitalism' (Gates 1995) frequently prophesised through the 1990s. Local media organisations across the world are generally ill-equipped to compete with the multinational behemoths who, themselves, sometimes struggle to shoulder the costs of network investment. The plight of TVNZ is sobering. New Zealand's largest broadcaster lacks the financial weight necessary to forge its own digital strategies or even, it seems, to play a significant role in any joint digital venture.

Just as the period of economic liberalisation in New Zealand led to its TV industry becoming one of the least regulated in the world, a parallel process took place within the IT industry. And just as the current Labour government has sought to stem the tide of commercialisation within the state-owned broadcaster, so it has taken some first steps towards addressing the lack of regulation in the realm of information technology. This took the form of an official inquiry early in 2000 that led to some key recommendations (Fletcher 2000) including: an Electronic Communications Commissioner's Office (sometimes referred to as a 'convergent regulator' in other countries); an Electronic Communications Industry Forum, bringing together major data, network, and content suppliers to act as the foundation for a system geared primarily towards industry self-regulation, drawing up 'codes and practices for regulated services for approval by the commissioner' (p. 2); an over-riding 'access objective' designed to 'promote the long term interests and potential end-users of electronic communication services by… facilitating efficient use of, and the efficient investment in, the infrastructure by which electronic communications are provided' (p. 2).

At the time of writing, the Forum and Commissioner have both yet to be established. However, the government has controversially rejected the Inquiry's recommendation that 'SKY's conditional access [set-top box digital decoder] system be specified [for regulation],…to enable the Forum…to develop a code to prevent any foreclosure to competition' (p. 3). This debate over 'open access' has occurred in various countries as the transition from analogue to digital transmission gets underway, especially where one company (often a content provider, such as SKY) controls the set-top box technology that acts as the gateway to digital reception. In New Zealand, the Minister of Telecommunications's stated reason for rejecting open access regulation (i.e. obligating SKY to carry signals from competing broadcasters such as TVNZ) is that: 'The Government considers that competition is only just developing in New Zealand in relation to telecommunication services using STBs, and it is too early to accurately assess whether there is a need to regulate any such service. I consider that regulation is only appropriate where it can be demonstrated that there is a need for it. At this point I am not convinced of such a need' (Swain 2000).

In December 2001, SKY (presumably because it suited its marketing strategy) agreed to carry TVNZ's two existing channels on its digital platform. With encouragement from the government, the first four buttons on the SKY remote-control unit now relate to the four national FTA channels (TV ONE, 2, 3, and 4 respectively). These measures may seem like crumbs from the table for TVNZ, which, until recently, harboured much greater ambitions for its transition to digital. Nevertheless, they are generally agreed to be important bulwarks against the threat of both public service and FTA television being swept aside in the digital age. Furthermore, the informal agreement between SKY and TVNZ now seems to allow for TVNZ's expansion beyond their two existing linear channels and, at some point in the future, into the domain of multi-channelling and interactive services (something SKY had previously refused in the earlier negotiations over a joint digital strategy). However, it's important to note that the current situation does not constitute a formal joint venture and appears to rely on the continued good will of SKY—something that can scarcely be assured indefinitely. In short, SKY has successfully leveraged its 'first-mover' advantage (and near monopoly of pay TV services) to become the de facto gatekeeper of digital television in New Zealand. Nevertheless, this is not (yet) regarded as sufficient grounds for regulation by the current government.

This situation is not unique to New Zealand. However, the longer-term implications can be contrasted with other countries undergoing the roll-out of digital television. By comparing the situation with that in the United Kingdom, for example, where digital television has advanced most rapidly by international standards, we can note at least two key differences. With severe financial crises besetting alternative (i.e. terrestrial and cable) digital platforms in the UK, BSkyB's digital platform is the dominant digital gateway and its future is far more secure than that of the existing terrestrial and cable platforms offered by competitors. However, the regulatory regime in the UK obligates BSkyB to carry signals from other existing broadcasters (while entitling BSkyB to make a 'reasonable' return for so doing, a clause that is the source of much discontent on both sides). What's more, with the looming crisis facing the existing terrestrial platform, the UK's main public service broadcaster, the BBC, has been exploring the possibility of establishing its own set-top box technology, in conjunction with other partners, to offset BSkyB's excessive dominance.[5] The feasibility of such a project arises from the financial weight attached to a large, powerful organisation such as the BBC. It is much harder to envisage a smaller public broadcaster such as TVNZ taking control of its technological environment to this extent. It is also, of course, much harder to threaten a multinational corporation with regulation in a small, marginal market such as New Zealand; the country needs SKY's investment every bit if not more than News Corp needs access to its consumer base. And while the wholesale digitisation of broadcasting (including analogue 'switch off') is more of a fait accompli in the UK,[6] this scarcely gives the government and local broadcasters in New Zealand more room for manoeuvre: with SKY and various Internet service providers busy developing new interactive services, and with the New Zealand government's broader economic strategy pinned on notions of a 'knowledge society' incorporating an advancing technological infrastructure, the technological status quo is not regarded as a viable option.

As a small population economy at the furthest reaches of the planet, New Zealand has always been subject to—and frequently at the mercy of—global trends and dynamics. It is in response to such trends that some of its most defining features have evolved. When Britain joined the European Economic Community in the early 1970s, for instance, New Zealand suddenly found that a guaranteed market for its primary exports at the time—lamb and butter—vanished overnight, and the national economy has been searching for a sense of direction ever since. For much of the time, this search has led to extremes of economic management, from excessive government subsidisation of heavy industry to the wholesale rationalisation and privatisation of government assets. New Zealand has found itself asking the question posed by communications theorist Eli Noam: 'after liberalization, then what?' (Noam 1996, p. 423). The state-owned broadcasting service perfectly embodies this dilemma. To Noam's question, we might respond 'digitisation, that's what'. That, of course, raises more questions than it answers.

'Local' culture, bandwidth, and bucks

The digitisation of New Zealand television is in its infancy and, as we have suggested, an initial failure at the level of public policy to rationalise, coordinate, and accelerate the transition points to a lengthy and uncertain road ahead (Littlewood 2001). Nevertheless, we aim in the remainder of this chapter to discuss some of the possible longer-term implications of this process for New Zealand. To some extent, of course, this is a necessarily speculative and hence risky enterprise. Debates within the country about the longer-term future have tended to be industry-focused. We intend here to offer some comment on the link between cultural issues and those associated with technology and with political economy.

Perceived threats to 'local culture' long pre-date the advent of digital broadcasting. Economics dictate that New Zealand, like so many other countries whose broadcast markets are either young or small, imports much of its programming, especially from the US, UK, and Australia. This process, often decried as 'cultural dumping' (see Dowmunt 1990; Tomlinson 1991) is highly visible in many developing and non-English-speaking nations. In New Zealand, by contrast, the binary between 'indigenous' and imported programming can seem less stark, given the majority Pākehā population and its strong cultural affinities with the US, UK, and Australia. This may, to some extent, have blunted the local content cause and its quest for wide-spread support. Nevertheless, as we have suggested, 'local content' has enjoyed growing prime-time prominence in recent years. The spectre of digitisation is problematic in this regard, though: local content, *traditionally understood*, may be more under threat in the digital age and foster an increase in calls for protectionism (in the form of local content quotas), while the very notion of 'local content' may become more difficult to pin down and sustain in future.

The virtual abolition of bandwidth scarcity afforded by digitisation cuts into the local content issue in a number of complex ways. At a simplistic level, however, digitisation simultaneously offers more space for local content (including innovative, lower-budget productions) on the airwaves whilst intensifying the economic pressures. Already, for example New Zealand households who buy into multi-channel television (via the SKY service) currently have access to more local content in absolute terms, compared to households still restricted to the five or so (depending on location) free-to-air terrestrial channels. But local content occupies a significantly lower proportion of the multi-channel schedules overall. This effect is magnified by the steady shift towards *digital* as opposed to analogue (UHF) multi-channel television offered by SKY in New Zealand.

A picture that is familiar across many countries is instructive here: multi-channelling tends to intensify competition and thus yield inflationary pressures within the broadcasting economy, pushing costs upwards. At the same time, somewhat inelastic sources of funding (advertising and subscription revenues,[7] plus public funding sources) tend to be spread more thinly. Established, international players who enjoy substantial economies of scale are generally much better equipped to survive and even displace these pressures than smaller, local producers.[8] As we shall see, though, greater complexity enters the picture when we consider some of the ways in which digitisation affects broadcasting beyond multi-channelling.

In order to really start examining the fate of local content in the digital age, some interrogation of the term 'local' itself is called for. By acknowledging that the term has always been contextual and contestable, it can perhaps be more easily appreciated that digitisation may not only impinge upon localism understood in a static sense, but may also contribute to a partial reconfiguration of the term itself. Consider, for example, that in New Zealand the term 'local culture' frequently approaches interchangeability with the term 'national culture': the terms are not fully synonymous but neither do they exist in a binary relationship as they tend to do in some societies considered close cultural neighbours of New Zealand, including Britain. Consider also that, in comparison to some larger advanced industrial societies, such as the UK and the US, the term 'local' is liable to carry less negative baggage: localism is less readily imbued with connotations of parochialism or insularity (see Tomlinson 1999; Keane 1991; Goode 1996).[9] Internally, moreover, in debates over local content quotas and the recent broadcasting Charter (discussed above), there is no immediate consensus over what really constitutes 'local' television: is it location, subject-matter, personnel, or 'cultural flavour' that counts, for example?[10] Digitisation, we tentatively suggest, may help to unsettle the notion of localism in New Zealand yet further in one or more of the ways sketched briefly below.

Where currently, in this sparsely and unevenly populated country, the distinction between the local and the national is somewhat unstable, it is possible to imagine the digitisation of broadcasting contributing to a greater uncoupling of the 'local' and the 'national' in some senses.[11] There are economic, cultural, and technological factors to consider here; some arrive with and some are simply magnified by the process of digitisation.

One phenomenon, which we will refer to here as 'everyday television', falls into the latter category, having seen rapid growth in recent years and seeming well-suited (economically, at least) to the advent of digital technology. We use the umbrella term 'everyday television' here to denote certain genres of television whose boundaries are somewhat fuzzy and which have grown in number in many countries. These include: 'reality television' shows that shine the spotlight on the 'everyday' lives of ordinary people and, especially, embattled professionals working in fields such as medicine, crime, transport, and tourism (see Misha Kavka's chapter in the current book); and 'lifestyle shows' that encompass the spectrum from the highly constructed home or garden or beauty 'makeover' show (still steeped in narrative conventions of drama, suspense, and resolution), to the shows basically offering footage of 'street culture' and amateur sports set to music, with intermittent narration (skateboarding, hip-hop music, and 'extreme' or dangerous sports are popular subjects in New Zealand). We shall return shortly to the question of hybridity but, for now, it is sufficient to note that 'everyday television' in New Zealand melds transnational formats with local content such that both aspects (form and content) bear the imprint of local and global influences.

It is also important here to note the interweaving of economic, technological, and cultural factors that give rise to these programs. Cheap, portable technologies such as digital cameras make such productions more practically and economically viable than before and, thus far at least, they appear to have resonated reasonably successfully with local audiences. Their continued cultural appeal may not be assured, but from a technological and economic vantage point, it would not be surprising to see an increasing proportion of local content given over to 'everyday television' in the multi-channel, digital environment.

This is not the place to begin trying to unpack the cultural significance of these televisual forms. At the very least, however, we should acknowledge the complex ways in which they *could* (perhaps only modestly) impact upon conceptions of localism in New Zealand. For example, they raise questions about the continued centrality of myth and story-telling to the 'imagined community' of a nation state (see Anderson 1991), not because they dispense with narrative altogether, but perhaps because they are less likely to emphasize 'meta-symbols', that is, people, places, images, and events—real or fictional—that speak to or for, and in some senses bind together, an otherwise heterogeneous and dispersed community. They are more likely to speak to and for relatively fluid interest and lifestyle communities than a territorially bounded 'community of fate' (Held 1987). And, while 'place' may continue to be central to the local 'flavour' of programs, the primacy of universal symbols (famous buildings and locations, for example) may begin to wane as the gaze turns more towards 'everyday' places: gardens, homes, streets, suburbs, and so on. What's more, the physical location of the audience may be only one of many factors determining the levels of identification with the people and places depicted. What's recognised as 'local' television may increasingly vary between households (and even within households) situated within the same localities.[12]

There is a more directly technological angle on this question of the 'deterritorialization of the local'. For the foreseeable future, at least, satellite looks to be the only platform on which digital television services are to be delivered in New Zealand. But other platforms, namely cable and terrestrial lend themselves more economically to regional variations in transmission (allowing for the regionalisation of advertisements and segments of the schedule, including local news services).[13] Jim Blackman, general manager of Auckland's local station, Triangle, which specialises in programming for the city's various ethnic minorities, recently sounded the alarm bell in this regard: should the digitisation of New Zealand broadcasting occur entirely via satellite technology, this may sound the death knell for small community stations that cannot shoulder the high cost of carriage on a platform oriented towards large-scale broadcast 'foot prints' (Blackman 2001).

Rather than furthering regional diversification, digital television in New Zealand may instead shift further and further towards a 'bespoke' model in which programs and schedules will be shaped at the level of individual households (and even individuals within those households, armed with their own 'PIN' codes). Some of this tailoring will be consciously shaped by viewers via subscriptions, pay-per-view events, selecting versions (such as a wide-screen format) and time-shifting, while other aspects will work within the traditional 'push' paradigm of broadcast television, including the targeting of advertisements (encompassing those for programs as well as for other products) to specific households, based on both demographic information and previous viewing behaviours.

In New Zealand, as elsewhere, the received wisdom is that digital technology threatens the continued existence of 'channels' and 'schedules', traditionally conceived, and raises instead the spectre of the 'me-channel' (see Negroponte 1995; Norris and Pauling 2001). At the time of writing, in fact, digital personal video recorders (PVRs), which are integral to these predictions, have not yet had any impact on the New Zealand market.[14] Nevertheless, while the World Wide Web experience may be instructive (that is, branded 'channels' are unlikely to disappear entirely in favour of an amorphous,[15] chaotic, and fully archival model, as 'users' and 'viewers' continue to value both convenience *and* serendipity), there are already signs that 'channels' are morphing into something other than discrete, unitary entities carrying a single, continuous, and linear broadcasting stream. SKY Digital's 'Mosaic' and 'Interactive Program Guide' (IPG) both work like televisual portals (or 'meta-channels'). 'Mosaic' splits the screen into windows, giving users a simultaneous view of current broadcasts on a selection of the channels available, with a 'point and click' interface: here there is a strong element of 'channelling' as channels not included in this visual interface are effectively screened out of viewers' field of vision. The textual interface of the

IPG doesn't screen out any of the channels but, in deciding which channels are assigned which on-screen numbers and positions, SKY effectively buries many channels too many 'clicks' away for most viewers to chance upon. (This is why it was important for New Zealand's FTA broadcasters to be granted a high position on the SKY remote handset.) Similarly, pay-per-view films with staggered start-times help to take the concept of the channel outside of its traditional parameters, giving the broadcast television the appearance, at least, of a 'pull' medium.

What might this morphing of the traditional channel concept mean for a country like New Zealand? We suggest, once again, that hybridity may become increasingly prominent and take on some novel features in the digital era.[16] Already, television is beginning to take on some of the 'cut and paste' characteristics that have helped earn the World Wide Web a reputation as the apotheosis of cultural bricolage.[17] At the production level, for example, intelligent software is being used to mine archived footage and prepare broadcast-ready clips without the intervention of skilled editing staff. At the network level, it is becoming increasingly common to see the same program shown on more than one channel with a minimal time difference.[18] Internationally, moreover, the practice of 'versioning' (preparing broadcasts for specific markets) has become increasingly prominent. Digital technology increases the economic attractiveness of versioning, the aim being to extract the maximum market value out of a product by increasing its flexibility and adaptability to local conditions. Digital technology is working to make existing techniques—such as multilingual versioning and altering program length to suit the local advertising schedules—easier and more cost-effective. But the 'localisation' of content is likely to take new forms as well. For example, the phenomenon of multiplexing in digital broadcasting creates the potential for broadcasters to utilise spare bandwidth to offer viewers material that is supplementary to its core content or, indeed, different versions of the same program (such as staggered start times). Depending on the eventual allocation of digital spectrum by the New Zealand government, it is feasible to imagine, for example, a mainstream public service broadcaster or a community channel offering viewers a range of permutations on Māori or English language and audio-dubbed or sub-titled versions of programs broadcast simultaneously. In a particularly optimistic scenario, this may even help to soften some of the most entrenched cultural dilemmas revolving around language, identity, and difference: we are not making such a grandiose (and media-centric) prediction here but do acknowledge at least the possibility of some positive, 'lubricating' impact on New Zealand's cultural politics.

Beyond language issues, the emergence of *interactive* television raises some interesting possibilities. At the time of writing, the 'interactivity' offered via digital television in New Zealand is restricted to the 'client-side' variety ('booking' pay-per-view events simply means unscrambling the signal, rather than interacting directly with the provider), though the infrastructure is in place for the imminent introduction of interactive services. The situation internationally tells us that interactivity via a television set is likely, in the near future at least, to mean email services, some degree of web access, online betting on televised sports events, and some 'point and click' advertising and online shopping services, often linked to broadcast content. Although there have been some interesting innovations in which viewers can directly influence narrative content, as in the internationally successful *Big Brother* format (see also www.urbanbedtimestories.com),[19] these are still generally regarded as 'special cases'. A less radical scenario is one in which there is a progressive bifurcation of television content into 'core' (and typically narrative-based) broadcast content, and 'supplementary' interactive content designed to enhance the core content.

From the point of view of New Zealand production, however, this process of bifurcation may, in fact, harbour some interesting implications. This depends in large part on the way in which local industry responds to the challenges of digitisation. At a recent conference on digital television in New Zealand (the first in the country dedicated to this topic), there were some interesting signs.[20] The head of one prominent local production company, making a strong case for the expansion of Māori *language* programming, told her audience how digital technology now enabled her company to offer a cheap and near-instantaneous translation service for creating Māori script versions, claiming that in the digital age time and money were no longer adequate excuses for failing to create Māori versions of programs and advertisements (Hoey 2001).[21] On another front, the conference highlighted a strong, emerging interest among media and new media companies and individuals in focusing their efforts on creating interactive content and services for digital television, and much discussion was given over to how New Zealand industry might grasp the new opportunities television offers in this direction.

It is certainly possible that, in the near future, interactivity will become a prominent site for the localisation of imported content. Internationally produced documentaries can be localised by offering on-screen information relating the issue to New Zealand (statistics, information sources, and so forth). International sports events can be localised with New Zealand oriented interactivity (player profiles, competitions to win autographed shirts, and so forth). We may also see more internationally produced advertisements, with locally specific information (store details, 'click here to book a test drive', and so forth) created as interactive add-ons. On top of all this, some interactive control over language (Māori/English, and audio/subtitles) may be overlaid. This raises the possibility that, rather than witnessing the simple erosion of local content in favour of more imported programming, digital television may become a site upon which the 'global' is increasingly *framed* by the 'local'. We use the term 'framing' here in a deliberate allusion to the techniques of framing commonplace on the World Wide Web, where a site gives users a windowed view of an external site, framed by elements (such as navigation buttons and logos) of the original site.[22]

If this is a plausible scenario, it is much less certain who will control this process of localisation. Perhaps we will witness the emergence of a vibrant, local 'versioning' industry, where 'versioning' means something more radical than before, and entails a *visible* and culturally significant impact on broadcast content. Alternatively, the large, global players, motivated by the desire to maximise the value of their products, may take ownership and control of these processes. This would not necessarily eliminate the creative input of local producers as, in line with other facets of the contemporary mediascape, such procedures would likely lend themselves to post-Fordist arrangements drawing on the expertise, 'flexibility',[23] and creativity of local organisations. But the extent to which such organisations operate simply at the behest of the global players, will surely in part be influenced by the speed with which local industry grasps this particular nettle.

Conclusion

The foregoing analysis lends itself to two, very broad-brush conclusions by way of a summary.

First, we suggest that if the history of broadcasting in New Zealand has been problematic, and if robust and mutually distinctive models of both commercial and public service television could scarcely be achieved in an era when the mediascape was simpler, the challenges will in all likelihood prevail and grow as digitisation brings about technological convergence and economic consolidation on a transnational scale.

Second, the one aspect of the public service ethos that has benefited from recent upheavals in broadcasting—namely, local content production— may be threatened by changes in the economic climate brought about in part, at least, by digitisation. But whatever the validity of such a statement, it remains fixed within a problematic binary that conceives the relationship between 'local' and 'imported' content as a zero-sum game. 'Imported' images and symbols are part of the local culture and influences upon it and the advent of interactivity (or, more generally, the bifurcation of core and supplementary content referred to above) creates some interesting new opportunities for conscious and direct localisation of imported content that needn't come at the expense of 'core' local productions, regardless of the economic pressures brought to bear on that sector.

References

Anderson, Benedict. 1991. *Imagined Communities: Reflections on the Origin and Spread of Nationalism.* London: Verso.

Barker, Chris. 1997. *Global Television: An Introduction.* Oxford: Blackwell.

Beck, Ulrich, Anthony Giddens & Scott Lash. 1994. *Reflexive Modernization.* Cambridge: Polity Press.

Bhabha, Homi. 1994. *The Location of Culture.* London: Routledge.

Blackman, Jim. 2001. Presentation to the El*ectronic Frontiers: Digital Television in New Zealand* Conference, Auckland, 30 November.

Briggs, Asa. 1985. *The BBC: The First 50 Years.* Oxford: Oxford University Press.

Cain, John. 1992. *The BBC: 70 Years of Broadcasting.* London: BBC.

Douglass, Susan. 1987. *Inventing American Broadcasting: 1899–1922.* Baltimore: John Hopkins University.

Dowmunt, Tony (ed.). 1990. *Channels of Resistance: Global Television and Local Empowerment.* London: BFI Books.

Fletcher, Hugh. 2000. *Ministerial Inquiry into Telecommunications: Executive Summary.* Available from: http://www.teleinquiry.govt.nz/reports/final/final#P47_8939 [Accessed 16 December 2001].

Gates, Bill. 1995. *The Road Ahead.* London: Viking Books.

Giddens, Anthony. 1991. *Modernity and Self-Identity: Self and Society in the Modern Age*, Cambridge, Polity Press.

Goode, Luke. 1996. 'Media Systems, Public Life and the Democratic Project', *Arena Journal* 7, pp. 65–97.

Held, David. 1987. *Models of Democracy.* Cambridge: Polity Press.

Hoey, Nicole. 2001. Presentation to the *Electronic Frontiers: Digital Television in New Zealand* Conference, Auckland, 30 November.

Horrocks, Roger. 1996. 'Conflicts and Surprises in New Zealand Television', *Continuum* 10 (1), pp. 51–63.

Jarvick, Lawrence. 1996. *PBS: Behind the Screen.* California: Prima Communications.

Keane, John. 1991. *The Media and Democracy.* Cambridge: Polity Press.

Ledbetter, James. 1997. *Made Possible By...: The Death of Public Service Broadcasting in the United States.* London: Verso.

Littlewood, James. 2001. Digital Television in New Zealand: Towards a Model of Public Service Datacasting. Thesis (MA), University of Auckland.

McLuhan, Marshall. 1964. *Understanding Media: The Extensions of Man.* London: Routledge & Kegan Paul.

MED (Ministry of Economic Development). 2001. *Size of the Internet*, Available from: http://www.med.govt.nz/pbt/infotech/itstats2000-05.htm [Accessed 16 December 2001].

Negroponte, Nicholas. 1995. *Being Digital.* London: Hodder & Stoughton.

New Zealand Government. 2000. *TVNZ Charter.* Available from: http://www.executive.govt.nz/minister/hobbs/tvnz/charter2.htm [Accessed 29 December 2001].

Noam, Eli. 1996. 'Beyond Liberalisation: From the Network of Networks to the System of Systems' in Eli Noam & A. Nishuilleabhain (eds) *Private Networks Public Objectives*. Amsterdam: Elsevier Science B.V., pp 423–30.

Norris, Paul & Brian Pauling. 2001. *New Technologies and the Digital Future: The Impact on New Zealand, Local Content and NZ On Air Funded Programmes*. Auckland: New Zealand On Air.

Owen, Bruce. 1999. *The Internet Challenge to Television*. Cambridge, MA: Harvard University Press.

Schiller, Dan. 1999. *Digital Capitalism: Networking the Global Market System*. Cambridge, MA: MIT Press.

Swain, Paul. 2000. Personal correspondence with James Littlewood.

Tomlinson, John. 1991. *Cultural Imperialism: A Critical Introduction*. London: Pinter.

Tomlinson, John. 1999. *Globalization and Culture*. Cambridge: Polity Press.

TVNZ. 2001. TVNZ Broadcast Funding Debate, TV ONE, 10 May.

Williams, Raymond. 1974. *Television: Technology and Cultural Form*, London: Fontana.

Notes

1   New Zealand is described by the US Postal Service as the furthest country on earth from America. It is also the direct polar antipode of Western Europe.

2   We use the term 'local content' here simply to denote programs produced in New Zealand. We acknowledge, however, that the term can be problematised and this is pertinent to the second section of this paper.

3   Sport—in particular, rugby and netball—plays a significant role in discourses of nationhood in New Zealand. Such discourses came to the fore when pay TV operator, SKY, controversially bought exclusive rights to live coverage of key rugby tournaments, for example.

4   It is important to acknowledge that local content is often denigrated for displaying low production values and having a low-cost look and feel, and this is used to question whether much of it is worthy of the label 'public service television'. However, most advocates of public service broadcasting would accept that the quantitative increase in local content represents at least a step in the right direction.

5   In the UK, the government has instigated an ambitious digitisation strategy with the end-game of ending all analogue broadcasting, at which point the unused spectrum can be auctioned off to the communications industries at a potentially great return. This cannot occur until a critical mass of consumers make the switch from analogue to digital television by subscribing to set-top box providers or purchasing a television set with a built-in digital decoder. The growth rate in digital TV consumers has been slowing up, and the UK government has been forced to put back its proposed date for analogue 'switch-off' from 2006 to 2010, and commentators agree it may slip further back still. The terrestrial digital platform was seen by the government as the one most likely to 'convert' analogue households that would be most resistant to the change-over, because it works via their existing roof-top aerials and offers FTA as well as pay TV services in contrast to the other platforms. As a public service broadcaster, the BBC has a vested interest in the success of the terrestrial platform because it is the only one likely to guarantee genuinely universal coverage (and therefore access) in the near future.

6 See note 5.

7 The current downturn in the global economy is exacerbating the pressures of falling advertising revenues.

8 The displacement of these economic pressures arises in large part from the asymmetrical relationship between the rights-owning corporations and the independent production companies (their 'suppliers') who are at their behest and are first to 'feel the squeeze'.

9 Discourses on national culture in New Zealand typically posit national distinctiveness and cosmopolitanism as two sides of the same coin. This does not contradict our earlier assertion that locally produced television is often denigrated as 'cheap': this does not amount to a denigration of the 'local' per se.

10 In the case of Māori production the issues may at times seem clearer, as many advocates for increased Māori content posit the prominence of the Māori *language* (a language under threat) as the sine qua non of cultural self-determination. However, within the Māori community itself, there is genuine disagreement over the primacy of language (Māori is a minority language even among Māori people) and over the community values and symbols that should be projected in Māori television.

11 This does not, of itself, imply that the 'local' takes on a more stable identity, however. On the contrary, as we suggest below, binaries between the 'local' and *all* its 'others' may become increasingly difficult to draw.

12 This, of course, connects with the discourse of 'deterritorialisation' prevalent in recent strands of social and cultural theory (Beck et al. 1994; Giddens 1991; Tomlinson 1999), which is not to be confused with a decline in the cultural significance of *place*: indeed, images, ideas, and symbols associated with 'place' have become increasingly prominent commodities circulating, especially via tourism and the media, in the global economy in recent times.

13 Some protagonists in New Zealand are still lobbying for the development of a digital terrestrial network, despite government inertia and some sobering tales from abroad, including the UK where the DTT network has been extremely unsuccessful in commercial terms (see note 5).

14 PVRs are essentially hard-disk drives that record broadcast programs from digital set-top boxes. They use compression technology to store many hours of programs without the need for removable media such as VHS tapes (though material can be exported to such media when permanent storage, as opposed to time-shifting, is required). Some leading brands incorporate 'smart' technology that can automatically record episodes of regularly watched programs and record and 'suggest' programs a viewer may be interested in watching. PVRs also make advertisements easier to skip than with VHS technology, though rumours of the death of spot advertising are probably greatly exaggerated: the long-term business model behind the development of PVRs was based not on providing consumers with black boxes that enabled them to skip advertisements but, rather, on selling a technology to the networks that would enable them to monitor viewing practices and trends (albeit anonymously) more finely than ever before, and to harness digital technology to target specific television advertisements to the types of household that would most likely be interested in the product. This is reflected in the fact that PVR technology is starting to become integrated into digital set-top box receivers supplied by the networks.

15   By branded channels, we refer here to popular web portals and directories, and not to the failed 'walled garden' model in which navigational convenience was offered only at the cost of highly restricted content. This model did not work on the World Wide Web, though it may have a future within the qualitatively different medium of television. Leading British digital provider, BSkyB, for example, currently offers subscribers 'walled garden' access to the Internet via the television.

16   On the central role of 'hybridity' to contemporary cultural theory, see especially Bhabha 1994. We acknowledge the problems associated with the discourse of hybridization (most importantly, the tendency to reproduce the very essentialism that it tries to transcend—see Tomlinson 1999, pp. 141ff), but use the term loosely in this context to refer to the visible (and largely intentional) *processes* by which disparate styles and influences are mixed together. Although the term carries some intellectual baggage that can't really be unpacked in a short essay such as this, it is nonetheless preferable to a term such as 'convergence' for at least two reasons. 1) The term 'convergence' has technicist and technologically determinist connotations that obscure the cultural dimensions of what is at stake here. 2) The term 'convergence' has always tended to imply a mythological collapsing of technological boundaries— a kind of digital soup in which distinctions between cultural/media forms disappear. In the context of television culture, the essay emphasises a 'cut and paste' model of digitisation rather than a 'seamless blending'. The notion of reversioning/localising supplementary material is clearly more about hybridity than convergence.

17   Of course, the very advent of television (as opposed to film and radio, for example) has long been associated with the emergence of a 'postmodern' (though not necessarily labelled as such) sensibility in this regard, from McLuhan's mosaic metaphor that he applied to television (McLuhan 1964) to Raymond Williams's focus on televisual 'flows' (Williams 1974; Barker 1997, pp. 153ff).

18   In New Zealand, for example, SKY News (which is an Australian service) switches over to New Zealand news provided by TV3 at specific times. Also, there has been much debate over the 'natural' home for Māori television, with some arguing for a dedicated Māori channel (a Māori Television Service, now being planned with government support) that can best represent the interests of the Māori community, and others arguing that such a channel would ghettoise Māori content and that it should, instead, find its rightful place in the schedules of the mainstream TVNZ channels. In a multi-channel environment, this looks less and less like a stark either/or option.

19   These formats have generally still demanded that viewers have Internet access via a PC as well as a television set, although *Big Brother* in the UK has offered digital TV subscribers the chance to participate via their TV set-top boxes.

20   'Electronic Frontiers: Digital Television in New Zealand', University of Auckland, November 30, 2001.

21   Of course, her claims cut into the debate over the 'core' of Māori culture (and, indeed, other cultures): does *language* have primacy, thereby making digital technology an excellent and economically viable vehicle for empowering indigenous cultures, or does narrative have primacy, thereby painting the economic implications of digitisation in a bleaker light?

22   We recognise that on the web this process is both controversial (creating copyright issues) and of waning credibility in terms of design and aesthetics. However, these

problems are not likely to carry over to the televisual arena to such a degree. Television is not an open technology like the web and copyright issues will be settled in advance. On the aesthetic and design fronts, the stakes are different again, as the medium lends itself more readily to simpler navigation and 'cleaner' interfaces.

23   The scare quotations here indicate that, in part at least, 'flexibility' often serves as a euphemism for the lower costs associated with project-based contracts.

Glossary

Te Reo (Māori language) terms

Aotearoa
New Zealand; the North Island

hāngi
a cooking oven set in the earth

hui
a meeting or gathering

iwi Māori
Māori people, tribe

kaikōrero
orators

kapa haka
haka group

karanga
a keening call or cry

kaumātua
elder

kōhanga reo
Māori language early education centre

kōrero
to speak; discussion

koroua
elderly man

kuia
elderly woman

kura kaupapa
Māori language school

mana
authority, prestige, respect

moko
tattoo

paepae
speaker's bench

te reo Māori
the Māori language; the voice of the Māori

Te Wai Pounamu
South Island

tikanga
custom, lore

tūpuna
ancestor(s)

wairua
spirit

whaikōrero
formal speech

whakapapa
genealogy

Television and cultural theory terms

ABC
Australian Broadcasting Corporation

active audience
a conception of the audience that assumes viewers to be highly active in the way they interpret and use what they watch on television, relating it to their own lives in ways that may not have been anticipated by the makers of programs

anti-siphoning laws/regulations
protective legislation to prevent pay television from gaining exclusive rights to sporting events judged to be of national cultural importance. Australia and the UK have regulations of this kind; New Zealand does not

BBC

British Broadcasting Corporation

Broadcasting Standards Authority

regulatory body

cable television

technology that delivers television signals to domestic sets through a cable (rather than an aerial)

CGI

computer-generated images

channel share

a channel's share of the viewers who were watching television at a particular time (that is, its proportion of the overall viewing audience)

channel surfing

flicking rapidly between channels, with the help of a remote control

cliffhanger

a dramatic or tense development in a story, at the end of a segment or episode, designed to hold the interest of viewers until the beginning of the next segment or episode

couch potato

colloquial term for a lazy television viewer who spends too much time 'blobbing out' in front of the set

content analysis

a method of analysis that seeks to measure, as objectively as possible, the ingredients of media messages—for example, to track the changing composition of news broadcasts

convergence

used to refer to both (a) the concentration and centralisation of media ownership and control (as, for example in the AOL/Time Warner merger)—that is, economic convergence—and (b) those technological changes through which television, computers, video, and telephones (or other media) become part of a single delivery system

cultural cringe

an insecure attitude to local culture, expressed either as embarrassment or as over-assertiveness. Seen by some critics as a product of New Zealand's colonial history

CUME

an estimate of the cumulative number of viewers who tuned in during a particular time period (say, over the course of the evening)

DBS
Direct Broadcasting Satellite. A satellite that sends television signals to homes (via a dish). This is an alternative to 'terrestrial' or 'cable' transmission

demographics
the social characteristics of a particular group—for example, the age, gender, region, and socioeconomic status of the audience for a particular television program. Also described as 'the audience profile'

digital television
a form of digital communication, based on the same principle as computers, whereby information (visual or verbal) is coded as binary signals—that is, as 'on' or 'off' (or as '1' or '0'). Previously television was based on an analogue system involving the manipulation of a continuous flow of electricity. Digital television permits higher definition images and greater compression of signals (so that the number of channels can increase)

flow
the continuous sequence of material broadcast by a television channel (incorporating adverts, promos, and interstitials as well as programs)

footprint
the region covered by the signals of a particular satellite

format
a term used in various ways to refer to the particular genre and organisation of a television program. Formats are imitated and traded internationally. The term is similar to 'genre' but is more closely linked with production

FTA
free-to-air. Broadcasting that is funded by either a licence fee, government subsidy, advertising revenue, or sponsorship, or some combination of these (It is distinguished from 'pay television', 'pay-per-view', etc.)

genre
a grouping of television programs that share similar characteristics in terms of theme, setting, mood, style, etc. The term is similar to 'format' but has broader application

globalisation
those cultural, economic, and political processes whereby money, people, technologies, images, and ideas are spread across the world, often with unanticipated and/or paradoxical effects. The international television industry offers many interesting examples

hegemony
the securing of general social consent by a dominant social group, such that their goals and values are made to appear natural and/or 'commonsense'. The term may

refer either to the process or to the particular orthodoxy that results from it. It involves the recognition that such consent is not simply given or guaranteed, but is negotiated, contested, and subject to change

hook

a striking sequence (e.g. at the beginning of a program) designed to catch the viewer's interest

ideology

systems of belief that are associated with particular social interests, and are employed to justify, promote, or protect those interests (compare *hegemony*)

imagined community

idea developed by Benedict Anderson that our sense of nation is curious and abstract since we do not know most of our fellow citizens. Nationalism creates a sense of nation and of belonging in various ways (through a common language, supposed common values, and traits, etc.). The media play an important role in this process of imagining the nation

independent industry

in New Zealand, 'independents' are those involved in television production who do not have a direct link with a broadcaster. The independent industry expanded when TVNZ increased its 'outsourcing' (or external commissioning) of program-making

infomercial

advertising that is packaged (or masquerades) as an information program

inheritance factor

the proportion of the audience that continues to watch the next program on the same channel (Broadcasters are always nervous about viewers switching channels, and hope there will be a flow-on of audience from one program to the next)

interactivity

the process of active participation in the construction, exchange of, and response to media messages. Digitisation has assisted the development of interactive forms of media

interstitials

short segments between programs (links, introductions, or fillers)

intertextuality

the complex relationships between television programs (or other *texts*), as experienced or interpreted by viewers

junction

the point at which a program starts or finishes (for example, on the hour or half-hour). Competing channels may have common junction points

local content

traditionally refers to locally produced (which in New Zealand means 'nationally produced') programs. The term has become more ambiguous as globalisation has complicated the opposition between 'local' and 'global' (e.g., there are programs made in New Zealand by companies based overseas)

mainstreaming

the practice of incorporating representations of minority interests into programs designed to appeal to majority audiences

media (or cultural) colonialism

the idea that certain countries (especially the USA or UK) dominate the global media environment to an unhealthy extent, with negative effects on other local or national cultures and production industries

mockumentary

a program made in the style of a documentary, but which is fictitious (e.g. Peter Jackson's *Forgotten Silver*)

narrowcasting

the transmission of specialised programs to small or niche audiences. Narrowcasting is the alternative to 'broadcasting', which is geared to larger audiences

neo-liberalism

an economic philosophy (or the policy associated with it) that prioritises market processes and the unfettered movement of capital, goods, and services

news values

the traditional criteria by which journalists decide which stories are worthy of inclusion in the day's news (e.g. local relevance, dramatic aspects, or up-to-the-minute immediacy)

nomadology

a process (and philosophy) of resistance to anything understood to be fixed or sedentary—including cultural meanings—in favour of freedom of movement and fluidity

NZBC

New Zealand Broadcasting Corporation. This organisation was once in charge of public radio and television

NZOA

New Zealand On Air (funding body)

OB

outside broadcast (i.e. outside the studio)

PBF

Public Broadcasting Fee. In 1999 this television 'licence fee' was replaced as the basis of public service broadcasting in New Zealand by direct government funding

PeopleMeter
device placed in a sample of New Zealand homes to collect information used in the construction of ratings (The sample consists of 470 households, comprising around 1150 people)

political economy
tradition of analysis that investigates the history, singularities, and future prospects of any social formation, drawing upon the ideas of politics and economics

postcolonialism
the study of what has happened to various parts of the world (including New Zealand) in the wake of colonisation. Postcolonialism focuses not on the achievement of independence, not on a period 'after', but rather on the continuing effects and implications of having once been a colony. Those effects are cultural and political as well as economic

postmodernism
a term—notoriously ill-defined—that refers to a broadly based cultural transformation linked with a perceived shift away from (or break with) 'the modern'. It has been associated with (a) the collapse of distinctions between high and popular culture, (b) a scepticism towards the notion of artistic originality or depth, and (c) stylistic promiscuity, playfulness, and *intertextuality*. Insofar as those characteristics are features of television, that medium may be interpreted as 'postmodern'

post-production
final stage in the making of a film or television program. Known in the industry as 'post', this phase includes the editing of images and sounds

pre-production
first stage in the making of a film or television program, this phase includes research, scripting, production planning, casting, etc.

prime time
period when the largest audiences are likely to be watching television. In New Zealand, this is from 6 to 10.30 pm

production values
the technical quality of a production, which is strongly influenced by the available budget (which determines how much time can be spent and what resources are available). A good production team will ensure that the available money is visible on screen (e.g. in the subtlety of the lighting, camerawork, editing, etc.)

programming
a term with two meanings: (a) the selection and arrangement of programs (a strategic activity that is also known as '*scheduling*'), and (b) a group of programs

promo
trailer (or 'teaser') designed to attract television viewers to a future program

public service broadcasting

a model of broadcasting that aims to 'inform, educate, and entertain'. The most famous example is the British Broadcasting Corporation (*BBC*). Public service broadcasting (PSB) tends to be organised through a state corporation, but one that is meant to enjoy a high degree of independence

public sphere

the realm of public opinion within any society, as conceived by the theorist Jurgen Habermas. Ideally this realm will encourage broad participation, freedom of speech, and rational debate. The contemporary public sphere, controlled by vested media interests, is much less democratic than this ideal version

'push and pull' media

a contrast between (a) traditional or 'push' media that have few producers and many consumers, and a slow and imperfect feedback process, and (b) new, interactive, or 'pull' media that invite each user to be involved in a more active process of choice and rapid feedback

PVR

personal video recorder with a hard-disk drive able to record broadcast programs via a digital set-top box (e.g. the TiVo system). This has much greater storage capacity than video cassette recorders and does not need videotape. It can allow viewers to 'customise' their viewing choices and to skip commercials in ways that some commentators have seen as a threat to the economic basis of commercial television

qualitative analysis

methods of analysis that are not limited to what can be translated into numbers. Qualitative approaches take subjective or textual elements into account (in contrast to 'quantitative' methods such as content analysis or ratings)

ratings

a measure of the size of the television audience for particular programs (see *'PeopleMeter'*). Overall ratings that attempt to estimate the total number of viewers over the age of five are further analysed according to such factors as age, gender, and region

reading

a term used broadly in Media Studies to refer to any process of interpretation. That is, one 'reads' not only books but also television programs, advertisements, etc. (Compare *'semiotics'*)

reception

the process by which audiences receive, interpret, and use media messages

reflectionism

an approach to the understanding of changes in media representations and texts that interprets them as direct reflections of changes in material (e.g. economic) circumstances

Reithian tradition

the tradition of public service broadcasting associated with Sir John (subsequently Lord) Reith, first Director-General of the BBC

schedule

the overall timetable of programs for a television channel

scheduling

see *'programming'*

semiotics/semiology

a particular approach to the study of communication that incorporates all visual as well as verbal forms. (That is, it promotes an expanded sense of 'language' and 'reading' that includes many types of sign and symbol.) It was first developed by the Swiss linguist Ferdinand de Saussure (who used the term 'semiology') and the American linguist C.S. Peirce (who used the term 'semiotics')

serial

a television drama program, running for many episodes, in which many of the storylines and key characters continue from one episode to the next (e.g. a *soap opera*). Compare *'series'*

series

a television program that runs for many episodes (often but not always in multiples of 13). In the case of a drama or comedy series, the stories are likely to be self-contained within each episode, but there is usually a core cast of characters throughout the series, and some continuing storylines (or 'story arcs'). Compare *'serial'*

signifier

a term in semiotics/semiology. Communication involves 'signs', each of which consists of a 'signifier' (the 'sound image' or visual form) and a 'signified' (the particular concept associated with it)

sitcom

the television genre of 'situation comedy', situated in a particular home, workplace, bar, or other context, and focusing on the comic interaction between a particular group of personalities

soap opera

a serial characterised by low-budget, fast turnaround methods of production. It is usually stripped across the week. Evening soaps are different in character to morning soaps since they aim at a wider audience

social imaginary

the way that people imagine their social context or surroundings, as this is reinforced by stories, legends, etc. Such shared understandings provide a basis for social life and contribute to a sense of legitimacy. A related term is 'national imaginary'

SOE

State Owned Enterprise. The type of public sector organisation created as a result of neo-liberal economic reforms. Government organisations (such as TVNZ) were restructured as SOEs to make them more responsive to market signals and (in commercial terms) more efficient

stripping

term used by programmers to describe the practice of running the same program at the same time each week day (so it is 'stripped' across the schedule). An example is *Shortland Street*

target audience

the type of viewers of particular interest to advertisers or to the makers or broadcasters of a television program (Compare *'demographics'*)

text

term now broadly used to refer to any message or communication seen as having an existence of its own separate from its producer

turnaround

the length of time available to make a program (i.e. the number of weeks allowed for pre-production, production, and post-production). 'Fast turnaround' is a way of keeping down costs

TVC

television commercial or 'ad'

TVNZ

Television New Zealand

UHF

Ultra High Frequency. A particular area of the electromagnetic spectrum used for broadcast transmission. Other areas used for transmission include VHF (Very High Frequency) and Microwave. Television channels are located on the UHF or the VHF band, similar to the way radio stations are 'AM' or 'FM'

vectorality

the idea that our experience and perception of space is powerfully influenced by the global media vectors (or lines) along which information is moved

versioning

the production of new, modified versions of a program (e.g. to sell in other countries)

vertical integration

strategy by which a commercial enterprise extends ownership or control, by going back to take over its sources of supply, and/or moving forward to take over marketing and distribution outlets. Such expansion is sometimes prohibited by law because it may give one company an unfair advantage

voiceover

passages of spoken word in a program where the speaker is not visible (e.g. commentary or narration)

Index